DK Travel Guides

SYDNEY

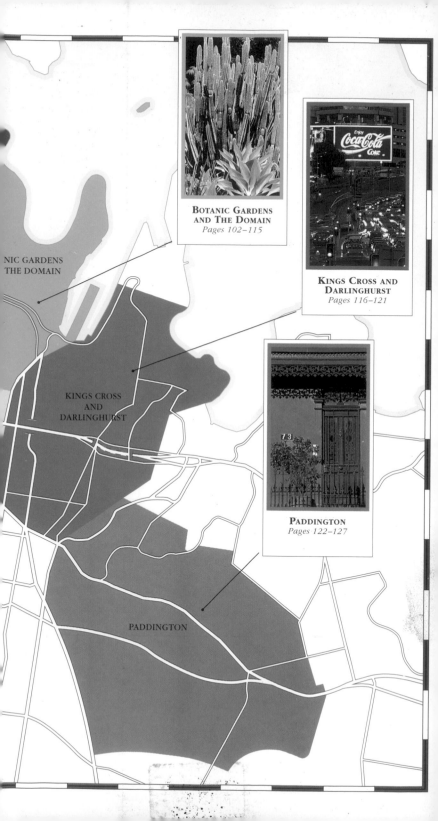

**BOTANIC GARDENS
AND THE DOMAIN**
Pages 102–115

**KINGS CROSS AND
DARLINGHURST**
Pages 116–121

PADDINGTON
Pages 122–127

NIC GARDENS
THE DOMAIN

KINGS CROSS
AND
DARLINGHURST

PADDINGTON

DORLING KINDERSLEY *TRAVEL GUIDES*

SYDNEY

Main Contributors: **KEN BRASS & KIRSTY MCKENZIE**

DORLING KINDERSLEY
LONDON • NEW YORK • SYDNEY • MOSCOW • DELHI
www.dk.com

A DORLING KINDERSLEY BOOK

www.dk.com

Produced by The Watermark Press
Sydney, Australia
PROJECT EDITOR Siobhán O'Connor
ART EDITOR Claire Edwards
EDITORS Robert Coupe, Leith Hillard, Jane Sheard
DESIGNERS Katie Peacock, Claire Ricketts, Noel Wendtman

Dorling Kindersley Limited
SENIOR EDITOR Fay Franklin
SENIOR ART EDITOR Jane Ewart

CONTRIBUTORS
Anna Bruechert, John Dengate, Carrie Hutchinson,
Graham Jahn, Kim Saville, Susan Skelly

PHOTOGRAPHERS
Max Alexander, Simon Blackall, Michael Nicholson,
Rob Reichenfeld, Alan Williams

ILLUSTRATORS
Richard Draper, Stephen Gyapay, Alex Lavroff Associates,
The Overall Picture, Robbie Polley

•

Reproduced by Colourscan, Singapore
Printed and bound by L. Rex Printing Company Limited, China

First published in Great Britain in 1996
by Dorling Kindersley Limited
9 Henrietta Street, London WC2E 8PS
Reprinted with revisions 1997, 1999, 2000

Copyright 1996, 2000 © Dorling Kindersley Limited, London

ISBN 0-7513-0311-9

**The information in every
Dorling Kindersley Travel Guide is checked annually**.
Every effort has been made to ensure that this book is as up-to-
date as possible at the time of going to press. Some details,
however, such as telephone numbers, opening hours, prices,
gallery hanging arrangements and travel information are liable to
change. The publishers cannot accept responsibility for any
consequences arising from the use of this book. We value the
views and suggestions of our readers very highly. Please write to:
Editorial Director, Dorling Kindersley Travel Guides,
Dorling Kindersley, 9 Henrietta Street, London WC2E 8PS.

CONTENTS

HOW TO USE THIS GUIDE 6

INTRODUCING SYDNEY

**A view of the Royal Botanic
Gardens and city skyline**

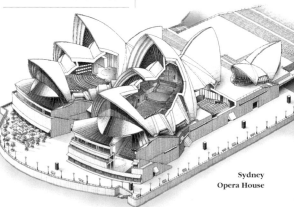

Sydney
Opera House

HOW TO USE THIS GUIDE

THIS GUIDE helps you to get the most from your visit to Sydney. It provides both expert recommendations and detailed practical information. *Introducing Sydney* locates the city geographically, sets modern Sydney in its historical and cultural context and describes events through the entire year. *Sydney at a Glance* is an overview of the city's main attractions, including a feature on the city shoreline and Sydney's best beaches. *Sydney Area*

Strolling at the Royal Easter Show

by Area is the main sightseeing section, covering all the sights, with photographs, maps and drawings. *Further Afield* looks at sights just outside the city centre while *Beyond Sydney* explores other places close to Sydney. Carefully researched tips on hotels, restaurants, pubs and entertainment venues are found in *Travellers' Needs*. The *Survival Guide* contains useful practical advice on everything from the Australian telephone system to public transport.

FINDING YOUR WAY AROUND THE SIGHTSEEING SECTION

The centre of Sydney has been divided into six sightseeing areas. Each area has its own chapter and is colour-coded for easy reference. Every chapter opens with a list of the

sights described. All sights are numbered and plotted on an *Area Map*. Detailed information for each sight is presented in numerical order, making it easy to locate within the chapter.

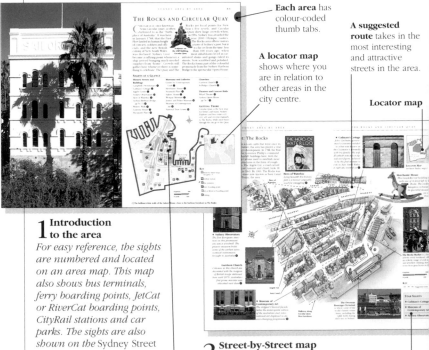

Each area has colour-coded thumb tabs.

A suggested route takes in the most interesting and attractive streets in the area.

A locator map shows where you are in relation to other areas in the city centre.

Locator map

1 Introduction to the area
For easy reference, the sights are numbered and located on an area map. This map also shows bus terminals, ferry boarding points, JetCat or RiverCat boarding points, CityRail stations and car parks. The sights are also shown on the Sydney Street Finder *on pages 240–45.*

The area shaded pink is shown in greater detail on the Street-by-Street map on the following pages.

2 Street-by-Street map
This gives a bird's eye view of the most important parts of each sightseeing area. The numbering of the sights ties in with the area map and the fuller descriptions on the pages that follow.

The list of star sights recommends the places that no visitor should miss.

SYDNEY AREA MAP

THE COLOURED areas shown on this map (see pp14–15) are the six main sightseeing areas – each covered by a full chapter in Sydney Area by Area (pp60–149). The six areas are highlighted on other maps throughout the book. In Sydney at a Glance (pp30–47), for example, they help locate the top sights, including art galleries and museums and parks and reserves. They are also used to show some of the top restaurants, cafés and pubs (pp184–5) and shopping areas (pp200–201).

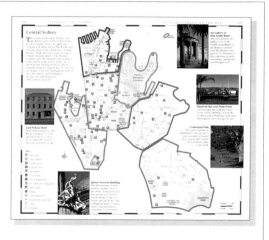

Façades of important buildings are often shown to help you recognize them quickly.

Practical information lists all the information you need to visit every sight, including a map reference to the Street Finder.(pp240–45).

Numbers refer to each sight's position on the area map and its place in the chapter.

The visitors' checklist provides all the practical information needed to plan your visit.

3 Detailed information on each sight

All the important sights in Sydney are described individually. They are listed in order, following the numbering on the area map. Addresses and practical information are provided. The key to the symbols used in the information block is on the back flap.

Stars indicate the features no visitor should miss.

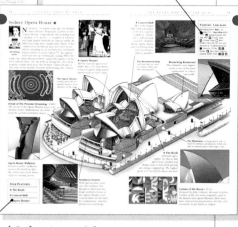

4 Sydney's top sights

Museums and galleries have colour-coded floorplans to help you locate the most interesting exhibits; historic buildings are dissected to reveal their interiors.

Introducing Sydney

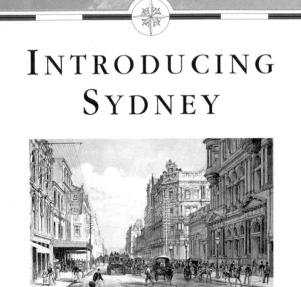

Putting Sydney on the Map

Situated on Australia's eastern coastline within the state of New South Wales, Sydney spreads with the rare luxury of space – 3,700 sq km (1,430 sq miles) in all – around what is often described as one of the finest harbours in the world. Greater Sydney is home to over 4 million people and, while it is not the nation's capital, it is Australia's oldest and largest city, as well as its media and financial centre. Sydney is also the main gateway to Australia and it enjoys good air, road and rail links to other major centres.

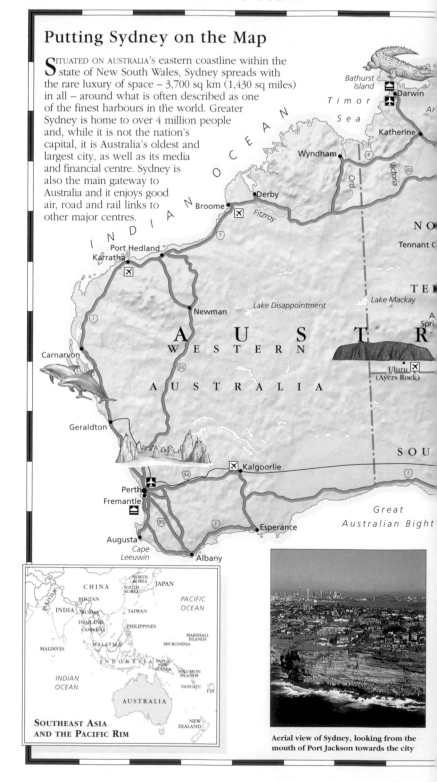

Bathurst Island
Darwin
Timor Sea
Katherine
Wyndham
Ord
Victoria
Derby
Broome
Fitzroy

N O

Tennant C

Port Hedland
Karratha

T E
Lake Mackay

Newman
Lake Disappointment

A U S T R
Spri

W E S T E R N
Uluru
(Ayers Rock)

Carnarvon

A U S T R A L I A

Geraldton

S O U

Kalgoorlie

Great Australian Bight

Perth
Fremantle

Augusta
Cape Leeuwin
Albany
Esperance

CHINA   JAPAN
NORTH KOREA
SOUTH KOREA
BHUTAN
INDIA   BURMA   TAIWAN
THAILAND   *PACIFIC OCEAN*
CAMBODIA   PHILIPPINES
MALDIVES   MARSHALL ISLANDS
MALAYSIA   MICRONESIA
INDONESIA PAPUA NEW GUINEA
INDIAN OCEAN   SOLOMON ISLANDS
VANUATU   FIJI
AUSTRALIA
NEW ZEALAND

SOUTHEAST ASIA AND THE PACIFIC RIM

Aerial view of Sydney, looking from the mouth of Port Jackson towards the city

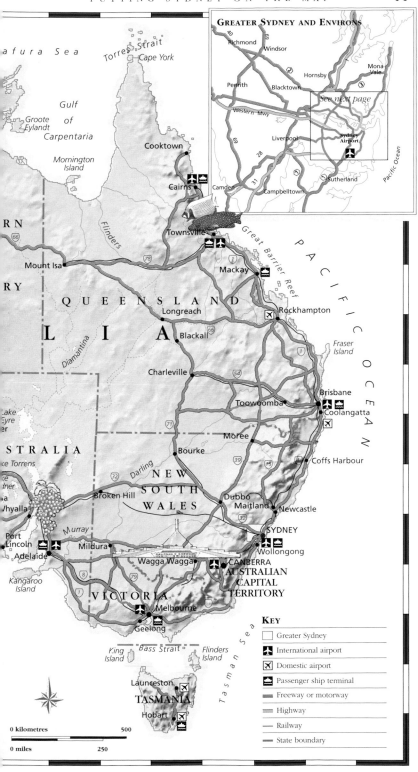

GREATER SYDNEY AND ENVIRONS

Richmond
Windsor
Hornsby
Mona Vale
Penrith
Blacktown
Western Mwy
See next page
Liverpool
Sydney Airport
Campbelltown
Camden
Sutherland
Pacific Ocean

Arafura Sea
Torres Strait
Cape York
Gulf of Carpentaria
Groote Eylandt
Mornington Island
Cooktown
Cairns
Townsville
Mackay
Great Barrier Reef
P A C I F I C
Mount Isa
QUEENSLAND
Longreach
Rockhampton
Flinders
Blackall
Fraser Island
Diamantina
Charleville
Brisbane
Coolangatta
Toowoomba
O C E A N
Moree
Bourke
Coffs Harbour
Darling
NEW SOUTH WALES
Dubbo
Maitland
Newcastle
Broken Hill
Murray
SYDNEY
Wollongong
Lake Eyre
STRALIA
Lake Torrens
Port Lincoln
Mildura
Wagga Wagga
CANBERRA
AUSTRALIAN CAPITAL TERRITORY
Adelaide
Kangaroo Island
VICTORIA
Melbourne
Geelong
King Island
Bass Strait
Flinders Island
T a s m a n   S e a
Launceston
TASMANIA
Hobart

KEY

☐	Greater Sydney
✈	International airport
✕	Domestic airport
⛴	Passenger ship terminal
▬	Freeway or motorway
▬	Highway
—	Railway
▬	State boundary

0 kilometres   500

0 miles   250

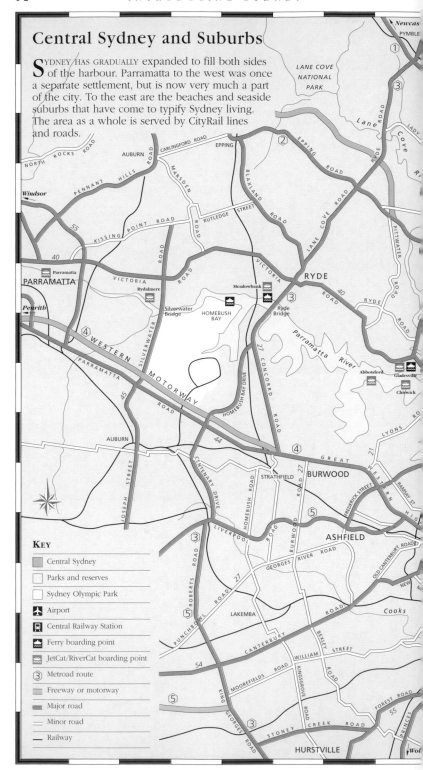

Central Sydney and Suburbs

SYDNEY HAS GRADUALLY expanded to fill both sides of the harbour. Parramatta to the west was once a separate settlement, but is now very much a part of the city. To the east are the beaches and seaside suburbs that have come to typify Sydney living. The area as a whole is served by CityRail lines and roads.

KEY

Central Sydney

Parks and reserves

Sydney Olympic Park

Airport

Central Railway Station

Ferry boarding point

JetCat/RiverCat boarding point

Metroad route

Freeway or motorway

Major road

Minor road

Railway

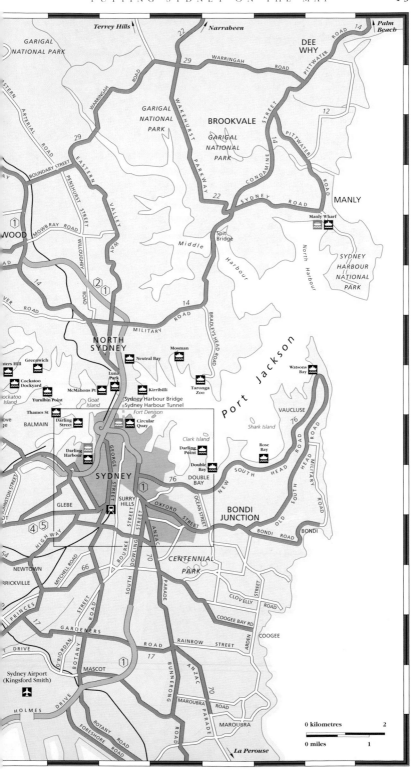

Central Sydney

THIS GUIDE DIVIDES inner Sydney into
six distinct areas, each of which has
its own chapter. Most city sights are
contained in these areas. The Rocks and
Circular Quay is the oldest part of inner
Sydney, while the City Centre is today's
central business district. The Botanic
Gardens and The Domain form a green
oasis almost in the heart of the city. To
the west lies Darling Harbour, which
includes Sydney's Chinatown. To the east
are Kings Cross and Darlinghurst, hub of
the café culture, and Paddington,
an area that still retains its
19th-century character.

Lord Nelson Hotel
*This traditional pub in The
Rocks (see pp62–77) first
opened its doors in 1834.
Its own specially brewed
beers are available on tap.*

KEY

	Major sight
	Other building
🚇	CityRail station
🚝	Monorail station
🚍	Bus terminus
🚌	Coach station
⛴	Ferry boarding point
🚤	JetCat/RiverCat boarding point
👮	Police station
P	Parking
🛈	Tourist information
✚	Hospital with casualty unit
✝	Church
✡	Synagogue

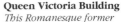

Queen Victoria Building
*This Romanesque former
produce market, built in
the 1890s, forms part of a
fine group of Victorian-
era buildings in the City
Centre (see pp78–89). Now
a shopping mall, it retains
many original features,
including its roof statues.*

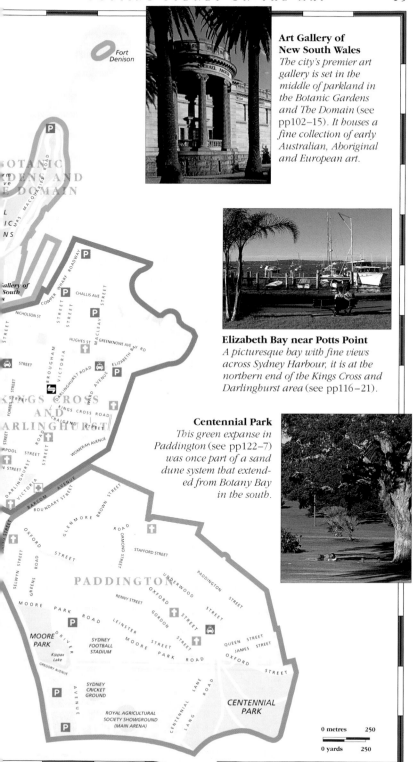

Art Gallery of New South Wales
The city's premier art gallery is set in the middle of parkland in the Botanic Gardens and The Domain (see pp102–15). It houses a fine collection of early Australian, Aboriginal and European art.

Elizabeth Bay near Potts Point
A picturesque bay with fine views across Sydney Harbour, it is at the northern end of the Kings Cross and Darlinghurst area (see pp116–21).

Centennial Park
This green expanse in Paddington (see pp122–7) was once part of a sand dune system that extended from Botany Bay in the south.

Fort Denison

BOTANIC GARDEN AND THE DOMAIN

Gallery of South

KINGS CROSS AND DARLINGHURST

PADDINGTON

MOORE PARK
Kippax Lake
SYDNEY FOOTBALL STADIUM
SYDNEY CRICKET GROUND
ROYAL AGRICULTURAL SOCIETY SHOWGROUND (MAIN ARENA)

CENTENNIAL PARK

0 metres   250
0 yards   250

THE HISTORY OF SYDNEY

**Sydney's coat of arms,
Sydney Town Hall**

THE FIRST inhabitants of Australia were the Aboriginal peoples. Their history began in a time called the Dreaming when the Ancestor Spirits emerged from the earth and gave form to the landscape. Anthropologists believe the Aboriginal peoples arrived from Asia more than 50,000 years ago. Clans lived in the area now known as Sydney, until the Europeans caused violent disruption to this world.

In 1768, Captain James Cook began a search for the fabled "great south land". Travelling in the wake of other European explorers, he was the first to set foot on the east coast of the land the Dutch had named New Holland, and claimed it for King and country. He landed at Botany Bay in 1770, naming the coast New South Wales.

At the suggestion of Sir Joseph Banks, Cook's botanist on the *Endeavour*, a penal colony was established here to relieve Britain's overflowing prisons. The First Fleet of 11 ships reached Botany Bay in 1788, commanded by Captain Arthur Phillip. He felt the land there was swampy and the bay wind-swept. Just to the north, however, he found "one of the finest harbours in the world," naming it Sydney Cove, after the Home Department's Secretary of State. Here, 1,485 convicts, guards, officers, officials, wives and children landed. This marked the beginning of the rapid decimation of the Aboriginal peoples, as they fell to introduced diseases and battled an undeclared war against the settlers. It is only in recent years that they have been granted full citizenship rights, and their traditions accorded respect.

In stark contrast, the city of Sydney flourished, with the construction of impressive public buildings befitting an emerging maritime power. In 1901, amid a burgeoning nationalism, the federation drew the country's six colonies together and New South Wales became a state of Australia.

In its two centuries of European settlement, Sydney has experienced alternating periods of growth and decline. It has weathered the effects of gold rush and trade booms, depressions and world wars, to establish a distinctive city marked by a vibrant eclecticism. The underlying British culture, married with Aboriginal influences and successive waves of Asian and European migration, has produced today's modern cosmopolitan city.

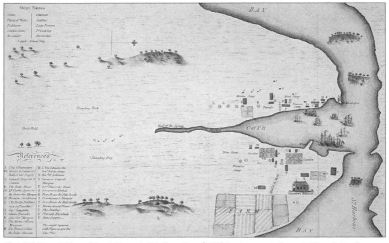

Sketch & Description of the Settlement at Sydney Cove **(1788) by transported convict Francis Fowkes**

◁ *Desmond, a New South Wales Chief* **(about 1825) by Augustus Earle**

Sydney's Original Inhabitants

ANTHROPOLOGISTS BELIEVE that Aboriginal peoples reached Sydney Harbour at least 40,000 years ago. One of the clans of coastal Sydney was the Eora. Their campsites were usually close to the shore, particularly in the summer when fish were plentiful. Plant and animal foods supplemented their seafood diet. Artistic expression was a way of life, with their shields decorated with ochre, designs carved on their implements, and their bodies adorned with scars, animal teeth and feathers. Sacred and social ceremonies are still important today. Oral traditions recount stories of the Dreaming *(see p17)* and describe the Eora's strong attachment to the land.

Hafted stone axe

Aborigines Fishing *(1819)*
Sixty-seven Eora canoes were counted in the harbour on a single day. Spears were used as tools and weapons.

This Berowra Waters carving is hard to interpret; experts believe that it may represent a koala.

The name Parramatta means place where eels lie down or sleep, or the head of the river.

Glenbrook Crossing
The Red Hand Caves near Glenbrook in the lower Blue Mountains contain stencils where ochre was blown over outstretched hands.

Glenbrook •

Glenbrook Caves ochre hand stencils

Parramatta •

Cabramatta •

Cabramatta means land where the *cobra* grub is found.

Red Ochre and Shell Paint Holder
Ochre was a commonly used material in rock painting. Finely ground, then mixed with water and a binding agent, it would be applied by brush or hand.

ABORIGINAL ROCK ART

There are approximately 5,500 known rock art sites in the Sydney basin alone. Early colonists such as Watkin Tench said that paintings and engravings were on every kind of surface. The history of colonization was also recorded in rock engravings, with depictions of the arrival of ships and fighting.

TIMELINE

43,000–38,000BC Tools found in a gravel pit beside Nepean River are among the oldest firmly dated signs of human occupation in Australia

Diprotodon

20,000 Humans lived in the Blue Mountains despite extreme conditions. Remains found of the largest mammal, *Diprotodon*, date back to this period

11,000 Burial excavat Victoria of than 40 indivi of this p

50,000 BC

20,000 BC

28,000 Funerary rites at Lake Mungo, NSW. Complete skeleton has been found of man buried at this time

23,000 One of the world's earliest known cremations carried out in Western NSW

18,000 People now inhabit the entire continent, from the deserts to the mountains

13,000 Final stages of Ice Age, with small glaciers in the Snowy Mountains

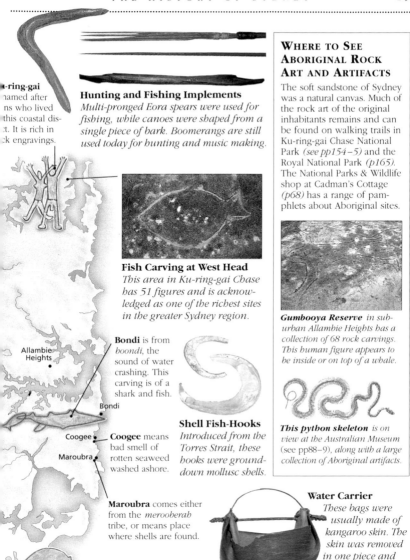

-ring-gai
named after
ns who lived
this coastal dis-
t. It is rich in
k engravings.

Hunting and Fishing Implements
Multi-pronged Eora spears were used for fishing, while canoes were shaped from a single piece of bark. Boomerangs are still used today for hunting and music making.

Fish Carving at West Head
This area in Ku-ring-gai Chase has 51 figures and is acknowledged as one of the richest sites in the greater Sydney region.

Allambie
Heights

Bondi is from *boondi*, the sound of water crashing. This carving is of a shark and fish.

Bondi

Shell Fish-Hooks
Introduced from the Torres Strait, these hooks were ground-down mollusc shells.

Coogee ● **Coogee** means bad smell of
Maroubra ● rotten seaweed washed ashore.

Maroubra comes either from the *merooberah* tribe, or means place where shells are found.

This carving of a leaping kangaroo is found in the Royal National Park.

Bundeena

WHERE TO SEE ABORIGINAL ROCK ART AND ARTIFACTS

The soft sandstone of Sydney was a natural canvas. Much of the rock art of the original inhabitants remains and can be found on walking trails in Ku-ring-gai Chase National Park *(see pp154–5)* and the Royal National Park *(p165)*. The National Parks & Wildlife shop at Cadman's Cottage *(p68)* has a range of pamphlets about Aboriginal sites.

Gumbooya Reserve *in suburban Allambie Heights has a collection of 68 rock carvings. This human figure appears to be inside or on top of a whale.*

This python skeleton *is on view at the Australian Museum (see pp88–9), along with a large collection of Aboriginal artifacts.*

Water Carrier
These bags were usually made of kangaroo skin. The skin was removed in one piece and either turned inside out or tanned with the sap from a gum tree.

8,000 BC The oldest returning boomerangs are in use in South Australia	**5,000 BC** Dingo reaches Australia, thought to have been brought by seafarers		*Captain James Cook*
		AD 1606 Dutch ship, *Duyfken*, records first European sighting of the continent. Lands on the eastern coast of Gulf of Carpentaria	
0,000 BC		AD 1	
			AD 1700 Macassans search for trepang or sea slugs off Australia's north coast
0,000–8,500 BC smania is separated om mainland ustralia by rising seas	*Copperplate print of a dingo*		**AD 1770** James Cook lands at Botany Bay

The Early Colony

Hat made from cabbage palm

THE COLONY'S BEGINNINGS were rugged and hungry, imbued with a spirit that would give Sydney its unique character. Convicts were put to work establishing roads and constructing buildings out of mud, reeds, unseasoned wood and mortar made from a crushed shell mixture. From these simple beginnings, a town grew. Officers of the New South Wales Corps became farmers, encouraged to work their land alongside convict labour. Because the soldiers paid for work and goods in rum, they soon became known as the Rum Corps, in 1808 overthrowing Governor Bligh (of *Bounty* fame) when he threatened their privileges. By the early 1800s farms were producing crops, with supplies arriving more regularly – as were convicts and settlers with more appropriate skills and trades.

GROWTH OF THE CITY

☐ *Today*　　■ *1810*

Boat building at the Government dockyard　　　　**Pitts Row**

First Fleet Ship *(c.1787)*
This painting by Francis Holman shows three angles of the Borrowdale, *one of the fleet's three commercial storeships.*

Scrimshaw
Engraving bone or shell was a skilful way to pass time during long months spent at sea.

Government House

A VIEW OF SYDNEY COVE
This idyllic image, drawn by Edward Dayes and engraved by F Jukes in 1804, shows the Aboriginal peoples living peacefully within the infant colony alongside the flourishing maritime and agricultural industries. In fact, they had been entirely ostracized from the life and prosperity of the town by this time.

TIMELINE

1787 The First Fleet leaves Portsmouth, bound for Botany Bay

1788 First white child born in the colony – and the first man hanged

Barrington, the convict and thespian star of The Revenge

1796 *The Revenge* opens Sydney's first, but short-lived, playhouse, simply named The Theatre

1785	1790	1795

Bennelong pictured in European finery

1789 The Aboriginal Bennelong is held captive and ordered to act as an intermediary between the whites and blacks

1790 First detachment of the New South Wales Corps arrives in the colony. Fears of starvation are lessened with the arrival of the supply ship *Lady Juliana*

1793 Arrival of the first free settlers

1797 Merino sheep a from Cape of Good H

The Arrest of Bligh
This shameful, and invented, scene shows the hated Governor William Bligh, in full regalia, hiding under a servant's bed to avoid arrest by the NSW Rum Corps in 1808.

WHERE TO SEE EARLY COLONIAL SYDNEY

The Rocks was the hub of early Sydney. Wharves, warehouses, hotels, rough houses and even rougher characters gave it its colour. Dramatic cuts were made in the rocky point to provide building materials and filling for the construction of Circular Quay, and allow for streets. The houses are gone, except for Cadman's Cottage *(see p68)*, but the irregular, labyrinthine lanes are still rich in the flavour of convict history.

The buildings may look impressive, but most were poorly built with inferior materials.

Male and female convicts housed separately

Waratah *(1803)*
John Lewin, naturalist and engraver, drew delicate and faithful representations of the local flora and fauna.

Barracks housing NSW Rum Corps

Elizabeth Farm (pp138–9) *at Parramatta is the oldest surviving building in Australia. It was built by convicts using lime mortar from the penal colony of Norfolk Island.*

Experiment Farm Cottage, *an early dwelling (see p139), displays marked convict-made bricks. Masons also marked each brick, as they were paid according to the number laid.*

Kangaroo *(1813)*
Naturalists were amazed at Sydney's vast array of strange plant and animal species. The first pictures sent back to England caused a sensation.

1799 Explorers Bass and Flinders complete their circumnavigation of Van Diemen's Land (now Tasmania), before returning to Port Jackson

1803 The first issue of the weekly *Sydney Gazette*, Australia's first newspaper, is published

1808 Rum Rebellion brings social upheaval. Estimated population of New South Wales stands at 9,100

1800	1805	1810

1801 Ticket-of-leave system introduced, enabling the convicts to work for wages and to choose their own master

1804 Irish convict uprising at Castle Hill

1802 Aboriginal leader Pemulwy is shot and killed following the killing of four white men by Aboriginal men

Love token

1810 New convict arrivals craft such items as love tokens

The Georgian Era

Merino sheep for export wool

Sydney's early decades were times of turbulence and growth. Lachlan Macquarie, governor from 1810 to 1821, was one of the most significant figures. He took over a town-cum-jail and left behind a fully fledged city with a sense of civic pride. Noted for his sympathetic attitude to convicts and freed women and men, he commissioned many fine buildings, including work by convict Francis Greenway *(see p114)*. When Macquarie left in 1822, Sydney boasted main roads, regular streets and an organized police system. By the 1830s, trade had expanded and labour and land were plentiful. In 1840, transportation of convicts was abolished. A decade of lively debate followed: on immigration, religion and education.

GROWTH OF THE CITY
☐ *Today*   ■ *1825*

The domed saloon is elliptical, and has a cantilevered staircase.

Bedroom

The breakfast room was used for informal dining.

View from the Summit
Blaxland, Lawson and Wentworth were the first Europeans to cross the Blue Mountains in 1813. Augustus Earle's painting shows convicts working on a road into this fertile area.

The Macquaries
Governor Macquarie and his wife Elizabeth arrived in the city with a brief to "improve the morals of the Colonists".

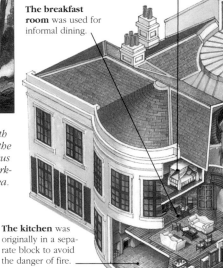

The kitchen was originally in a separate block to avoid the danger of fire.

ELIZABETH BAY HOUSE
This extravagant Regency villa was built from 1835–9 for Colonial Secretary Alexander Macleay *(see p120)*. After only six years' occupancy, lavish building and household expenses forced him into bankruptcy.

TIMELINE

1814 Holey dollar eases coin shortage

Holey dollar and dump, made from Spanish coins

1820 Macquarie Chair crafted of she-oak and wallaby skin

1830 Sir Thomas Mitchell discovers megafauna fossils in New South Wales

Macquarie Chair

| 1810 | 1815 | 1820 | 1825 | 1 |

1816 Convict architect Francis Greenway designs his first building, Macquarie Lighthouse

1817 The Bank of NSW opens. Macquarie recommends adoption of the name Australia for the continent, as suggested by explorer Matthew Flinders

1824 Hume and Hovell are the first Europeans to see the Snowy Mountains

1831 First Australian nov *Quintus Servinton*, printed and publish

Lyrebird *(1813)*
As the colony continued to expand, more exotic birds and animals were found. The male of this species has an impressive tail that spreads into the shape of a lyre.

Servants' quarters

Aboriginal Explorer
Bungaree took part in the first circumnavigation of the continent, sailing with Matthew Flinders.

Drawing room

The Classical design was to be complemented by a colonnade, but money ran out.

The dining room was furnished in a florid style out of keeping with the Neo-Classical architecture.

WHERE TO SEE GEORGIAN SYDNEY

Governor Macquarie designated the street now bearing his name *(see pp112–15)* as the ceremonial centre of the city. It has an elegant collection of buildings: the Hyde Park Barracks, St James' Church, the Sydney Mint, Parliament House and Sydney Hospital. Other fine examples are the Victoria Barracks *(p127)*, Vaucluse House *(p136)* and Macquarie Lighthouse *(p137)*.

Old Government House, *the oldest surviving public building in Australia (see p139), was erected in 1799. Additions ordered by Governor Macquarie were completed in 1816.*

High Fashion, 1838
Stylish ladies would promenade through Hyde Park (see pp86–7) in the very latest London fashions, now available from the recently opened David Jones department store.

Naturalist and author, Charles Darwin

1842 Sydney town becomes a city

1837 Victoria is crowned Queen of England

1844 Edward Geoghegan's Australian musical comedy, *The Currency Lass*, first performed

1848 Parramatta's Female Factory, a notorious women's prison, closes down

1835	**1840**	**1845**	**1850**

1836 Charles Darwin visits Sydney on HMS *Beagle*

1838 Myall Creek massacre of Aboriginal peoples

1841 Female Immigrants' Home established in Sydney by Caroline Chisholm. Gas lights illuminate Sydney

1840 Transportation of convicts to NSW is abolished

Caroline Chisholm, philanthropist

1850 Work begins on NSW's first railway line, from Sydney to Parramatta

Victorian Sydney

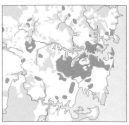

Gold rush memorabilia

IN THE 1850s, gold was discovered in New South Wales and Sydney came alive with gold seekers, big spenders and a new wave of settlers. It was the start of a peaceful period of solid growth. Education became compulsory, an art gallery was opened and the Australian Academy of Arts held its first exhibition. The city skyline became more complex, with spires and "tall" buildings. Terrace houses proliferated. Victorian decorum and social behaviour borrowed from the mother country flourished, with much social visiting and sporting enthusiasm. It was an age of pleasure gardens and regattas, but also a time of unruliness and political agitation. In the 1890s, as the country moved towards Federation, fervent nationalism and an Australian identity began to take shape.

The structure was built of hollow pine.

The dome was 30 m (98 ft) in diameter.

Mrs Macquaries Chair *(1855)*
This prime harbour viewing spot (see p106), *with the seat carved from rock for the governor's wife, was "the daily resort of all the fashionable people in Sydney".*

Boer War
The 1st Australian Horse division was praised for its bushcraft, horsemanship and accurate shooting.

THE GARDEN PALACE
Built in the Botanic Gardens especially for th occasion, in 1879–80, the Garden Palace host the first international exhibition held in the southern hemisphere. Twenty nations took pa Sadly, the building and most of its contents were destroyed by fire in 1882.

TIMELINE

Henry Parkes

1851 The discovery of gold near Bathurst, west of the Blue Mountains, sparks a gold rush

1868 The Duke of Edinburgh visits and survives an assassination attempt. The Prince Alfred Hospital is later named in his honour

1872 He Parkes elected N Premier

1850	1860	1870

1857 *Dunbar* wrecked at The Gap with the loss of 121 lives and only one survivor

Henry Lawson, notable poet and author of short stories

1867 Henry Lawson born

1869 Trend in the colony towards the segregation of Aboriginal peoples on reserves and settlements

1870 The last British troops withdraw from the colony

The Waverly
This clipper brig, with its extra sails and tall masts, enabled the fast transport of wool exports and fortune seekers hastening to newly discovered colonial gold fields.

WHERE TO SEE VICTORIAN SYDNEY

Sydney's buildings reflect the spirit of the age. The Queen Victoria Building *(see p82)*, Sydney Town Hall *(p87)* and Martin Place *(p84)* mark grand civic spaces. In stark contrast, the Argyle Terraces and Susannah Place *(p67)* in The Rocks give some idea of the cramped living conditions endured by the working class.

The "Strasburg" Clock
In 1887, Sydney clockmaker Richard Smith began work on this astronomical model now in the Powerhouse Museum (see pp100–101).

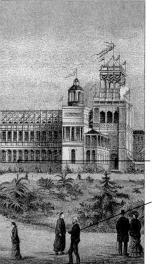

Some of the exhibits held in the Powerhouse Museum *(see pp100–101)* were rescued from this burning building.

The exhibition attracted over one million people.

St Mary's Cathedral (see p86), *built in Gothic Revival style, is thought to be the largest Christian church in the former "Empire", outside Britain.*

Victorian terrace houses, *decorated with iron lace, began to fill the streets of Paddington (see pp122–7) and Glebe (p131) from the 1870s onwards.*

Arthur Streeton
In 1891, Streeton and Tom Roberts, both Australian Impressionist painters, set up an artists' camp overlooking Sydney Harbour in Mosman.

1880 The *Bulletin* is launched, and becomes a literary icon. Captain Moonlight, a notorious bushranger, is hanged

1890 First electric trams run between Bondi Junction and Waverley

Tivoli Theatre programme

1896 Moving pictures come to the Tivoli Theatre

1880

1890

1879 Steam tram-way travels from the city to Redfern

Steam tram

1891 Labor Party enters the political arena

1888 Louisa Lawson's journal *Dawn* published

1900 Queen Victoria consents to the formation of the Commonwealth of Australia. Bubonic plague breaks out

77 Caroline Chisholm, a ilanthropist who helped migrant women, dies

Sydney Between the Wars

Vegemite spread created in 1923

FEDERATION TOOK PLACE on 1 January 1901 and New South Wales became a state of the Australian nation. In Sydney, new wharves were built, roads widened and slums cleared. The 1920s were colourful and gay in "the city of pleasure". The skyline bristled with cranes as modern, functional structures replaced their ornate predecessors. The country was hit hard by the Great Depression in 1931, but economic salvation came in the form of rising wool prices and growth in manufacturing. The opening of the Sydney Harbour Bridge in 1932 was a consolidation of all the changes brought by Federation and urbanization.

GROWTH OF THE CITY

☐ *Today*   ▨ *1945*

The poster depicts the youthful vigour of the nation.

Surf lifesaver

Home in the Suburbs
The Federation bungalow became a unique architectural style (see p37). *Verandas, gables and chimneys featured amid much red brick.*

"Making Do"
This chair, made in 1910, used packing case timber, cotton reels, fencing wire and the mouldings of picture frames.

Bronzed Lifesavers
No surf beach was complete without these icons, forever looking to sea.

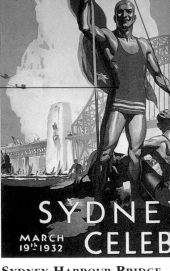

SYDNE
MARCH
19ᵗʰ 1932
CELEB

SYDNEY HARBOUR BRIDGE
After nine years of construction, the larg crowd ever seen in Sydney greeted the bridge's opening. Considered a wonde of engineering at the time, it linked the harbour's north and south shores.

TIMELINE

1901 Miles Franklin's *My Brilliant Career* is published

Miles Franklin

1912 High-rise era begins in Sydney with the erection of the 14-storey Culwulla Chambers in Macquarie Street. First surfboard arrives in Sydney from Hawaii

1920 Prince Edward, the Prince of Wales, visits

1918 Sydneysiders greet the Armistice riotously

1900   **1910**   **192**

1902 Women win the right to vote in New South Wales

1901 Proclamation of the Commonwealth of Australia. Edmund Barton elected as first prime minister

1907 Trunk line between Melbourne and Sydney opens

Poster for telephone trunk line

1919 The Archibald Prize for portraiture is first awarded. Influenza epidemic hits Sydney

1915 Anzacs land at Gallipoli

Luna Park
This harbourside amusement park opened in 1935 (see p132). A maniacally grinning face loomed at the entranceway. Millions of Australians recall the terrifying thrill of running the gauntlet through the gaping mouth as children.

One million people crossed the bridge on its opening day.

Donald Bradman
The 1932 English team used "dirty" tactics to outsmart this brilliant cricketer, almost causing a diplomatic rift with Great Britain.

Australian Women's Weekly
This magazine, first published in 1933, becomes a family institution full of homespun wisdom, recipes, stories and handy hints.

WHERE TO SEE EARLY 20TH-CENTURY SYDNEY

The years after Federation yielded stylish and sensible buildings like Central Railway Station, the Commonwealth Bank in Martin Place *(see pp38–9)* and the State Library of New South Wales. The suburbs of Haberfield and Strathfield best exemplify the Federation style of gentrified residential housing.

The Anzac Memorial *(1934) is in Hyde Park (see pp86–7). The Art Deco memorial, with its reflecting pool, commemorates all Australians killed in wars.*

The wireless *became almost a fixture in sitting rooms in the 1930s. This 1935 AWA Radiolette is held at the Powerhouse Museum (see pp100–101).*

1924 Sydney swimmer Andrew "Boy" Charlton wins a gold medal at the Paris Olympics	**1937** Heyday of painted glass pub art depicting local heroes	**1938** Sydney celebrates her 150th anniversary
		1939 Australia declares war on Germany

Painted glass pub sign

1930 **1940**

1928 Kingsford Smith and Ulm make first flight across Pacific in the *Southern Cross*	**1935** Luna Park opens	**1941** Australia declares war on Japan	**1942** Japanese midget submarines enter Sydney Harbour
1932 Sydney Harbour Bridge opens		**1945** Street celebrations mark the end of World War II

Kingsford Smith, Ulm

Postwar Sydney

1950s Holden sedan

THE POSTWAR baby boom was accompanied by mass immigration and the suburban sprawl. The hippie movement gave youth an extrovert voice that imbued the 1960s with an air of flamboyance. Australian involvement in the Vietnam War led to political unrest in the early 1970s, relieved for one seminal moment by the 1973 opening of the Sydney Opera House *(see pp74–7)*. In the 1980s, vast sums were spent on skyscrapers and glossy redevelopments like Darling Harbour, and on bicentennial celebrations. The city's potential was recognized in 1993 with the announcement that Sydney would host the year 2000 Olympics.

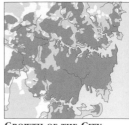

GROWTH OF THE CITY

□ *Today*	▥ *1966*

Drag queens pose in their Hollywood-style sequined finery or lampoon public figures of the day.

Sydney to Hobart Yacht Race
Australia's most prestigious and treacherous yacht race runs over 1,167 km (725 miles). Each Boxing Day since 1945, spectators have watched yachts jostle at the starting line.

Elaborate floats and costumes can take a year to make, with prizes given to the best.

Bicentenary
The re-enactment of the First Fleet's journey ended in Sydney Harbour on Australia Day, 1988. A chaotic flotilla greeted the "tall ships".

GAY AND LESBIAN MARDI GRAS

What began as a protest march involving 1,000 people in 1978 is now a multi-million dollar boost for Australian tourism. While the parade lasts for one rude and riotous night only *(see p49)*, the surrounding international festival offers a month of art, sporting and community events.

TIMELINE

Johnny O'Keefe

Patrick White

1950		1960		1970
1950 Petrol, butter and tea rationing ends	**1958** Qantas Airlines embarks on its first round-the-world flights		**1965** Conscription re-introduced; first regular army battalion sent to Vietnam	**1973** Office opening the Sydn Opera Hou
1954 Elizabeth II is the first reigning monarch to visit Australia	**1959** Population of Australia reaches 10 million	**1964** Rocker Johnny O'Keefe, "The Wild One", continues to top the music charts		**1973** Patri White wins Nobel Prize Literatu
1956 TV launched in Sydney. By the 1960s, the most popular show is *The Mickey Mouse Club*				

Green Bans
In the 1970s, the militant building union placed work bans on developments in the inner city considered destructive to the environment or cultural heritage.

The parade of ornate floats and showy dance troupes stretches for over 2 km (1¼ miles).

MR ETERNITY

Arthur Stace (1885–1967), a reformed alcoholic, was inspired by an evangelist who said that he wanted to "shout eternity through the streets of Sydney". "I felt a powerful call from the Lord to write 'Eternity'." At least 50 times a day, for over 30 years, he chalked this word in perfect copperplate on the footpaths and walls of the city. A plaque in Sydney Square pays tribute to Mr Eternity's endeavours.

Arthur Stace and "Eternity", 1963

Dame Mary Gilmore
This 1957 portrait is by William Dobell, one of the most influential postwar artists. He won the coveted Archibald Prize three times.

Floats are marshalled in Elizabeth Street, before travelling along Oxford and Flinders Streets.

Oz Magazine, 1963–73
This satirical magazine, which had a major international influence, was the mouthpiece of an irreverent generation. It was declared obscene in 1964.

Aboriginal Land Rights
In 1975, the first handover of land was made to Vincent Lingiari, representative of the Gurindji people, by Prime Minister Gough Whitlam.

1977 Kerry Packer launches World Series Cricket	**1978** Sydney artist Brett Whiteley wins Archibald Prize, Wynne Prize and Sulman Prize for three different works of art	*Façade detail of the Brett Whiteley Studio (see p130)*		**2000** Sydney plays host to the first Olympic Games of the new millennium
	1980		**1990**	
1976 Nude sunbathing allowed on two Sydney beaches	**1979** Sydney's Eastern Suburbs Railway opens	**1988** Monorail begins operation	**1989** Earthquake strikes Newcastle causing extensive damage	**1992** Sydney Harbour Tunnel opens **1990** Population of Australia reaches 17 million

SYDNEY AT A GLANCE

THERE ARE MORE THAN 100 places of interest described in the *Area by Area* section of this book. A broad range of sights is covered: from the colonial simplicity of Hyde Park Barracks *(see p114)* to the ornate Victorian terraces of Paddington; from the tranquillity of Centennial Park *(see p127)* to the bustle of the cafés and shops of Oxford Street. To help you make the most of your stay, the following 16 pages are a time-saving guide to the best Sydney has to offer. Museums and galleries, architecture and parks and reserves all have sections of their own. There is also a guide to the diverse cultures that have helped to shape the city into what it is today. Below is a selection of attractions that no visitor should miss.

SYDNEY'S TOP TEN ATTRACTIONS

The Rocks
See pp62–77

Sydney Opera House
See pp74–7

Art Gallery of New South Wales
See pp108–11

Royal Botanic Gardens
See pp104–5

AMP Tower
See p83

Oxford Street and Paddington
See pp116–27

Darling Harbour and Chinatown
See pp90–101

Taronga Zoo
See pp134–5

Harbour ferries
See pp234–5

Sydney's beaches
See pp54–5

◁ **Sydney Harbour Bridge, opened in 1932** *(see pp70–71)*

Sydney's Best: Museums and Galleries

Sydney is well endowed with museums and galleries, and, following the current appreciation of social history, much emphasis is placed on the lifestyles of past and present Sydneysiders. Small museums are also a feature of the Sydney scene, with a number of historic houses recalling the colonial days. These are covered in greater depth on pages 34–5. Most of the major collections are housed in architecturally significant buildings – the Classical façade of the Art Gallery of NSW makes it a city landmark, while the MCA or Museum of Contemporary Art has given new life to a 1950s Art Deco-style building at Circular Quay.

Bima figure, Powerhouse Museum

Museum of Sydney
The Edge of the Trees is an interactive installation by the entrance.

THE ROCKS AND CIRCULAR QUAY

Djamu Gallery
This gallery, set in the Customs House, celebrates Australia's indigenous cultures in art and performances.

CITY CENTRE

Museum of Contemporary Art
The excellent Aboriginal art section at this museum includes Mud Crabs *by Tony Dhanyula Nyoka.*

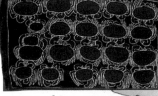

DARLING HARBOUR

National Maritime Museum
The museum is the home port for HMB Endeavour, *a replica of the vessel that charted Australia's east coast in 1770, with Captain Cook in command.*

Powerhouse Museum
The sun and moon design in the terrazzo floor of the foyer of the King's Cinema is a 1980s tribute to 1930s style, with tiles laid using techniques of the period. Films are shown each day.

0 metres	500
0 yards	500

Art Gallery of New South Wales
The Australian collection includes colonial watercolours which, to avoid deterioration, are only shown for a few weeks each year. Charles Meere's Australian Beach Pattern *(1940) is among more recent works.*

Elizabeth Bay House
The dining room is elegantly furnished to the 1840s period, when the Colonial Secretary Alexander Macleay briefly lived in the house that ultimately caused his bankruptcy.

BOTANIC GARDENS AND THE DOMAIN

KINGS CROSS AND DARLINGHURST

Hyde Park Barracks
Originally built by convicts for their own incarceration, these barracks were later home to poor female immigrants. Exhibits recall the daily life of these occupants.

PADDINGTON

Australian Museum
At Australia's largest natural history museum, dinosaurs such as this large mammal or "megafauna" Diprotodon skeleton are a major attraction.

Sydney Jewish Museum
The history of the city's Jewish community is documented here. Included is a reconstruction of George Street in 1848, a major location for Jewish businesses.

Exploring Museums and Galleries

SYDNEY BOASTS a rich variety of museums and galleries that reflects the cultural, artistic and historical heritage of this, the country's oldest city – and of Australia as a whole. The growth of such institutions in recent years parallels a corresponding growth in public interest in all things cultural, a phenomenon that seems at odds with Sydney's predominantly hedonistic image. In fact, Sydney has a long-standing cultural tradition, one that has not always been widely recognized. It may even surprise some people that museums and galleries attract more people than do high-profile football matches.

Nautilus scrimshaw, National Maritime Museum

Detail from *Window of Dreams* at the National Maritime Museum

Collage on one of the internal doors of the Brett Whiteley Studio

VISUAL ARTS

THE TRADITIONALLY conservative curatorial policy of the **Art Gallery of NSW** has been abandoned in recent times, and it now has one of the finest existing collections of modern Australian and Aboriginal art. Thanks to its former policy, however, it also possesses an outstanding collection of late 19th- and early 20th-century English and Australian works. Thematic temporary exhibitions are also a regular feature.

The far newer **Museum of Contemporary Art** (MCA) is best known for blockbuster exhibitions. Many of these take advantage of its prime harbour site to create a fine sense of spectacle. It also has a considerable permanent collection, and hosts mini film festivals, literary readings and talks.

The **Brett Whiteley Studio** opened even more recently. Housed in the studio of the late artist, it commemorates the life and works of perhaps the most celebrated and controversial Sydney painter of the late 20th century.

The substantial collection of Australian painting and sculpture held by the **SH Ervin Gallery** is supplemented by frequent thematic and other specialized exhibitions.

TECHNOLOGY AND NATURAL HISTORY

THE UNDISPUTED leader in this area is the **Powerhouse**, with traditional and interactive displays covering fields as diverse as space travel, silent films and solar energy. The **National Maritime Museum** has the world's fastest boat, *Spirit of Australia*, as part of its extensive indoor and outdoor displays. The **Harris Street Motor Museum** has regularly changing exhibitions of classic vehicles, from vintage cars to contemporary designs.

The **Australian Museum**, in contrast, emphasizes natural history with its displays of the exotic and extinct: from birds, insects and rock samples to giant Australian megafauna.

ABORIGINAL CULTURE

WITH MORE THAN 200 works, both traditional and contemporary, on display, the **Art Gallery of NSW**'s Yiribana Gallery has the best and most

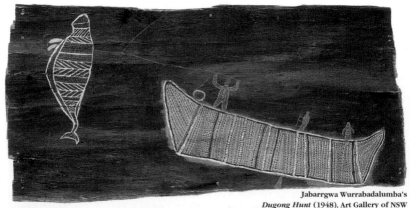

Jabarrgwa Wurrabadalumba's
Dugong Hunt (1948), Art Gallery of NSW

The Georgian-style front bedroom in the cottage at Elizabeth Farm

comprehensive collection of Aboriginal art in the country. The **Australian Museum**, has displays ranging from the prehistoric era to the start of European settlement. Its innovative **Djamu Gallery** at the Customs House features exhibitions on indigenous Australian and Pacific Island cultures.

The First Australians exhibit at the **National Maritime Museum** includes audio and video material, with traditional tools made by present-day Aboriginal communities.

The **Museum of Sydney** uses images, artifacts and oral histories to evoke the life of the Eora, the indigenous people of the Sydney region, up to the years of first contact with the European colonists.

COLONIAL HISTORY

THE SUPERB interior of **Elizabeth Bay House** has been furnished to show early colonial life at its most elegant, but while at first the house may appear to celebrate a success story, the enormous cost of its construction brought bankruptcy to its owner. Also built in grand style, **Vaucluse House** celebrates the life and times of WC Wentworth, explorer and politician.

Experiment Farm Cottage, **Hambledon Cottage** and **Elizabeth Farm** in

Water dip at Experiment Farm Cottage

and around Parramatta are testament to the crucial role of agriculture in the survival of a colony that was brought to the brink of starvation. The former has been restored as a gentleman's cottage of the mid-19th century, while the latter two have been furnished to the period of 1820–50. Parramatta's **Old Government House** was once the vice-regal "inland" residence when Parramatta had more people than Sydney. The colonial furniture on display predates 1855.

The **Museum of Sydney** is built on the site of the first Government House, close to Sydney Cove. On display are

recently unearthed relics of that building, some of which are visible under windows at the entrance to the museum.

Susannah Place provides an insight into working-class life in the 19th century. **Cadman's Cottage**, also in The Rocks, is a simple stone dwelling dating from 1816 and the city's oldest extant building. Adjacent is the **Sailors' Home**, built in 1864 and now The Rocks Visitors Centre. It also has permanent exhibitions detailing the area's architectural, archaeological and social heritage. The important role of gold in Australia's history and how it determined patterns of migration and expansion are shown at the **Powerhouse Museum**.

Hyde Park Barracks evokes the often brutal lives and times of the convicts who were housed there in the early 19th century, while not neglecting its other place in Australia's history as an immigration depot.

Side view of the veranda at Elizabeth Farm, near Parramatta

SPECIALIST MUSEUMS

AUTHOR MAY GIBBS' home on the harbour, **Nutcote**, has been refurbished in the style of the 1930s. The **Justice and Police Museum** examines a far less comfortable history, investigating Australian crime and punishment, while the **Westpac Museum** traces local financial transactions from first coins through to credit cards. Experiences of Jewish migrants to Australia and the story of the Holocaust are examined at the **Sydney Jewish Museum**.

Sydney's Best: Architecture

For such a young city, Sydney possesses a remarkable diversity of architectural styles. They range from the simplicity of Francis Greenway's Georgian buildings *(see p114)* to Jørn Utzon's Expressionist Sydney Opera House *(see pp74–7)*. Practical Colonial structures gave way to elaborate Victorian edifices such as Sydney Town Hall and the same passion for detail is seen on a smaller scale in Paddington's terraces. Later, Federation warehouses and bungalows brought in a particularly Australian style.

Contemporary
Governor Phillip Tower is a modern commercial building incorporating a historical site (see p85).

Colonial Convict
The first structures were very simple yet formal English-style cottages with shingled roofs and no verandas. Cadman's Cottage is a fine representative of this style.

Colonial Georgian
Francis Greenway's court house design was ordered to be adapted to suit the purposes of a church. St James' Church is the result.

American Revivalism
Shopping arcades connecting streets, such as the Queen Victoria Building, were 1890s vogue.

THE ROCKS AND CIRCULAR QUAY

CITY CENTRE

Victorian
The Town Hall interior includes Australia's first pressed metal ceiling, installed for fear that the organ would vibrate a plaster one loose.

DARLING HARBOUR

Contemporary Expressionism
Innovations in sports stadiums and museum architecture, such as the National Maritime Museum, emphasize roof design and the silhouette.

Interwar Architecture
Bruce Dellit's Anzac Memorial in Hyde Park, with sculptures by Rayner Hoff, encapsulates the spirit, form and detail of Art Deco.

| 0 metres | 500 |
| 0 yards | 500 |

Modern Expressionism
One of the world's greatest examples of 20th-century architecture, Jørn Utzon's Sydney Opera House beat 234 entries in a design competition. Work commenced in 1958 and, despite the architect's resignation in 1966, it was opened in 1973.

Early Colonial
The first buildings of character and quality, such as Hyde Park Barracks, were for the government.

BOTANIC GARDENS AND THE DOMAIN

Australian Regency
During the 1830s, the best designed villas were the work of John Verge. Elizabeth Bay House was his masterpiece.

KINGS CROSS AND DARLINGHURST

Colonial Military
Victoria Barracks, designed by engineers, is an impressive example of a well-preserved Georgian military compound.

PADDINGTON

Colonial Grecian
Greek Revival was the major style for public buildings, such as the Darlinghurst Court House, designed by the Colonial Architect in the 1820–50 period.

Victorian Iron Lace
Festooned with a filigree of cast-iron lace in a wide range of prefabricated patterns, Paddington verandas demonstrate 1880s workmanship.

Exploring Sydney's Architecture

Federation era stained glass

WHILE EUROPEAN SETTLEMENT in Sydney has a relatively short history, architectural styles have rapidly evolved from provincial British buildings and the simplicity of convict structures. From the mid-19th century until the present day, architectural innovations have borrowed from a range of international trends to create vernacular styles more suited to local materials and conditions. The signs of affluence and austerity, from gold rush to depression, are also manifested in bricks and mortar.

Entrance detail from the Victorian St Patrick's Seminary in Manly

Façade of the Colonial Susannah Place, with corner shop window

COLONIAL ARCHITECTURE

LITTLE REMAINS of the Colonial buildings from 1790–1830. The few structures still standing have a simple robustness and unassuming dignity. They rely more on form, proportion and mass than on detail.

The Rocks area has one of the best collections of early Colonial buildings: **Cadman's Cottage** (1816), the **Argyle Centre** (1826) and **Susannah Place** (1844). The Georgian **Hyde Park Barracks** (1819) and **St James' Church** (1820), by Francis Greenway *(see p114)*, as well as the Greek Revival **Darlinghurst Court House** (1835) and **Victoria Barracks** (1841–8) are excellent examples of this period.

AUSTRALIAN REGENCY

JUST AS THE Colonial style was reaching its zenith, the city's increasingly moneyed society abandoned it as undignified and unfashionable. London's residential architecture, exemplified by John Soane under the Prince Regent's patronage, was in favour from the 1830s to the 1850s. Fine examples of this shift towards Regency are John Verge's stylish town houses at **39–41 Lower Fort Street** (1834–6), The Rocks, and the adjoining **Bligh House** built for a wealthy merchant in 1833 in High Colonial style complete with Greek Classical Doric veranda columns.

Regency-style homes often had Grecian, French and Italian details. **Elizabeth Bay House** (1835–8), internally the finest of all John Verge's works, is particularly noted for its cantilevered staircase rising to the arcaded gallery. The cast-iron Ionic-columned **Tusculum Villa** (1831) by the same architect at Potts Point *(see p118)* is unusual in that it is encircled by a double-storeyed veranda, now partially enclosed.

VICTORIAN

THIS PROSPEROUS ERA featured confident business people and merchants who designed their own premises. Tracts of the city west of York Street and south of Bathurst Street are testimony to these self-assured projects. The cast-iron and glass **Strand Arcade** (1891) by JB Spencer originally included a gas and electricity system, and hydraulic lifts.

Government architect James Barnet's best work includes the "Venetian Renaissance" style **General Post Office**, Martin Place (1864–87), and the extravagant **Lands Department Building** (1877–90) with its four iron staircases and, originally, patent lifts operated by water power. The **Great Synagogue** (1878), **St Mary's Cathedral** (1882), **St Patrick's Seminary** (1885), **Sydney Town Hall** and **Paddington Street** are also of this period.

AMERICAN REVIVALISM

AFTER FEDERATION in 1901, architects looked to styles such as Edwardian, American Romanesque and Beaux Arts from overseas for commercial buildings. The former **National Mutual Building** (1892) by Edward Raht set the change of direction, followed by warehouse buildings in Sussex and Kent Streets. The Romanesque **Queen Victoria Building**

The Australian Regency-style Bligh House in Dawes Point

(1893–98) was a grand council project by George McRae. The Beaux Arts **Commonwealth Savings Bank** (1928) features an elaborate chamber in Neo-Classical style.

INTERWAR ARCHITECTURE

ARCHITECTURE BETWEEN World Wars I and II produced skyscrapers such as the **City Mutual Life Assurance Building** (1936), by Emil Sodersten. This building exhibits German Expressionist influences such as pleated or zigzag windows.

Two important structures are the **ANZAC Memorial** (1929–34) in Hyde Park and **Delfin House** (1938–40), by the Art Deco architect Bruce Dellit. The latter, a skyscraper, features a vaulted ceiling and a granite arch decorated with an allegory of modern life.

MODERN ARCHITECTURE

Modern MLC Centre, Martin Place

FROM THE mid-1950s, modern architecture was introduced to the city through glass-clad curtain-walled office blocks, proportioned like matchboxes on their ends. The contrasting expressed frame approach of **Australia Square** (1961–7) gives structural stability to one of the world's tallest light-weight concrete office towers. This city block was formed by amalgamating 30 properties. Harry Seidler's **MLC Centre** (1975–8) is a 65-storey office

FEDERATION ARCHITECTURE

This distinctly urban style of architecture was developed to meet the demands of the prosperous and newly emerging middle classes at the time of Federation in 1901. Particular features are the high-pitched roofs, which form a picturesque composition or architectural tableau, incorporating intricate gables, wide verandas and chimneys. The decorative timber fretwork of the verandas and archways and the leadlight windows reveal the influence of the Art Nouveau period, as do the vibrant red roof tiles. The patriotic references are seen throughout, and Australian flora and fauna are recurring decorative motifs.

"Verona" in The Appian Way, Burwood

tower comprising a reinforced concrete tube structure with column-free floors.

Jørn Utzon's **Sydney Opera House** (1959–73) is widely regarded as one of the architectural wonders of the world.

CONTEMPORARY ARCHITECTURE

DRAMATIC DESIGNS in recent sports and recreation buildings, such as the elliptical **Sydney Football Stadium** (1985–8) by Philip Cox, use advanced steel engineering systems. Beneath the vast roof of the **National Maritime Museum** (1986–9), also by Cox, there is ample space for a wide range of exhibitions.

Detailed masonry has made a return to commercial buildings such as the very highly regarded **Governor Phillip Tower** (1989–94). The dictates of office design do not detract from the historical Museum of Sydney, ingeniously sited on the lower floors.

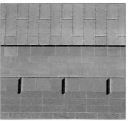

Masonry detail from the contemporary Governor Phillip Tower

WHERE TO FIND THE BUILDINGS

Anzac Memorial *p86*
Argyle Centre *p68*
Australia Square, Cnr George & Bond Sts. **Map** 1 B3.
Bligh House, 43 Lower Fort St, Dawes Point. **Map** 1 B2.
Cadman's Cottage *p68*
City Mutual Life Assurance Building, Cnr Hunter & Bligh Sts. **Map** 1 B4.
Commonwealth Savings Bank of Australia, Martin Place *p84*
Darlinghurst Court House *p121*
Delfin House, 16–18 O'Connell St. **Map** 1 B4.
Elizabeth Bay House *p120*
General Post Office, Martin Place *p84*
Governor Phillip Tower *p85*
Great Synagogue *p86*
Hyde Park Barracks *pp114–15*
Lands Department Building *p84*
39–41 Lower Fort Street, Dawes Point. **Map** 1 A2.
MLC Centre, Martin Place *p84*
National Maritime Museum *pp94–5*
National Mutual Building, 350 George St. **Map** 1 B4.
Paddington Street *p126*
Queen Victoria Building *p82*
St James' Church *p115*
St Mary's Cathedral *p86*
St Patrick's Seminary *p147*
Strand Arcade *p84*
Susannah Place *p67*
Sydney Football Stadium, Moore Park. **Map** 5 C4.
Sydney Opera House *pp74–7*
Sydney Town Hall *p87*
Tusculum Villa *p118*
Victoria Barracks *p127*

Sydney's Many Cultures

SYDNEY HAS ONE of the world's most cosmopolitan societies, reflected in the extraordinary variety of restaurants, religions, community centres and cultural activities to be found throughout the city and its environs. Over 235 birthplaces outside Australia were named in the last census. Indeed, the Sydney telephone directory lists interpreting services for 22 languages, including Greek, Italian, Spanish, Chinese, Vietnamese, Turkish, Korean and Arabic, and many of these groups have their own newspapers. While immigrants have settled all over the city, there are still pockets of Sydney that retain a distinctive ethnic flavour.

Thai Community
Thai culinary traditions have caused a revolution in Sydney eating houses. The Loy Krathong Festival in Parramatta celebrates the transplanted Thai culture.

Auburn Mosque
This lavish mosque rises above the thriving Turkish businesses nearby. Halal meat markets and sweet shops are proof of their influence.

Thailand

Turkey

Cambodian
Cabramatta is the hub of the Cambodian community. Songkran, the three-day new year celebration is held at Bonnyrigg.

Cambodia

Vietnam

Filipinos
Over 60 per cent of this rapidly expanding migrant group arrive as the brides of Australian men.

Philippines

Lebar

Vietnamese
This sculpture of a cow stands in Cabramatta's Freedom Plaza, an area offering all the sights, smells and street life of Southeast Asia.

Lakemba
A living monument to Islam, the fastest growing religion in Australia, this centre is a meeting place for local Lebanese people.

0 kilometres 4
0 miles 2

Irish Parade
Sydney's first settlers, many of them Irish, made their home in The Rocks. With its proliferation of pubs, it is the focal point for jubilant St Patrick's Day celebrations on 17 March each year.

Little Italy
Long home to the Italian community, Leichhardt evokes the flavour of Europe with its bars, cafés, restaurants and a sprawling annual street fair.

Jewish Delicatessen
The sizeable Jewish community in the city's eastern suburbs, about half of whom were born in Australia, is well served by kosher supermarkets and butchers' shops.

Ireland

China

Italy

Israel

Greece

Indigenous Australia

Aboriginal Peoples
Yarra Bay in Bondi hosts the Survival concert every 26 January, the culmination of a week of cultural exchange.

St Nicholas Church
Marrickville's Greek Orthodox church is the home of worship for the community, mostly based in the southern suburbs.

Chinese New Year
Each year, revellers pack Dixon Street, at the heart of Chinatown, to celebrate with fireworks and Chinese dragons.

Exploring Sydney's Many Cultures

IN THE MID-20TH CENTURY, most Australians could trace their ancestry back to the British Isles. The building of postwar Australia, dependent as it was on skilled migrant labour, changed all that. Between 1947 and 1972, there were more than two million arrivals and soon communities of Italians, Greeks, Croatians, Macedonians and Turks had been established. As the

Poster to tempt migrants

country looked to its close neighbours for trade in the 1970s and 1980s, and wars wreaked havoc in Asian countries, priorities changed. Today, more than 8 per cent of New South Wales's population is Asian-born and a large proportion have settled in Sydney.

The Aboriginal Bangarra Dance Theatre, based in Sydney

ABORIGINAL PEOPLES

SYDNEY CONTAINS the largest urban Aboriginal population in Australia. The largest communities are at La Perouse and Redfern. The richness of the Aboriginal culture in a variety of fields is, however, far more pervasive. Indigenous artwork is now much sought after and there are several specialist Aboriginal art shops in the city (see pp206–7). The Yiribana Gallery is a permanent exhibition space at the Art Gallery of New South Wales (p111). The Bangarra Dance Theatre (p213) and Aboriginal Islander Dance Theatre, both based in Sydney, are noted for their innovative blends of traditional and contemporary dance.

In 1988, indigenous peoples around Australia replaced the term "Aborigines" with names from their own languages. "Koori", defined as "people", is now in common usage in New South Wales.

THE BRITISH

FOR MORE THAN 150 years, Sydney lifestyle was influenced by Great Britain. From the "mother country" came art, literature, fashion, morals, administration and manners – not to mention breakfast sausages, meat pies, stewed fruit and steamed plum pudding. Many rituals and celebrations have their roots in British tradition, which may explain why a lot of Sydneysiders persist with hot Christmas dinners in the midst of summer, approach cricket with almost religious fervour and take pride in the brewing of many fine local beers.

THE CHINESE

THE FIRST CHINESE arrivals were almost all men who came to seek their fortune when gold was discovered in the 1850s. At the end of the gold rushes, many settled in tight-knit communities with undeservedly dubious reputations. In the cities and towns where they settled, there were many cultural conflicts with the predominantly Anglo-Celtic settlers. Eventually, the Chinese were deterred by taxes and then excluded from settlement after the introduction of the Immigration Restriction Act in 1901. Entry restrictions for non-European migrants were only relaxed in the 1960s.

Many Chinese students were allowed to remain in Australia after the Tiananmen Square massacre in 1989. Today, the

The Chinese Garden (see p98)

Chinese are the fastest growing community in Sydney, with most new arrivals from China, Hong Kong and Taiwan. It is not only Chinese Australians who throng to Chinatown. All locals browse, sample the delicacies and treat themselves to lunchtime yum cha (see p180).

THE GREEKS

SEVEN CONVICTS transported for piracy in 1829, two of whom stayed on, were probably the first Greek arrivals. Although the early pioneers in the 19th century were mainly from islands such as Kythera, many Greeks also arrived from Cyprus and North Africa.

In the 1940s, new migrants began to set up small businesses such as cafés, fish-and-chip shops and greengrocers. The Greek community gradually grew and has maintained its strong networks through the church and social and sporting organizations. Every year, on the Sunday following 6 January, the Greek Orthodox

Dancers in traditional Greek costume at the Opera House

Church celebrates the Feast of the Epiphany with the Blessing of the Waters at Yarra Bay in Sydney's south. The nearby suburb of Sutherland is becoming the city's "Little Athens".

The Irish

THE IRISH HAVE HAD a profound impact on politics, literature, music, religion and law in Australia. About one-third of the convicts transported here were Irish, and many more migrated later. In 1831, Cork's Foundling Hospital sent 50 girls, the first government-assisted migrants. The idea was that "in consequence of the very great disproportion of males to females in New South Wales it would be extremely beneficial to . . . have introduced there some females properly educated and of virtuous habits".

"St Patrick" in St Patrick's Day Parade

While the Irish are much dispersed today, a St Patrick's Day parade runs through the city streets each year *(see p50)*. Many pubs, particularly those in The Rocks, draw boisterous crowds to mark the occasion.

The Italians

ITALIAN IMMIGRATION peaked in the 1950s and 1960s, but the strong Italian community has been established since the gold rushes of the 1850s. The Italians brought with them much-needed industrial labour, as well as cheese-making skills and wine-growing expertise.

Although Italians now live all over Sydney, Leichhardt's Norton Street, with its restaurants, cafés and nightspots, is still the Italian heartland. East Sydney's Stanley Street is the "Little Italy" of the inner city and pasta and cappuccino are as much a part of Sydney life as meat pies and beer.

One of the most important Italian festivals is the Blessing of the Fleet in October *(p48)*. The community also makes its presence felt whenever Italy advances through to the finals of the soccer World Cup.

The Lebanese

LEBANESE MIGRANTS first began arriving in the 1840s with the majority being Orthodox Christians or Catholics. It was not until 1976, as a result of Lebanon's civil war, that Muslims began to migrate in large numbers. While early settlers largely comprised shopkeepers living in rural areas, later migrants, being the largest group of Arabic-speaking citizens in the city, established it as the Lebanese centre. In the southwest of Sydney, Punchbowl and Lakemba have a high Lebanese profile. They have places of worship for all Lebanese Australians wishing to maintain their religious and cultural traditions. The city's Arabic-language newspapers are also based there.

The Vietnamese

FROM 1976 TO 1981, 54 boats laden with refugees from war-torn Vietnam reached Darwin in Australia's north. Tens of thousands of "boat people" and other refugees risked rough seas, pirates, starvation and imprisonment to escape.

A number of suburbs have large Vietnamese communities, notably Cabramatta in Sydney's southwest, where they are the most numerous of 109 nationalities. Along with Cambodians, they have made Cabramatta a dynamic commercial centre.

New Zealand Maori dancers taking part in the Te Aroha Festival

The Melting Pot

AFTER THE CHINESE community, the fastest-growing migrant group in New South Wales is the Filipinos, living predominantly in the western suburbs of Fairfield and Blacktown.

Fairfield also has a booming South American, particularly Chilean, community, as well as a significant group of East Timorese living in exile.

Don Moon, a highly successful Korean businessman, saw huge potential in the run-down suburb of Campsie not far from the city. He encouraged other Korean immigrants to invest in the area, which now has a popular shopping district.

The restaurants and cafés in Randwick show the presence of an Indonesian and Malay community. As a cosmopolitan South Pacific city, Sydney has migrants from Tonga, Western Samoa and Fiji, as well as New Zealanders, including Maoris, dispersed throughout the city.

Pailau Gate at the entrance to Freedom Plaza in Cabramatta

Sydney's Best: Parks and Reserves

Flannel flower

SYDNEY IS ALMOST completely surrounded by national parks and intact bushland. There are also a number of national parks and reserves within Greater Sydney itself. Here, the visitor can gain some idea of how the landscape looked before the arrival of European settlers. The city parks, too, are filled with plant and animal life. The more formal plantings of both native and exotic species are countered by the indigenous birds and animals that have adapted and made the urban environment their home. One of the highlights of a trip to Sydney is the huge variety of birds to be seen, from large birds of prey such as sea eagles and kites, to the shyer species such as wrens and tiny finches.

Garigal National Park
Rainforest and moist gullies provide shelter for superb lyrebirds and sugar gliders.

North Arm Walk
In spring, grevilleas and flannel flowers bloom profusely on this foreshore walk.

Lane Cove National Park
The open eucalypt forest is dotted with grass trees, as well as fine stands of red and blue gums. The rosella, a type of parrot, is common.

Bicentennial Park
Situated at Homebush Bay on the Parramatta River, the park features a mangrove habitat. It attracts many water birds, including pelicans.

Hyde Park
Situated on the edge of the city centre, the park provides a peaceful respite from the hectic streets. The native iris is just one of the plants found in the lush gardens. The sacred ibis, a water bird, is often seen.

Middle Head and Obelisk Bay
Gun emplacements, tunnels and bunkers built in the 1870s to protect Sydney from invasion by sea dot the area. The superb fairy wren lives here and water dragons can at times be seen basking on rocks.

North Head
Coastal heathland, with banksias, tea trees and casuarinas, dominates the cliff tops. On the leeward side, moist forest surrounds tiny harbour beaches.

Grotto Point
Bottlebrushes, grevilleas and flannel flowers line paths winding through the bush to the lighthouse.

Bradleys Head
The headland is a nesting place for the ringtail possum. Noisy flocks of rainbow lorikeets are also often in residence.

South Head
Unique plant species such as the sundew cover this heathland.

Neilsen Park
The kookaburra is easily identified by its call, which sounds like laughter.

The Domain
Palms and Moreton Bay figs are a feature of this former common. The Australian magpie, with its black and white plumage, is a frequent visitor.

Moore Park
Huge Moreton Bay figs provide an urban habitat for the flying fox.

Centennial Park
Open expanses and groves of paperbark and eucalypt trees bring sulphur-crested cockatoos en masse. The brushtail possum is a shy creature that comes out at night.

0 kilometres   4

0 miles   2

Exploring the Parks and Reserves

DESPITE 200 YEARS of European settlement, Sydney's parks and reserves contain a surprising variety of native wildlife. Approximately 2,000 species of native plants, 1,000 cultivated and weed species and 300 bird species have managed to adapt favourably to the changes.

Several quite distinct vegetation types are protected in the bushland around Sydney, and these in turn provide shelter for a wide range of birds and animals. Even the more formal parks such as Hyde Park and the Royal Botanic Gardens are home to many indigenous species, allowing the visitor a glimpse of the city's diverse wildlife.

Colourful and noisy rainbow lorikeets at Manly's Collins Beach

COASTAL HINTERLAND

ONE REASON Sydney has so many heathland parks, such as those found at South Head and North Head, is that the soil along the city's coastline is deficient in almost every known nutrient. What these areas lack in fertility, they make up for in species diversity.

Heathland contains literally hundreds of species of plants, including some unique flora that have adapted to the poor soil. The most surprising ones are the carnivorous plants, which rely on passing insects for their food. The tiny sundew (*Drosera spathulata*), so called because of its sparkling foliage, is the commonest of the carnivorous species. This low-growing plant snares insects on its sticky, reddish leaves, which lie flat on the ground. You will often stumble across them where walking tracks pass through swampy ground, waiting patiently for a victim.

Red bottlebrush (*Callistemon* sp.)

Two other distinctive plants are casuarinas (*Allocasuarina* species) and banksias (*Banksia* species), both of which attract smaller birds such as honey-eaters and blue wrens.

RAINFOREST AND MOIST FOREST

RAINFOREST REMNANTS do exist in a few parts of Sydney, especially in the Royal National Park to the south of the city (*see pp164–5*). Small pockets can also be found in Garigal National Park, Ku-ring-gai Chase (*see pp154–5*) and some gullies running down to Middle Harbour. The superb lyrebird (*Menura novaehollandiae*) is a feature of these forest areas. The sugar glider (*Petaurus breviceps*), a small species of possum, can sometimes be heard calling to its mate during the night.

The deadliest spider in the world, the funnel-web (*Atrax robustus, see p89*), also lives here, but you are unlikely to see one unless you go poking under rocks and logs. A common plant in this habitat is the cabbage tree palm (*Livistona australis*). The heart of this palm was used as a vegetable by the early European settlers.

The soft tree fern (*Dicksonia antartctica*) decorates the gullies and creeks of moist forest. You may see a ringtail possum (*Pseudocheirus peregrinus*) nest at the top of one of these ferns at Bradleys Head. The nest looks rather like a hairy football and is found in hollow trees or ferns and shrubs.

Rainbow lorikeets (*Tricholglossus haematodus*) also inhabit Bradleys Head, as well as Clifton Gardens and Collins Beach. Early in the morning, they shoot through the forest canopy like iridescent bullets.

OPEN EUCALYPT FOREST

SOME of the finest Sydney red gums (*Angophora costata*) can be seen in the Lane Cove National Park. The centuries-old trees, with their gnarled pinkish trunks, give the area an almost "lost world" feeling.

Tall and straight blue gums (*Eucalyptus saligna*) stand in the lower reaches of the park, where the soil is better, while the smaller yellowish scribbly gum (*Eucalyptus racemosa*), with its distinctive gum veins, lives on higher slopes. If you examine the markings on a scribbly gum closely, you will see they start out thin, gradually become thicker, then take a U-turn and stop. This is the track made by an *ogmograptis* caterpillar the previous year. The grubs that made the track

Coastal heathland lining the cliff tops at Manly's North Head

become small, brownish-grey moths and are commonly seen in eucalypt or gum forests.

Grass trees (*Xanthorrhoea* species), also common in open eucalypt forest, are an ancient plant species with a tall spike that bears white flowers in spring. Lyrebirds, echidnas, currawongs and black snakes are predominant wildlife. The snakes, although beautiful, should be treated with caution.

A Sydney red gum, with gnarled limbs, in Lane Cove National Park

WETLANDS

Mᴏʀᴇ ᴛʜᴀɴ 60 per cent of New South Wales' coastal wetlands have been lost. This makes the remaining areas of wetland especially important. Most of Sydney's wetlands are mangrove swamps, with some of the best-preserved examples at Bicentennial Park and the North Arm Walking Track.

Mangrove swamps are one of the most hostile places for a plant or animal to live. There

A grey mangrove swamp near the Lane Cove National Park

is no fresh water and, unlike soil, the mud has no oxygen whatsoever below the very surface level. Mangroves have developed some fascinating ways around these problems.

First, excess salt is excreted from their leaves. Secondly, they get oxygen to the roots by pushing special peg-like roots, called pneumatophores, into the air. At low tide, these can be clearly seen around the base of most mangroves. They allow air to diffuse down into the roots so that they can survive the stifling conditions under the mud. The Sydney rock oyster (*Faccoftrea commercialis*), a popular local delicacy, is found in mangrove areas, particularly around the Hawkesbury and Botany Bay.

CITY PARKS

Aɴ ᴀᴍᴀᴢɪɴɢ number of birds and animals make the city parks their home. Silver gulls (*Larus novaehollandiae*) and sulphur-crested cockatoos (*Cacatua galerita*) are frequent daytime visitors to Hyde Park, Centennial Park, The Domain and the Botanic Gardens.

After dark, brushtail possums (*Trichosurus vulpecula*) come out in search of food and may be seen scavenging in rubbish bins. Also a night creature, the fruit-eating grey-headed flying fox (*Pteropus poliocephalus*) can be seen swooping through the trees. There is sometimes

The nocturnal grey-headed flying fox, at rest during the daytime

a temporary colony of these marsupials in the Botanic Gardens, where they hang upside down from trees in the park. Most of Sydney's flying foxes come from a large colony in Gordon, in the city's north.

Moore Park and The Domain are good places to spot flying foxes and they also have wonderful specimens of Moreton Bay and other fig species.

While paperbarks (*Melaleuca* species) are a feature of Centennial Park, a range of palms can be seen in the Botanic Gardens. The exquisite superb fairy wren (*Malurus cyaneus*) can also be seen here, flitting between shrubs, while overhead honeyeaters dart after each other in the tree canopy.

STRANGLER FIGS

The majestic figs in the city parks hide a dark secret. While most of the Moreton Bay figs (*Ficus macrophylla*) you see have been grown by gardeners long past, in the wild these trees have a different approach. They start as a tiny seedling, sprouted from a seed dropped by a bird in the fork of a tree. Over decades, the pencil-thin roots grow downwards. Once they reach the ground, new roots are sent down, forming a lacy network around the trunk of the host tree. They eventually become an iron-hard cage around the host tree's trunk so that it dies and rots away, leaving the fig with a hollow trunk.

The Moreton Bay fig, with its massive spreading canopy

SYDNEY THROUGH THE YEAR

SYDNEY'S TEMPERATE CLIMATE allows for the enjoyment of outdoor activities throughout the year. Seasons in Sydney are the opposite of those in the northern hemisphere. September ushers in the three months of spring; summer stretches from December to February; March, April and May are the autumn months; while the shorter days and falling temperatures of June announce the onset of winter. In reality, however, Sydney seasons often merge

Reveller at the Mardi Gras

into one another with little to mark their changeover. Balmy nights, the sweet, pervasive scent of jasmine blossom and the colourful blooming of shrubs and flowers are typical of spring. Summer caters for sun- and surf-lovers as well as being Sydney's festival season. Autumn, with its warm days and cooler nights, is often perfect for bushwalks and picnics. And the crisp days of winter are ideal for going on historic walks and exploring art galleries and museums.

SPRING

WITH THE WARMER weather, the profusion of spring flowers brings the city's parks and gardens excitingly to life. Food, art and music festivals abound. Footballers finish their seasons with action-packed grand finals, professional and backyard cricketers warm up for their summer competitions and the horse-racing fraternity gets ready to place its bets.

SEPTEMBER

David Jones Spring Flower Show *(first two weeks)*, Elizabeth Street department store. Breathtaking floral artwork fills the ground floor.
Festival of the Winds *(second Sun)*, Bondi Beach *(see p137)*. Multicultural kite-flying festival; music, dance.
Spring in the Gardens *(late Sept)*, Royal Botanic Gardens. Among glorious displays of spring blooms, enjoy the minstrels, brass bands, dance displays, sculpture exhibits and food stalls *(see pp104–5)*.

Sacred ibis stilt-dancer at the Royal Botanic Gardens Festival

Traditional costumes at the Blessing of the Fleet, Darling Harbour

Spring Racing Carnival *(early Sep–early Oct)*. The horse-racing action is shared between Rosehill and Royal Randwick racecourses.
Australian Rugby League Grand Final, Stadium Australia, Homebush.
New South Wales Rugby Union Grand Final, Sydney Football Stadium *(see p52)*.
Carnivale *(last three weeks)*, various venues. Multicultural festival featuring theatre, art, music, dance, films, story-telling, talks and food from a multitude of nations.
Aurora New World Festival *(late Sep–early Oct)*, Darling Harbour *(see pp92–3)*. Fiestas, parades and festivals from all nations, including music, arts, dance, puppets and fireworks.

OCTOBER

Manly International Jazz Festival *(Labour Day weekend)*. World-class jazz at a variety of venues *(see p133)*.

Aurora Blessing of the Fleet *(Labour Day weekend, Sun)*, Darling Harbour *(pp92–3)*. An Italian and Greek tradition: a fleet of gaily decorated fishing boats is officially blessed.
Leura Garden Festival *(from second to third weekends)*, Blue Mountains *(pp160–61)*. A village fair launches the festival, when magnificent private gardens may be viewed.

NOVEMBER

Melbourne Cup Day *(first Tue)*. The city almost grinds to a halt mid-afternoon to tune in to Australia's most popular horse race. Restaurants and hotels offer special luncheons.
Kings Cross Carnival *(first Sun)*, Darlinghurst Road. Street fair: stalls, bargains and food.
Sydney to the Gong Bicycle Ride *(first Sun)*. From Sydney's Moore Park to Flagstaff Point in Wollongong. Over 10,000 cyclists of all standards line up for this 92-km (57-mile) ride.

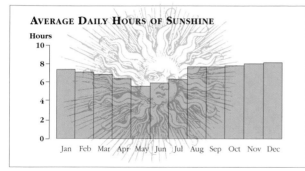

AVERAGE DAILY HOURS OF SUNSHINE

Hours

Jan Feb Mar Apr May Jun Jul Aug Sep Oct Nov Dec

Sunshine Hours
A sunny climate is one of Sydney's main attractions. There are very few days with no sunshine at all, even in the middle of winter. An up-to-date weather forecast is available by telephoning 1196. Coastal weather conditions can be obtained by dialling 11541.

SUMMER

SYDNEY TURNS FESTIVE in the summer months. Christmas pageants and open-air carol singing in The Domain mark the start of the season. Then there is the Sydney Festival, a month of cultural events and other popular entertainment, culminating in Australia Day celebrations on 26 January. Summer, too, brings a feast for sport lovers, with surfing and lifesaving events, yacht races and a host of local and international cricket matches.

"Santa Claus" at the surf: Christmas Day celebrations on Bondi Beach

DECEMBER

Carols in The Domain *(Sat before Christmas)*. Carols by candlelight in the parkland of the city's favourite outdoor gathering spot *(see p107)*.
Christmas at Bondi Beach *(25 Dec)*. Holidaymakers hold their own unofficial party on this famous beach *(see p137)*.
Sydney to Hobart Yacht Race *(26 Dec)*. The harbour teems with small craft as they escort racing yachts out to sea for the start of their journey.
New Year's Eve *(31 Dec)*. Street parties in The Rocks and Circular Quay and fireworks displays on Sydney Harbour.

JANUARY

Opera in the Park *(first or second Sat)*, The Domain *(see p107)*. A free performance of highlights from productions by the Australian Opera.
Cricket Test matches and one-day internationals are held at the Sydney Cricket Ground *(see p52)*.
Symphony under the Stars *(second or third Sat)*, The Domain *(see p107)*. Free concert performed by the Sydney Symphony Orchestra.
Ferrython *(26 Jan)*, Sydney Harbour. Ferries compete fiercely for line honours, as do rigged competitors in the Tall Ships Race held on the same day.
Australia Day Concert *(26 Jan)*, The Domain *(p107)*. Free evening concert featuring the best of Australian rock acts.
Chinese New Year *(late Jan or early Feb)*. Lion dancing, firecrackers and other typical New Year festivities take

Chinese New Year lion

place in Chinatown *(see p99)*, Cabramatta *(p40)* and the city's many Chinese restaurants.

FEBRUARY

Gay and Lesbian Mardi Gras Festival, various inner-city venues *(see pp28–9)*. A month of events culminating in a flamboyant street parade, concentrated on Oxford Street, usually held in early March.
Perspecta *(until late Mar, odd-numbered years)*, Art Gallery of NSW *(see pp108–11)*. A prestigious biennial exhibition of the very best contemporary art.
Tropfest *(third Sun)*, Darlinghurst and The Domain. Hugely popular short film festival.
Bondi Beach Cole Classic *(first Sun)*, North Bondi *(see p137)*. A 2-km (1½-mile) race for any swimmer aged from 13 to 70 game enough to enter.
Coogee Surf Carnival *(Sat in early Feb)*, Coogee *(see p55)*.

Australia Day Tall Ships race in Sydney Harbour

Average Monthly Rainfall

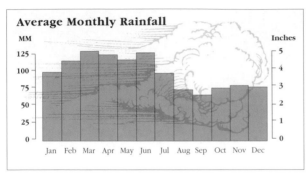

MM		Inches
125		5
100		4
75		3
50		2
25		1
0		0

Jan Feb Mar Apr May Jun Jul Aug Sep Oct Nov Dec

Rainfall
Autumn is Sydney's rainiest season, with March being the wettest month, while spring is the driest time of year. Rainfall, however, can often be unpredictable. Long stretches of sunny weather are common, but so, too, are periods of unrelenting rain.

AUTUMN

AFTER THE HUMIDITY of the summer, autumn brings fresh mornings and cooler days that are tailor-made for outdoor pursuits. There are many sporting and cultural events – some of them colourful and eccentric – to tempt the visitor. For many, the Royal Easter Show is the highlight of the season. Anzac Day (25 April) is a national holiday on which Australians commemorate their war dead.

MARCH

St Patrick's Day Parade *(17 Mar, or Sun before)*. Hyde Park *(see pp86–7)* to Prince Alfred Park. Pubs serve green beer on the day.
Kings Cross Bed Race *(Sun in mid-Mar)*, Darlinghurst Road, Potts Point. Fund-raisers push their beds through a challenging but fun 100-m (110-yd) obstacle course.

St Patrick's Day beer

Dragon Boat Races Festival *(first weeken after Easter)*, Darling Harbour *(see pp92–3)*. Brilliantly decorated Chinese dragon boats race across Cockle Bay.
Autumn Racing Carnival *(six weeks during Mar and Apr)*. Top-class races and big prize money, at Rosehill and Royal Randwick racecourses.

EASTER

Royal Easter Show *(starts one week before Good Friday)*, Olympic Park. Homebush. Country meets city in 12 days of ring events, livestock and produce judging, woodchopping competitions, sheepdog trials, arts and crafts displays and sideshow alley attractions.
Darling Harbour Circus and Street Theatre Festival *(Easter school holidays)*, Darling Harbour *(see pp92–3)*. Street theatre by magicians, acrobats, mime and performance artists.

Woodchopping at the Easter Show

APRIL

National Trust Heritage Week *(dates vary)*. Celebration of the natural, architectural and cultural heritage of Sydney.
Archibald, Wynne, Sulman and Dobell exhibitions *(six weeks mid-autumn)*, Art Gallery of NSW *(pp108–11)*. Annual exhibition of that year's entries in the portraiture, landscape, genre works and drawing competitions.
Anzac Day *(25 Apr)*. Dawn remembrance service held at the Cenotaph, Martin Place *(see p84)*, with a parade by war veterans along George Street.

MAY

Sydney Writers' Festival *(third week)*, State Library of New South Wales *(see p112)*.
Bridge to Bridge Power Boat Classic *(first Sun)*. Race from Brooklyn Bridge to Upper Hawkesbury Power Boat Club, Windsor *(see pp156–7)*.
Sydney Morning Herald Half Marathon *(fourth Sun)*, from Pier One, The Rocks. An open 21-km (13-mile) run.

Traditional decorative dragon boats on Darling Harbour's Cockle Bay

Average Monthly Temperature

Temperature
This chart gives the average minimum and maximum temperatures for Sydney. Spring and autumn are generally free of extremes, but be prepared for sudden cold snaps in winter and occasional bursts of oppressive humid heat in summer.

WINTER

WINTER IN SYDNEY can be cold enough to require warm jackets; temperatures at night may drop dramatically away from the coast. The days are often clear and sometimes surprisingly mild. Arts are a major feature of winter. There are lots of exhibitions and the Sydney Film Festival, which no film buff will want to miss.

JUNE

A Taste of Manly *(first weekend)*, Manly Beach *(see p133)*. Annual food and wine festival.
Home Computer Show *(fours days over the long weekend)*, Convention and Exhibition Centre, Darling Harbour *(see p98)*. The very latest in personal computer software, hardware and entertainment.
Darling Harbour Jazz Festival *(mid-Jun to mid-Jul)*, Darling Harbour *(see pp92–3)*. Constantly changing line-up of jazz, blues, country, gospel and world music bands and performers.
Sydney Film Festival *(two weeks mid-Jun)*, State Theatre *(see p82)*. The latest short and feature films, as well as retrospectives and showcases.

JULY

Biennale of Sydney *(two months, mid-year)*, various venues. International festival, held in even-numbered years, encompassing many forms of visual art, from painting and

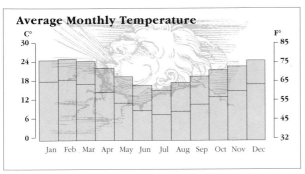

Australian soldiers or "Diggers" at an Anzac Day ceremony

installations to photography and performance art.
Yulefest *(throughout July)*, Blue Mountains *(see pp160–61)*. Hotels, guesthouses and some restaurants celebrate a midwinter "Christmas" with log fires and all the yuletide trimmings.
Australian Book Fair *(mid-Jul)*, Convention and Exhibition Centre, Darling Harbour *(see p98)*. Australian book publishers' trade fair. Open to the general public on the weekend, with plenty of attractions, including author appearances, book discussion panels and lots of lively entertainment for children.
Sydney International Boat Show *(late Jul)*, Convention and Exhibition Centre, Darling Harbour *(p98)*.
NAIDOC (National Aboriginal and Torres Strait Islander) Week *(ends 11 Jul)*. Week-long celebrations to build awareness and understanding of Aboriginal culture and history.

The familiar logo of the Film Festival

PUBLIC HOLIDAYS

New Year's Day (1 Jan)
Australia Day (26 Jan)
Good Friday (variable)
Easter Monday (variable)
Anzac Day (25 Apr)
Queen's Birthday (second Mon in Jun)
Bank Holiday (first Mon in Aug: only banks and some financial institutions are closed)
Labour Day (first Mon in Oct)
Christmas Day (25 Dec)
Boxing Day (26 Dec)

AUGUST

City to Surf Race *(second Sun)*. From the city to Bondi Beach *(see p137)*. A 14-km (9-mile) community event that attracts all types, from amateurs to leading marathon runners.
Japan Festival *(third week)*, various venues. Ikebana, tea ceremonies, sports and music, with visiting acts of all kinds.

Runners in the City to Surf Race, surging down William Street

SPORTING SYDNEY

SPORT IS INTEGRAL to the Australian lifestyle and Sydney is no exception. On any day you'll see the locals on golf courses at dawn, running along the streets keeping fit, or having a quick set of tennis after work. And at the weekend, during both summer and winter, there is no

Horse-riding in a Sydney park

end to the variety of sports you can watch. Thousands of people regularly gather at the Sydney Football Stadium and the Sydney Cricket Ground to catch their favourite teams in action while, for those who cannot make it to the ground, sport reigns supreme on weekend television.

Australia versus the All Blacks, SFS

RUGBY LEAGUE AND RUGBY UNION

RUGBY LEAGUE is what Australians are referring to when they talk about "the footie". There are three major competition levels: local, State of Origin and Tests. Matches are held all over Sydney, but the Sydney Football Stadium (SFS) is by far the biggest venue. Tickets are available from **Ticketek**.

Rugby union is the second most popular game. Tests are held at Homebush's Stadium Australia, with regional games in the Super 12 series at the Sydney Football Stadium.

CRICKET

DURING THE SUMMER, Test cricket and one-day internationals are played at the Sydney Cricket Ground (SCG). Tickets for weekday sessions can often be bought at the gate. Book through **Ticketek** for weekend sessions.

BASKETBALL

BASKETBALL has grown in popularity as both a spectator and recreational sport in recent years. Sydney has male and female teams competing in the National Basketball League. The games, held at the Sydney Entertainment Centre, have much of the excitement of American basketball. Tickets can be purchased from Ticketek or at the box office.

AUSTRALIAN RULES FOOTBALL

THERE IS a strong "Aussie Rules" following in Sydney. The local team, the Sydney Swans, plays its home games at the Sydney Cricket

Ground. Tickets can usually be bought at the ground on the day of the game.

GOLF, TENNIS AND CYCLING

THERE ARE many golf courses throughout Sydney where visitors are welcome at all times. These include **Moore Park** and **St Michael's** golf courses. Book ahead, especially at weekends.

Tennis is another favoured sport. Courts available for hire can be found all over Sydney. Many centres also have floodlit courts for night hire.

Sydney boasts excellent locations for the whole family to go cycling. One of the most frequented is Centennial Park (see p127). You can hire bikes and safety helmets from **Centennial Park Cycles**.

Aerial view of Sydney Football Stadium at Moore Park

Sydney 2000 Olympic Games

THE HIGHLIGHT of the millennium celebrations in Australia will be the 27th Summer Olympic Games, the second time the country has hosted the competition. Twenty-eight sports are due to be contested, two of which, tae kwon do and triathlon, are featured for the first time. Sydney Olympic Park *(see p138)* is situated on the Parramatta River at Homebush Bay, 14 km (8.5 miles) west of the city centre. Sydney 2000 is the first Olympiad to take the environment into account. Areas of nature will be protected, with water and energy conservation being key aspects of every new design. The purpose-built Olympic Village will accommodate 15,000 athletes during the games, while international visitors and sports fans in attendance will be served by some 35,000 hotel rooms in the city.

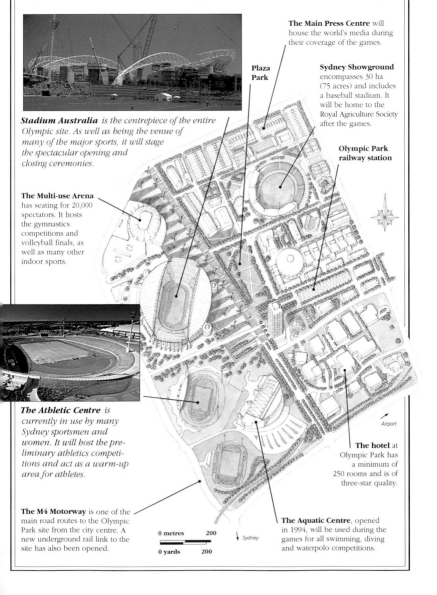

Stadium Australia is the centrepiece of the entire Olympic site. As well as being the venue of many of the major sports, it will stage the spectacular opening and closing ceremonies.

The Main Press Centre will house the world's media during their coverage of the games.

Plaza Park

Sydney Showground encompasses 30 ha (75 acres) and includes a baseball stadium. It will be home to the Royal Agriculture Society after the games.

Olympic Park railway station

The Multi-use Arena has seating for 20,000 spectators. It hosts the gymnastics competitions and volleyball finals, as well as many other indoor sports.

The Athletic Centre is currently in use by many Sydney sportsmen and women. It will host the preliminary athletics competitions and act as a warm-up area for athletes.

Airport

The hotel at Olympic Park has a minimum of 250 rooms and is of three-star quality.

The M4 Motorway is one of the main road routes to the Olympic Park site from the city centre. A new underground rail link to the site has also been opened.

0 metres   200

0 yards   200

↓ Sydney

The Aquatic Centre, opened in 1994, will be used during the games for all swimming, diving and waterpolo competitions.

Sydney's Beaches

BEING A CITY BUILT AROUND THE WATER, it is no wonder that many of Sydney's recreational activities involve the sand, sea and sun. There are many harbour and surf beaches throughout Sydney, most of them accessible by bus *(see p231)*. Even if you're not a swimmer, the beaches offer a chance to get away from it all for a day or weekend and enjoy the fresh air and relaxed way of life.

Scuba diving at Gordons Bay

SWIMMING

YOU CAN SWIM at either harbour or ocean beaches. Harbour beaches are generally smaller and are sheltered and calm. Popular harbour beaches include Camp Cove, Shark Bay and Balmoral Beach.

One of the most distinctive features of the ocean beaches is the surf lifesavers in their red and yellow caps. Surf life-saving carnivals are held throughout the summer. Call **Surf Life Saving NSW** for a calendar of events.

Well-patrolled, safer surf beaches include Bondi, Manly and Coogee. Bondi is a great place for "people watching", as is its neighbour Tamarama, although the surf can be rough with a strong rip *(see p223)*.

SURFING

SURFING IS MORE a way of life than a leisure activity for some Sydneysiders. If you're a beginner, try Bondi, Bronte, Palm Beach or Collaroy.

Two of the best surf beaches are Maroubra and Narrabeen. Bear in mind that local surfers know one another well and do not take kindly to "intruders" who drop in on their waves

or leave litter on their beaches. If you'd like to learn, local surf shops should be able to help. To hire a surfboard, try **Bondi Surf Co.** or **Aloha Surf**.

If you'd like to catch some of the action but stay dry, there are plenty of vantage points on the walk from Bondi Beach to Tamarama *(see pp144–5)*.

WINDSURFING AND SAILING

THERE ARE LOCATIONS around Sydney suitable for every level of windsurfer. Boards can be hired from **Balmoral Windsurfing, Sailing and Kayaking School and Hire**. Good spots include Palm Beach, Narrabeen Lakes, La Perouse, Brighton-Le-Sands and Kurnell Point (for beginner and intermediate boarders) and Long Reef Beach, Palm Beach and Collaroy (for the more experienced windsurfer).

One of the best ways to see the harbour is while sailing. A sailing boat, including skipper, can be hired for the afternoon from the **Australian Sailing Academy**. If you'd like to learn how to sail, the **Sirsi Newport Marina** has two-day courses and also hires out sailing boats and motor cruisers to experienced sailors.

SCUBA DIVING

THE GREAT BARRIER REEF it may not be, but there are some excellent dive spots around Sydney, especially in winter when the water is clear, if a little cold. More favoured spots are Shelly Beach, Gordons Bay and Camp Cove.

Pro Dive Coogee offers a complete range of courses, escorted dives, introductory dives for beginners, and hire equipment. **Dive Centre Manly** also runs courses, hires equipment and conducts boat dives seven days a week.

DIRECTORY

Aloha Surf
44 Pittwater Rd, Manly.
(9977 3777.

Australian Sailing Academy
The Spit, Mosman. **(** 9960 3999.

Balmoral Windsurfing, Sailing and Kayaking School and Hire
2 The Esplanade, Balmoral Beach.
(9960 5344.

Beach Watch Info Line
(9901 7996.

Bondi Surf Co.
Shop 2, 72–76 Campbell Pde,
Bondi Beach. **(** 9365 0870.

Dive Centre Manly
10 Belgrave St, Manly.
(9977 4355.

Pro Dive Coogee
27 Alfreda St, Coogee.
(9665 6333.

Sirsi Newport Marina
122 Crescent Rd, Newport.
(9979 6213.

Surf Life Saving NSW
(9984 7188.

Rock baths and surf lifesaving club at Coogee Beach

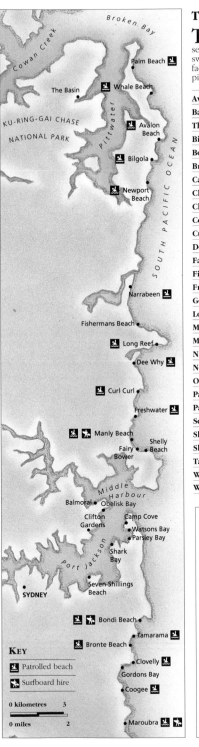

TOP 30 BEACHES

THE BEACHES shown here have been selected for their safe swimming, water sports, facilities available or their picturesque setting.

	Swimming Pool	Surfing	Windsurfing	Fishing	Scuba Diving	Picnic/Barbecue	Restaurant/Café
Avalon	●	■	●			■	
Balmoral	●		●	●		■	
The Basin	●					■	
Bilgola							
Bondi Beach	●	■			●	●	●
Bronte	●	■		■		●	●
Camp Cove					●		
Clifton Gardens	●		●	■	●		
Clovelly				■	●		
Coogee	●		●	■	●	■	●
Curl Curl	●	■		■			
Dee Why	●	■		■		●	●
Fairy Bower					●		
Fishermans Beach		■	●	■			
Freshwater	●	■		■		●	■
Gordons Bay				●	●		
Long Reef		■	●	■			
Manly Beach	●	■			●	■	●
Maroubra		■	●	■			
Narrabeen	●	■	●	■		■	
Newport Beach	●	■		■		■	●
Obelisk Bay *(naturist)*							
Palm Beach	●	■	●	■		■	●
Parsley Bay						■	
Seven Shillings Beach	●					■	
Shark Bay	●					■	●
Shelly Beach					●	●	●
Tamarama		■	●	■		●	●
Watsons Bay	●					■	●
Whale Beach	●	■	●	■		■	●

THE TYPES OF WAVES

Cresting waves *can be identified by the foam that is created as they break from the top. These waves are ideal for board riding and body surfing.*

Plunging waves *curl into a tube before breaking close to the shore. Fondly known as "dumpers", these waves should only be tackled by experienced surfers.*

Surging waves *are those that don't appear to break. They often travel all the way into the beach before breaking and can easily sweep a toddler or child off its feet.*

KEY

⚑ Patrolled beach

🏄 Surfboard hire

0 kilometres   3

0 miles   2

Garden Island to Farm Cove

Waterlily in the Royal Botanic Gardens

Sydney's vast harbour, also named Port Jackson after a Secretary in the British Admiralty who promptly changed his name, is a drowned river valley which was transformed over millions of years. Its intricate coastal geography of headlands and secluded bays can sometimes confound even life-long residents. This waterway was the lifeblood of the early colony, with the maritime industry a vital source of wealth and supply. The legacies of alternate recessions and booms can be viewed along the shoreline: a representative story in a nation where an estimated 70 per cent of the population cling to the coastal cities, especially along the eastern seaboard.

The city skyline is a result of random development. The 1960s indiscriminate destruction of architectural history was halted, and towers now stand amid Victorian buildings.

Two harbour beacons, known as "wedding cakes" because of their three tiers, are solar powered and equipped with a fail-safe back-up service. There are around 350 buoys and beacons now in operation.

The barracks for the naval garrison date from 1888.

Garden Island marks a 1940s construction project with 12 ha (30 acres) reclaimed from the harbour.

Sailing on the harbour is a pastime not exclusively reserved for the rich and elite. Of the several hundred thousand pleasure boats registered, some are available for hire while others take out groups of inexperienced sailors.

0 metres	250
0 yards	250

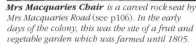

Mrs Macquaries Chair is a carved rock seat by Mrs Macquaries Road (see p106). In the early days of the colony, this was the site of a fruit and vegetable garden which was farmed until 1805.

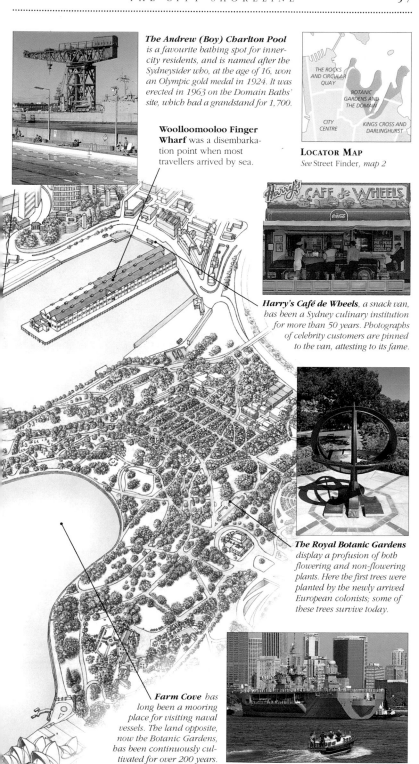

The Andrew (Boy) Charlton Pool *is a favourite bathing spot for inner-city residents, and is named after the Sydneysider who, at the age of 16, won an Olympic gold medal in 1924. It was erected in 1963 on the Domain Baths' site, which had a grandstand for 1,700.*

Woolloomooloo Finger Wharf was a disembarka-tion point when most travellers arrived by sea.

LOCATOR MAP
See Street Finder, *map 2*

Harry's Café de Wheels, *a snack van, has been a Sydney culinary institution for more than 50 years. Photographs of celebrity customers are pinned to the van, attesting to its fame.*

The Royal Botanic Gardens *display a profusion of both flowering and non-flowering plants. Here the first trees were planted by the newly arrived European colonists; some of these trees survive today.*

Farm Cove *has long been a mooring place for visiting naval vessels. The land opposite, now the Botanic Gardens, has been continuously cul-tivated for over 200 years.*

Sydney Cove to Walsh Bay

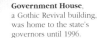

Conservatorium
of Music

IT IS ESTIMATED that over 70 km (43 miles)
of harbour foreshore have been lost as
a result of the massive land reclamation
projects carried out since the 1840s. That
the 13 islands existing when the First Fleet
arrived in 1788 have now been reduced to
just eight is a startling indication of rapid
and profound geographical transformation.
Redevelopments around the Circular Quay
and Walsh Bay area from the 1980s have
opened up the waterfront for public use

**Detail from
railing at
Circular Quay**

and enjoyment, acknowledging that it is the city's
greatest natural asset. Environmental and architectural aspirations for Sydney recognize
the need to integrate city and harbour.

1857 Man
O'War Steps

*The Sydney Opera House was
designed to take advantage of its
spectacular setting. The roofs
shine during the day and seem
to glow at night. The building
can appear as a visionary landscape to the pedestrian onlooker.*

Government House,
a Gothic Revival building,
was home to the state's
governors until 1996.

*Harbour cruises regularly depart
from Circular Quay, taking visitors out
and about both during the day and in
the evening. They are an incomparable
way to see the city and its waterways.*

0 metres	250
0 yards	250

*The Sydney Harbour
Bridge was also known
as the "Iron Lung" at the
time of its construction.
During the Great Depres-
sion it provided on-site
work for approximately
1,400, while many more
were employed in the
specialist workshops.*

The Rocks' *narrow but stalwart streets have managed to hold out since 1788 against the encroaching city. Three streets, however, were demolished to make room for Harbour Bridge foundations.*

The Tank Stream, the colony's first water supply, now runs underground and spills into the quay.

LOCATOR MAP
See Street Finder, *maps 1 & 2*

Cahill Expressway

Circular Quay, *originally and more accurately known as Semi-Circular Quay, was the last and arguably greatest convict-built structure. Tank Stream mudflats were filled in to shape the quay, and sandstone from The Rocks formed the sea wall.*

The Wharf Theatre *resides on a pier that took six years to build, mostly due to the diversion of labour and materials during World War I. The theatre was opened in 1984.*

The wharves were completed in 1922.

Imports and exports to and from the city were stored in these wharves until 1977.

The wharves' design *included a rat-proof sea wall around the port. This was an urgent response to the 1900 bubonic plague outbreak, attributed to rats on the wharves.*

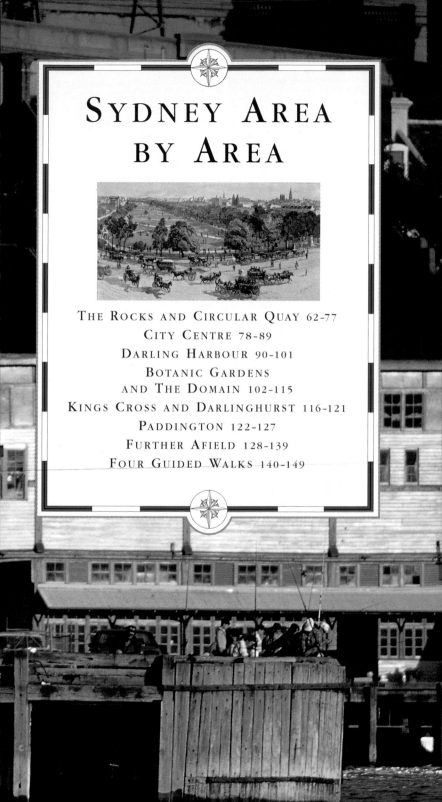

SYDNEY AREA
BY AREA

THE ROCKS AND CIRCULAR QUAY

CIRCULAR QUAY, once known as Semi-Circular Quay, is often referred to as the "birthplace of Australia". It was here, in January 1788, that the First Fleet landed its human freight of convicts, soldiers and officials, and the new British colony of New South Wales was declared. Sydney Cove became a rallying point whenever a ship arrived bringing much-needed supplies from "home". Crowds still gather here whenever there is something to celebrate. The Quay and The

Sculpture on the AMP Building, Circular Quay

Rocks are focal points for New Year's Eve revels, and Circular Quay drew huge crowds when, in 1994, Sydney was awarded the year 2000 Olympic Games. The Rocks area offers visitors a taste of Sydney's past, but it is a far cry from the time, less than 100 years ago, when most inhabitants lived in rat-infested slums and gangs ruled its streets. Now scrubbed and polished, The Rocks forms part of the colourful promenade from the Sydney Harbour Bridge to the spectacular Opera House.

SIGHTS AT A GLANCE

Historic Streets and Buildings
Campbell's Storehouses **1**
George Street **2**
Cadman's Cottage **6**
Argyle Centre **8**
Sydney Observatory **10**
Hero of Waterloo **11**
*Sydney Harbour Bridge
pp70–71* **13**
Writers' Walk **15**

Customs House **17**
Macquarie Place **18**

Museums and Galleries
Merchants' House **3**
Susannah Place **4**
Sailors' Home **5**
Westpac Museum **7**
Justice and Police Museum **16**
Museum of Contemporary
Art **19**
National Trust Centre **20**

Churches
Garrison Church **9**
St Philip's Church **21**

Theatres and Concert Halls
Wharf Theatre **12**
*Sydney Opera House
pp74–7* **14**

GETTING THERE

Circular Quay is the best stop for ferries and trains. Sydney Explorer and bus routes 431, 432, 433 and 434 run regularly to The Rocks, while most buses through the city go to the Quay.

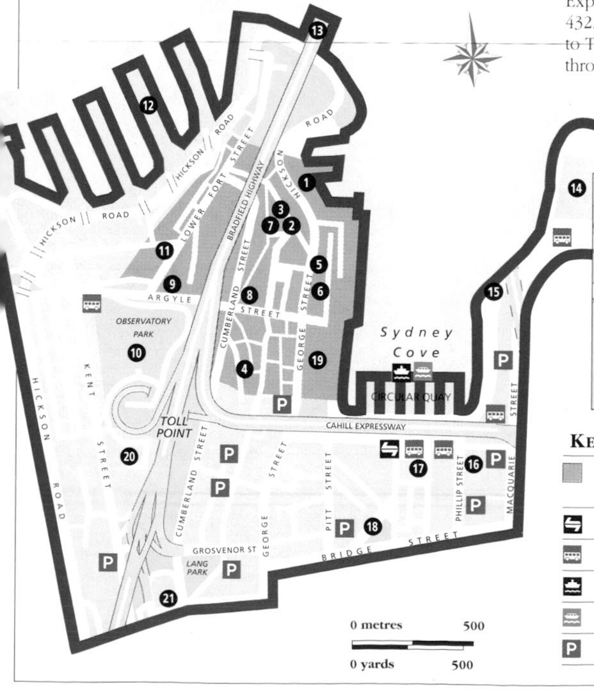

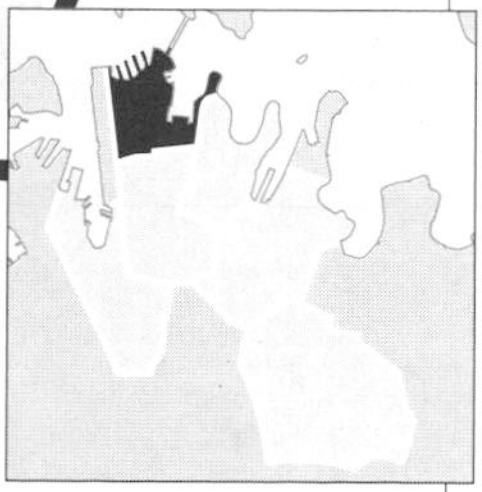

KEY

▭	Street-by-Street map *See pp64–5*
🚇	CityRail station
🚌	Bus terminus
⛴	Ferry boarding point
🛥	JetCat/RiverCat boarding point
P	Parking

◁ **The brilliant white walls of the Sailors' Home, close to the harbour foreshore in The Rocks**

Street-by-Street: The Rocks

Named for the rugged cliffs that were once its dominant feature, this area has played a vital role in Sydney's development. In 1788, the First Fleeters under Governor Phillip's command erected makeshift buildings here, with the convicts' hard labour used to establish more permanent structures in the form of rough-hewn streets. The Argyle Cut, a road carved through solid rock using just hammer and chisel, took 18 years to build, beginning in 1843. By 1900, The Rocks was overrun with disease; the street now known as Suez Canal was once Sewer's Canal. Today, the area is still rich in colonial history and colour.

Governor Arthur Phillip

Hero of Waterloo
Lying beneath this historic pub is a tunnel originally used for smuggling **11**

★ **Sydney Observatory**
The first European structure on this prominent site was a windmill. The present museum holds some of the earliest astronomical instruments brought to Australia **10**

Garrison Church
Columns in this church are decorated with the insignia of British troops stationed here until 1870. Australia's first prime minister was educated next door **9**

Hero of Waterloo ↑

WATSON ROAD

ARGYLE STREET

UPPER FORT STREET

TRINITY AVENUE

BRADFIELD HIGHWAY

CUMBERLAND STREET

GLOUCESTER

ARGYLE STREET

HARRINGTON STREET

GEORGE STREET

LOW

Argyle Cut

Suez Canal

★ **Museum of Contemporary Art**
The stripped Classical façade belies the avant-garde nature of the Australian and international art displayed in an ever-changing programme **19**

Walkway along Circular Quay West foreshore

★ **Cadman's Cottage**
John Cadman, government coxswain, resided in what was known as the Coxswain's Barracks with his family. His wife Elizabeth was also a significant figure, believed to be the first woman to vote in New South Wales, a right she insisted on **6**

LOCATOR MAP
See Street Finder, *map 1*

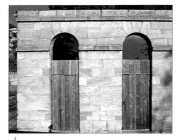

Merchants' House
For many years this and the other historic buildings on George Street were neglected – now they house cultural institutions **3**

The Rocks Market is a hive of activity every weekend, offering an eclectic range of craft items and jewellery utilizing Australian icons from gum leaves to koalas.

0 metres	100
0 yards	100

KEY

– – – Suggested route

The Overseas Passenger Terminal is where some of the world's luxury cruise liners, including the *QEII*, berth during their stay in Sydney.

STAR SIGHTS

★ **Cadman's Cottage**

★ **Museum of Contemporary Art**

★ **Sydney Observatory**

Campbell's Storehouses ❶

7–27 Circular Quay West, The Rocks. **Map** 1 B2. 🚌 *Sydney Explorer, 431, 432, 433, 434.* 🅾 ♿

In 1798, the Scottish merchant Robert Campbell sailed into Sydney Cove and soon established himself as a founding father of commerce for the new colony. With trade links already established in Calcutta, his business blossomed. In 1839, Campbell began constructing a private wharf and stores to house the tea, sugar, spirits and cloth he imported from India. Twelve sandstone bays had been built by 1861 and a brick upper storey was added in about 1890. Part of the old sea wall and 11 of the original stores still remain. The area soon took on the name of Campbell's Cove, which it retains to this day.

Today the bond stores contain galleries and harbourside restaurants catering for a range of tastes, from contemporary to Chinese and Italian. It is a delightful area in which to relax with a meal and watch the bustling boats in the harbour go by. The pulleys that were used to raise cargo from the wharf can still be seen on the outside, near the top of the building.

George Street ❷

Map 1 B2. 🚌 *Sydney Explorer, 431, 432, 433, 434.*

Formerly the preserve of wealthy merchants, sailors and the city's working class, George Street today is a popular attraction with visitors to Sydney, who are drawn to its restaurants, art galleries, museums, jewellery stores and craft souvenir shops. For one-stop memento and gift shopping it is ideal, with little of the mass-produced and tacky, but a great deal in the way of modern Australian craft of a very high calibre, with many unique pieces.

One of Sydney's original thoroughfares – some say Australia's first street – it ran from the main water supply, the Tank Stream, to the tiny community in the Rocks, and was known as Spring Street. In 1810 it was renamed in honour of George III. George Street today runs all the way from the Harbour Bridge to the Central Railway Station north of Chinatown.

Many 19th-century building remain, such as the 1844 Counting House at No. 43, the Old Police station at No. 127 (1882), and the Russell Hotel at No. 143 (1887).

But it is The Rocks end that most reflects what the early colony must have looked like, characterized by cobbled pavements, narrow side streets, warehouses, bond stores, pubs and shop fronts that reflect the area's early maritime history. Even the Museum of Contemporary Art *(see p73)*, constructed during the 1950s, began its life as the Maritime Services Board's administration offices.

In the early 1970s union workers placed "green bans" on the demolition of The Rocks *(see p29)*. These streets had been considered slum areas by the government of the day. However many of the buildings in George Street were restored and are now listed by the National Trust. The Rocks remains a vibrant part of the city, with George Street at its hub. A market is held here every weekend, when part of the street is closed off to traffic *(see p203)*.

Merchants' House ❸

43 George St, The Rocks. **Map** 1 B2. 📞 9241 5099. 🚌 *Sydney Explorer, 431, 432, 433, 434.* ■ *until further notice.*

The land on which this late-Georgian town house is built was originally owned by Robert Campbell of the nearby

Umbrellas shade the terrace restaurants overlooking the waterfront at Campbell's Storehouses

Old-style Australian products at the corner shop, Susannah Place

Campbell's Storehouses. He sold it to James Combes and John Martyn, painters, glaziers and plumbers in 1841. In 1848, they commissioned architect John Bibb to design a Greek Revival sandstone, hardwood and cedar house that would also be used as a storehouse. The building has been restored by the Sydney Cove Authority to its original state. It is now run by the National Trust of Australia (NSW) as an historic house, shop and function centre, though its much-loved museum of childhood has sadly closed.

Billy Tea on sale at the Susannah Place shop

Susannah Place ❹

58–64 Gloucester St, The Rocks.
Map 1 B2. 🄲 9241 1893. 🚌 Sydney Explorer, 431, 432, 433, 434. 🄾 Jan: 10am–5pm daily; Feb–Dec: 10am–5pm Sat & Sun. ⬤ Good Fri, 25 Dec.
🖳 📷 🖊

THIS 1844 TERRACE of four brick and sandstone houses has a rare history of continuous domestic occupancy from the 1840s right through to 1990. The museum now housed here examines this working-class domestic history, evoking the living conditions of its inhabitants. Rather than re-creating a single period, the museum retains the many renovations made by successive tenants.

Built for Edward and Mary Riley, who arrived from Ireland with their niece Susannah in 1838, these solid houses have basement kitchens and backyard outhouses. Connections to piped water and sewerage had probably arrived by the mid-1850s. The museum surveys the houses' development over the years, from wood and coal to gas and electricity, which enables the visitor to gauge the gradual lightening of the burden of domestic labour.

The terrace, including a corner grocer's shop, escaped the wholesale demolitions that occurred after the outbreak of bubonic plague in 1900, as well as later clearings of land to make way for the Sydney Harbour Bridge and the Cahill Expressway. In the 1970s, it was saved once again when the Builders Labourers' Federation, under the leadership of activist Jack Mundey, imposed a conservation "green ban" on The Rocks (see p29), temporarily halting all demolition and redevelopment work.

Sailors' Home ❺

106 George St, The Rocks.
Map 1 B2. 🄲 9255 1788. 🚌 Sydney Explorer, 431, 432, 433, 434. 🄾 9am–6pm daily. 📷 ♿

BUILT IN 1864 as lodgings for visiting sailors, the building now houses The Rocks Visitors Centre at street level, with exhibitions on the two upper levels. The L-shaped wing that fronts onto George Street was added in 1926.

At the time it was built, the Sailors' Home was a welcome alternative to the many seedy inns and brothels in the area, saving sailors from the perils of "crimping". "Crimps" would tempt newly arrived men into lodgings and bars providing much-sought-after entertainment. While drunk, the sailors would be sold on to departing ships, waking miles out at sea and returning home in debt.

Sailors used the home until 1980, when it was adapted for use as a puppet theatre. In 1994, it opened as a heritage centre and a tourist information and tour bookings facility.

On the second level, a permanent exhibition outlines the archaeological, architectural and social heritage of The Rocks. The third level hosts temporary exhibitions. On the same level, at the eastern end, a re-creation of a 19th-century sleeping cubicle gives visitors a good impression of the spartan nature of the original accommodation available to sailors.

Interior of the Sailors' Home, looking down to the shop

Façade of Cadman's Cottage, the oldest extant building in the city

Cadman's Cottage ⑥

110 George St, The Rocks. **Map** 1 B2. 📞 9247 8861. 🚌 431, 432, 433 434. ⏰ 9am–5pm daily. ⬤ Good Fri, 25 Dec. 📷

DWARFED BY the adjacent Sailors' Home, of which it was once part, this sandstone cottage once housed the Sydney Water Police and now serves as the city's information centre for the Sydney Harbour National Park. Built in 1816 as a barracks for the crews of the governor's boats, it is Sydney's oldest surviving dwelling.

The cottage is named after John Cadman, a convict who was transported in 1798 for horse-stealing. By 1813, he was coxswain of a timber boat and the following year received a conditional pardon. In 1821, he was appointed coxswain of government craft and granted a full pardon. Six years later, he was made boat superintendent and took up residence in the four-room cottage that now bears his name.

Cadman married Elizabeth Mortimer in 1830. She had also arrived in Sydney as a convict, sentenced to seven years transportation for the theft of one hairbrush. The couple, along with Elizabeth's two daughters, lived in the cottage until 1846.

When Cadman's Cottage was built it stood on the foreshore of Sydney Harbour. At high tide, the water used to lap just 2.5 m (8 ft) from the door.

Now, as a result of successive land reclamations such as the filling-in of Circular Quay in the 1870s, it is set well back from the waterfront.

Westpac Museum ⑦

6–8 Playfair St, The Rocks. **Map** 1 B2. 📞 9736 5670. 🚌 Sydney Explorer, 431, 432, 433, 434. ⏰ 10am–5pm Mon–Fri, 10am–4pm Sat & Sun. ⬤ Good Fri, 25–26 Dec.

FROM 1817, WHEN the "holey" dollar was in circulation and Sydney's first bank opened, to present-day plastic credit cards, this museum, located on the first floor, traces the history of banking in Australia. In an incongruous pairing, it also covers Olympic history from 1956 to 2000. There is a self-guided tour with interactive and holographic displays. A wonderful re-creation of a working branch of the 1890s is on the ground floor.

Argyle Centre ⑧

18–24 Argyle St, The Rocks. **Map** 1 B2. 🚌 Sydney Explorer, 431, 432, 433, 434. ⏰ 9am–8pm daily. ⬤ Good Fri, 25 Dec. 📷 ♿

THE FORMER Argyle Bond Stores consists of a number of warehouses surrounding a cobbled courtyard. They have been converted into a retail complex of mostly fashion and accessories shops that retains its period character and charm.

Built between 1826 and the early 1880s, the stores held imported goods such as spirits. All goods forfeited for the non-payment of duties were auctioned in the courtyard. The oldest store was built for Captain John Piper, but it was confiscated and sold after his arrest for embezzlement.

Argyle Centre from the courtyard

Garrison Church ⑨

Cnr Argyle and Lower Fort Sts, Millers Point. **Map** 1 A2. 📞 9247 2664. 🚌 431, 433. ⏰ 9am–6pm daily. 📷 ♿

OFFICIALLY NAMED the Holy Trinity Church, this was dubbed the Garrison Church because it was the colony's first military church. Officers and men from various British

Bank of New South Wales one pound note from around 1830

regiments, stationed at Dawes Point fort, attended morning prayers here until 1870.

Henry Ginn designed the church and, in 1840, the foundation stone was laid. In 1855, the architect Edmund Blacket was engaged to enlarge the church to accommodate up to 600 people. These extensions, minus the spire that Blacket proposed, were completed in 1878. Regimental plaques hung along interior walls recall the church's military associations.

Other features to look out for are the brilliantly coloured east window and the carved red cedar pulpit. The window was donated by the devout parishioner, Dr James Mitchell, father of David Scott Mitchell, the principal benefactor of the State Library of New South Wales' Mitchell Library wing *(see p112)*.

East window, Garrison Church

Sydney Observatory ⓾

Watson Rd, Observatory Hill, The Rocks. **Map** 1 A2. 9217 0485. *Sydney Explorer, 431, 432, 433, 434.* 10am–5pm daily. **Night viewings** 8:30pm daily (bookings essential). 25 Dec, 31 Dec.

I N 1982, THIS DOMED building, which had been a centre for astronomical observation and research for almost 125 years, became the city's astronomy museum. It has interactive equipment and games, along with night sky viewings; it is essential to book for these.

The building began life in the 1850s as a time-ball tower. At 1pm daily, the ball on top of the tower dropped to signal the correct time. A cannon was fired simultaneously at Fort Denison. This custom continues today *(see p107)*.

In the 1880s, some of the first astronomical photographs of the southern sky were taken here. From 1890–1962, the observatory mapped 750,000 stars as part of an international project that produced an atlas of the entire night sky.

Hero of Waterloo ⓫

81 Lower Fort St, Millers Point. **Map** 1 A2. 9252 4553. *431, 432, 433, 434.* 10am–11pm Mon–Sat, 10am–10pm Sun. 25–26 Dec.

T HIS PICTURESQUE old inn is especially welcoming in the winter, when its log fires and cosy ambience offer respite from the chill outside. Built in 1844 from sandstone excavated from the Argyle Cut, this was a favourite drinking place for the nearby garrison's soldiers. Unscrupulous sea captains were said to use the hotel to recruit. Patrons who drank themselves into a stupor were pushed into the cellars through a trapdoor. From here they were carried along underground tunnels to the wharves close by and then on to waiting ships.

Wharf Theatre ⓬

Pier 4, Hickson Rd, Millers Point. **Map** 1 A1. 9250 1700. *431, 432, 433, 434.* **Box office** 9am–8:30pm Mon–Sat; **Wharf** 9am–11pm daily. phone in advance. See **Entertainment** p210.

T HE THEN RECENTLY formed Sydney Theatre Company took possession of this early 20th-century finger wharf at Walsh Bay in 1984. Pier 4/5 is

The corner façade of the Hero of Waterloo hotel in Millers Point

one of four finger wharves at Walsh Bay, reminders of the time when this was a busy part of the city's maritime industry.

Pier 4/5 fulfilled the Sydney Theatre Company's need for a base large enough to hold theatres, rehearsal rooms and administration offices. The ingenious conversion of the once-derelict heritage building into a modern theatre complex is recognized as an outstanding architectural achievement.

Since then, the main theatre, a small and intimate space, has been a venue for many of the company's productions. It has seen premieres of plays from leading Australian playwrights such as Michael Gow and David Williamson, as well as performances of new works from overseas and plays from the standard repertoire.

At the tip of the wharf, the bar area and Wharf Restaurant *(see p189)* command superb harbour views across to the Harbour Bridge *(see pp70–71).*

The Wharf Theatre, a former finger wharf, jutting on to Walsh Bay

Sydney Harbour Bridge ⓭

COMPLETED IN 1932, the construction of the Sydney Harbour Bridge was an economic feat, given the depressed times, as well as an engineering triumph. Prior to this, the only links between the city centre on the south side of the harbour and the residential north side were by ferry or a circuitous 20-km (12½-mile) road route with five bridge crossings. Known as the "Coathanger", the single-span arch bridge was manufactured in sections and took eight years to build, including the railway line. Loans for the total cost of approximately 6.25 million Australian pounds were paid off in 1988. Intrepid visitors can make the vertiginous climb to its summit, with spectacular views as reward.

Ceremonial scissors

The 1932 Opening
The ceremony was disrupted when zealous royalist Francis de Groot rode forward and cut the ribbon, in honour, he claimed, of King and Empire.

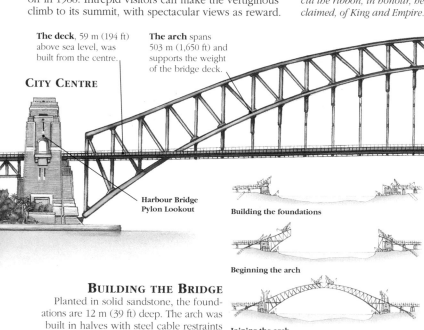

The deck, 59 m (194 ft) above sea level, was built from the centre.

The arch spans 503 m (1,650 ft) and supports the weight of the bridge deck.

CITY CENTRE

Harbour Bridge Pylon Lookout

Building the foundations

Beginning the arch

BUILDING THE BRIDGE

Planted in solid sandstone, the foundations are 12 m (39 ft) deep. The arch was built in halves with steel cable restraints initially supporting each side. Once the two halves met, work began on the deck.

Joining the arch

Deck under construction

Anchoring tunnels are 36 m (118 ft) long and dug into rock at each end.

Support cables were slackened over a 12-day period, enabling the two halves to join.

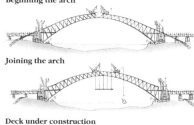

Temporary attachment plate

The Bridge Design
The steel arch of the bridge supports the deck, with hinges at either end bearing the bridge's full weight and spreading the load to the foundations. The hinges allow the structure to move as the steel expands and contracts in response to wind and extreme temperatures.

The Bridge in Curve *(1930) The bridge has inspired many artists. The huge structure towers over the nearby houses in this work by Grace Cossington Smith.*

Over 150,000 vehicles cross the bridge each day, about 15 times as as many as in 1932.

Bridge Workers *The bridge was built by 1,400 workers, 16 of whom were killed in accidents during construction.*

NORTH SHORE

Maintenance *Painting the bridge has become a metaphor for an endless task. Approximately 30,000 litres (6,593 gal) of paint are required for each coat, enough to cover an area equivalent to 60 soccer pitches.*

The vertical hangers support the slanting crossbeams which, in turn, carry the deck.

FATHER OF THE BRIDGE Chief engineer Dr John Bradfield shakes the hand of the driver of the first train to cross the bridge. Over a 20-year period, Bradfield supervised all aspects of the bridge's design and construction. At the opening ceremony, the highway linking the harbour's south side and northern suburbs was named in his honour.

Paying the Toll *The initial toll of sixpence helped pay off the construction loan. The toll is now used for maintenance and to pay for the 1992 Sydney Harbour Tunnel.*

Strolling along a section of the Writers' Walk at Circular Quay

Sydney Opera House ⑭

See pp74–7.

Writers' Walk ⑮

Circular Quay. **Map** 1 C2.
🚌 *Circular Quay routes.*

THIS SERIES OF PLAQUES is set in the pavement at regular intervals between East and West Circular Quay. It gives the visitor the chance to ponder the observations of famous Australian writers, both past and present, on their home country, as well as the musings of some noted literary visitors.

Each plaque is dedicated to a particular writer, with a quotation and a brief biographical note. Australian writers include novelists Miles Franklin and Peter Carey, poets Oodgeroo Noonuccal and Judith Wright, humorists Barry Humphries and Clive James, and the influential feminist writer Germaine Greer. Among visiting writers are Charles Darwin, Joseph Conrad and Mark Twain.

Justice and Police Museum ⑯

8 Phillip St. **Map** 1 C3. 📞 *9252 1144.*
🚌 *Circular Quay routes.* ◻ *Jan: 10am–5pm Sun–Thu; Feb–Dec: 10am–5pm Sat & Sun.* ● *Good Fri, 25 Dec.* 🖼
📷 ♿

THE MUSEUM'S buildings were originally the Water Police Court, designed by Edmund Blacket in 1856; Water Police Station, designed by Alexander Dawson in 1858; and Police Court designed by James Barnet in 1885. Here the rough-and-tumble underworld of quayside crime, from the petty to the violent, was dealt swift and, at times, harsh justice. The museum exhibits bear vivid testimony to that turbulent period, as they document and re-create legal and criminal history. Late-Victorian legal proceedings can be easily imagined in the fully restored courtroom.

Menacing implements from knuckledusters to bludgeons are displayed as the macabre relics of violent and notorious crimes. Other aspects of policing and justice are highlighted in regularly changing exhibitions. The charge room, austere remand cell, prison uniforms, prison artifacts and slideshow evoke powerful images of the penal code of the time.

Montage of criminal "mug shots", Justice and Police Museum

Customs House ⑰

Alfred St, Circular Quay. **Map** 1 B3.
📞 *9247 2285.* 🚌 *Circular Quay routes.* ◻ **Customs House** *phone to check.* ◻ **Djamu Gallery** *9:30am–5pm daily.* ◻ **Objects Gallery and Store** *10am–5pm daily.* 📷 ♿

COLONIAL ARCHITECT James Barnet designed this 1885 sandstone Classical Revival building, on the same site as a previous Customs House. It recalls the days when trading ships berthed at the quay to load and unload their goods. Veranda columns in polished granite, a finely sculpted coat of arms and a clock face, added in 1897, featuring a pair of tridents and dolphins, are among its fine features. The Objects Gallery and Store, displaying a range of design and craft objects, is found here, as well as shops, a performance space and cafés. The Djamu Gallery exhibits indigenous and Pacific Islander artifacts, art and objects.

Detail from Customs House

Macquarie Place ⑱

Map 1 B3. 🚌 *Circular Quay routes.*

IN 1810, GOVERNOR Lachlan Macquarie created this park on what was once part of the vegetable garden of the first Government House. The sandstone obelisk, designed by convict architect Francis Greenway *(see p114)*, was erected in 1818 to mark the starting point for all roads in the colony. The gas lamps recall the fact that this was also the site of Sydney's first street lamp, installed in 1826.

Also in this little triangle of history are the remains of the bow anchor and cannon from HMS *Sirius*, flagship of the First Fleet. There is also a statue of Thomas Mort, a 19th-century industrialist whose vast business interests embraced gold, coal and copper mining, dairy and cotton farming, wool auctioning and ship repair. These days his statue is a marshalling place for the city's somewhat kamikaze bicycle couriers.

Façade of the Museum of Contemporary Art

Museum of Contemporary Art ⓳

Circular Quay West, The Rocks.
Map 1 B2. **(** 9252 4033. ☷ Sydney Explorer, 431, 432, 433 434. ◯ 10am–6pm daily. ● 25 Dec. 🎦 🖭 🖳 🖉

Sydney's substantial collection of contemporary art has grown steadily, but largely out of public view, since 1943. This was the year John Power died, leaving his art collection and a financial bequest to the University of Sydney.

In 1991 the collection, which by then included works by Hockney, Warhol, Christo and Lichtenstein, was transferred to this 1950s mock Art Deco former Maritime Services Board Building at Circular Quay West. As well as showing selections from its permanent collection, the museum hosts exhibitions by local and overseas artists. At the front of the building the MCA Fish Café *(see p194)* spills out onto a terrace with superb views across to the Sydney Opera House. The MCA Store sells distinctive gifts by Australian designers.

National Trust Centre ⓴

Observatory Hill, Watson Rd, The Rocks.
Map 1 A3. **(** 9258 0123. ☷ Sydney Explorer, 343, 431, 432, 433, 434. ◯ 9am–5pm Mon–Fri. **Gallery** ◯ 11am–4pm daily. ● some public hols. 🖳

The buildings that form the headquarters of the conservation organization, the National Trust of Australia, date from 1815, when Macquarie chose the site on Observatory Hill for a military hospital.

Today they house tea rooms, a National Trust shop and the SH Ervin Gallery, containing works by prominent 19th- and 20th-century Australian artists such as Thea Proctor, Margaret Preston and Conrad Martens.

St Philip's Church ㉑

3 York St (enter from Jamison St). **Map** 1 A3. **(** 9247 1071. ☷ George St routes. ◯ 9am–5pm Mon–Fri (apply at office). ● 26 Jan, 25 Apr. 🖭 🖉

Despite its elevated site, this Victorian Gothic church seems overshadowed in its moden setting. Yet, when it was first built, the tall square tower with its decorative pinnacles was a local landmark.

Begun in 1848, St Philip's is by Edmund Blacket, dubbed "the Christopher Wren of Australia" for the 58 churches he designed. In 1851, work was disrupted when its stonemasons left for the gold fields, but by 1856 the building was finally completed.

A peal of bells was donated in 1858, with another added in 1888 to mark Sydney's centenary. These bells still announce the services each Sunday.

The interior and pipe organ of St Philip's Anglican church

A FLAGPOLE ON THE MUDFLATS

It is easy to miss the modest flagpole in Loftus Street near Customs House. It flies a flag, the Union Jack, on the spot where Australia's first ceremonial flag-raising took place. On 26 January 1788, Captain Arthur Phillip came ashore to hoist the flag and declare the foundation of the colony. A toast to the King was drunk and a musket volley fired. On the same day, the rest of the First Fleet arrived from Botany Bay to join Phillip and his men. (On this date each year, the country marks Australia Day with a national holiday.) In 1788, the flagpole was on the edge of mudflats on Sydney Cove. Today, because of the large amount of land reclaimed to build Circular Quay, it is some distance from the water's edge.

The Founding of Australia by Algernon Talmage, which hangs in Parliament House *(see pp112–13)*

Sydney Opera House 🄐

NO BUILDING ON EARTH looks like the Sydney Opera House. Popularly known as the "Opera House" long before the building was complete, it is, in fact, a complex of theatres and halls linked beneath its famous shells. Its birth was long and complicated. Many of the construction problems had not been faced before, resulting in an architectural adventure which lasted 17 years *(see p77)*. An appeal fund was set up, eventually raising $900,000, while the Opera House Lottery raised the balance of the $102 million final cost. As well as being the city's most popular tourist attraction, the Sydney Opera House is also one of the world's busiest performing arts centres.

★ Opera Theatre
Mainly used for opera and ballet, this 1,547-seat theatre is big enough to stage grand operas such as Verdi's Aida.

Detail of The Possum Dreaming *(1988)*
The mural in the Opera Theatre foyer is by Michael Tjakamarra Nelson, an artist from the central Australian desert.

The Opera Theatre
ceiling and walls are painted black to focus attention on the stage.

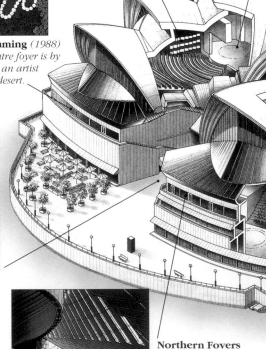

Opera House Walkway
Extensive public walkways around the building offer the visitor views from many different vantage points.

STAR FEATURES

★ **The Roofs**

★ **Concert Hall**

★ **Opera Theatre**

Northern Foyers
With spectacular views over the harbour, the Reception Hall and the large northern foyers of the Opera Theatre and Concert Hall can be hired for conferences, lunches, parties and weddings.

★ Concert Hall

This is the largest hall, with seating for 2,679. It is used for symphony, choral, jazz, folk and pop concerts, chamber music, opera, dance and everything from body building to fashion parades.

VISITORS' CHECKLIST

Bennelong Point. **Map** 1 C2.
📞 9250 7111. *Box office* 9250 7777. 🚌 Sydney Explorer, 324, 438, 440. ⛴ Circular Quay.
🚆 Circular Quay. 🅿 for performances and tours only.
📷 ♿ limited (9250 7209).
🎫 9am– 4pm daily (except Good Fri, 25 Dec). Check in advance (9250 7250). 🎦 🍴 🛍 🏛

The Monumental Steps and forecourt are used for outdoor entertainment.

Bennelong Restaurant
This dramatic and elegant venue is one of the finest restaurants in Sydney (see p188).

The Playhouse, seating almost 400, is ideal for intimate productions while also able to present plays with larger casts.

★ The Roofs

Although apocryphal, the theory that Jørn Utzon's arched roof design came to him while peeling an orange is appealing. The highest point is 67 m (221 ft) above sea level.

Curtain of the Moon *(1972)*
Designed by John Coburn, this and its fellow Curtain of the Sun were originally used in the Drama and Opera Theatres. Both have been removed for preservation.

Exploring Sydney Opera House

THE SYDNEY OPERA HOUSE covers almost 2 ha (4.5 acres), and is the fourth building to stand on this prominent site. Underneath the ten spectacular roofs of varying planes and textures lies a complex maze of more than 1,000 rooms, some oddly shaped to fit into niches and nooks created by the angular exterior. The power supply alone could easily support a town of 25,000 people.

Sydney Dance Company poster

Coppelia **in the Opera Theatre**

OPERA THEATRE

THE RELATIVELY compact size of this venue is a bonus for patrons who savour intimacy. Stage designers continue to demonstrate the opera theatre's great versatility for both opera and dance. The proscenium opening is 12 m (39 ft) wide, and the stage extends back 21 m (69 ft), while the orchestra pit accommodates up to 70–80 musicians. It is rumoured that Box C plays host to a resident ghost.

CONCERT HALL

THE RICH concert acoustics under the vaulted ceiling of this venue are much admired. Sumptuous Australian wood panelling and the 18 acoustic rings above the stage clearly reflect back the sound. The 10,500 pipe Grand Organ was designed and built by Ronald Sharp from 1969–79.

DRAMA THEATRE AND PLAYHOUSE

THE DRAMA THEATRE was not in the original building plan, so jackhammers were brought in to hack it out of the concrete. Its stage is 15 m (160 ft) square, and can be clearly viewed from every seat in the auditorium. Refrigerated aluminium panels in the ceiling control the temperature.

Fine Australian art hangs in the Playhouse foyer, notably Sidney Nolan's eye-catching *Little Shark* (1973) and a fresco by Salvatore Zofrea (1992–3), inspired by the play *Summer of the Seventeenth Doll.*

BACKSTAGE

ARTISTS PERFORMING at the Opera House have the use of five rehearsal studios, 60 dressing rooms and suites and a green room complete with restaurant, bar and lounge.

The scene-changing machinery works on very well-oiled wheels; most crucial in the Opera Theatre where there is regularly a nightly change of performance, with an average of 16 operas being performed in repertoire each year.

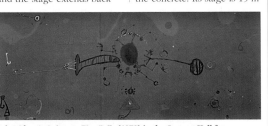

John Olsen's *Salute to Five Bells* (1973) in the Concert Hall foyer

TIMELINE

1945	1950	1955	1960	1965	1970

1955 International design competition announced

1948 Sir Eugene Goossens lobbies government and Bennelong Point is chosen as opera house site

1957 Utzon's design wins and a lottery is established to finance the building

1963 Building of roof shells begins

Roof in mid-construction

1973 Opera House officially opened by Queen Elizabeth II

1959 Construction begins

Old tram shed at Bennelong Point

1963 Utzon opens Sydney office

1966 Utzon resigns. Australian architects appointed to complete interior design

1967 Concrete roof shells completed

1973 Prokofiev's opera *War and Peace* is the first public performance in Opera House

The Design of the Opera House

Jørn Utzon

IN 1957, JØRN UTZON won the international competition to design the Sydney Opera House. He envisaged a living sculpture that could be viewed from any angle – land, air or sea – with the roofs as a "fifth façade". It was boldly conceived, posing architectural and engineering problems that Utzon's initial compendium of sketches did not begin to solve. When construction began in 1959, the intricate design proved impossible to execute and had to be greatly modified. The project remained so controversial that Utzon resigned in 1966 and an Australian design team completed the building's interior. Over the years, the Opera House has been variously described as "one of the modern wonders of the world" and "a ruck of nuns".

The Red Book, as submitted for the 1957 design competition, contains Utzon's original concept sketches for the Sydney Opera House.

Segmented globe

Segments separated

Roof comes into view

Several pieces cut out of a globe were used in an ingenious manner by architect Jørn Utzon to make up the now familiar shell roof structure.

UTZON'S OPERA HOUSE MODEL

Shell membrane roof

The northern foyers overlook Sydney Harbour.

Utzon visualized a building that "floated" on water.

The construction materials remain clearly exposed.

Stepped base

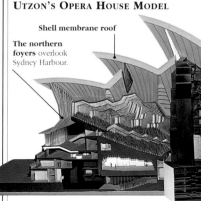

Utzon's original interiors and many of his design features now exist only in model form. The architect donated his models and plans to the State Library of NSW (see p112).

The pre-cast roof has its inspiration in nature. The basic idea for the formwork of the roof was taken from the fanlike ribs of a palm. Realizing this deceptively simple idea took Utzon six years of design work.

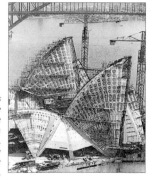

The roof tiles were not fixed in place individually, but installed in panels to create the smooth and continuous roof surface.

CITY CENTRE

USTRALIA'S first thoroughfare, George Street, was originally lined with clusters of mud and wattle huts. The gold rushes brought bustling prosperity, and by the 1880s shops and the architecturally majestic edifices of banks dominated the area.

Mosaic floor detail, St Mary's Cathedral

The city's first skyscraper – Culwulla Chambers in Castlereagh Street – was completed in 1913, but the city council then imposed a 46-m (150-ft) height restriction which remained in place until 1956. Hyde Park, on the edge of the city centre, was first used as a race-course, attracting illegal betting and gambling taverns to Elizabeth Street. The park went on to host other amusements: wrestling matches, circuses, public hangings and, from 1804 onwards, cricket matches between the army and the town. Today the park provides a surprisingly peaceful oasis, while the city's commercial centre is an area of glamorous boutiques, department stores, extravagant arcades and malls. Excellent shopping and browsing is on offer for all budgets with plenty of diversions to occupy the casual visitor.

SIGHTS AT A GLANCE

Historic Streets and Buildings
Marble Bar ❶
Queen Victoria Building ❷
Strand Arcade ❺
Martin Place ❻
Lands Department Building ❼
Sydney Town Hall ⓬

Museums and Galleries
Museum of Sydney ❽
Australian Museum pp88–9 ⓮

Landmarks
AMP Tower p83 ❹

Cathedrals and Synagogues
St Mary's Cathedral ❾
Great Synagogue ⓫
St Andrew's Cathedral ⓭

Parks and Gardens
Hyde Park ❿

Theatres
State Theatre ❸

GETTING THERE
Town Hall, Wynyard, Martin Place, St James and Museum railway stations serve the area. There are frequent buses, particularly along Elizabeth and George Streets. Monorail stops are at City Centre, Park Plaza and World Square.

KEY

	Street-by-Street map See pp80–81
🚆	CityRail station
🚝	Monorail station
🚌	Bus terminus
P	Parking

0 metres 500
0 yards 500

◁ **Mythological figures in the Archibald Fountain, Hyde Park**

Street-by-Street: City Centre

Sculpture outside the MLC Centre

ALTHOUGH CLOSELY RIVALLED by Melbourne, this is the business and commercial capital of Australia. Vibrant by day, at night the streets are far less busy when office workers and shoppers have gone home. The comparatively small city centre of this sprawling metropolis seems to be almost jammed into a few city blocks. Because Sydney grew in such a haphazard fashion, with many of today's streets following tracks from the harbour originally made by bullocks, there was no allowance for the expansion of the burgeoning city into what has become a major international centre. A colourful night scene of cafés, restaurants and theatres is emerging, however, as more people return to the city centre to live.

★ **Queen Victoria Building**
Taking up an entire city block, this 1898 former produce market has been lovingly restored and is now a shopping mall ❷

State Theatre
A gem from the era when the movies reigned, this glittering and richly decorated 1929 cinema was once hailed as "the Empire's greatest theatre" ❸

To Sydney Town Hall

The Queen Victoria Statue was found after a worldwide search in 1983 ended in a small Irish village. It had lain forgotten and neglected since being removed from the front of the Irish Parliament in 1947.

STAR SIGHTS

★ Queen Victoria Building

★ Sydney Tower

★ Martin Place

0 metres   100

0 yards   100

KEY

– – – Suggested route

Marble Bar
Once a landmark bar in the 1890 Tattersalls hotel, it was dismantled and re-erected in the Sydney Hilton in 1973 ❶

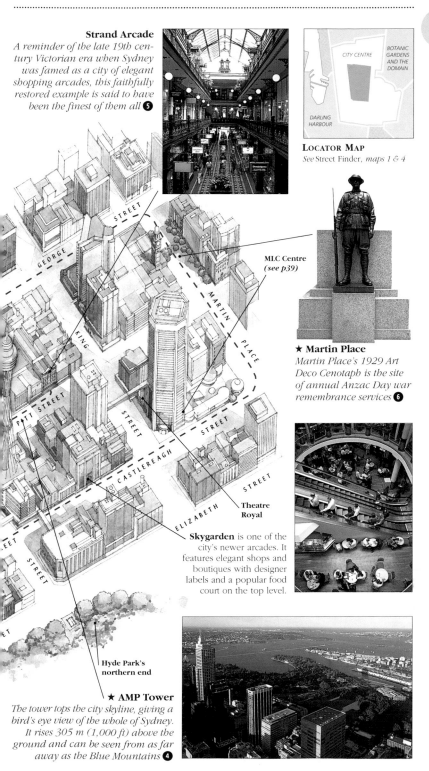

Strand Arcade
A reminder of the late 19th century Victorian era when Sydney was famed as a city of elegant shopping arcades, this faithfully restored example is said to have been the finest of them all **5**

LOCATOR MAP
See Street Finder, *maps 1 & 4*

MLC Centre
(see p39)

★ **Martin Place**
Martin Place's 1929 Art Deco Cenotaph is the site of annual Anzac Day war remembrance services **6**

Theatre Royal

Skygarden is one of the city's newer arcades. It features elegant shops and boutiques with designer labels and a popular food court on the top level.

Hyde Park's northern end

★ **AMP Tower**
The tower tops the city skyline, giving a bird's eye view of the whole of Sydney. It rises 305 m (1,000 ft) above the ground and can be seen from as far away as the Blue Mountains **4**

Entrance to the Marble Bar

The Marble Bar **❶**

259 Pitt St. **Map** 1 B5. 🚌 *George St routes.* ⏰ *noon–11pm Mon–Wed, noon–midnight Thu, noon–2am Fri, 3pm–3am Sat, 5–11pm Sun.* ⏺ *public hols.* 📷 *See **Restaurants, Cafés and Pubs** p197.*

T HE MARBLE BAR, originally part of George Adams' Tattersalls Hotel built in 1893, is an inspired link with the Sydney of an earlier era. The bar, whose rich and decadent Italian Renaissance style had made it a local institution, was dismantled before the demolition of the hotel in 1969. Its colonnade entrance, fireplaces and counters were re-erected in the Sydney Hilton basement and reopened in 1973.

During the week, the bar attracts a broad range of city workers for lunch and after-work drinks. On Fridays and at weekends if a band is playing, the bar bustles with a younger crowd who come to hear the mostly jazz and rhythm and blues music.

Queen Victoria Building **❷**

455 George St. **Map** 1 B5. 📞 *9264 9209.* 🚌 *George St routes.* ⏰ *9am–6pm Mon–Wed, 9am–9pm Thu, 9am–6pm Fri & Sat, 11am–5pm Sun & public hols.* 📷 ♿ 🛍 *See **Shops and Markets** pp198 and 200.*

F RENCH DESIGNER Pierre Cardin called the Queen Victoria Building "the most beautiful shopping centre in the world". Yet this spacious and ornate Romanesque building, better known as the QVB, began life as the Sydney produce market. The dust, flies, grime and shouts as horses struggled with heavy loads on the slippery ramps are now difficult to imagine. Completed to the design of City Architect George McRae in 1898, the dominant features are the central dome, sheathed in copper as are the 20 smaller domes, and the glass barrel vault roof which lets in a flood of natural light.

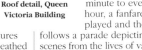
Roof detail, Queen Victoria Building

The market closed at the end of World War I and the building fell into disrepair. It had various roles during this time, including that of City Library. By the 1950s, after extensive remodelling and neglect, it was threatened with demolition.

Refurbished at a cost of over $75 million, the QVB reopened in 1986 as today's grand shopping gallery, housing over 190 shops and boutiques on four levels. At the Town Hall end a wishing well incorporates a stone from Blarney Castle, Ireland and a sculpture of Islay, beloved dog of Queen Victoria. In 1983, a worldwide search began for a statue of the queen herself. One was finally found in the village of Daingean, Republic of Ireland, where it had lain forgotten since its removal from the front of the Irish Parliament in 1947.

Now fully restored, the Queen Victoria Statue stands near the wishing well. Inside the QVB, suspended from the ceiling, is the Royal Clock. Weighing more than 1 tonne and over 5 m (17 ft) tall, the clock was designed by Neil Glasser in 1982. The upper structure features part of Balmoral Castle above a copy of the four dials of Big Ben. At one minute to every hour, a fanfare is played and there follows a parade depicting six scenes from the lives of various kings and queens of England.

State Theatre **❸**

49 Market St. **Map** 1 B5. 📞 *9373 6655.* **Tours** *9231 4629.* 🚌 *George St routes.* **Box office** ⏰ *9am–5:30pm Mon–Sat.* ⏺ *Good Fri, 25 Dec.* ♿ 🛍 *bookings necessary.*

W HEN IT OPENED in 1929, this picture palace was hailed as the finest that local craftsmanship could achieve. The State Theatre is one of the best examples in Australia of the Architectural fantasies used to entice people to the movies.

Its Cinema Baroque style is evident right from the Gothic foyer, with its vaulted ceiling, mosaic floor, richly decorated marble columns and statues. Inside the brass and bronze doors, the auditorium which seats over 2,000 people is lit by a 20,000-piece chandelier. The Wurlitzer organ rises from below stage just before performances. Now one of Sydney's premier concert, live theatre and special events venues, it is also the main base for the Sydney Film Festival, held in June of each year *(see p51).*

The ornately decorated Gothic foyer of the State Theatre

AMP Tower **4**

THE HIGHEST OBSERVATION DECK in the Southern Hemisphere, the AMP Tower, formerly known as the Sydney Tower, was conceived as part of the 1970s Centrepoint shopping centre, but was not completed until 1981. More than a million people visit the turret each year to appreciate stunning 360-degree views, often stretching for over 85 km (53 miles). A landmark in itself, it can be seen from almost anywhere in the city, and far beyond.

Observation Level
Views from Level 4 stretch to Pittwater in the north, Botany Bay to the south, westwards to the Blue Mountains, and along the harbour out to the open sea.

The 30-m (98-ft) spire completes the total 305 m (1,000 ft) of the tower's height.

The water tank holds 162,000 litres (35,500 gallons) and acts as an enormous stabilizer on very windy days.

Level 4: Observation

Level 3: Coffee shop

Level 2: Buffet restaurant

Level 1: A la carte restaurant

The turret's nine levels, with room to hold almost 1,000 people at a time, include two revolving restaurants, a coffee shop and the Observation Level.

The windows comprise three layers. The outer has a gold dust coating. The frame design prevents panes falling outwards.

The 56 cables weigh seven tonnes each. If laid end to end, they would reach from New Zealand to Sydney.

The shaft is designed to withstand wind speeds expected only once in 500 years, as well as unprecedented earthquakes.

The stairs are two separate, fireproofed emergency escape routes. Each year in September or October Sydney's fittest race up the 1,474 stairs.

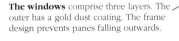

Construction of Turret
The eight turret levels were erected on the roof of the base building, then hoisted up the shaft using hydraulic jacks.

Double-decker lifts can carry up to 2,000 people per hour. At full speed, a lift takes only 40 seconds to ascend the 76 floors to the Observation Level.

New Year's Eve
Every year, fireworks are set off on top of the AMP Tower as part of the official public fireworks displays to mark the New Year.

Strand Arcade **5**

412–414 George St. **Map** 1 B5.
C 9232 4199. **E** George St routes.
O 9am–5:30pm Mon–Wed & Fri,
9am–9pm Thu, 9am–4pm Sat,
11am–4pm Sun. **C** most public
hols. **O** **&** See **Shops and
Markets** pp198–201.

Victorian Sydney was a city
of grand shopping arcades.
The Strand, joining George and
Pitt Streets and designed by
English architect John Spencer,
was the finest jewel in the city's
crown. The blaze of publicity
surrounding its opening in
April 1892 was equalled only
by the natural light pouring
through the glass roof and the
artificial glare from the chandeliers, each carrying 50 jets
of gas as well as 50 lamps.

The boutiques and shops in
the galleries make window
shopping a delight in this airy
building which, after a fire in
1976, was restored to its original splendour. Be sure to stop,
as shoppers have done since
opening day, for light refreshments at Harris Coffee & Tea
near the Pitt Street entrance.

**The Pitt Street entrance to the
majestic Strand Arcade**

Martin Place **6**

Map 1 B4. **E** George St & Elizabeth
St routes.

Running from George Street
across Pitt, Castlereagh and
Elizabeth Streets to Macquarie
Street, this plaza was opened
in 1891 and made a traffic-free
precinct in 1971. It is busiest at
lunchtime when city workers
enjoy their sandwiches while
watching free entertainment,

Interior of National Australia Bank, George Street end of Martin Place

sponsored by the Sydney City
Council, in an amphitheatre
near Castlereagh Street.

Every Anzac Day, a national
day of war remembrance on
25 April, the focus moves to
the Cenotaph at the George
Street end. Thousands of past
and present servicemen and
women attend a dawn service
and wreath-laying ceremony,
followed by a march-past. The
shrine, with bronze statues of a
soldier and a sailor on a granite
base, by Bertram MacKennal,
was unveiled in 1929.

On the southern side of the
Cenotaph is the symmetrical
façade of the Renaissance-
style General Post Office,
considered to be the finest
building by James Barnet,
Colonial Architect. Con-
struction of the GPO, as
Sydneysiders call it, took
place between 1866 and
1874, with additions in
Pitt Street between 1881
and 1885. Most contro-
versial were the relief
figures executed by
Tomaso Sani. Although **Statue of explorer**
Barnet declared that　　**Gregory Blaxland**
the figures represented
Australians in realistic form,
they were labelled "grotesque".

A stainless steel sculpture
of upended cubes, the Dobell
Memorial Sculpture stands
above a waterfall which was

funded by public subscription
following a donation by artist
Lloyd Rees. The sculpture, a
tribute to the artist William
Dobell (see p29), was created
by Bert Flugelman in 1979.

Lands Department
Building **7**

23 Bridge St. **Map** 1 B3. **E** 325,
George St routes. **O** only 2 weeks in
the year, dates vary. **&**

Designed by the Colonial
Architect James Barnet, the
three-storey Classical Revival
sandstone edifice was built
between 1877 and 1890.
As for the GPO building,
Pyrmont sandstone was
used for the exterior.
Decisions about the sub-
division of much of rural
eastern Australia were
made in offices within.
Statues of explorers and
legislators who "pro-
moted settlement" fill
23 of the façade's 48
niches; the remainder
are still empty. The
luminaries include the
explorers Hovell and Hume,
Sir Thomas Mitchell, Blaxland,
Lawson and Wentworth (see
p136), Ludwig Leichhardt, Bass
and Matthew Flinders and the
botanist Sir Joseph Banks.

Museum of Sydney ❽

37 Phillip St. **Map** 1 B3. 📞 9251 5988. 🚌 Circular Quay routes. 🕐 9:30am–5pm daily. 🔴 Good Fri, 25 Dec. 📷 🚻 ♿

Sɪᴛᴜᴀᴛᴇᴅ ᴀᴛ the bottom of Governor Phillip Tower, the Museum of Sydney is on the site of the first Government House, the home, office and seat of authority for the first nine governors of NSW from 1788 until its demolition in 1846. The design assimilates a valuable archaeological site into a modern office block. The museum itself traces the city's turbulent history, from the 1788 arrival of the British colonists until the present day.

The Eora People

The museum sits on Cadigal land. A new gallery explores the culture, history, continuity and place of Sydney's original Aboriginal inhabitants, and the "turning point" of colonization/ invasion. Collectors' chests hold items of daily use such as flint and ochre, each piece painstakingly catalogued and evocatively interpreted.

Eora stories are recounted by today's Sydney Kooris; just some of the voices in the whispering soundscape that

The Lookout, Level 3, overlooking the piazza towards Circular Quay

permeates the museum. In the square at the front of the complex, the acclaimed *Edge of the Trees* sculpture, with its collection of 29 sandstone, steel and wooden pillars, symbolizes the first contact between the Aboriginal peoples and Europeans. Haunting voices in the Eora tongue fill the space. Inscribed in the wood are signatures of the First Fleeters and names of botanical species in both the indigenous language and Latin. Incisions made in the pillars are filled with organic materials such as ash, feathers, bone, shells and human hair.

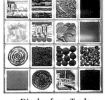

Display from Trade exhibition on Level 3

European Settlement

Outside the museum, a paving pattern outlines the site of first Government House. Original foundations, lost under street level for many years, can be seen here through a window. Inside the entrance a viewing floor reveals more foundations. A segment of wall has been reconstructed using sandstone excavated during archaeological exploration of the site.

Exhibits draw on pre-1850s resources from both local and overseas museums, ranging from the Australian Museum *(see pp88–9)* to the British Natural History Museum.

The displays are brought to life by the use of multimedia. On Level 2, holographic ghosts tell their stories, supported by artifacts such as dinner plates and bone dominoes. A video screen, stretching up through all three levels, shows the Sydney bush as it was in 1788. Tales of colonial places, people and events are told through the materials and goods displayed, from bric-a-brac to letter fragments, in the collectors' chests. Panoramic images of the developing city provide a vivid backdrop.

Edge of the Trees **sculptural installation by Janet Laurence and Fiona Foley (1995)**

Terrazzo mosaic floor in the crypt of St Mary's Cathedral

St Mary's Cathedral ❾

Cathedral St. **Map** 1 C5. ☎ *9220 0400.* ▦ *Elizabeth St routes.* ⬭ *6:30am–6:30pm daily.* ♿ *with advance notice.* 🎦 *noon Sun.*

ALTHOUGH Catholics arrived with the First Fleet, the celebration of Mass was at first prohibited because of fears that the priests would provoke civil strife among the colony's large Irish Catholic population. It was not until 1820 that the first priests were appointed and regular services allowed. In 1821, Governor Macquarie

laid the foundation stone for St Mary's Chapel on the site where the cathedral is today. This was the first land granted to the Catholic Church in Australia.

The initial section of this Gothic Revival style cathedral was opened in 1882. In 1928, the building was completed, but without the twin southern spires originally proposed by the architect William Wardell. By the entrance steps are statues of Australia's first cardinal, Moran, and Archbishop Kelly who laid the stone for the final stage in 1913. They

were sculpted by Bertram MacKennal, also responsible for the Martin Place Cenotaph (*see p84*) and the Shakespeare group outside the State Library (*see p112*). The crypt's Celtic-inspired terrazzo mosaic floor took 15 years to complete.

Great Synagogue ⓫

187 Elizabeth St. **Map** 1 B5. ☎ *9267 2477.* ▦ *394, 396, 380, 382.* ⬭ *for services and tours only.* ◕ *public & Jewish hols.* ♿ 🎦 *noon Tue, Thu.*

THE LONGEST established Jewish Orthodox congregation in Australia, consisting of more than 900 families, assembles in this synagogue. The building was consecrated in 1878. Although Jews had arrived with the First Fleet, worship did not commence until the 1820s. With its carved entrance columns and wrought iron gates, the synagogue is perhaps the finest work of Thomas Rowe, the architect of Sydney Hospital (*see p113*). Among the interior features is a panelled ceiling, decorated with many hundreds of tiny gold leaf stars.

Candelabra from the Great Synagogue

Hyde Park ❿

Map 1 B5. ▦ *Elizabeth St routes.*

FENCED AND NAMED after its London equivalent by Governor Macquarie in 1810, Hyde Park marked the outskirts of the township. It was a popular exercise field for garrison troops and later incor-

porated a racecourse and a cricket pitch. Though much smaller today than the original park, it still provides a peaceful haven in the middle of the bustling city centre.

Anzac Memorial
The 30-m (98-ft) high Art Deco memorial, reflected in the poplar-lined Pool of Remembrance, commemorates those Australians who were killed at war in the service of their country. Opened in 1934, the Anzac Memorial now includes a photographic and military artifact exhibition downstairs.

Sandringham Garden
In spring, the pergola in this sunken garden is a cascade of mauve-flowering wisteria. The garden, a memorial to the English kings George V and George VI, was opened by Queen Elizabeth II in 1954.

Tomb of the Unknown Soldier in the Art Deco Anzac Memorial

Diana, goddess of purity and the chase, Archibald Fountain

Archibald Fountain
This bronze and granite fountain commemorates the French and Australian World War I alliance. It was completed by François Sicard in 1932 and donated by JF Archibald, one of the founders of the *Bulletin*, a popular literary magazine which encouraged the work of Henry Lawson and "Banjo" Paterson, among many others. It was Archibald's bequest that established the Archibald Prize for portraiture (*see p50*).

The Grand Organ in Sydney Town Hall's Centennial Hall

Sydney Town Hall ⑫

483 George St. **Map** 4 E2.
☎ 9265 9333. 🚌 George St routes.
🕐 8:30am–6pm Mon–Fri. ● 1 Jan,
25 Dec. 🚻 ♿ 9231 4629.

THE STEPS of this sandstone building, central to George Street's Victorian architecture, have been a favourite Sydney meeting place since it opened in 1869. Walled burial grounds had originally covered the site.

It is a fine example of high Victorian architecture, even though the plans of the original architect, JH Wilson, proved

beyond the builders' capabilities. A rapid succession of designers was brought in. The vestibule – an elegant salon with intricate plasterwork, lavish stained glass and a crystal chandelier – is the work of Albert Bond. The Bradbridge brothers completed the clock tower in 1884. From 1888–9, other architects were used for the Centennial Hall, with its coffered zinc ceiling and an imposing 19th-century organ with more than 8,500 pipes.

On the façade, you will see numerous carved lion heads. Just to the north of the main entrance, facing George Street, a lion has been carved with one eye shut. This oddity appeared because of the head stonemason's habit of checking the line of the stonework by closing one eye. The sly joke was not found until work was finished.

Some people have concluded that Sydney Town Hall became the city's most elaborate building by accident, as each architect strove to outdo his predecessors. Today, it makes a magnificent venue for concerts, dances and balls.

The Great Bible, St Andrew's Cathedral

St Andrew's Cathedral ⑬

Sydney Square, Cnr George & Bathurst Sts. **Map** 4 E3. ☎ 9265 1661.
🚌 George St routes. 🕐 7:30am–6pm Mon–Fri, 9:30am–4pm Sat, 8am–8pm Sun. 🅿 ♿ 🚻 11am & 1:45pm Mon–Fri, after 10:30am service on Sun.

WHILE THE FOUNDATION stone for the country's oldest cathedral was laid in 1819, almost 50 years elapsed before the building was consecrated in 1868. The Gothic Revival design is by Edmund Blacket, whose ashes are interred here. Inspired by York Minster in England, the twin towers were completed in 1874. In 1949, the main entrance was moved to the eastern end near George Street.

Inside are memorials to Sydney pioneers, including Thomas Mort (see p72). A 1539 bible and beads collected in the Holy Land are among the religious memorabilia.

The southern wall incorporates stones from London's St Paul's Cathedral, Westminster Abbey and the House of Lords.

Obelisk
This monument was dubbed "Thornton's Scent Bottle" after the mayor of Sydney who had it erected in 1857. The mock-Egyptian edifice is in fact a ventilator for a sewer.

Emden **Gun**
Standing at the corner of College and Liverpool Streets, this monument commemorates a World War I naval action. HMAS *Sydney* destroyed the German raider *Emden* off the Cocos Islands on 9 November 1914, and 180 crew members were taken prisoner.

City Circle Railway
The park we see today bears very little resemblance to the Hyde Park of old. In fact, the dictates of city railway tunnels have largely created its present landscape. Tunnels were excavated through an open cut that

ran through the park, and after the rail system was opened in 1926 the entire area had to be remodelled and replanted.

Busby's Bore Fountain
This is a reminder of Busby's Bore, the city's first piped water supply opened in 1837.

John Busby, a civil engineer, conceived and supervised the construction of the 4.4-km (2¾-mile) tunnel. It carried water from bores on Lachlan Swamp, now within Centennial Park (see p127), to horse-drawn water carriers on the corner of Elizabeth and Park Streets.

Game in progress on the giant chessboard, near Busby's Bore Fountain

Australian Museum

Model head of
Tyrannosaurus rex

THE AUSTRALIAN MUSEUM, founded in 1827, was the first museum established in Australia and remains the premier showcase of Australian natural history. The main building, an impressive sandstone structure with a marble staircase, faces Hyde Park. Architect Mortimer Lewis was forced to resign his position when building costs began to far exceed the budget. Construction was completed in the 1860s by James Barnet. The collection provides a visual and audio journey across Australia and the near Pacific, covering prehistory, biology, botany, environment and cultural heritage. Australian Aboriginal cultures and traditions are celebrated in a community access space also used for dance and other performances. Touring exhibitions are a regular and popular museum feature.

Museum Entrance
The façade features massive Corinthian square pillars or piers.

Planet of Minerals
This section features a walk-through re-creation of an underground mine with a display of gems and minerals.

Crocoite   **Azurite**

Agate   **Education Centre**

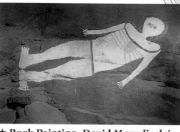

★ Rock Painting, David Mowaljarlai
In 1984, this Aboriginal artist painted an interpretation of the Wandjina, Ancestor Spirit of nature, rain-bearing clouds and law who can punish by cyclone and flood.

Skeletons

Ground floor

Main entrance

Aboriginal Australia
displays artifacts of daily use, like spears and grinding stones, as well as grave posts.

STAR EXHIBITS

★ **Afrovenator**

★ **"Eric", the Opalized Pliosaur**

★ **Rock Painting, David Mowaljarlai**

MUSEUM GUIDE
Aboriginal Australia is on the ground floor, as is the skeleton display. Mineral and rock exhibits are in two galleries on Level 1, with dinosaurs on Level 2. Birds and insects are also found on Level 2, along with human evolution, Indonesia and marine invertebrate displays.

Search & Discover
Sydneysiders bring bugs, rocks and bones to this area for identification. The public can also access CD-Roms for research.

VISITORS' CHECKLIST

6 College St. **Map** 4 F3.
☎ 9320 6000. 🚌 Sydney Explorer, 323, 324, 325, 327, 389.
🚆 Museum, St James. 🅿 Park Plaza. ◯ 9:30am–5pm daily.
● 25 Dec. 🖼 🅿 ♿ 🛒 🍴
🔲 🎫 **Concerts, films.**

Level 2

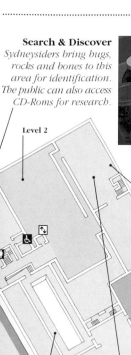

Human evolution

★ **"Eric", the Opalized Pliosaur**
The extinct marine reptile was found in a mineral field where it was in the process of turning into solid opal.

Marine invertebrates

Discovery Space

Indonesia
The gamelan orchestra on display comprises xylophones for melody and gongs for rhythm. The gallery sometimes hosts performances.

Level 1

★ **Afrovenator**
The almost complete skeleton of the predatory "African hunter", Afrovenator, is about 9 m (30 ft) long. The dinosaur was discovered and subsequently unearthed in Niger, Africa, in 1993.

Birds and Insects
Australia's most poisonous spider, the male of the funnel-web species, dwells exclusively in the Greater Sydney region.

KEY TO FLOORPLAN

☐ Australian Environments
▨ Indonesia
▨ More than Dinosaurs
☐ Peoples of Australia
☐ Temporary exhibition space
☐ Non-exhibition space

"WELCOME STRANGER" GOLD NUGGET

In 1869, the largest gold nugget ever found in Australia was discovered in Victoria. It weighed 71.06 kg (156 lb). The museum holds a cast of the original in a display examining the impact of the gold rush, when the Australian population doubled in ten years.

◀———— 67.5 cm (26½ in) wide ————▶

DARLING HARBOUR

Named in honour of the seventh governor of New South Wales, Ralph Darling, this area was originally called Cockle Bay because of the molluscs early European settlers collected here. Darling Harbour was an unsavoury place in the late 19th century, known for its thieves' dens and bawdy houses. Its docks, backed by a railway yard, were an embarkation point for wool and other exports. The country's industrial age began here in 1815 with the opening of a steam mill. Darling Harbour continued as, first, a grimy workplace and, later, with the industrial decline of Sydney Harbour, an obsolete and run-down backwater. In the 1980s, it was decided to make this prime city site a focal point of the 1988 Bicentenary. The project was the largest urban redevelopment ever carried out in Australia. Today Darling Harbour is an extension of the city centre with a mixture of fine museums, shopping and open space. It has become a popular and lively area of Sydney.

Horatio Nelson, National Maritime Museum

SIGHTS AT A GLANCE

Historic Districts and Buildings
Pyrmont Bridge ❸
Chinatown ❼

Museums and Galleries
National Maritime Museum pp94–5 ❶
Harris Street Motor Museum ❹
Powerhouse Museum pp100–101 ❿

Parks and Gardens
Chinese Garden ❻

Entertainment
Sydney Aquarium pp96–7 ❷
Convention and Exhibition Centre ❺

Theatres
Capitol Theatre ❽

Markets
Paddy's Market ❾

GETTING THERE

Harbourside, Convention and Haymarket monorail stations are convenient. Ferries run to Darling Harbour wharf, while the most useful buses are the Sydney Explorer, 456 and 501.

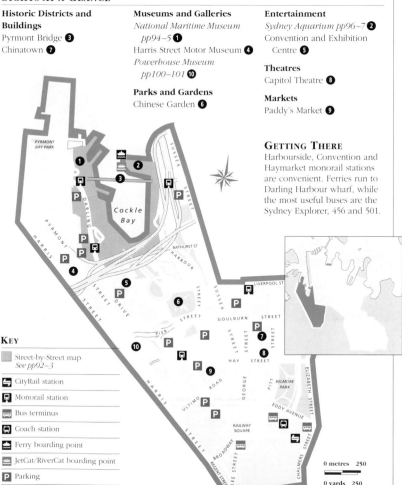

KEY

▨	Street-by-Street map *See pp92–3*
🚉	CityRail station
▣	Monorail station
🚌	Bus terminus
▣	Coach station
⛴	Ferry boarding point
⛴	JetCat/RiverCat boarding point
🅿	Parking

0 metres 250
0 yards 250

◁ **View from Harbourside Shopping Centre looking east towards the city**

Street-by-Street: Darling Harbour

**Carpentaria lightship,
National Maritime Museum**

Dᴀʀʟɪɴɢ ʜᴀʀʙᴏᴜʀ was New South Wales' bicentennial gift to itself. This imaginative urban redevelopment covers a 54-ha (133-acre) site that was once a busy industrial centre and international shipping terminal catering for the developing local wool, grain, timber and coal trades. The advent of container shipping proved to be the end of the area's commercial viability and it gradually fell into ruin. In 1984, however, the Darling Harbour Authority was formed to examine the area's commercial options. The resulting complex opened in 1988, complete with the National Maritime Museum and Sydney Aquarium, two of the city's tourist highlights. Free outdoor entertainment, appealing to children in particular, is a regular feature.

The Harbourside Shopping Centre offers a wide range of unusual gifts and Australian souvenirs. Clothing and record shops also vie for attention alongside busy eating houses.

Walkway to Harris Street Motor Museum

Convention and Exhibition Centre
This complex presents an alternating range of trade shows displaying everything from home decorating suggestions to bridal wear ❺

DARLING DRIVE

WESTERN DISTRIBUTOR

WESTERN DISTRIBUTOR

The Tidal Cascades sunken fountain was designed by Robert Woodward, also responsible for the El Alamein Fountain *(see p120)*. The double spiral of water and paths replicates the circular shape of the Convention Centre.

IMAX large-screen cinema

The Dragon Boat Festival, which takes place each April, is now an international event. Over 2,000 people from around the world compete in a dragon boat race that accompanies other Chinese cultural and social events.

Sᴛᴀʀ Sɪɢʜᴛs

★ **Sydney Aquarium**

★ **National Maritime Museum**

Pyrmont Bridge
The swingspan bridge opens for vessels up to 14 m (46 ft) tall. The monorail track running above the walkway also opens up to allow access for even taller boats ❸

LOCATOR MAP
See Street Finder, maps 3 & 4

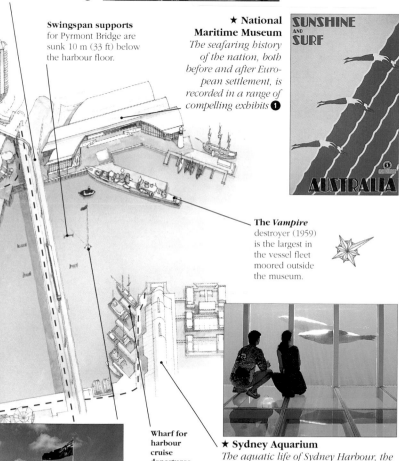

Swingspan supports for Pyrmont Bridge are sunk 10 m (33 ft) below the harbour floor.

★ **National Maritime Museum**
The seafaring history of the nation, both before and after European settlement, is recorded in a range of compelling exhibits ❶

The *Vampire* destroyer (1959) is the largest in the vessel fleet moored outside the museum.

Wharf for harbour cruise departures

★ **Sydney Aquarium**
The aquatic life of Sydney Harbour, the open ocean and the Great Barrier Reef is displayed in massive tanks which can be seen from underwater walkways ❷

The flagpole in Cockle Bay was erected in 1988, the year of the Australian bicentennial. Every year in late July, these calm waters fill with all manner of marine craft on display at the International Boat Show.

0 metres		100
0 yards		100

KEY

‒ ‒ ‒ Suggested route

National Maritime Museum ❶

1602 Willem Blaeu Celestial Globe

BOUNDED AS IT IS by the sea, Australia's history is inextricably linked to maritime traditions. The museum displays material in a broad range of permanent and temporary thematic exhibits, many with interactive elements. As well as artifacts relating to the enduring Aboriginal maritime cultures, the exhibits survey the history of European exploratory voyages in the Pacific, the arrival of convict ships, successive waves of migration, water sports and recreation, and naval life. Historic vessels on show at the wharf include a flimsy Vietnamese refugee boat, sailing, fishing and pearling boats, a navy patrol boat and a World War II commando raider.

Museum Façade
The billowing steel roof design by Philip Cox suggests both the surging sea and the sails of a ship.

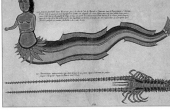

Passengers
The model of the Orcades reflects the grace of 1950s liners. This display also charts harrowing sea voyages made by migrants and refugees.

Merana Eora Nora – First People traces the seafaring traditions of Aboriginal peoples and Torres Strait Islanders.

The Tasman Light was used in a Tasmanian lighthouse.

★ Navigators
This 1754 engraving of an East Indian sea creature is a European vision of the uncharted, exotic "great south".

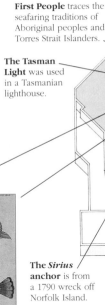

The *Sirius* anchor is from a 1790 wreck off Norfolk Island.

Main entrance (sea level)

The Navy exhibit examines naval life in war and peace, as well as the history of colonial navies.

KEY TO FLOORPLAN

☐	Navigators and Merana Eora Nora
☐	Passengers
☐	Commerce
☐	Leisure
☐	Navy
▨	Linked by the Sea: USA Gallery
☐	Temporary exhibitions
☐	Non-exhibition space

STAR EXHIBITS

- ★ **Navigators and Merana Eora Nora**
- ★ **Leisure**
- ★ **Vampire**

Linked by the Sea honours enduring links between the US and Australia. American traders stopped off in Australia on their way to China.

Commerce
This 1903 Painters' and Dockers' Union banner was carried by waterfront workers in marches. It shows the Niagara *entering the dry dock at Cockatoo Island (see p106).*

★ Leisure
The world's fastest boat, a 1.5 tonne hydroplane named Spirit of Australia, *set the world water speed record in 1978, travelling at 511 km/h (317 mph). It was powered by an anti-submarine aircraft engine.*

Level 1

Mazda Gallery

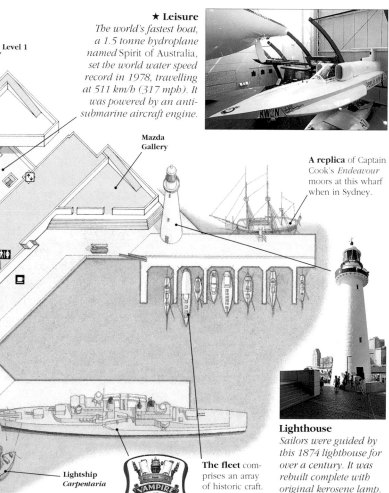

A replica of Captain Cook's *Endeavour* moors at this wharf when in Sydney.

The fleet comprises an array of historic craft.

Lightship *Carpentaria*

Lighthouse
Sailors were guided by this 1874 lighthouse for over a century. It was rebuilt complete with original kerosene lamp.

★ Vampire
The museum's largest vessel is the 1959 Royal Australian Navy destroyer, whose insignia is shown here. Tours of "The Bat" are accompanied by simulated battle action sounds.

MUSEUM GUIDE
The Leisure, Navy and Linked by the Sea: USA Gallery exhibits are located on the main entrance level (sea level). The First Australians, Discovery, Passengers and Commerce sections are found on the first level. There is access to the fleet from both levels.

Sydney Aquarium ❷

Tropical
sea star

SYDNEY AQUARIUM contains the country's most comprehensive collection of Australian aquatic species. Over 5,000 animals from 600 species are held in a series of re-created marine environments. For many visitors, the highlight is a walk "on the ocean floor" through two floating oceanaria with 145 m (480 ft) of acrylic underwater tunnels. These allow close observation of sharks, stingrays and schools of fish. Fur and harbour seals may be viewed above and below water in a special seal sanctuary. None of the displays is harmful to the creatures, and many of the tanks display practical information about marine environmental hazards.

Saltwater Crocodiles
The largest and most dangerous species of crocodile, "salties" live in the swamps and estuaries of Australia's north.

Platypus
Exhibit

Entrance

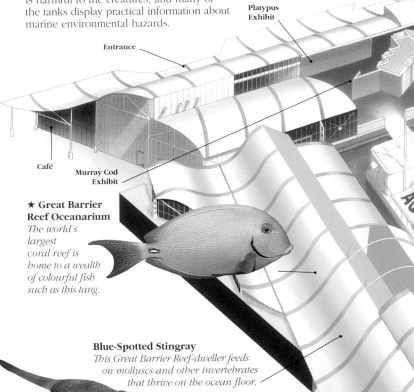

Café

Murray Cod
Exhibit

★ Great Barrier Reef Oceanarium
The world's largest coral reef is home to a wealth of colourful fish such as this tang.

Blue-Spotted Stingray
This Great Barrier Reef-dweller feeds on molluscs and other invertebrates that thrive on the ocean floor.

Aquarium Building and Pier
The stark white design of the aquarium is Structuralist (see p39), an architectural style that dominates Darling Harbour.

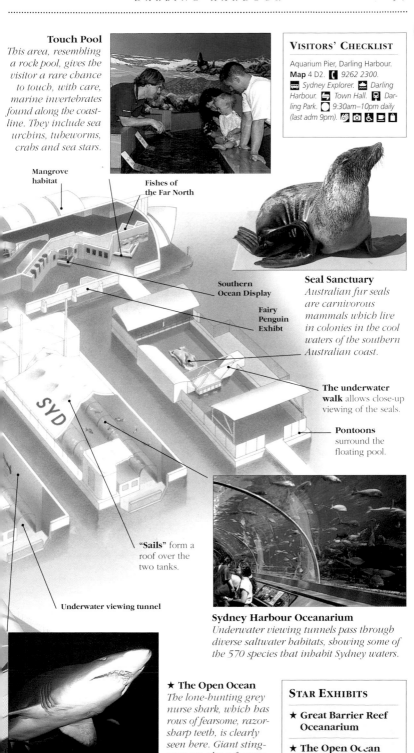

Touch Pool
This area, resembling a rock pool, gives the visitor a rare chance to touch, with care, marine invertebrates found along the coastline. They include sea urchins, tubeworms, crabs and sea stars.

VISITORS' CHECKLIST

Aquarium Pier, Darling Harbour.
Map 4 D2. 9262 2300.
Sydney Explorer. Darling Harbour. Town Hall. Darling Park. 9:30am–10pm daily (last adm 9pm).

Mangrove habitat

Fishes of the Far North

Southern Ocean Display

Fairy Penguin Exhibt

Seal Sanctuary
Australian fur seals are carnivorous mammals which live in colonies in the cool waters of the southern Australian coast.

The underwater walk allows close-up viewing of the seals.

Pontoons surround the floating pool.

SYD

"Sails" form a roof over the two tanks.

Underwater viewing tunnel

Sydney Harbour Oceanarium
Underwater viewing tunnels pass through diverse saltwater habitats, showing some of the 570 species that inhabit Sydney waters.

★ The Open Ocean
The lone-hunting grey nurse shark, which has rows of fearsome, razor-sharp teeth, is clearly seen here. Giant stingrays are also a feature.

STAR EXHIBITS

★ **Great Barrier Reef Oceanarium**

★ **The Open Ocean**

Pyrmont Bridge ❸

Darling Harbour. **Map** 1 A5.
🚉 *Darling Park, Harbourside.* 📷
♿ 🚻

P YRMONT BRIDGE opened in
1902. The world's oldest
electrically operated swingspan
bridge, it was fully functional
before Sydney's streets were
lit by electricity. It was the
second Pyrmont Bridge and
provided access to what, at
the time, was a busy international shipping terminal with
warehouses and wool stores.
Electricity for the new bridge
came from the Ultimo power
station, the building that now
houses the city's Powerhouse
Museum *(see pp100–101)*.

Percy Allan, the bridge's
designer, achieved overseas
recognition for his two central
steel swingspans and went on
to design 583 more bridges in
the course of his career. JJ
Bradfield, the designer of the
Sydney Harbour Bridge *(see
pp70–71)*, was also involved
in construction of this bridge.

The 369-m (1,200-ft) long
Pyrmont Bridge has 14 spans,
with only the two central
swingspans being made of
steel. The remaining spans
are made of ironbark, an
Australian hardwood timber.
The bridge was permanently
closed to road traffic in 1981,
but reopened to pedestrians
when the Darling Harbour
complex opened in 1988. A
portion of the monorail route
travels along the bridge. The

**The view from Pyrmont Bridge
looking up towards the city centre**

central steel swingspans are
still driven by their original
motor. The bridge is opened
regularly to allow boats access
to and from Cockle Bay.

**Anthony Quinn's 1959 Chevrolet,
Harris Street Motor Museum**

Harris Street Motor Museum ❹

320 Harris St, Pyrmont. **Map** 3 C3.
📞 9552 3375. 🚉 *Convention
Centre.* 🕙 *10am–5pm Wed–Sun
(9:30am–6:30pm daily in school hols).*
🎫 📷 ♿

C ELEBRATING A CENTURY of
automotive history, the
museum has more than 150
classic motor cars, commercial
vehicles and motorcycles on
display, along with stories of
the great car designers, their
successes and failures. Exhibits
include an Edward VII Garden-
er's Serpollet steam car, the
unique Delorean, a Model T
BP tanker and actor Anthony
Quinn's 1959 Chevrolet. In the
midst of the exotic cars are
everyday vehicles such as the
Morris, Vauxhall and Buick.

Housed in a former 1890s
woolstore, the museum also
has the country's largest international standard slot car track.
Two eight-lane tracks run over
67 m (220 ft), with the "driver"
racing against the clock.

The architectural geometry of the Convention and Exhibition Centre

Convention and Exhibition Centre ❺

Darling Drive, Darling Harbour.
Map 3 C3. 📞 9282 5000.
🚉 *Convention.* 🕙 *7am–7pm daily
(check in advance).* 📷 ♿

T HIS PURPOSE-BUILT facility
was completed in 1988.
Major international and local
conventions are held in the
main auditorium. For trade
shows and exhibitions, the
Exhibition Centre's five halls
can be combined to form a
column-free area the size of
five sports fields. The roof is
supported by a system of sail-
like masts and rigging, which
reflects the maritime history
of Darling Harbour. Works of
art by such noted Australian
artists as Brett Whiteley and
John Olsen hang within.

Chinese Garden ❻

Darling Harbour. **Map** 4 D3. 📞 9281
6863. 🚉 *Haymarket.* 🕙 *9:30am–
5:30pm Mon–Fri (4:30pm in winter),
9:30am–6pm Sat & Sun.* 🎫 📷 ♿

K NOWN AS the Garden of
Friendship, the Chinese
Garden was built in 1987. It is
a tranquil refuge from the city
streets. The garden's design
was a gift to Sydney from its
Chinese sister city of Guangdong. The Dragon Wall is in
the lower section beside the
lake. It has glazed carvings of
two dragons, one representing
Guangdong province and the
other the state of New South
Wales. In the centre of the wall,
a carved pearl, symbolizing
prosperity, is lifted by the

waves. The lake is covered with lotus and water lilies for much of the year and a rock monster guards against evil. On the other side of the lake is the Twin Pavilion. Waratahs (New South Wales's floral symbol) and flowering apricots are carved into its woodwork, and also grow at its base.

A tea house, found at the top of the stairs in the Tea House Courtyard, serves traditional Chinese tea and cakes.

Chinatown ❼

Dixon St Plaza, Sydney. **Map** 4 D4.
🚉 *Haymarket.*

Oᴿɪɢɪɴᴀʟʟʏ concentrated around Dixon and Hay Streets, Chinatown is expanding to fill Sydney's Haymarket area, stretching west to Harris Street, south to Broadway and east to Castlereagh Street. It is close to the Sydney Entertainment Centre, where some of the world's best-known rock and pop stars perform and indoor sporting events are held.

For years, Chinatown was a run-down district at the edge of the city's produce markets where many Chinese migrants worked. Today Dixon Street, its main thoroughfare, has been

Chinatown entrance, Dixon Street

spruced up, with street lanterns and archways, and a new wave of Asian migrants fills the now up-market restaurants.

Chinatown is a distinctive area with greengrocers, traditional herbalists and butchers' shops with wind-dried ducks hanging in their windows. Jewellers, clothing shops and confectioners fill the arcades. There are also two Chinese-language cinema complexes.

Capitol Theatre ❽

13 Campbell St, Haymarket. **Map** 4 E4.
📞 9320 5000. 🚌 *George St routes.*
⭕ *performances only.* **Box office**
⭕ *9am–8pm Tue–Sun, 9am–5pm Mon.* 🚻

Iɴ ᴛʜᴇ ᴍɪᴅ-1800s a cattle and corn market was situated here. It became Paddy's Market Bazaar with sideshows and an outdoor theatre, which were

in turn replaced by a circus with a floodable ring. The present building was erected in the 1920s as a luxurious picture palace. In the mid-1990s, the cinema was restored, in keeping with the original theme of a Florentine Garden.

The Capitol reopened as a lyric theatre with productions of *West Side Story* and *Miss Saigon* being staged beneath its Mediterranean-blue ceiling studded with twinkling stars reflecting the southern sky.

The lavishly renovated Capitol Theatre in Chinatown

Paddy's Market ❾

Cnr Thomas & Hay Sts, Haymarket.
Map 4 D4. 📞 9212 2428.
🚉 *Haymarket.* ⭕ *9am–4:30pm Fri–Sun.* ⚫ *25 Apr, 25 Dec.* 📷 🚻
*See also **Shops and Markets** p203.*

Hᴀʏᴍᴀʀᴋᴇᴛ, ɪɴ Chinatown, is home to Paddy's Market, Sydney's oldest and best-known market. It has been in this area, on a number of sites, since 1869 (with only one five-year absence). The origin of the name is uncertain, but is believed to have come from either the Chinese who originally supplied much of its produce, or the Irish who were their main customers.

Once the shopping centre for the inner-city poor, Paddy's Market is now an integral part of an ambitious development including residential apartments, specialist retail fashion shops and a five-screen cinema complex. Despite this transformation, the familiar clamour and chaotic bargain-hunting atmosphere of the original marketplace remain. Every weekend the market is filled with up to 800 stalls selling everything from fresh produce such as vegetables and flowers, to chickens, puppies, electrical products and leather goods.

Pavilion in the grounds of the Chinese Garden

Powerhouse Museum ⑩

Thomas Hope Egyptian chair

THIS FORMER POWER STATION, completed in 1902 to provide power for Sydney's tramway system, was redesigned to cater for the needs of a modern, hands-on museum. Revamped, the Powerhouse opened in 1988. The early collection was held in the Garden Palace hosting the 1879 international exhibition of invention and industry from around the world *(see pp24–5)*. Few exhibits survived the devastating 1882 fire, and today's huge and ever-expanding holdings were gathered after this disaster. The buildings' monumental scale provides an ideal context for the epic sweep of ideas encompassed within: everything from the realm of space and technology to the decorative and domestic arts. The museum emphasizes Australian innovations and achievements celebrating both the extraordinary and the everyday.

★ **Kings Cinema**
Visitors can watch newsreels, early sound classics and silent films in this Art Deco cinema which, with its many original fittings, re-creates 1930s film-going.

Soviet Organic Satellite Model
Replica spacecraft and a "habitation module", complete with kitchenette and sleeping area, detail the past and future of space exploration.

Level 3

Autogiro Aircraft
This rare 1934 precursor to the helicopter has a rotor powered by the movement of air rather than by a motor. The rotor's design provides vertical lift and controls direction.

Level 2

MUSEUM GUIDE

The museum is two buildings: the former powerhouse and the Neville Wran building. There are over 20 exhibitions on four levels, descending from Level 5, the restaurant level. The shop, entrance and main exhibits are on Level 4. Level 3 has thematic exhibits, a Design Gallery and the Kings Cinema. Level 2 has experiments and displays on space, computers and transport.

KEY TO FLOORPLAN

- ☐ Level 5: Asian Gallery
- ☐ Level 4: Decorative Arts, Innovation & Temp. Exhibitions
- ☐ Level 3: Social History & Design
- ☐ Level 2: Science & Technology
- ☐ Non-exhibition space

★ **Boulton & Watt Engine**
The oldest surviving rotative steam engine in the world, it powered a London brewery for 102 years from 1875. It is regularly put into operation in the museum.

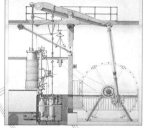

Level 5

Ken Done Restaurant
Artist Ken Done designed and painted the hibiscus and frangipani flower motifs that cover the restaurant walls.

Level 4

The Neville Wran Building, a 1980s addition, is based on the design of grand exhibition halls and railway stations of the 19th century.

Interactive Displays
More than 100 interactive units engage visitors in play while teaching them about science.

Main entrance

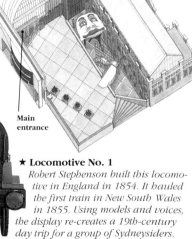

★ **Locomotive No. 1**
Robert Stephenson built this locomotive in England in 1854. It hauled the first train in New South Wales in 1855. Using models and voices, the display re-creates a 19th-century day trip for a group of Sydneysiders.

STAR EXHIBITS

★ **Boulton & Watt Engine**

★ **Locomotive No. 1**

★ **Kings Cinema**

BOTANIC GARDENS AND THE DOMAIN

THIS TRANQUIL PART of Sydney can seem a world away from the bustle of the city centre. It is rich in the remnants of Sydney's convict and colonial past: the site of the first farm, and the boulevard-like Macquarie Street where the barracks, hospital, church and mint – bastions of civic power – are among the oldest surviving public buildings in Australia. This street continues to assert its dominance today as the home of the state government of New South Wales. The Domain, an

Wooden angel, St James' Church

open, grassy space, was originally set aside by the colony's first governor for his private use. Today it is a democratic place with joggers and touch footballers sidestepping picnickers. In January, during the Festival of Sydney, it hosts outdoor concerts with thousands of people enjoying fine music. The Botanic Gardens, which with The Domain was the site of Australia's first park, is a haven where visitors can stroll around and enjoy the extensive collection of native and exotic flora.

SIGHTS AT A GLANCE

Historic Streets and Buildings
Conservatorium of Music ❷
Government House ❸
Woolloomooloo Finger Wharf ❻
State Library of NSW ❾
Parliament House ❿
Sydney Hospital ⓫
Sydney Mint ⓬
Hyde Park Barracks ⓭

Museums and Galleries
Art Gallery of New South Wales pp108–11 ❼

Churches
St James' Church ⓮

Islands
Fort Denison ❺

Monuments
Mrs Macquaries Chair ❹

Parks and Gardens
Royal Botanic Gardens pp104–5 ❶
The Domain ❽

GETTING THERE
Visit on foot, if possible. St James and Martin Place train stations are close to most of the sights. The 311 bus from Circular Quay runs near the Art Gallery of NSW and past the Woolloomooloo Finger Wharf. The Sydney Explorer also stops at several sights.

| 0 metres | 500 |
| 0 yards | 500 |

KEY

Royal Botanic Gardens
See pp104–5

P Parking

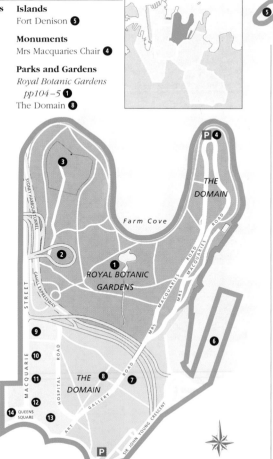

◁ Succulents and cacti from the Succulent Garden in the Royal Botanic Gardens

Royal Botanic Gardens ❶

The royal botanic gardens, an oasis of 30 ha (74 acres) in the heart of the city, occupy a superb position, wrapped around Farm Cove at the harbour's edge. Established in 1816 as a series of pathways through shrubbery, they are the oldest scientific institution in the country and house an outstanding collection of plants

Statue in the Botanic Gardens

from Australia and overseas. A living museum, the gardens are also the site of the first farm in the fledgling colony. Fountains, statues and monuments are today scattered throughout. Plant specimens collected by Joseph Banks on Captain James Cook's epic voyage along the east coast of Australia in 1770 are displayed in the National Herbarium of New South Wales, an important centre for research on Australian plants.

LOCATOR MAP
See Street Finder, maps 1 & 2

Government House (1897)

★ Palm Grove
Begun in 1862, this cool summer haven is one of the world's finest outdoor collections of palms. There are about 180 species. Borders planted with kaffir lilies make a colourful display in springtime.

★ Herb Garden
Herbs from around the world used for a wide variety of purposes – culinary, medicinal and aromatic – are on display here. A sensory fountain and a sundial modelled on the celestial sphere are also features.

0 metres   200

0 yards   200

★ Sydney Tropical Centre
Two glasshouses contain tropical ecosystems in miniature. Native vegetation is displayed in the Pyramid, while the Arc holds plants not found locally, commonly known as exotics.

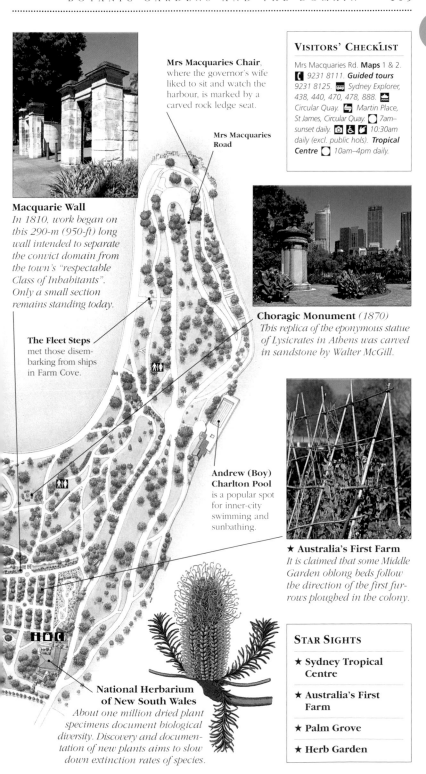

Macquarie Wall
*In 1810, work began on
this 290-m (950-ft) long
wall intended to separate
the convict domain from
the town's "respectable
Class of Inhabitants".
Only a small section
remains standing today.*

The Fleet Steps
met those disem-
barking from ships
in Farm Cove.

Mrs Macquaries Chair,
where the governor's wife
liked to sit and watch the
harbour, is marked by a
carved rock ledge seat.

**Mrs Macquaries
Road**

Choragic Monument *(1870)*
*This replica of the eponymous statue
of Lysicrates in Athens was carved
in sandstone by Walter McGill.*

**Andrew (Boy)
Charlton Pool**
is a popular spot
for inner-city
swimming and
sunbathing.

★ **Australia's First Farm**
*It is claimed that some Middle
Garden oblong beds follow
the direction of the first fur-
rows ploughed in the colony.*

**National Herbarium
of New South Wales**
*About one million dried plant
specimens document biological
diversity. Discovery and documen-
tation of new plants aims to slow
down extinction rates of species.*

STAR SIGHTS

★ **Sydney Tropical
Centre**

★ **Australia's First
Farm**

★ **Palm Grove**

★ **Herb Garden**

Conservatorium of Music ❷

Macquarie St. **Map** 1 C3.
☎ 9230 1222. ➡ Sydney Explorer,
Circular Quay routes. ☐ 9am–5pm
Mon–Fri, 9am–4pm Sat (grounds
only in school hols). ● public hols,
Easter Sat. ◻ ♿

WHEN IT WAS finished in
1821, this striking castellated Colonial Gothick building
was meant to be stables and
servants' quarters for Government House, but construction
of the latter was delayed for
almost 25 years. That stables
should be built in so grand a
style, and at such great cost,
brought forth cries of outrage
and led to bitter arguments
between the architect, Francis
Greenway (see p114), and
Governor Macquarie – and a
decree that all future building
plans be submitted to London.
Between 1908 and 1915,
"Greenway's folly" underwent
a dramatic transformation. A
concert hall, roofed in grey
slate, was built on the central
courtyard and the building in
its entirety was converted for
the use of the new Sydney
Conservatorium of Music.
The "Con" is still a training
ground for future musicians.
While picturesque, it is not
the ideal location for the flourishing musical talent of Sydney,
and there are plans to extend
and improve the site. For now,
though, this idiosyncratic old
building continues to house the
city's premier music school.

The Conservatorium of Music at the edge of the Royal Botanic Gardens

THE HISTORY OF COCKATOO ISLAND

HMS *Orlando* in dry dock at
Cockatoo Island in the 1890s

Now completely deserted,
the largest of the 12 Sydney
Harbour islands was used to
store grain from the 1830s.
It was a penal establishment
from the 1840s to 1908, with
prisoners being put to work
constructing dock facilities.
The infamous bushranger
"Captain Thunderbolt" made
his escape from Cockatoo in
1863 by swimming across to
the mainland. From the 1870s
to the 1960s, Cockatoo
Island was a thriving naval
dockyard and shipyard, the
hub of Australian industry.

Government House ❸

Macquarie St. **Map** 1 C2. ☎ 9931
5222. 📠 9931 5200. ➡ Sydney
Explorer, Circular Quay routes. **House**
☐ 10am–3pm Fri–Sun. ● public hols.
Garden ☐ 10am–4pm daily.
◻ ♿ 📷

WHAT USED to be the official
residence of the governor
of New South Wales overlooks
the harbour from within the
Royal Botanic Gardens, but the
grandiose, somewhat sombre,
turreted Gothic Revival edifice
seems curiously out of place
in its beautiful park setting.
It was built of local sandstone and cedar between
1837 and 1845. A fine
collection of 19th- and early
20th-century furnishings and
decoration is housed within.

Resting on the carved stone seat
of Mrs Macquaries Chair

Mrs Macquaries Chair ❹

Mrs Macquaries Rd. **Map** 2 E2.
➡ Sydney Explorer, 888. ♿

THE SCENIC Mrs Macquaries
Road winds alongside much
of what is now the city's Royal
Botanic Gardens, from Farm
Cove to Woolloomooloo Bay
and back again. The road was
built in 1816 at the instigation
of Elizabeth Macquarie, wife
of the Governor. In the same
year, a stone bench, inscribed
with details of the new road,
was carved into the rock at the
point where Mrs Macquarie
would stop to admire the view
on her daily constitutional.
Although today the outlook
from this famous landmark is
much changed, it is just as
arresting, taking in the broad
sweep of the harbour and foreshore with all its landmarks.

Dilapidated old buildings on the historic Woolloomooloo Finger Wharf on the harbour foreshore

Fort Denison **5**

Sydney Harbour. **Map** 2 E1. 9247 5033. from Circular Quay. **Departures** noon & 2pm Sun. for restoration, except Sun. 9206 1166 (booking essential).

FIRST NAMED Rock Island, this prominent, rocky outcrop in Sydney Harbour was very quickly dubbed "Pinchgut". This was probably because of the meagre rations given to convicts who were confined there as punishment. It had a grim history of incarceration in the early years of the colony.

In 1796, convicted murderer Francis Morgan was hanged on the island in chains. His body

Fort Denison in 1907

was left to rot on the gallows for three years as a grisly warning to the other convicts.

Between 1855 and 1857, the Martello tower (the only one in Australia), gun battery and barracks that now occupy the island were built as part of Sydney's defences and the site was renamed after the governor of the time. The gun, still fired at 1pm each day, was an important aid for navigation, allowing mariners to set their ships' chronometers.

Today the island is the perfect setting for watching the many public harbour activities,

such as fireworks displays. To explore Fort Denison, book on one of the daily boat tours that leave from Circular Quay.

Woolloomooloo Finger Wharf **6**

Cowper Wharf Roadway, Woolloomooloo. **Map** 2 E4. Sydney Explorer, 311.

THIS IS THE LARGEST of several finger wharves that jut out into the harbour. The wharf, completed in 1914, was one of the points of embarkation for soldiers bound for both world wars. Following World War II, it was a landing place for many of the thousands of immigrants who came to Australia.

The wharf was the subject of public controversy in the late 1980s and early 1990s. Plans to demolish it were thwarted by the protests of conservation groups. This important maritime site is now undergoing refurbishment and plans for it include a marina, quayside flats and perhaps a hotel.

Art Gallery of New South Wales **7**

See pp108–11.

The Domain **8**

Art Gallery Rd. **Map** 1 C4. Sydney Explorer, 888.

PEOPLE WHO SWARM to the January concerts and other Festival of Sydney events in The Domain (see p49) are part of a long-standing tradition.

This extensive public space has long been a rallying point for crowds of Sydneysiders whenever emotive issues of public importance have arisen, such as the attempt in 1916 to introduce military conscription or the dismissal of the elected federal government by the then governor-general in 1975.

Ever since the 1890s, part of The Domain has also been used as the Sydney version of "Speakers' Corner". Here, on any Sunday, visitors can watch and listen as soapbox orators hold forth about any subject that takes their fancy.

A dramatic view of Sydney Opera House from The Domain

Art Gallery of New South Wales ❼

Established in 1874, the art gallery has occupied its present imposing building since 1897. Designed by the Colonial Architect WL Vernon, the gallery doubled in size following 1988 building extensions. Two equestrian bronzes – *The Offerings of Peace* and *The Offerings of War* – greet the visitor on entry. The gallery itself houses some of the finest works of art in Australia. It has sections devoted to Australian, Asian, European, photographic and contemporary and photographic works, along with a strong collection of prints and drawings. The Yiribana Gallery, the largest in the world to exclusively exhibit Aboriginal and Torres Strait Islander art and culture, was opened in 1994.

Cycladic figure (c.2,500 BC)

Sofala *(1947)*
Russell Drysdale's visions of Australia show "ghost" towns laid waste by devastating natural forces such as drought.

Sunbaker *(1937)*
Max Dupain's iconic, almost abstract, Australian photograph of hedonism and sun worship uses clean lines, strong light, and geometric form. The image's power lies in its simplicity.

The Sculpture Terrace is a small outdoor area which has large-scale sculptures on display.

Madonna and Child with Infant St John the Baptist
This oil on wood (c.1541) is the work of Siena Mannerist artist Domenico Beccafumi.

Level 5

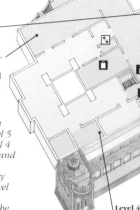

Temporary exhibitions, often by much-acclaimed Australian artists, are held here throughout the year.

Level 4

STAR EXHIBITS

★ **The Golden Fleece – Shearing at Newstead by Tom Roberts**

★ **Pukumani Grave Posts**

GALLERY GUIDE
The collection is housed on five descending levels. Level 5 displays photography. Level 4 contains many European and Australian features of the collection. Major temporary exhibitions are held on Level 3, 20th-century European prints are on Level 2 and the Yiribana Gallery is on Level 1.

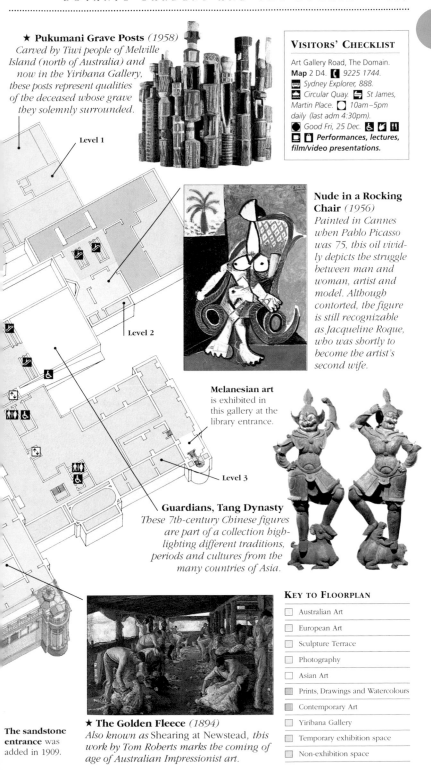

★ **Pukumani Grave Posts** *(1958)*
Carved by Tiwi people of Melville Island (north of Australia) and now in the Yiribana Gallery, these posts represent qualities of the deceased whose grave they solemnly surrounded.

Level 1

VISITORS' CHECKLIST

Art Gallery Road, The Domain.
Map 2 D4. 9225 1744.
Sydney Explorer, 888.
Circular Quay. St James, Martin Place. 10am–5pm daily (last adm 4:30pm).
Good Fri, 25 Dec. **Performances, lectures, film/video presentations.**

Nude in a Rocking Chair *(1956)*
Painted in Cannes when Pablo Picasso was 75, this oil vividly depicts the struggle between man and woman, artist and model. Although contorted, the figure is still recognizable as Jacqueline Roque, who was shortly to become the artist's second wife.

Level 2

Melanesian art is exhibited in this gallery at the library entrance.

Level 3

Guardians, Tang Dynasty
These 7th-century Chinese figures are part of a collection highlighting different traditions, periods and cultures from the many countries of Asia.

The sandstone entrance was added in 1909.

★ **The Golden Fleece** *(1894)*
Also known as Shearing at Newstead, *this work by Tom Roberts marks the coming of age of Australian Impressionist art.*

KEY TO FLOORPLAN

☐ Australian Art
☐ European Art
☐ Sculpture Terrace
☐ Photography
☐ Asian Art
☐ Prints, Drawings and Watercolours
☐ Contemporary Art
☐ Yiribana Gallery
☐ Temporary exhibition space
☐ Non-exhibition space

Exploring the Art Gallery's Collection

ALTHOUGH LOCAL WORKS had been collected since 1875 the gallery did not seriously begin seeking Australian and non-British art until the 1920s, and not until the 1940s did it begin acquiring Aboriginal and Torres Strait Islander paintings. These contrasting collections are now its great strength. Major temporary exhibitions are also regularly staged, with the annual Archibald, Wynne and Sulman prizes being most controversial and highly entertaining.

Grace Cossington Smith's 1955 *Interior with wardrobe mirror*

AUSTRALIAN ART

AMONG THE MOST important colonial works is John Glover's *Natives on the Ouse River, Van Diemen's Land* (1838), an image of doomed Tasmanian Aborigines.

The old wing holds paintings from the Heidelberg school of Australian Impressionism. Charles Conder's *Departure of the Orient – Circular Quay* (1888) and Tom Robert's *The Golden Fleece – Shearing at Newstead* (1894) hang alongside fine works by Frederick McCubbin and Arthur Streeton. Rupert Bunny's sensuous *Summer Time* (c.1907) and *A Summer Morning* (c.1908), and

George Lambert's heroic *Across the black soil plains* (1899), impress with their huge size and complex compositions.

Australia was slow to take up Modernism. *Implement blue* (1927) and *Western Australian Gum Blossom* (1928), both by Margaret Preston, are her most assertive of the 1920s. Sidney Nolan's works range from *Boy in Township* (1943) to *Burke* (c.1962), exploiting myths of early Australian history. There are fine holdings of William Dobell and Russell Drysdale, as well as important collections of Arthur Boyd, Fred Williams, Grace Cossington Smith and Brett Whiteley *(see p130).*

EUROPEAN ART

THE SCOPE OF the scattered European collection ranges from the medieval to the modern. British art from the late 19th to the early 20th centuries forms an outstanding component.

Among the Old Masters are some significant Italian works that reflect Caravaggio's influence. There are also several notable works from the Renaissance in Sienese and Florentine styles.

***Study for Self Portrait*, a Francis Bacon painting from 1976**

Hogarth, Turner and Joshua Reynolds are represented, as are Neo-Classical works. *The Visit of the Queen of Sheba to King Solomon* (1884–90) by Edward Poynter has been on display since 1892. Ford Madox Brown's *Chaucer at the Court of Edward III* (1845–51) is the most commanding work in the Pre-Raphaelite collection.

The Impressionists and Post-Impressionists, represented by late-1880s Pissarro and Monet, are housed in the new gallery wing. Bonnard, Kandinsky, Braque and many other well-known European artists are also here. *Old Woman in Ermine* (1946) by Max Beckmann and *Three Bathers* (1913) by Ernst Kirchner are strong examples of German Expressionism. The gallery's first Picasso, *Nude in a Rocking Chair* (1956), was purchased in 1981. Among distinguished sculptures is Henry Moore's *Reclining Figure: Angles* (1980), found resting by the side of the entrance.

Henry Moore's *Reclining Figure: Angles* (1980)

PHOTOGRAPHY

AUSTRALIAN photography from 1975 to today, represented in all its various forms, is a major part of the collection. In recent years, however, the emphasis has been on building up a body of 19th-century Australian work in a range of early mediums. Nearly 3,000

Brett Whiteley's vivid *The Balcony (2)* from 1975

prints constitute this collection with pieces by Charles Kerry, Charles Bayliss and Harold Cazneaux, the latter a major figure of early 20th-century Pictorialism. Such international photographers as Muybridge, Robert Mapplethorpe and Man Ray are also represented here.

ASIAN ART

THIS COLLECTION is one of the finest in Australia. Chinese art is represented by a chronological presentation of works from the pre- Shang dynasty (c.1600–1027 BC) to the 20th century. The Ming porcelains, earthenware funerary pieces *(mingqi)* and the sculptures deserve close attention.

The Japanese painting collection contains fine examples by major artists of the Edo period (1615–1867). The Indian and Southeast Asian holdings consist of lacquer, ceramics and sculptures, with painting displays changing regularly.

PRINTS AND DRAWINGS

AS SO MANY of the works in this collection are fragile, the exhibitions are changed frequently. The collection represents the European tradition from the High Renaissance to the 19th and 20th centuries, with work by Rembrandt, Constable, William Blake and Edvard Munch. A strong bias towards Sydney artists from the past 100 years has resulted in a fine gathering of work by Thea Proctor, Norman and Lionel Lindsay and Lloyd Rees.

Egon Schiele's *Poster for the Vienna Secession* (1918)

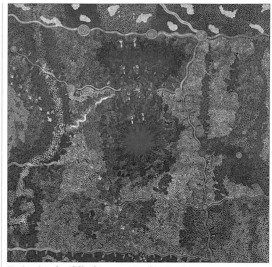

***Warlugulong* by Clifford Possum Tjapaltjarri and Tim Leura Tjapaltjarri**

CONTEMPORARY ART

THE SIGNIFICANCE of the art of our time is reflected in the dynamic collection of recent work by international and Australian artists. The collection highlights the artistic themes that have been central to art practice of the last two decades. Works of Australian artists such as Imants Tillers, Ken Unsworth and Susan Norrie are on display alongside pieces by notable international artists of the calibre of Cindy Sherman, Yves Klein, Philip Guston and Anselm Kiefer. The gallery also has a contemporary project space that features temporary experimental installations.

***Fruit Bats* (1991) by Lin Onus**

YIRIBANA GALLERY

DEVOTED TO the exhibition of Aboriginal and Torres Strait Islander artworks bought since the 1940s, traditional bark paintings hang alongside innovative works from both desert and urban areas. The ability of contemporary artists to apply traditional ceremonial body and sand painting styles to new media forms, and the endurance of "Aboriginality",

are repeatedly demonstrated. The significant early purchases are mainly natural pigment paintings on bark and card, often containing a simple, figurative motif of everyday life. Also of interest are two sandstone carvings by Queenslanders Linda Craigie and Nora Nathan, the only women artists in the collection until 1985. Topographical, geographical and cultural mapping of the land is displayed in a number of intricate landscapes. The qualities and forms of the natural world, and the actions and tracks of Ancestral Beings, are coded within the images. These paintings are maps of Ancestral journeys and events. The bark painting *Three Mimis Dancing* (1964) by Samuel Wagbara examines the habitation of the land by Spirits and the recurrence of the Creation Cycles.

Pukumani Grave Posts Melville Island (1958) is a solemn ceremonial work dealing with death, while the eminent Emily Kame Kngwarreye honours the land from which she comes. The canvases of her intricate dot paintings, created using new tools and technology, appear to move and shimmer, telling stories of the animals and food to be found there.

Mosaic replica of the Tasman Map in the State Library of NSW

State Library of NSW **❾**

Macquarie St. **Map** 4 F1.
📞 9273 1414. 🚌 *Sydney Explorer, Elizabeth St routes.* 🕐 *9am–9pm Mon–Fri, 11am–5pm Sat & Sun.* ⬤ *most public hols.* ♿ 🎫

T HE STATE LIBRARY is housed in two separate buildings connected by a passageway and a glass bridge. The older building, the Mitchell Library wing (1906), is a majestic sandstone edifice facing the Royal Botanic Gardens. Huge stone columns supporting a vaulted ceiling frame the impressive vestibule. On the vestibule floor is a mosaic replica of an old map illustrating the two voyages made to Australia by Dutch navigator Abel Tasman in the 1640s. The original Tasman Map is held in the Mitchell Library as part of its large collection of historic Australian paintings, books, documents and pictorial records.

The Mitchell wing's vast reading room, with its huge skylight and oak panelling, is just beyond the main vestibule. The newest section is an attractive contemporary structure that faces Macquarie Street. It houses the General Reference Library, open to anyone who wishes to use it.

Outside the library, also facing Macquarie Street, is a statue of explorer Matthew Flinders. Behind him on the windowsill is a statue of his co-voyager, his faithful cat, Trim.

Parliament House **❿**

Macquarie St. **Map** 4 F1.
📞 9230 2135. 🚌 *Sydney Explorer, Elizabeth St routes.* 🕐 *10am, 11am and 2pm; it is necessary to book in advance by calling the booking office.* ⬤ *most public hols.* ♿

T HE CENTRAL SECTION of this building, which houses the state parliament, is part of the original Sydney Hospital built from 1811–16. It has been a seat of government since the 1820s when the newly appointed Legislative Council first held meetings here. The building was extended twice during the 19th century and again during the 1970s and 1980s. The current building contains the chambers for both houses of state parliament, as well as parliamentary offices.

Malby's celestial globe, Parliament House

MACQUARIE STREET

Described in the 1860s as one of the gloomiest streets in Sydney, this could now claim to be the most elegant. Open on the northeastern side to the harbour breezes and the greenery of The Domain, a leisurely walk down this tree-lined street is one of the most pleasurable ways to view the architectural heritage of Sydney.

__The new wing__ of the library was built in 1988 and connected to the old section by a glass walkway.

The Mitchell Library wing's portico (1906) has Ionic columns.

***The Legislative Assembly**, the lower house of state parliament, is furnished in the traditional green of the British House of Commons.*

Parliament House was once the convict-built Rum Hospital's northern wing.

STATE LIBRARY OF NSW *(1906–41)*   **PARLIAMENT HOUSE** *(1811*

Parliamentary memorabilia is on view in the Jubilee Room, as are displays showing Parliament House's development and the legislative history of New South Wales.

The corrugated iron building with a cast-iron façade tacked on at the southern end was a pre-fabricated kit from England. It was originally intended as a chapel for the gold fields, but was diverted from this purpose and sent to Sydney. In 1856, this dismantled kit became the chamber for the new Legislative Council. Its packing cases were used to line this chamber; the rough timber is still on view inside.

Stained glass at Sydney Hospital

builders were paid by being allowed to import rum for resale. Both the north and south wings of the Rum Hospital survive as Parliament House and the Sydney Mint. The central wing, which was in danger of collapsing, was demolished in 1879 and the new hospital, which still functions today, was completed in 1894. The Classical Revival building boasts a Baroque staircase and elegant floral stained-glass windows in its entrance hall. Florence Nightingale approved the design of the 1868 nurses'

wing. In the inner courtyard, there is a brightly coloured Art Deco fountain (1907), somewhat out of place among the surrounding heavy stonework.

At the front of the hospital sits *Il Porcellino*, a brass boar. It is a copy of a 17th-century fountain in Florence's Mercato Nuovo. Donated in 1968 by an Italian woman whose relatives had worked at the hospital, the statue is an enduring symbol of the close friendship between Italy and Australia.

Like his Florentine counterpart, *Il Porcellino* is supposed to bring good luck to all those who rub his snout. All coins tossed in the shallow pool at his feet for luck and fortune are collected for the hospital.

Sydney Hospital ⑪

Macquarie St. **Map** 1 C4.
📞 9382 7111. 🚌 *Sydney Explorer, Elizabeth St routes.* ⬤ *daily.* 🎫 *for tours.* 📷 ♿ ✍ *upon request.*

THIS IMPOSING COLLECTION of Victorian sandstone buildings stands on the site of what was once the central section of the original convict-built Sydney Hospital – known as the Rum Hospital because the

Il Porcellino, the brass boar in front of Sydney Hospital

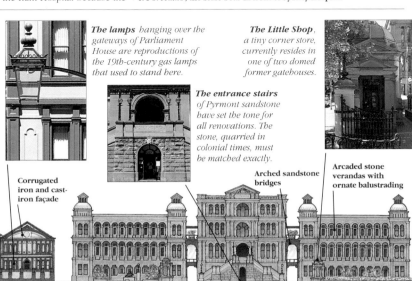

The lamps *hanging over the gateways of Parliament House are reproductions of the 19th-century gas lamps that used to stand here.*

The Little Shop, *a tiny corner store, currently resides in one of two domed former gatehouses.*

The entrance stairs *of Pyrmont sandstone have set the tone for all renovations. The stone, quarried in colonial times, must be matched exactly.*

Corrugated iron and cast-iron façade

Arched sandstone bridges

Arcaded stone verandas with ornate balustrading

SYDNEY HOSPITAL *(1868–94)*

Sydney Mint ⓬

Macquarie St. **Map** 1 C5. 🚌 *Sydney Explorer, Elizabeth St routes.* ⬤ *for refurbishment.*

THE GOLD RUSHES of the mid-19th century transformed colonial Australia. The Sydney Mint opened in the 1816 Rum Hospital's south wing in 1854 to turn recently discovered gold into bullion and currency.

It was the first branch of the Royal Mint to be established outside London. The Mint was closed in 1927 as it was no longer competitive with the Melbourne and Perth Mints. The Georgian building went into its own decline after it was converted into government offices. In the 1950s, the front courtyard was even used as a car park. In 1982, after restoration, it opened as a branch of the Powerhouse Museum (*see pp100–101*), but the collection has now been moved on a permanent basis to the Powerhouse Museum in Harris Street.

This building has been taken over by the Historic Houses Trust who intend to open it as a library and resource centre. There are also plans for a shop or a café. Once development work has finished, it should be possible to view parts of the original building.

Replica convict hammocks on the third floor of Hyde Park Barracks

FRANCIS GREENWAY, CONVICT ARCHITECT

Until recently, Australian $10 notes bore the portrait of the early colonial architect Francis Greenway, the only currency in the world to pay tribute to a convicted forger. Greenway was transported to Sydney in 1814 to serve a 14-year sentence for his crime. Under the patronage of Governor Macquarie, who appointed him Civil Architect in 1816, Greenway designed more than 40 buildings, of which only 11 remain today. He received a full pardon in 1819, but soon fell out of favour because he persisted in charging large fees while still on a government salary. Greenway died in poverty in 1837.

Francis Greenway (1777–1837)

Hyde Park Barracks ⓭

Queens Square, Macquarie St. **Map** 1 C5. 🕿 *9223 8922.* 🚇 *St James, Martin Place.* ◻ *9:30am–5pm daily.* ⬤ *Good Fri, 25 Dec.* 📷 📀 ♿ 📋 *book in advance for all tours.*

DESCRIBED BY Governor Macquarie as "spacious" and "well-aired", the beautifully proportioned barracks are the work of Francis Greenway and are considered his masterpiece. They were completed in 1819 by convict labour and designed

MACQUARIE STREET

Fine examples of Francis Greenway's Georgian style are within an easy walk of one another at the Hyde Park end of Macquarie Street. The brick and sandstone of Hyde Park Barracks, St James' Church and the Old Supreme Court Building form a harmonious group on the site the governor envisaged as the city's civic centre.

Sydney Mint, like its twin, Parliament House, has an unusual double-colonnaded, two-storeyed veranda.

The roof of the Mint has now been completely restored to replicate the original wooden shingles in casuarina (she-oak).

The stone wall of Hyde Park Barracks' northwest pavilion still bears the marks of the convicts' chisels.

Hyde Park Barracks Café

SYDNEY MINT *(1816)*

to house 600 convicts who had previously been forced to find their own lodgings after their day's work. The building housed Irish orphans and then single female immigrants, before becoming courts and legal offices. Refurbished in 1990, it reopened as a museum on the site and its occupants.

The displays include a room reconstructed as convict quarters of the 1820s, as well as pictures, models and artifacts. Many objects recovered during archaeological digs at the site and now on display had been dragged away by rats to their nests; the scavenging rodents are acknowledged as valuable agents of preservation.

The Greenway Gallery on the second floor holds temporary exhibitions on history, ideas and culture. From the Barracks Café, which incorporates the original confinement cell area, the visitor can gaze out over the now serene gravel courtyard, once the scene of brutal convict floggings.

Intermittently during school holidays, visitors can stay for a night in a convict dormitory, sleeping in a hammock and enjoying a convict-style breakfast in the morning.

Detail from the Children's Chapel mural in the St James' Church crypt

St James' Church ⓮

179 King St. **Map** 1 B5.
📞 9232 3022. 🚇 St James, Martin Place. ⏰ 9am–5pm daily. 📷

THIS FINE GEORGIAN building, constructed with convict-made bricks, was designed as a courthouse in 1819. The architect, Francis Greenway, was forced to convert it into a church in 1820, when plans to build a grand cathedral on George Street were abandoned.

Greenway was unhappy about the change, but nevertheless designed a simple yet elegant church. Consecrated in 1824 by Samuel Marsden, the infamous "flogging parson", it is Sydney's oldest church. Many additions have been carried out, including designs by John Verge in which the pulpit faced towards high-rent pews, while convicts and the military sat behind the preacher where the service would have been inaudible. A Children's Chapel was added in 1930.

Prominent members of early 19th-century society, many of whom died violently, are commemorated in marble tablets. These tell the full and bloody stories of luckless explorers, the governor's wife dashed to her death from her carriage, and shipwreck victims.

The stained-glass windows in St James' Church are mostly 20th century, and represent the union formed by air, earth, fire and water.

This clock, dating from 1817 and one of Sydney's oldest, is on the Hyde Park Barracks façade.

Georgian sandstone façade

Statue of Prince Albert

PARK BARRACKS (1817–19)

The Land Titles Office, a W.L. Vernon building from 1908, has a Classical form with some fine Tudor Gothic detailing.

LAND TITLES OFFICE (1908–13)

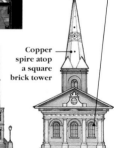

Copper spire atop a square brick tower

ST JAMES' (1820)

KINGS CROSS AND DARLINGHURST

**Façade detail,
Del Rio** *(see p119)*

SITUATED ON the eastern fringe of the city, Kings Cross, known as "The Cross", and Darlinghurst are a couple of Sydney celebrities. Their allure is tarnished – or enhanced, perhaps – by trails of scandal and corruption. Kings Cross, particularly, is still regarded as a hotbed of vice; both areas still bear the taint of 1920s gangland associations. In fact, both are now cosmopolitan areas – among the most densely populated parts of

Sydney, famed as much for their street life and thriving café culture as for their unsavoury features. Kings Cross exudes a welcome breath of bohemia, in spite of the sleaze of Darlinghurst Road and the flaunting of its red light district. Darlinghurst comes brilliantly into its own every March, when the flamboyant Gay and Lesbian Mardi Gras parade, supported by huge crowds of spectators, makes its triumphant way along Oxford Street.

SIGHTS AT A GLANCE

Historic Streets and Buildings
Victoria Street **2**
Elizabeth Bay House **3**
Old Gaol, Darlinghurst **6**
Darlinghurst Court House **7**

Museums and Galleries
Sydney Jewish Museum **5**

Parks and Gardens
Beare Park **4**

Monuments
El Alamein Fountain **1**

GETTING THERE
Kings Cross railway station serves the area. Bus number 311 travels through Kings Cross and Darlinghurst, while the 324, 325 and 389 are also useful. Buses 378, 380 and 382 travel along Oxford Street.

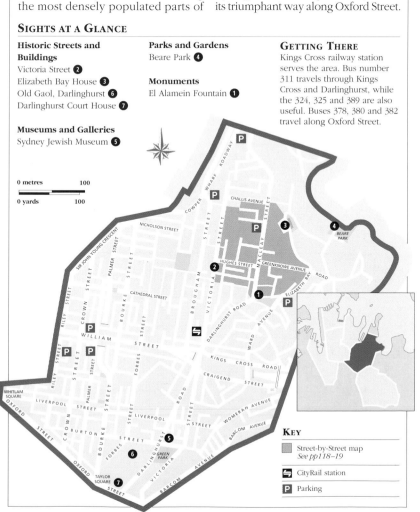

| 0 metres | 100 |
| 0 yards | 100 |

KEY

▦	Street-by-Street map *See pp118–19*
⬆	CityRail station
P	Parking

◁ **The large neon sign at the top of William Street marking the entrance to Kings Cross**

Street-by-Street: Potts Point

Beare Park fountain detail

T HE SUBSTANTIAL VICTORIAN houses filling the streets of this old suburb are excellent examples of the 19th-century concern with architectural harmony. New building projects were designed to enhance rather than contradict the surrounding buildings and general streetscape. Monumental structures and fine details of moulded stuccoed parapets, cornices and friezes, even the spandrels in herringbone pattern, are all integral parts of a grand suburban plan. (This plan included an 1831 order that all houses cost at least £1,000.) Cool and dark verandas extend the street's green canopy of shade, leaving an impression of cool drinks enjoyed on hot summer days in fine Victorian style.

The McElhone Stairs were preceded by a wooden ladder that linked Woolloomooloo Hill, as Kings Cross was known, to the estate far below.

Horderns Stairs

These villas, from the Georgian and Victorian eras, can be broadly labelled as Classical Revival and are fronted by leafy gardens.

★ **Victoria Street**
In 1972–4, residents of this historic street fought a sometimes violent battle against developers wanting to build high-rise office towers, motels and blocks of flats ❷

Kings Cross Station

Werrington, a mostly serious and streamlined building, also has flamboyant Art Deco detailing which is now subdued under brown paint.

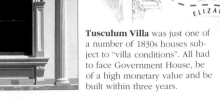

Tusculum Villa was just one of a number of 1830s houses subject to "villa conditions". All had to face Government House, be of a high monetary value and be built within three years.

STAR SIGHTS

★ **Victoria Street**

★ **Elizabeth Bay House**

Challis Avenue is a fine and shady complement to nearby Victoria Street. This Romanesque group of terrace houses has an unusual façade, with arches fronting deep verandas and a grand ground floor colonnade.

LOCATOR MAP
See Street Finder, *map 2*

Rockwall, a symmetrical and compact Regency villa, was built to the designs of the architect John Verge *(see p120)* in 1830–7.

Landmark Hotel

Del Rio is a finely detailed high-rise apartment block. It clearly exhibits the Spanish Mission influence that filtered through from California in the first quarter of the 20th century.

★ **Elizabeth Bay House**
A contemporary exclaimed over the beauty of the 1830s garden: "trees from Rio, the West Indies, the East Indies, China . . . the bulbs from the Cape are splendid" ❸

The Arthur McElhone Reserve

Art Deco Birtley Towers

0 metres 50
0 yards 50

KEY

– – – Suggested route

Elizabeth Bay was part of the original land grant to Alexander Macleay *(see p120)*. He created a botanist's paradise with ornamental ponds, quaint grottoes and promenades winding all the way down to the harbour.

El Alamein Fountain, commemorating the World War II battle

El Alamein Fountain ❶

Fitzroy Gardens, Macleay St, Potts Point. **Map** 2 E5. 🚌 *311.*

THIS DANDELION of a fountain in the heart of the Kings Cross district has a reputation for working so spasmodically that passers-by often murmur facetiously, "He loves me, he loves me not." Built in 1961, it commemorates the Australian army's role in the siege of Tobruk, Libya, and the battle of El Alamein in Egypt during World War II. At night, when it is brilliantly lit, the fountain looks surprisingly ethereal.

Victoria Street ❷

Potts Point. **Map** 5 B2. 🚌 *311, 324, 325.*

AT THE POTTS POINT end, this street of 19th-century terrace houses, interspersed with a few incongruous-looking high-rise blocks, is, by inner-city standards, almost a boulevard. The gracious street you see today was once at the centre of a bitterly fought conservation struggle, one which almost certainly cost the life of a prominent heritage campaigner.

In the early 1970s, many residents, backed by the "green bans" *(see p29)* put in place by the Builders' Labourers Federation of New South Wales, fought to prevent demolition of old buildings for high-rise

development. Juanita Nielsen, publisher of a local newspaper and heiress, vigorously took up the conservation battle. On 4 July 1975, she disappeared without trace. A subsequent inquest into her disappearance returned an open verdict.

As a result of the actions of the union and residents, most of Victoria Street's superb old buildings still stand. Ironically, they are now occupied not by the low-income residents who fought to save them, but by the well-off professionals that eventually displaced them.

Juanita Nielsen

Elizabeth Bay House ❸

7 Onslow Ave, Elizabeth Bay. **Map** 2 F5. 📞 9356 3022. 🚌 *Sydney Explorer, 311.* 🕐 *10am–4:30pm Tue–Sun.* ● *Good Fri, 25 Dec.* 🎟️ 📷

ELIZABETH BAY HOUSE *(see pp22–3)* contains the finest colonial interior on display in Australia. It is a potent expression of how the depression of the 1840s cut short the 1830s' prosperous optimism. Designed in the fashionable Greek Revival style by John Verge, it was built for Colonial Secretary Alexander Macleay, from 1835–39. The domed oval saloon with its cantilevered staircase is recognized as Verge's masterpiece. The exterior is less satisfactory, as the intended colonnade and portico were not finished owing to a crisis in Macleay's financial affairs. The present portico dates from

1893. The interior is furnished to reflect Macleay's occupancy from 1839–45, and is based on inventories drawn up in 1845 for the transfer of the house and contents to Macleay's son, William Sharp. He took the house in return for payment of his father's debts, leading to a rift that was never resolved.

Macleay's original 22-hectare (54-acre) land grant was subdivided for flats and villas from the 1880s to 1927. In the 1940s, the house itself was divided into 15 flats. In 1942, the artist Donald Friend, standing on the balcony of his flat – the former morning room – saw the ferry *Kuttabul* hit by a torpedo from a Japanese midget submarine.

The house was restored and opened as a museum in 1977. It is a property of the Historic Houses Trust of NSW.

The sweeping staircase under the oval dome, Elizabeth Bay House

Beare Park ❹

Ithaca Rd, Elizabeth Bay. **Map** 2 F5. 🚌 *311, 350.*

ORIGINALLY A PART of the Macleay Estate, Beare Park is now encircled by a jumble of apartment blocks. A refuge from hectic Kings Cross, it is one of only a handful of parks serving a densely populated area. In the shape of a natural amphitheatre, the park puts Elizabeth Bay on glorious view.

The family home of JC Williamson, a famous theatrical entrepreneur who came to Australia from America in the 1870s, formerly stood at the eastern extremity of the park.

Star of David in the lobby of the Sydney Jewish Museum

Sydney Jewish Museum ❺

146 Darlinghurst Rd, Darlinghurst. **Map** 5 B2. 9360 7999. *Sydney Explorer, Bondi & Bay Explorer, 311, 378.* 10am–4pm Mon–Thu, 10am–2pm Fri, 11am–5pm Sun. *Sat, Jewish hols.*

SIXTEEN JEWISH convicts were on the First Fleet and many more were to be transported before the end of the convict era. As with other convicts, most would endure and some would thrive, seizing all the opportunities the colony had to offer for those wishing to make something of themselves.

The Sydney Jewish Museum relates stories of Australian Jewry within the context of the Holocaust. The ground floor display explores present-day Jewish traditions and culture within Australia. Ascending the stairs to mezzanine levels 1–6, the visitor passes through chronological and thematic exhibitions which unravel the history of the Holocaust.

From Hitler's rise to power and *Kristallnacht*, through the evacuation of the ghettos and the Final Solution, to the ultimate liberation of the infamous death camps and Nuremberg Trials, the harrowing events are graphically documented. This horrific period is recalled using photographs and relics, some exhumed from mass graves, as well as audiovisual exhibits and oral testimonies.

Holocaust survivors act as guides on each level. Their presence, bearing witness to the recorded events, lends considerable power and moving authenticity to the exhibits throughout the museum.

Old Gaol, Darlinghurst ❻

Cnr Burton & Forbes Sts, Darlinghurst. **Map** 5 A2. 9339 8666. *378, 380, 382* 7:30am–10pm Mon–Fri. *public hols.*

ORIGINALLY KNOWN as the Woolloomooloo Stockade and later as Darlinghurst Gaol, this complex is now part of the Sydney Institute of Technology. It was constructed over a 20-year period from 1822.

Surrounded by walls almost 7 m (23 ft) high, the cell blocks radiate from a central roundhouse. The jail is built of stone quarried on the site by convicts which was then chiselled by them into blocks.

No fewer than 67 people were executed here between 1841 and 1908. Perhaps the most notorious hangman was Alexander "The Strangler" Green, after whom Green Park, outside the jail, is thought to have been named. Green lived near the park until public hostility forced him to live in relative safety inside the jail.

Some of Australia's most noted artists, including Frank Hodgkinson, Jon Molvig and William Dobell, trained or taught at the art school which was established here in 1921.

The former Governor's house, Old Gaol, Darlinghurst

Darlinghurst Court House ❼

Forbes St, Darlinghurst. **Map** 5 A2. 9368 2947. *378, 380, 382.* Feb–Dec: 10am–4pm Mon–Fri. *Jan, public hols.*

ABUTTING THE GRIM old jail, to which it is connected by underground passages, and facing tawdry Taylors Square, this unlikely gem of Greek Revival architecture was begun in 1835 by Colonial Architect Mortimer Lewis. He was only responsible for the central block of the main building with its splendid six-columned Doric portico with fine Greek embellishments. The balancing side wings were not added until the 1880s.

The court house is still used by the state's Supreme Court mainly for criminal cases, and these are open to the public.

Beare Park, a quiet inner-city park with harbour views

PADDINGTON

ADDINGTON IS JUSTLY celebrated for its handsome terraces, but this "village in the city", as it is often dubbed, is also famed for its interesting speciality shops full of oddities and collectables, fine restaurants, small hotels, fashionable art galleries and antique dealers' shops. Paddington boasts a lively street culture, especially on Saturdays when people from far and wide flock to the famous weekly Paddington Bazaar, spilling out into the streets, pubs and cafés of the surrounding area. Stretching from the Victoria Barracks at its western end, along Oxford Street to the green haven of Centennial Park, Paddington slopes

Clock tower on Paddington Town Hall

away from this bustling central thoroughfare into the narrow lanes and elegant, leafy streets. The suburb has undergone a series of radical transformations. The first Paddington was built in the 1830s as a Georgian weekend retreat for the moneyed class. These gracious homes had a short life, before being knocked down and subdivided. The terraces succeeding them fell into ruin by the 1920s, but are now admired as finely restored Victorian homes with their distinctive wrought-iron "lace" verandas. The glimpses of harbour found in the quiet streets make Paddington one of Sydney's most sought-after residential areas.

SIGHTS AT A GLANCE

Historic Streets and Buildings
Paddington Street ❶
Five Ways ❸
Juniper Hall ❹
Paddington Town Hall ❺
Paddington Village ❻
Victoria Barracks ❼

Parks and Gardens
Centennial Park ❽

Markets
Paddington Bazaar ❷

GETTING THERE
The best way to travel to and around this area is by bus. Buses 378, 380 and 382 run along Oxford Street on their way between the city and beach suburbs, while bus 389 cuts through the back streets.

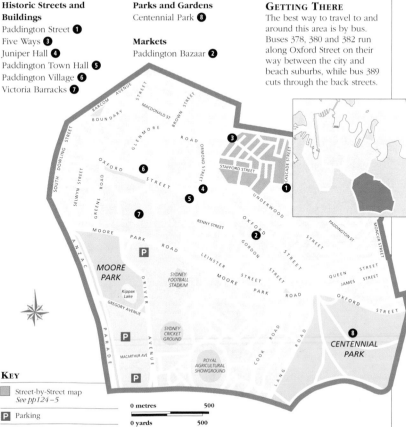

KEY

▨	Street-by-Street map *See pp124–5*
🅿	Parking

0 metres 500
0 yards 500

◁ **The front entrance to a lovingly restored Victorian terrace house in Paddington**

Street-by-Street: Paddington

Paddington began to flourish in the 1840s, when the decision was made to build the Victoria Barracks. At the time much of it was "the most wild looking place . . . barren sand-hills with patches of scrub, hills and hollows galore". The area began to fill rapidly, as owner builders bought into the area and built short rows of terrace houses, many extremely narrow because of the lack of building regulations. After the Depression, most of Paddington was threatened with demolition, but was saved and restored by the large influx of postwar migrants.

Victorian finial in Union Street

★ **Five Ways**
This shopping hub was established in the late 19th century on the busy Glenmore roadway trodden out by bullocks ❸

Duxford Street's terrace houses in toning pale shades constitute an ideal of town planning: the Victorians preferred houses in a row to have a pleasingly uniform aspect.

"Gingerbread" houses can be seen in Broughton and Union Streets. With their steeply pitched gables and fretwork barge-boards, they are typical of the rustic Gothic Picturesque architectural style.

The London Tavern opened for business in 1876, making it the suburb's oldest pub. Like many of the pubs and delicatessens in this well-serviced suburb, it stands at the end of a row of terraces.

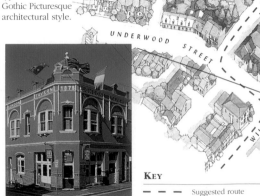

STAR SIGHTS

★ **Paddington Street**

★ **Five Ways**

KEY

– – – Suggested route

The **Sherman Gallery** is housed in a strikingly modern building. It is designed to hold Australian and international contemporary sculpture and paintings. Suitable access gates and a special in-house crane enable the movement of large-scale artworks, including textiles.

The **Sotheby's Gallery** is a renowned gallery and auction house. It is housed in a typical Paddington corner building, with an iron-lace balcony.

LOCATOR MAP
See Street Finder, maps 5 & 6

Warwick, built in the 1860s, is a minor castle lying at the end of a row of humble terraces. Its turrets, battlements and assorted decorations, in a style somewhat fancifully described as "King Arthur", even adorn the garages at the rear.

Windsor Street's terrace houses are, in some cases, a mere 4.5 m (15 ft) wide.

Street-making in Paddington's early days was often an expensive and complicated business. A cascade of water was dammed to build Cascade Street.

★ Paddington Street
Under the established plane trees, some of Paddington's finest Victorian terraces exemplify the building boom of 1860–90. Over 30 years, 3,800 houses were built in the suburb ❶

| 0 metres | 50 |
| 0 yards | 50 |

Paddington Street terrace house

Paddington Street ❶

Map 6 D3. 🚌 *378, 380, 382.*

WITH ITS HUGE PLANE trees shading the road and fine two-, three- and four-storey terrace houses on each side, Paddington Street is one of the oldest, loveliest, and at the same time most typical of the suburb's streets.

Paddington grew rapidly as a commuter suburb in the late 19th century and most of the terraces were built for renting to the city's artisans. They were cheaply decorated with iron lace (some of which had arrived in ships as ballast), as well as Grecian-style friezes, worked parapets, swagged urns, lions rampant, cornices, pilasters, scrolls and other fancy plastering. Façades were proudly emblazoned with the house and terrace names.

By the 1900s, these terraces had become unfashionable as people who could afford to moved further out of the city to newly emerging "garden suburbs" such as Haberfield, Croydon and Strathfield.

In the 1960s, however, tastes changed once more: the architectural appeal of the terraces, as well as the many advantages of living near the city, came to be appreciated. Paddington experienced a renaissance.

Paddington Street now offers the perennial browser plenty of opportunities to indulge. Small art galleries and interior design studios operate out of shopfronts both quaint and grand.

Paddington Bazaar ❷

395 Oxford St. **Map** 6 D4.
📞 *9331 2646.* 🚌 *378, 380, 382.*
🕙 *10am–4pm (5pm daylight saving)* Sat. ● *25 Dec.* 📷 ♿ *See Shops and Markets p203.*

THIS MARKET, which began in 1973, takes place every Saturday, come rain or shine, in the grounds of Paddington Village Uniting Church. It is probably the most colourful and varied in Sydney; a place to meet and be seen as much as to shop. Stallholders come from all over the world, and many young designers, hoping to launch their careers, display their wares. Among the myriad offerings are jewellery, pottery and an array of other arts and crafts, as well as both new and secondhand clothing.

Whatever you are looking for, from organic bananas to a full Oriental massage, you are likely to find it here.

Five Ways ❸

Cnr Glenmore Rd & Heeley St.
Map 5 C3. 🚌 *389.*

AT THIS PICTURESQUE junction, where three streets cross on Glenmore Road, a busy shopping hub developed by the tramline that ran from the city to Bondi Beach. On the five corners stand Victorian and early 20th-century shops, one now a restaurant.

Occupying another corner is the impressive, three-storey Royal Hotel (see p196), which was completed in 1888. This mixed Victorian and Classical

Revival building, with its intricately worked cast-iron "lace" screen balcony offering distant harbour views, is quite typical of the hotel architecture to be found in Sydney at that time.

Balcony of the Royal Hotel

Juniper Hall ❹

250 Oxford St. **Map** 5 C3.
📞 *9258 0123.* 🚌 *378, 380, 382.*
🕙 *twice yearly (dates vary).* 📷

THE EMANCIPIST gin distiller Robert Cooper built this superb example of Colonial Georgian architecture for his third wife Sarah. He named it after the main ingredient of the gin that made his fortune.

Completed in 1824, the two-storey home is the oldest still standing in Paddington and is probably the largest house ever built in the suburb. It had to be: Cooper already had 14 children when he declared that Sarah would have the finest house in Sydney, and he subsequently fathered 14 more.

Juniper Hall was saved from demolition in the mid-1980s and restored in fine style. Now under the auspices of the National Trust, the building is used as private office space.

The Colonial Georgian façade of the superbly restored Juniper Hall

Paddington Town Hall ❺

Cnr Oxford St & Oatley Rd. **Map** 5 C3.
🚌 378, 380, 382. ⬦ 10am–4pm
Mon–Fri. ⬤ public hols. 📷

THE PADDINGTON Town Hall was completed in 1891. An international competition which, in a spirit of Victorian self-confidence, was intended to produce the state's finest town hall, was won by local architect JE Kemp. His Classical Revival building, to which a clock tower was later added, still dominates the surrounding area, although it is no longer a centre of local government.

The building now houses Chauvel Cinema (see p210), run by the Australian Film Institute, Paddington Library, a radio station, commercial offices and a large ballroom that is available for hire.

Paddington Town Hall

Paddington Village ❻

Cnr Gipps & Shadforth Sts. **Map** 5 C3.
🚌 378, 380, 382.

PADDINGTON BEGAN its life as a working-class suburb. The community comprised the carpenters, quarrymen and stonemasons who supervised the convict gangs that built Victoria Barracks in the 1840s.

The artisans and their families occupied a tight huddle of spartan houses, a few of which still remain, crowded into the narrow streets nearby. Like the barracks, these dwellings and surrounding shops and hotels were built mainly of locally quarried stone.

The lush green expanse of Centennial Park

Victoria Barracks ❼

Oxford St. **Map** 5 B3. 📞 9339 3000.
🚌 378, 380, 382. **Museum** 📞 9339
3330. ⬦ 10am–12:30pm Thu, 10am–3pm Sun. ⬤ summer school hols.
📷 ♿ 🎫 **Parade & tour:** 10am Thu.

VICTORIA BARRACKS is the largest and best-preserved group of late Georgian architecture in Australia, covering almost 12 ha (29 acres). It is widely considered to be one of the best examples of a military barracks in the world.

Designed by the Colonial Engineer, Lieutenant Colonel George Barney, the barracks were built between 1841 and 1848 using local sandstone quarried by mainly convict labour. Originally intended to house 800 men, it has been in continuous military use ever since, and still operates as a centre of military planning, administration and command.

The main block is 225 m (740 ft) long and has symmetrical two-storey wings with cast-iron verandas flanking a central archway. The perimeter walls, which are designed to

The archway at the Oxford Street entrance to Victoria Barracks

repel surprise attacks, have foundations 10 m (40 ft) deep in places. Occupying a former jail block, the museum traces Australia's military heritage.

Centennial Park ❽

Map 6 E5. 📞 9339 6699. 🚌 Clovelly, Coogee, Maroubra, Randwick, Bronte, City, Bondi Beach & Bondi Junction routes. ⬦ Mar–Apr: 6am–6pm daily, May–Aug: 6:30am–5:30pm daily, Sep–Oct: 6am–6pm daily, Nov–Feb 6am–8pm daily. 🎫 on request.

ENTERING THIS 220-ha (544-acre) park through one of its sandstone and wrought-iron gates, the visitor may wonder how such an extensive and idyllic place has survived so close to the centre of the city.

Formerly a common, it was dedicated "to the enjoyment of the people of New South Wales forever" on 26 January 1888, the centenary of the foundation of the colony. On 1 January 1901, more than 100,000 people gathered here to witness the Commonwealth of Australia come into being, when Australia's first federal ministry was sworn in by the first governor-general.

Today picnickers, painters, runners, and those on horses, bikes and in-line skates (all of which can be hired nearby) use this vast recreation area.

Once the source of Sydney's water supply, the swamps are now home to many waterbirds. Within the park are ornamental ponds, cultivated gardens, an Avenue of Palms with 400 trees, a sports ground and a café (see p194).

FURTHER AFIELD

BEYOND THE INNER CITY, numerous places vie for the visitor's attention. Around the harbour foreshores are picturesque suburbs, secluded beaches, scenic outlooks and cultural and historic sights. Taronga Zoo is worth a visit as much for its incomparable setting as for its birds and animals. Manly, stretching between harbour and ocean, is the

Mr and Mrs Luna Park

city's northern playground, while Bondi is its eastern counterpart. In Balmain, Glebe and Surry Hills, the visitor can experience the character of the inner suburbs. Still further afield, out west at Parramatta, there are sights that recall and evoke the first days of European settlement and the colony's initially unsteady steps towards agricultural self-sufficiency.

SIGHTS AT A GLANCE

Historic Districts and Buildings
University of Sydney ❸
Balmain ❻
Kirribilli Point ❽
North Head ⓲
Vaucluse House ⓭
Watsons Bay ⓯
Macquarie Lighthouse ⓰
Captain Cook's Landing Place ⓲
Elizabeth Farm ⓴
Hambledon Cottage ㉑
Experiment Farm Cottage ㉒
Old Government House ㉔

16 km = 10 miles

Parks and Gardens
Nielsen Park ⓮
Museums and Galleries
Brett Whiteley Studio ❶
Nutcote ❾
Entertainment
Luna Park ❼
Taronga Zoo pp134–5 ❿
Sydney Olympic Park ⓳
Beaches
Manly ⓫
Bondi Beach ⓱
Restaurants and Pubs
Surry Hills ❷
Glebe ❹

Markets
Sydney Fish Market ❺

Cemeteries
St John's Cemetery ㉓

KEY

▨	Main sightseeing areas
☐	Park or reserve
✈	Airport
③	Metroad route
▬	Freeway or motorway
▬	Major road
▭	Minor road

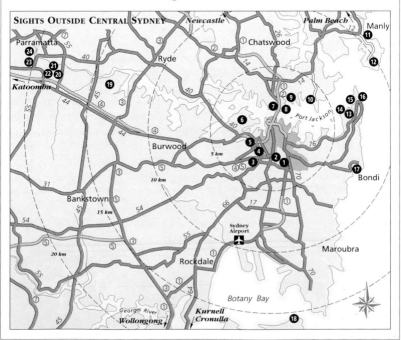

SIGHTS OUTSIDE CENTRAL SYDNEY

◁ **The majestic clock tower rising above the main quadrangle at the University of Sydney**

Brett Whiteley Studio ❶

2 Raper St, Surry Hills. **Map** 5 A4.
📞 *9225 1881*. 🚌 *343, 372, 393*.
🕐 *10am–4pm Sat & Sun*. ⬤ *Easter Sun*. 🈺 ♿ 🎦

IN JUNE 1992, Brett Whiteley, *enfant terrible* of Australian contemporary art, died unexpectedly at the age of 53. An internationally acclaimed and prolific artist, he produced some of the most sumptuous images of Sydney and its distinctive harbour ever painted.

In 1985, Whiteley bought a former factory and converted it into a studio and residence. The studio is now a public museum and art gallery. It features the work of Whiteley and other artists. Visitors have the opportunity to gain an insight into Whiteley's life and work through changing exhibitions and displays of personal effects and memorabilia. The studio is under the administration of the Art Gallery of New South Wales (*see pp108–11*).

Surry Hills ❷

Map 5 A3. 🚌 *301, 302, 303, 304, 339, Oxford St routes. See **Shops and Markets** pp200–201*.

THIS WAS ONCE one of the more depressed areas of the inner city. In the 1920s, Surry Hills was a haunt of the razor gangs that terrorized inner-city Sydney. The 1940s slums were vividly described in Ruth Park's celebrated novels *Poor Man's Orange* and *The*

Shop in Crown Street, Surry Hills

Harp in the South. In the post-war years, the low property and rental prices attracted a large number of new migrants to the already-hectic district.

In recent decades, young professionals have moved into the area, lured by the charm of its Victorian terraces and closeness to the city. Many of the suburb's traditional inhabitants have since been displaced.

Today Surry Hills is a curious mixture of fashion and seediness. Newly renovated houses stand alongside dilapidated dwellings, while streets of elegant Victorian terraces abut modern high-rise flats and factory warehouses.

For the visitor, the suburb offers a wide range of ethnic cuisines, often at bargain prices. It is famed for the Lebanese and Turkish restaurants that cluster near the intersection of Cleveland and Elizabeth Streets. You will also find Indian, Chinese, Thai,

French and numerous Italian eateries scattered around the suburb, along with smart and casual cafés and stylish pubs.

Once the centre of Sydney's garment trade, it still has factory outlets where clothing, lingerie and haberdashery can be purchased at below retail prices. Alternative fashion and retro clothing shops are found at the Oxford Street end of Crown Street. These boutiques attract the street-smart crowd.

University of Sydney ❸

Parramatta Rd, Camperdown.
Map 3 B5. 📞 *9351 2222*. 🚌 *343, Parramatta Rd & City Rd routes*. 🕐 *daily*. 📷 ♿ 🎦 *10:30am Tue–Thu (essential to book one week in advance)*.

INAUGURATED IN 1850, this is Australia's oldest university. The campus is a sprawling hotchpotch of buildings from different eras, of often dubious architectural merit. However, the original Victorian Gothic main building still stands on its elevated site, dominating its surroundings. The work of the Colonial Architect Edmund Blacket, it is scrupulously modelled on the architecture of Cambridge and Oxford.

Statue of Hermes, Nicholson Museum

It features intricate stone tracery, a clock tower with carved pinnacles, gargoyles (one, in the quadrangle, represents a crocodile) and a cloistered main quadrangle.

The gem of the complex, and probably Blacket's finest work, is the Great Hall at the main building's northern end. This grandly sombre hall, with its carved cedar ceiling and stained-glass windows depicting famous philosophers and scientists, is often used for public concerts as well as for university ceremonies.

The Nicholson Museum of antiquities, the natural history Macleay Museum and the War Memorial Art Gallery, which houses the university's art collection, are all within the grounds. They are open to the public on most weekdays.

Brett Whiteley Studio: former artist's studio, now a museum

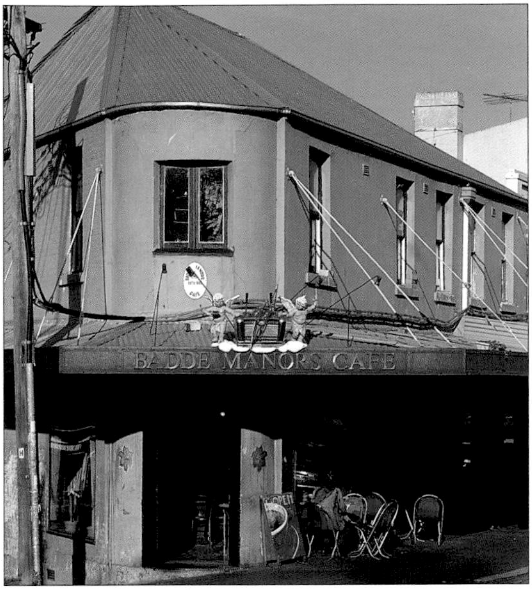

Corner view of Badde Manors Café on Glebe Point Road, Glebe

Glebe ❹

Map 3 A4. 🚌 *431, 433. See* ***Shops and Markets*** *p203.*

THE WORD "GLEBE" means land assigned to a clergyman as part of his benefice. In 1789, Governor Phillip granted 162 ha (400 acres) to Richard Johnson, the First Fleet chaplain, and his wife Mary. Almost all of the present suburb was once part of that Glebe Estate. Many of its streets wind down to the working harbour and contain terrace houses with Sydney wrought-iron "lace" in varying states of repair.

The once-grand residences of the 19th-century élite were mostly towards the harbour end of Glebe Point Road, with workers' cottages clustered nearer Parramatta Road. It is a mix that survives to this day. Glebe is partly a gentrified member of the café society and partly a humble address, while also being a dormitory suburb for students at the nearby University of Sydney.

It is densely populated and lively, with many restaurants and cafés in all price ranges, traditional and trendy pubs, good bookshops, an art-house cinema and shops selling everything from antique clocks to New Age goods and chattels. Glebe Market is held every Saturday and has stalls ranging from second-hand clothing and silver jewellery to bric-a-brac.

Sydney Fish Market ❺

Cnr Pyrmont Bridge Rd & Bank St, Pyrmont. **Map** 3 B2. ☎ *9660 1611.* 🚌 *501.* 🕐 *7am–4pm daily.* ● *25 Dec.* 📷 ♿ ☕ *See* ***Shops and Markets*** *pp202–3.*

EVERY WEEKDAY, about 200 seafood retailers and other dealers arrive at this cooperative fish market to bid for the previous day's catch. It is sold by Dutch auction, with prices starting high and decreasing, which halves the sale time. The catch consists of a quantity and variety of fish and other seafood species many times that offered at the London or San Francisco markets.

A fair amount of this catch ends up, later in the morning, in the fish market's numerous large retail outlets which, for the general public, are its main attraction. As well as fresh fish, these retailers sell smoked salmon and roe, sushi, marinated baby octopus and many other ready-to-eat delicacies. Visitors watch the experts as they tenderize octopus and squid in concrete mixers. As well as fishmongers, there are a number of other fresh food shops, several restaurants and, of course, purveyors of fish and chips for the connoisseur.

Balmain ❻

🚌 *433, 434, 442. See* ***Shops and Markets*** *p203 and* ***Four Guided Walks*** *pp142–3.*

BALMAIN WAS ONCE one of Sydney's most staunchly working-class areas, with shipyards, a dry dock and repair yards, a coal mine, numerous rough-and-ready pubs and an intimidating criminal element. Its late 19th-century town hall, post office, court house and fire station in Darling Street reflect the civic pride of the suburb in the Victorian era.

In recent years, the many stone and timber cottages of what had become a slum have transformed into a charming, bustling suburb that still retains its village character, with interesting shops, galleries, cafés, restaurants and pubs.

The quietness of the Balmain peninsula, its proximity to the city and its bohemian ambience perhaps account for the many prominent writers – including the novelist Kate Grenville and playwright David Williamson – who live and work here.

The Saturday market, held at St Andrews Congregational Church in Darling Street, is one of Sydney's best. Antiques, estate jewellery and ingenious art and craft items are on sale.

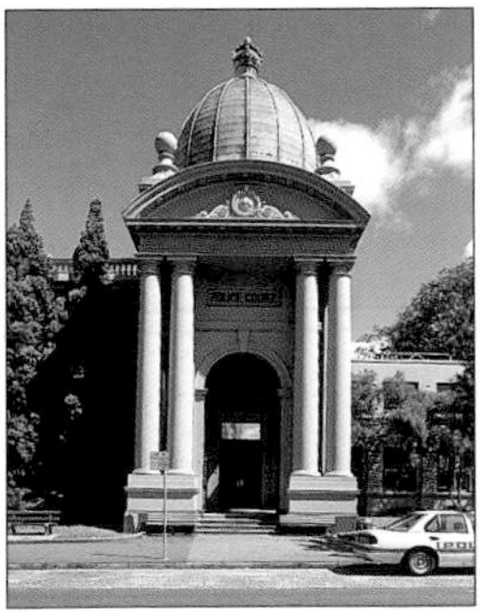

Imposing entrance to Balmain court house on Darling Street

THE COLOURFUL FACES OF LUNA PARK

The gateway to Luna Park is the gaping mouth of a huge laughing face, flanked by two 36-m (129-ft) Art Deco towers. Between 1935 and 1945, four successive canvas, wire and plaster faces fell to the ravages of time. Built in the 1950s, the fifth face was replaced in 1973 with one designed by the Sydney artist Martin Sharp. The seventh, from the 1980s, is now at the Powerhouse Museum (*see pp100–101*). Today's face is made of polyurethane and painted fibreglass.

The present Luna Park face, crossing the harbour by barge

The Big Dipper at Luna Park

Luna Park ❼

1 Olympic Drive, Milsons Point.
🚢 Milsons Point. 🅾 ♿

THIS FAMOUS FUN FAIR, built on the site of former Harbour Bridge construction workshops, was modelled on Luna Park at Coney Island, New York. Built in South Australia, Sydney's Luna Park was dismantled and re-erected on its present site in 1935. For the next 43 years it was one of the most conspicuous landmarks on the harbour foreshores. Except during the compulsory blackouts of World War II, its brilliant illuminations were a feature of the city's night scene.

In 1979, seven people were killed in a ghost train fire, a tragedy that led to the park's eventual closure in April 1988. In the early 1990s, Luna Park was refurbished. In 1995, it reopened briefly as a fun fair, but this has since closed down and Luna Park's future remains uncertain. Redevelopment proposals for the site are currently being considered.

Luna Park retains many of its extravagant features. Las Vegas glitz and 1940s Futurism are just two of the styles decorating one of Sydney's most treasured icons. The old-style fun house Coney Island, Crystal Palace and the gateway face are all protected by heritage listing.

Kirribilli Point ❽

Kirribilli Ave, Kirribilli. 🚢 Kirribilli North Sydney.

THE TWO HOUSES occupying this prominent headland, in their delightful garden settings, are typical of the magnificent homes in sprawling grounds that once ringed the harbour. Most have been demolished

now and the land subdivided for apartment living. Kirribilli, meaning "place for fishing", is the most densely populated suburb in Australia.

The larger, more dominant of the two houses is Admiralty House, built as a single-storey residence in 1843. Between 1885 and 1913 it served as the residence of the commanding officer of Britain's Royal Navy Pacific Squadron, which was based in Sydney. Fortifications on the shoreline recall its military history. Now the official Sydney home of Australia's governor-general, it is said that even its shed could be considered the city's best address.

In 1855, the charming Gothic Kirribilli House, with its steep gables and decorative fretwork, was built in the grounds of Admiralty House. Today it is the official Sydney residence of Australia's prime minister.

Nutcote ❾

5 Wallaringa Ave, Neutral Bay.
📞 9953 4453. 🚢 Kurraba Point, Neutral Bay. 🕙 11am–3pm Wed–Sun. 🚫 Good Fri, 25–26 Dec. 🎫 🅾 🛍

ONE OF THE CLASSICS of Australian children's literature, *Snugglepot and Cuddlepie*, was published in 1918. Since then, these two characters – known as the "gumnut" babies along with the cartoon creatures Bib and Bub – have been loved by countless young Australians.

Nutcote was, for 44 years, the home of their creator, illustrator and author May Gibbs. Saved from demolition then

Admiralty House and Kirribilli House, near Sydney Harbour Bridge

Shop façades featuring decorative gables along Manly's Corso

restored and refurbished in the style of the 1930s, it opened in 1994 as an historic house museum. Visitors can view the author's painstakingly kept notebooks and other memorabilia (including the table at which she worked), as well as original editions of her books. There is a garden tea room, with views across the harbour and a shop that sells a range of May Gibbs' souvenirs.

May Gibbs' studio at Nutcote

Taronga Zoo ⓾

See pp134–5.

Manly ⓫

🚢 Manly. **Oceanworld** West Esplanade. 🕿 9949 2644. ◯ 10am–5:30pm daily. ● 25 Dec. 🖼 🗘 ♿ 🖍 See **Four Guided Walks** pp146–7.

L ONG AFTER Australia's conversion to the metric system, the slogan "seven miles from Sydney and a thousand miles from care" is still current. It refers to Manly and the 7-mile (11-km) journey from Circular Quay by harbour ferry. If asked to suggest a single excursion,

most Sydneysiders would nominate a ferry ride to Manly. This narrow stretch of land lying between the harbour and the ocean was named by Governor Phillip, even before the township of Sydney got its name, for the impressive bearing of the Aboriginal men.

As the ferry pulls in to the rejuvenated Manly wharf you will notice, on the right, the lively fun fair that occupies the adjacent pier, and on the left, the tranquil harbourside beach known as Manly Cove.

At the far end of Manly Cove is Oceanworld, where visitors can see sharks, giant stingrays and other species in an underwater viewing tunnel. You can also dive with the sharks here if you are brave enough.

The Corso is a lively pedestrian thoroughfare of souvenir shops and fast food outlets. It leads to Manly's ocean beach, with its promenade lined by towering Norfolk pines. Nearby stands a monument to a local newspaper proprietor who, in 1902, defied bans on daytime

bathing and promptly found himself arrested. By the following year, however, Australia's bathing laws were liberalized.

In October each year, Manly plays host to the prestigious Manly Jazz Festival *(see p48).*

North Head ⓬

📞 9977 6522. 🚢 Manly. **Quarantine Station** ◯ 1:10pm Wed, Fri–Mon, or as arranged. Bookings essential. **Ghost tours** Wed, Fri–Sun. Bookings essential (starting times vary). ● public hols. 🖼 🗘 ♿ 🖍 See **Parks and Reserves** pp44–7.

T HE MAJESTIC CLIFFS of North Head afford the finest views in Sydney Harbour National Park, providing vistas along the coastline, across to Middle Harbour and towards the city. North Head is also the ideal place for observing the movements of harbour and seagoing craft and especially for seeing off the yachts at the start of the annual Sydney to Hobart race *(see p49).*

The Quarantine Station nestles just above Spring Cove within the national park. Here, between 1832 and the 1960s, many ships, with their crews and passengers, were quarantined to protect Sydneysiders from the spread of epidemic diseases such as smallpox, plague, influenza and typhoid fever. Over 500 people died here, leading some people to believe the area is haunted.

Countless migrants spent their first months in Australia in this place of splendid isolation. Many of its internees left poignant messages and poems carved in the sandstone.

First-class quarters at the Quarantine Station, North Head

Taronga Zoo ⑩

Red kangaroo

THIS FAMOUS HARBOURSIDE zoo is home to almost 4,000 animals, with a special emphasis placed on unique Australian wildlife exhibits. Conspicuous iron bars and fences have been dispensed with, as many of the large enclosures use moats to separate the wandering public from the curious animal onlookers contained in environments closely resembling their natural habitat. The zoo is involved in the breeding of endangered animals, and readily donates or exchanges animals to capitalize on the worldwide "gene pool".

Asian Elephant
This relatively large enclosure encourages more natural behaviour as the elephants are freely able to interact.

Australian Birds

Athol Wharf Road

⑬

Lower entrance

Bradleys Head Road

0 metres 100
0 yards 100

The platypus is one of only three species of egg-laying mammals.

⑫

⑪

⑩

⑨

⑧

⑤

⑥

④

②

③

①

⑦

Bradleys Head Road

Common Wombat
This ground-dwelling animal is a powerful burrower able to move quickly if disturbed. It feeds on roots and has a pouch for carrying its young.

Upper entrance

Performing seal theatre

STAR DISPLAYS

★ **White Tiger**

★ **Orang-utan Rainforest**

★ **Koala House**

Upper Entrance
This edifice has greeted visitors since the opening in 1916. By 1917, more than half of Sydney's population had paid a visit.

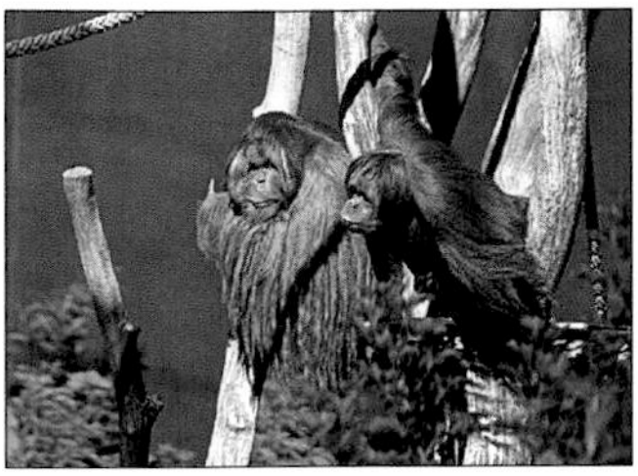

★ Orang-utan Rainforest
Threatened by widespread destruction of their natural habitat in the Sumatran and Borneo rainforests, these primates are on the world's endangered species list.

Visitors' Checklist
Bradleys Head Rd, Mosman.
☎ 9969 2777. 🚌 238, 247, 250. ⛴ Taronga Zoo. 🕘 9am–5pm daily (last adm 4:30pm).
📷 ♿ 🍴 ☕ 🛍
Concerts, talks, performances.

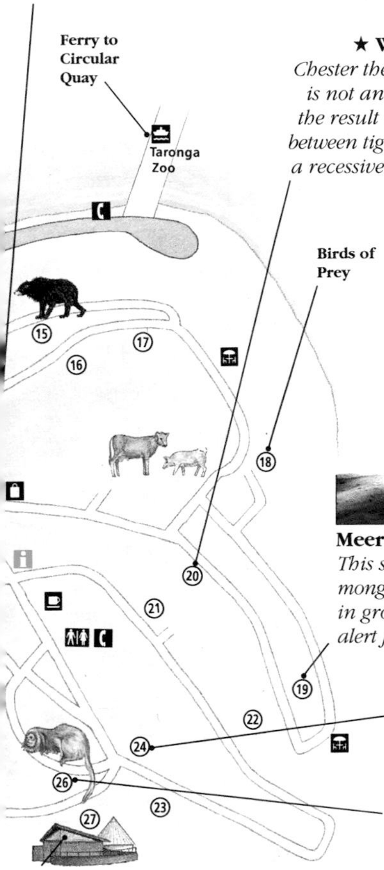

Ferry to Circular Quay
Taronga Zoo
Birds of Prey
[15]
[16]
[17]
[18]
[20]
[21]
[19]
[22]
[24]
[26]
[23]
[27]

★ White Tiger
Chester the white tiger is not an albino, but the result of a mating between tigers carrying a recessive white gene.

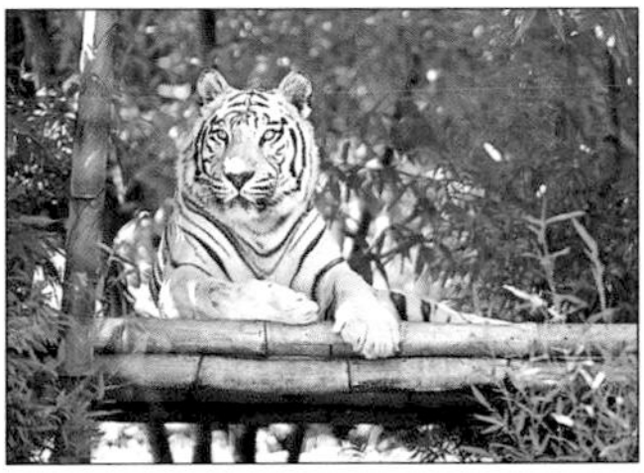

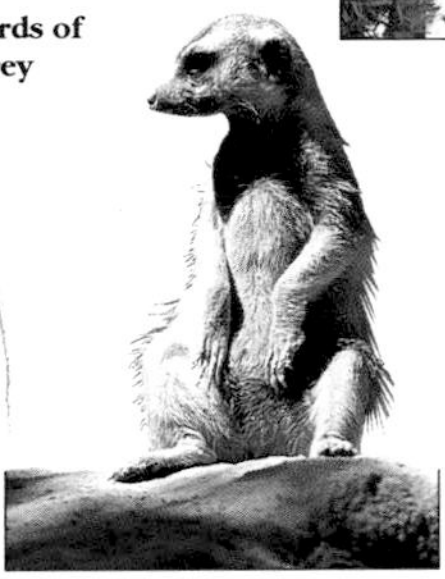

Meerkat
This southern African mongoose always forages in groups, with a guard alert for signs of danger.

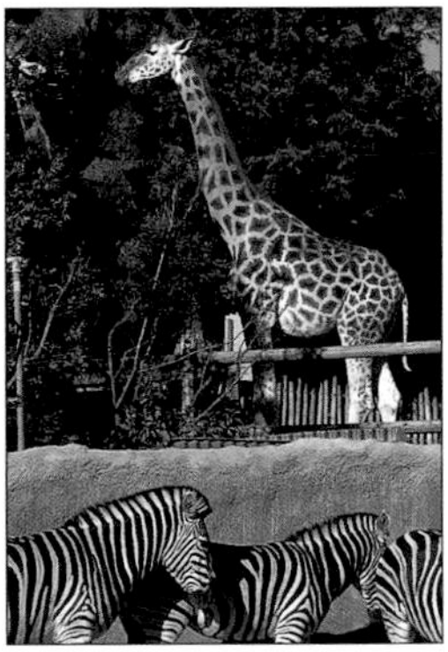

African Waterhole
Savannah waterholes are visited by many species. The zoo recreates that environment as giraffes, zebras and hippopotami roam together.

The golden lion tamarin is the most endangered primate in the world today.

The Serpentaria has amphibians, invertebrates and reptiles.

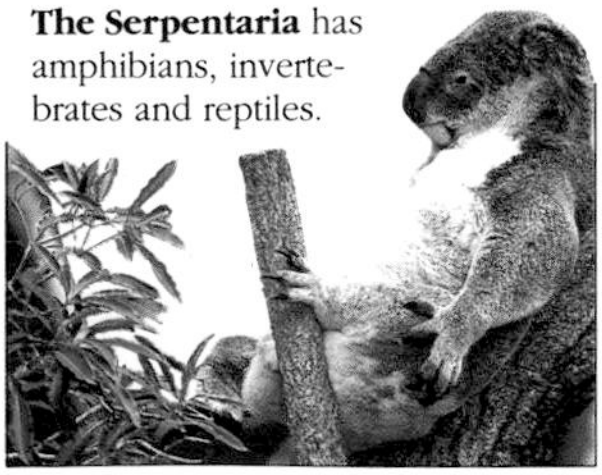

★ Koala House
Visitors can see the koalas in their eucalypt habitat at tree level. The spiral ramp allows you to get close to feeding and sleeping animals.

Key to Animal Enclosures

African Waterhole [24]	Orang-utan Rainforest [25]
Asian elephant [10]	Otter [16]
Australian Birds [13]	Penguin [8]
Australian Walkabout [3]	Red panda [17]
Australia's Night Life [5]	Saltwater crocodile [9]
Birds of Prey [18]	Seals and sea-lions [14]
Chimpanzee Park [23]	Serpentaria [27]
Dingo & Tasmanian devil [7]	Snow leopard [22]
Echidna & platypus [4]	Sun bear [15]
Golden lion tamarin [26]	Walk-through Rainforest [6]
Gorilla [29]	Wetlands [1]
Jungle Cats [12]	White tiger [20]
Koala House [28]	Wombat [2]
Lion [21]	Yellow-footed rock wallaby [11]
Meerkat [19]	

Façade of Vaucluse House, with its garden and fountain

Vaucluse House ⑬

Wentworth Rd, Vaucluse.
[9388 7922. ▤ 325. ○ 10am–
4:30pm Tue–Sun. ● Good Fri,
25 Dec. ▨ ▣ ▤ ▨

TRADITION HAS IT that the
most riotous party colonial
Sydney ever saw took place
on the Vaucluse House lawns
in 1831. WC Wentworth and
4,000 of his political cronies
gathered there to celebrate the
recall to England of Governor
Ralph Darling, the arch-enemy.
  WC Wentworth was a major
figure in the colony, being one
of the first three Europeans to
cross the Blue Mountains *(see
pp160–61)*. He was the son of
a female convict and a physi-
cian forced to "volunteer" his
services to the new colony in
order to avoid conviction on
a highway robbery charge.
  The younger Wentworth
became an author, barrister and
statesman who stood for the
Australian-born "currency" lads
and lasses against the "sterling"
English-born. He lived here
with his family from 1829–53,
during which time he drafted
the Constitution Bill, giving
self-government to the state.
  Vaucluse House was begun
in 1803 by Sir Henry Browne
Hayes, a knight of the realm
transported for kidnapping a
Quaker heiress. Sitting comfortably in 11 ha (27 acres) of
parkland, natural bush and
cultivated gardens, this Gothic
Revival house, with its many
idiosyncratic additions, has
been compared to a West
Indian plantation house. The
interior and grounds have been
restored to 1840s style and the

house contains some furniture
that originally belonged to the
Wentworth family. A popular
tea house is in the grounds.

**Greycliffe House, in the tranquil
grounds of Nielsen Park**

Nielsen Park ⑭

▤ 325. ○ Sunrise–10pm daily.

PART OF THE Sydney Harbour
National Park, Nielsen Park,
with its grassy expanses, sandy
beach and netted swimming
pool, is the perfect spot for a
family picnic. Here visitors can

savour the unusual peace that
descends on many harbour
beaches on an endless sunny
day. It is also an ideal vantage
point from which to enjoy a
spectacular summer sunset or
simply to observe the coming
and going of ferries and the
meandering harbour traffic.
  In the midst of this tranquil
setting, enhancing its charm,
stands Greycliffe House with
its decorative gables and ornate
chimney stacks. This Victorian
Gothic mansion was completed
in 1852 for WC Wentworth's
daughter and now offers local
national park information.

Watsons Bay ⑮

[9391 7100. ⛴ Watsons Bay.
See **Four Guided Walks** pp148–9.

AS THE BASE FOR the boats
that take the pilots out to
arriving ships, this pretty bay
has long been a vital part of
the working harbour. It is also
the home of Doyle's famous
waterfront seafood restaurant,
long a magnet for Sydneysiders
and visitors alike.
  Just up the hill and almost
opposite the bay on the ocean
side is The Gap, a spectacular
cliff with tragic associations.
Many troubled people have
taken a suicidal leap from this
rugged cliff on to the wave-
lashed rocks below.
  It was here that the ill-fated
ship *Dunbar* was wrecked in
1857, with the loss of all but
one of its 122 passengers and
crew. Treacherous conditions
had led to miscalculation of
the ship's distance from the
Heads. All hands were ordered

View over Watsons Bay, looking southwest towards the city

The crescent-shaped Bondi Beach, Sydney's most famous beach, looking towards North Bondi

on deck as The Gap's rock walls loomed. The recovered anchor is now set into the cliff near the shipwreck site.

The 1883 Macquarie Lighthouse overlooking the Pacific Ocean

Macquarie Lighthouse ⑯

🚌 324, 325. 📷 ♿

THIS IS THE SECOND lighthouse on this windswept site that is attributed to the convict architect Francis Greenway *(see p114)*. He supervised the construction of the first tower, which was completed in 1818 and described by Governor Macquarie as a "noble magnificent edifice". The colony's first lighthouse, it replaced the previous system of bonfires lit up along the headland and earned Greenway a conditional pardon. When the sandstone

eventually crumbled away, the present lighthouse was built. Although designed by Colonial Architect James Barnet, it was based on Greenway's original and was illuminated for the first time in 1883.

Bondi Beach ⑰

🚌 380, 382, 389, 321. See **Four Guided Walks** *pp144–5.*

THIS LONG CRESCENT of golden sand, so close to the city, has long been a mecca for the sun and surf set *(see pp54–5)*. Throughout the year, surfing enthusiasts visit from far and

wide in search of the perfect wave, and inline skaters hone their skills on the promenade. But the beach life that once defined many Australians has declined in recent times, partly as a result of growing awareness of the dangers of sun exposure *(see p223)*, but also because of a shift in cultural attitudes and preoccupations.

People now seek out Bondi for its trendy seafront cafés and cosmopolitan milieu as much as for the beach. The pavilion, built in 1928 as changing rooms, has been a community centre since the 1970s. It is now a busy venue for festivals, plays, films and craft displays.

BONDI SURF BATHERS' LIFE SAVING CLUB

The founding of the surf lifesaving club at Bondi Beach in 1906 gave impetus to the formation of other local clubs, and ultimately to a global movement. An early club member demonstrated his new lifesaving reel, designed using hair pins and a cotton reel. Now updated, it is standard equipment on beaches worldwide. In 1938, Australia's largest surf rescue was mounted at Bondi, when more than 200 people were washed out to sea by freak waves. Five died, but lifesavers rescued more than 180, establishing their highly dependable reputation.

Bondi surf lifesaving team at the Bondi Surf Carnival, 1937

Captain Cook's Landing Place ⑱

Captain Cook Drive, Kurnell.
9668 9111. 987. **Toll Gate**
7am–7pm daily. **Discovery**
Centre 11am–3pm Mon–Fri,
10am–4:30pm Sat & Sun. 25 Dec.

ALTHOUGH DIFFICULT to get to,
visitors will find this place
worth the effort. It is, after all,
one of Australia's most important European historic sites.
Here James Cook, botanists
Daniel Solander and Joseph
Banks and the crew of HMS
Endeavour landed on 29 April
1770. Aboriginal peoples
waving spears at the invaders
were shot at. One, hit in the
legs, returned with a shield to
defend himself from attack.

Nowadays people can cast
a fishing line from the rock
where the Europeans stepped
ashore. Nearby are the site of

**Cook's Obelisk, overlooking Botany
Bay, Captain Cook's Landing Place**

a well where, Cook recorded,
a shore party "found fresh
water sufficient to water the
ship" and a monument which
marks the first recorded European burial in Australia.

There are also monuments
to Solander, Banks and Cook,
but it is the peaceful ambience
that is most impressive. Now
part of Botany Bay National
Park, Captain Cook's Landing
Place has lovely walks, some
accessible to wheelchairs,
where visitors may roam and
observe the flora which led to
the naming of Botany Bay.

The Discovery Centre in the
park focuses on a number of
themes: the bay's wetlands

Pampas grass and banana plants in the garden at Elizabeth Farm

and the importance of their
conservation; an interesting
exhibition detailing Cook's
exploration of the area; and
an introduction to Aboriginal
customs and culture.

Sydney Olympic Park ⑲

Homebush Bay. Olympic Park.
Homebush Bay Corporation (9735
4800).

THE HIGHLIGHT of millennium
celebrations in Australia
will be the 27th Summer
Olympic Games, the second
time the country has hosted the
competition. Sydney Olympic
Park is situated at Homebush
Bay, 14 km (8.5 miles) west
of the city centre. This 760-ha
(1,900-acre) waterfront site is
the venue for 14 sports,
including the football final,
gymnastics and pentathlon.

The centrepiece of the
games is Stadium Australia,
measuring 52 m (170 ft) from
ground level to its translucent
roof. It has seating for 110,000
spectators – the largest
capacity of any Olympiad. The
Sydney International Aquatic
Centre, with seating for 12,000,
is the venue for swimming
and other indoor water sports.
The Indoor Arena, with its
15,000 seats, hosts the gymnastics competition and the
volleyball and handball finals.

The first Olympiad to
consider the environment,
areas of nature will be
protected, with water and
energy conservation being
key aspects of the design.

Elizabeth Farm ⑳

70 Alice St, Rosehill. **9635 9488.**
Harris Park. 10am–5pm
daily. Good Fri, 25 Dec.

THE DISCOVERY of fertile land
at Parramatta, and the har-
vesting of its first successful
grain crop in 1790, helped save
the fledgling colony from starvation and led to the rapid
development of the area.

This zone was the location
of several of Australia's first
colonial land grants. In 1793,
John Macarthur, a wealthy
farmer and sheep breeder,
was granted 40 ha (100 acres)
of land at Parramatta. He
named the property after his
wife and this was to be
Elizabeth's home for the rest
of her life. Macarthur was
often absent from the farm as
the centre of his wool opera-
tions had moved to Camden.

Part of the house, a simple
stone cottage built in 1793, still
remains and it is the oldest
European building in Australia.
As it was added to over the
next 50 years, it developed into

John Macarthur, 1766–1834

a substantial home with many features of a typical Australian homestead. Simply furnished to the period of 1820–50, with reproductions of paintings and other Macarthur possessions, the house is now a museum strongly evoking the original inhabitants' life and times.

The kitchen, Hambledon Cottage

Hambledon Cottage ㉑

63 Hassall St, Parramatta. ☎ 9635 6924. 🚆 Parramatta. ◯ 11am–4pm Wed, Thu, Sat, Sun & public hols. ♿ ♿ 📷

THIS DELIGHTFUL cottage, with its walls of rendered and painted sandstock, was built in 1824 as the retirement home for Penelope Lucas, governess to the Macarthur daughters. It is set in a park containing trees brought to Australia in 1817 by John Macarthur.

Visitors can wander through rooms that have been restored to the period 1820–50. An 1830 Broadwood piano is one of the furniture exhibits. The kitchen has walls of convict-made bricks. It contains such original appliances and utensils as a handmill for grinding wheat and a bread oven.

Experiment Farm Cottage ㉒

9 Ruse St, Parramatta. ☎ 9635 5655. 🚆 Parramatta. ◯ 10am–4pm Tue–Thu, 11am–4pm Sun & public hols. ● Good Fri, 18–31 Dec. ♿ 📷 ♿ 📷

WHEN HIS SENTENCE expired in 1789, convict farmer James Ruse was given 0.6 ha (1½ acres) of land at Parramatta on which to start a farm, along with a hut, grain for sowing, vital farming tools, two sows and six hens. He successfully planted and harvested a substantial wheat crop with his wife Elizabeth's help. She was the first female convict to be emancipated in New South Wales. In 1791, they were rewarded with a grant of 12 ha (30 acres), the colony's first land grant. Arthur Phillip, governor of the day, called it Experiment Farm.

In 1793, Ruse sold this farm to surgeon John Harris for £40. The date of the cottage is not certain, but it is believed to be early 1830s. The woodwork is Australian red cedar and the cottage is furnished according to an 1838 inventory.

Medicine chest (c.1810), Experiment Farm

St John's Cemetery ㉓

O'Connell St, Parramatta. ☎ 9635 5904. 🚆 Parramatta. 📷 ♿

THIS WALLED cemetery – the oldest in Australia – houses the graves of many convicts and settlers who arrived on the First Fleet in 1788. The oldest grave that can be identified is the flat sandstone slab simply inscribed, "H.E. Dodd 1791". Henry Edward Dodd, known to be Governor Phillip's butler, was the tenth person buried in the cemetery, but the location of the other nine graves is unknown. The first recorded burial was of a child on 31 January 1790. One prominent grave here is that of pioneer churchman Samuel Marsden, who earned the unfortunate title of the "flogging parson" during his period as magistrate general because of his harsh judgments. The merchant Robert Campbell (see p66) and the father of the explorer and patriot William Charles Wentworth (see p136), D'Arcy Wentworth, are also buried here.

Old Government House ㉔

Parramatta Park (entry by Macquarie St gates), Parramatta. ☎ 9635 8149. 🚆 Parramatta. ◯ 10am–4pm Mon–Fri, 11am–4pm Sat, Sun & most public hols. ● Good Fri, 25 Dec. ♿ ♿ limited. 📷

THE CENTRAL BLOCK of Old Government House is the oldest intact public building in Australia. This elegant brick structure, plastered to resemble stone, was built by Governor Hunter in 1799 on the site of a cottage constructed in 1790 for Governor Phillip. Wings to the side and rear were added between 1812 and 1818. The Doric porch, added in 1816, has been attributed to Francis Greenway (see p114).

Australia's finest collection of early 19th-century furniture is now housed inside. A structure on the site, once thought to be a dairy, has been identified as an early worker's cottage.

The drawing room of Old Government House, Parramatta

FOUR GUIDED WALKS

Mural on a Manly surf shop

SYDNEY'S TEMPERATE CLIMATE and natural beauty make it an ideal city for walking. The following walks have been chosen for their distinct character; they all capture a view of the essential Sydney. You can follow the paths that trace the headlands and inlets around Watsons Bay; enjoy an invigorating clifftop walk at Bondi; catch glimpses of the original landscape in Manly's unspoilt bushland; or explore the narrow streets of historic Balmain. Three of the walks incorporate ocean or harbourside beaches, so be prepared in warmer weather by packing a swimsuit, towel and hat and wearing a reliable sunscreen. Please remember when in Sydney's national parks and bushland that all the indigenous flora and fauna is protected. The best sign of appreciation is to leave the bush as you found it. The *Tips for Walkers* provide practical information about each walk, listing accessibility by bus, train or ferry and estimated distance of the walk, along with scenic rest areas, picnic spots, cafés and restaurants en route. The NSW Travel Centre *(see p218)* can supply visitors with information on the many accompanied walking tours available in Sydney.

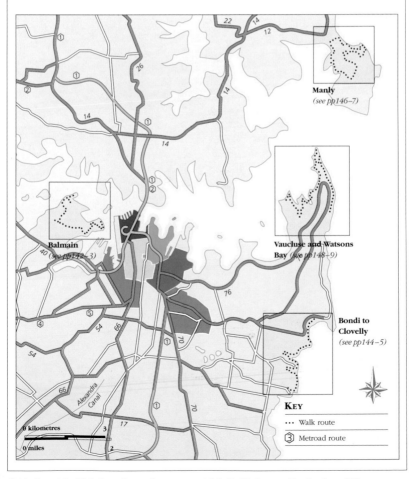

Manly
(see pp146–7)

Balmain
(see pp142–3)

Vaucluse and Watsons Bay *(see pp148–9)*

Bondi to Clovelly
(see pp144–5)

Alexandra Canal

0 kilometres   3

0 miles   2

KEY

··· Walk route

③ Metroad route

◁ A lookout rising high above the treacherous waters of the Pacific Ocean at The Gap *(see p148)*

A Two-Hour Walk Around Balmain

HISTORIC BALMAIN VILLAGE was named after William Balmain, a ship's surgeon on the First Fleet. In 1800, he was granted rights to 223 ha (550 acres) of the peninsula, which he later sold for a paltry 5 shillings in a dubious business transaction. From the mid-1800s, much of the land was subdivided for housing to support the then flourishing mining and maritime industries. Today, grand colonial and Victorian buildings stand side by side with tiny workers' cottages, adding variety to every street.

Colourful shopfront on Darling Street, Balmain

The Waterman's Cottage ③

East Balmain

Begin from the Darling Street Wharf ①. By the 1840s, when the ferry service began, shipyards dotted these foreshores. The sandstone building at No. 10 Darling Street ②, once the Dolphin Hotel then the Shipwright's Arms, was a watering hole for sailors and ferrymen. On the opposite corner is The Waterman's Cottage (1841) ③, home to Henry McKenzie, whose boat ferried residents to and from Sydney Town.

Turn left into Weston Street and walk through the Illoura Reserve for views of the city and Darling Harbour. Leave the park via William and Johnston Streets, stopping in the latter to view Onkaparinga ④, the colonial residence at No. 12. When building started in 1860, mussel shells from Aboriginal feasts stood in mounds upon the harbour foreshore beyond.

Turn left onto Darling Street then right into Duke Street. Gilchrist Place then leads down to Mort Bay Reserve ⑤. Ship's propellers stand as monuments to the area's working past. A path leads up to The Avenue's timber workers' cottages.

Back on Darling Street, turn left down Killeen Street. Take the path across Ewenton Park to Ewenton ⑥ (c.1854). Past the park, Hampton Villa ⑦ at 12B Grafton Street was home to state premier Henry Parkes.

Turn right into Ewenton Street and then left into Wallace Street, with its variety of early Australian architecture. The rough stone home at No. 1 is called the Railway Station as its narrow frontage makes it resemble one. The charming Clontarf ⑧ is at No. 4, while Maitland House ⑨ has a symmetry worth a second glance. Return to Darling Street.

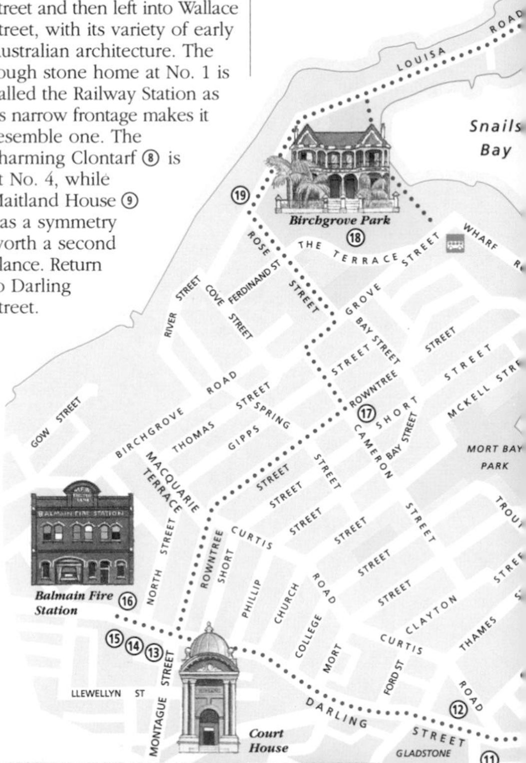

The domestic grandeur of Louisa Road

Historic Links

Sydney's oldest extant lock-up, The Watch House (1854) ⑩ at No. 179 Darling Street, has been restored, but a ghostly female form remains. Further along, enjoy a drink at The London Hotel (1870) ⑪, where the balcony stools are made of old-fashioned tractor seats.

After the roundabout, visit St Andrew's Church ⑫ before losing yourself to the bookshops, cafés and delicatessens of Balmain. Every Saturday, Balmain Market fills the churchyard *(see p203)*. At the shops' far end, the Victorian Post Office (1887) ⑬ and neighbouring Court House ⑭ reflect 1880s Sydney's prosperity. The Town Hall ⑮ dome was removed during World War II for fear of air raids. Across the street is the Fire Station ⑯ (1894). Set on the crest of a hill, its horse-drawn vehicles always travelled downhill on their outward journey.

Distant views of the city and Sydney Harbour Bridge from Snails Bay

Balmain to Birchgrove

Retrace your steps to Rowntree Street. Turn left and wander down to Birchgrove (about 10 minutes' walk). From Birchgrove shops ⑰, take Cameron Street left and Grove Street right, to Birchgrove Park ⑱ and Snails Bay. Walk down Rose Street to Louisa Road. Two of the most notable homes are Nos. 12 and 14, Keba (1878) and Vidette (1876) ⑲, where deep verandas and iron-lace balconies hint at colonial opulence. A poem in praise of the nearby park is inscribed on a plaque at Keba's entrance. Amid Vidette's formal greenery, a deep well is still fed by a natural spring.

There is a wealth of interest in the homes that follow: a tiny porch, Victorian entrance tiles, ornate iron lace – plus occasional glimpses of water frontage and private moorings. At the road's end, the reserve at Yurulbin Point ⑳ marks the mouth of Parramatta River. A fishing nook on its eastern corner is a perfect vantage point for taking in the city skyline and passing harbour traffic.

Shops nestled in the quiet Birchgrove village ⑰

Balmain War Memorial

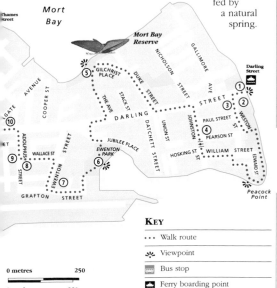

KEY

- ••• Walk route
- ☀ Viewpoint
- 🚌 Bus stop
- ⚓ Ferry boarding point

0 metres 250

0 yards 250

TIPS FOR WALKERS

Starting point: Darling Street Wharf.

Length: 5.5 km (3½ miles).

Getting there: Ferries regularly leave Circular Quay for Darling Street Wharf. The 442 bus from the Queen Victoria Building stops in Darling Street. To return, there is a 15-minute ferry ride at hourly intervals from Birchgrove (pick up a schedule at Circular Quay). Alternatively, take Bus 441 from Grove Street (Snails Bay) back to the city (weekdays only).

Stopping-off points: Darling Street, in particular, has many good delicatessens, pâtisseries, restaurants and cafés. Places to picnic include Mort Bay Reserve, Gladstone Park, Birchgrove Park and Yurulbin Point.

A Two-Hour Walk from Bondi Beach to Clovelly

THIS INVIGORATING OCEANSIDE and clifftop walk explores the beautiful shoreline and surfing beaches of eastern Sydney. The local colour along this scenic trail is at its most vibrant at weekends, when people flock to the cafés and beaches. The Victorian cemetery at the walk's end bears witness to Sydney's multicultural heritage.

Pool at North Bondi Beach

A Seaside Community

Walk north along Campbell Parade ①, passing a colourful array of hotels, beachwear shops and lively cafés that give the street a raffish atmosphere. The stylish Gelato Bar at No. 140 makes an indulgent pit-stop. Keep walking until the Hotel Bondi ②, the parade's most significant building and easily spotted by its pretty clock tower. Opened as a first-class hotel in 1920, it initially stood quite alone by what was then a bush-fringed beach. Turn right, crossing the road in front of the hotel, and walk down to Queen Elizabeth Drive leaving the traffic and noise of Campbell Parade behind as you reach Sydney's most famous beach, Bondi.

Statue of lifesaver near Bondi Pavilion

Bondi's popularity dates back to the 1880s. Although daylight bathing was banned at the time, the beach was considered a fashionable place to stroll. Bondi trams came into use shortly after and, by the time bathing restrictions were lifted in 1902, the red and white trams were filled with beach-goers. Just ahead you will see Bondi Pavilion ③. Built in 1928 to replace a modest timber building, it was designed on a grand scale and originally housed a ballroom, gymnasium, restaurant, café, Turkish baths and open-air theatre. Although decidedly less glamorous today, the complex is still a thriving local community centre hosting cultural events. Photographs inside recall the romance of Bondi Beach in earlier times.

Next to the Pavilion is the home of arguably Australia's oldest surf life saving club, the Bondi Surf Bathers ④ *(see p137)*. Follow the sweep of the beach to its southern end.

Climb a flight of steps to continue on Notts Avenue, above Bondi Baths ⑤ and alongside the Bondi Icebergs clubhouse. Prospective members must swim every Sunday, regardless of weather, 50 weeks of the year for four years to join.

Tips for Walkers

Starting point: *Campbell Parade, southern end.*
Length: *4 km (2½ miles).*
Getting there: *Take the train to Bondi Junction, then Bus 380 to Bondi Beach. Bus 339 runs from Clovelly Beach to Circular Quay. Waverley Cemetery is open from 8am to dusk every day.*
Stopping-off points: *Public toilets, showers and food and refreshments are available at Bondi, Tamarama and Bronte Beaches. Take-away cuisine can be bought along Bondi's Campbell Parade as the walk begins. Tamarama's beach café serves refreshing drinks. In warm weather, make the most of four of Sydney's best beaches by packing your swimming gear.*

Tamarama Surf Life Saving Club, at the beach's northern end

Bronte's swimming baths

Bondi to Bronte

Veer left off Notts Avenue as the path drops down and skirts sharp rock formations, the result of years of erosion. Take the steep steps to Mackenzies Point lookout ⑥ on the headland. The magnificent view stretches for 180 degrees from Ben Buckler in the north to Malabar in the distant south.

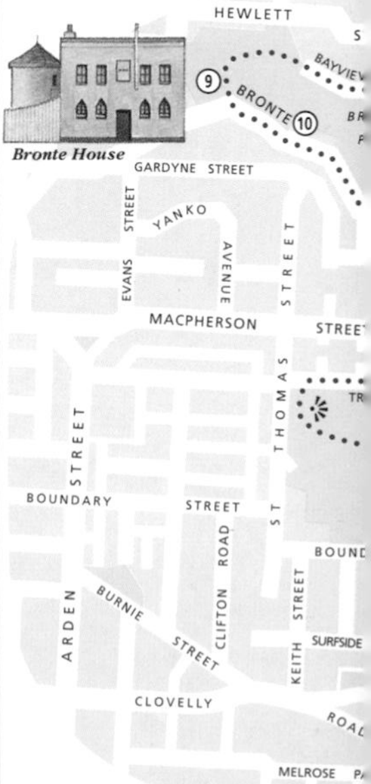

Key

- ••• Walk route
- Viewpoint
- Bus stop
- [P] Parking

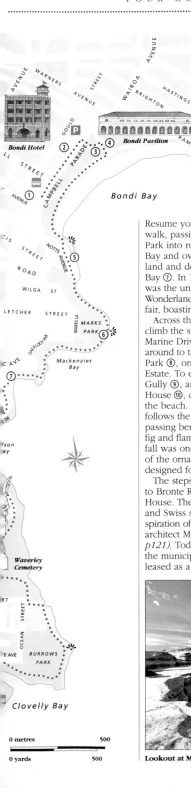

Bondi Hotel

Bondi Pavilion

Bondi Bay

Mackenzies Bay

Waverley Cemetery

Clovelly Bay

0 metres   500

0 yards   500

Resume your walk, passing through Marks Park into rocky Mackenzies Bay and over the next headland and down to Tamarama Bay ⑦. In 1906–11, this beach was the unlikely home of Wonderland City – a rowdy fun fair, boasting a roller coaster.

Across the beach and park, climb the steps to Tamarama Marine Drive. Follow the road around to the slopes of Bronte Park ⑧, once part of Bronte Estate. To explore Bronte Gully ⑨, and glimpse Bronte House ⑩, continue away from the beach. Take the track that follows the creek into a valley, passing beneath a canopy of fig and flame trees. The waterfall was once a natural feature of the ornamental gardens designed for Bronte Estate.

The steps on your left lead to Bronte Road and Bronte House. The mixture of Gothic and Swiss styling was the inspiration of the original owner, architect Mortimer Lewis *(see p121)*. Today it is owned by the municipal council and is leased as a private residence.

Bronte to Waverley

Continue down Bronte Road towards the southern end of Bronte Beach. After passing Bronte's cafés, walk through the car park and follow the road uphill, through a cutaway originally dug for trams. As the road winds through the cutting and veers right, take the steps through Calga Reserve. Walk down Trafalgar Street to the Waverley Cemetery ⑪.

In grand displays of Edwardian and Victorian monumental masonry, English, Italian and Irish residents have been laid to rest. Among notable Australians buried here are writers Henry Lawson and Dorothea Mackellar; Fanny Durack, the

Irish Memorial, Waverley Cemetery

first woman to win an Olympic gold medal (in 1912), and do the Australian crawl swimming stroke; and aeronautical pioneer Lawrence Hargrave.

The Irish Memorial honours the 1798 Irish Rebellion and its leader Michael Dwyer, who was transported to Australia for his part in the uprising.

Leave the cemetery at the southern end and walk through Burrows Park. Hug the coast around to Eastbourne Avenue, which leads down to Clovelly Beach ⑫ and the walk's end.

Lookout at Mackenzies Point, a popular spot for watching surfers ⑥

A Three-Hour Walk Around Manly

THIS WALK TAKES IN THE holiday atmosphere of downtown Manly and its splendid surf beach, before passing along quieter shorelines and clifftop streets, and through unspoilt bushland replete with native flora and fauna. It features marvellous views, the commanding architecture of Manly's most significant building, St Patrick's Seminary, and the charm of Collins Beach and Fairy Bower.

Houses rising above Fairy Bower

Brass band plays in The Corso

From Harbour to Ocean

Start at Manly Wharf ①. This suburb was little more than a cosy fishing village until 1852, when entrepreneur Henry Gilbert Smith's vision of a resort similar to fashionable Brighton in his native England started to take shape. The ferry service began in 1855, operating from the same spot in use today.

Leaving Manly Cove, cross The Esplanade and walk down The Corso, a pedestrian mall. At the end of The Corso, to the left, stands the New Brighton Hotel ② in striking Egyptian Classical Revival Style. In 1926, it replaced the original New Brighton, built in 1880 as the resort's first att. ıction.

Head towards the rolling surf and sweeping sands of Manly Beach ③ then continue south along the promenade. From the 1950s-style Surf Pavilion, follow Marine Parade walkway around to Cabbage Tree Bay. The pretty area around the rock pool was named Fairy Bower ④ for the delicate wildflowers and maidenhair ferns that once grew on the hillside. Beyond the rock pool, continue on the pathway around to Shelly Beach ⑤, a secluded scuba diving and snorkelling spot, which is also ideal for child swimmers. The 1920s beach kiosk has now been stylishly restored and converted into the smart Le Kiosk restaurant.

Detail on the New Brighton Hotel

Shelly Beach to St Patrick's Seminary

Across the park, take the steps to your left to Shelly Beach Headland. A path further left loops around the headland. Viewing platforms ⑥ overlook the vast South Pacific Ocean.

Take the carpark exit into Bower Street. Follow the road as it rounds high above Fairy Bower, passing by homes of diverse architectural styles, from Spanish Mission to Neo-Georgian. Turn left into College Street, then right into Reddall Street, and left again

> **TIPS FOR WALKERS**
>
> ***Starting point:*** *Manly Wharf*
> ***Length:*** *7.5 km (4½ miles).*
> ***Getting there:*** *Regular ferry and JetCat services depart from Wharf 2 at Circular Quay.*
> ***Stopping-off points:*** *The wide range of fresh food counters at Manly Pier make it an ideal place to stock up on picnic fare. Restaurants and cafés line The Corso and Manly Beach Promenade. A kiosk at Shelly Beach offers the choice of a smart restaurant, barbecue or snack bar. In warm weather, come prepared with a swimsuit, hat, towel and sunscreen.*

The clear waters of sheltered Shelly Beach ⑤

into Addison Road. Opposite the Victorian buildings at Nos. 97–99 and 95, a lane into Fairy Bower Road leads to views of the old St Patrick's Seminary ⑦. Both Romanesque and Neo-Gothic architecture are in evidence in this 1885 Catholic seminary, built only after much deliberation by the essentially Protestant government.

Leave Fairy Bower Road by Vivian Street to turn left into Darley Road and arrive at the seminary. On the opposite side of the road, the Archbishop's House is partially hidden by Norfolk Island pines. Known as the Cardinal's Palace for its lavish interiors, it is, sadly, not open to the public.

The grand Victorian architecture of St Patrick's Seminary ⑦

North Head Reserve

At the top of Darley Road, turn right beneath the Parkhill Sandstone Arch ⑧ into North Head

Reserve. Follow the right-hand fork onto Collins Beach Road down through bushland alive with bird calls. Paperbarks, Sydney red gums and banksias are just some of the native flora growing in abundance.

At the road's end, follow the track to your right across two footbridges, then down steps to Collins Beach ⑨. A stone cairn between the second foot-bridge and the beach marks where Governor Arthur Phillip was speared by the Aboriginal Wil-ee-ma-rin after a misunderstanding. The quiet waterfall and dense bushland make it possible to imagine this beach in pre-colonial days.

Leave this peace and quiet via a rough hillside track onto a concrete pathway, then out into Stuart Street. Beyond the street, Little Manly Point gently nudges out into the harbour.

Back to the Present

For memorable harbour views, follow the direction of Stuart Street through Little Manly Point Reserve, passing by the baths of Little Manly Cove ⑩. If you are reluctant to end this charming walk, turn left and proceed to the end of Addison Road. Manly Point Peace Park offers a quiet place to take in a panorama of the distant city.

Return down Addison Road, making your way back to the wharf via Stuart Street and the East Esplanade. With its boat sheds and bleached timber yacht clubs, the East Esplanade Park has a nautical amosphere and is a relaxing place to meander. Continue past the attractions of the amusement pier to Manly Wharf, which was your starting point.

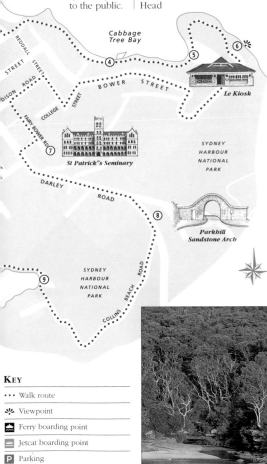

KEY

•••	Walk route
☀	Viewpoint
⛴	Ferry boarding point
⛴	Jetcat boarding point
P	Parking

0 metres   250

0 yards   250

Collins Beach ⑨ on the edge of Sydney Harbour National Park

A Three-Hour Walk in Watsons Bay and Vaucluse

TRACING THE PERIMETERS of spectacular South Head, this walk touches on the area's colonial connections and takes in a variety of ocean and harbourside terrain, from headlands with sweeping views and crashing waves, to secluded coves, white sandy beaches and the streets of one of Sydney's most desirable neighbourhoods.

Signal Station ② at Dunbar Head

Macquarie Lighthouse to Camp Cove

The start of this walk is majestic Macquarie Lighthouse (1883) ①. A copy of the country's first lighthouse built in 1818 *(see p137)*, it stands on the same site.

Take the walk northwards, passing by the Signal Station ② following Old South Head Road. Before the station was built in 1848, a flag was hoisted to warn the colony of ships entering the harbour.

Continue along the footpath, where a plaque marks the location of Australia's worst maritime disaster. It was here that the migrant ship *Dunbar* crashed onto the rocks in a gale in 1857 *(see pp136–7)*. The only survivor was hauled to safety up the treacherous cleft in the cliff face known as Jacob's Ladder ③. From here, follow the descending path, arriving at the turbulent seas and jutting stony ledges of The Gap ④. The *Dunbar*'s anchor is here set into concrete, while salvaged personal effects are displayed at the National Maritime Museum *(see pp94–5)*.

Taking the steps down from The Gap, bear right into the entrance of Sydney Harbour National Park. This single-lane roadway leads through natural bushland into HMAS *Watson* Military Reserve. Follow the road up to visit the Naval Memorial Chapel ⑤. A large clear window inside the chapel offers spectacular views of North Head and the Pacific Ocean. Resume your walk by taking the road out of the reserve, and then turn right into Cliff Street. Passing a row of weatherboard cottages on your left, follow the street to its end and onto Camp Cove Beach ⑥. It was here in 1788 that Captain Arthur Phillip first stepped ashore after leaving Botany Bay to explore the coastline.

Bust, Macquarie Lighthouse ①

Camp Cove to Watsons Bay

Take the wooden steps at the northern end of the cove to make the 40-minute return walk to South

Nudist Lady Bay Beach

Doyle's well-known restaurant at Watsons Bay ⑧

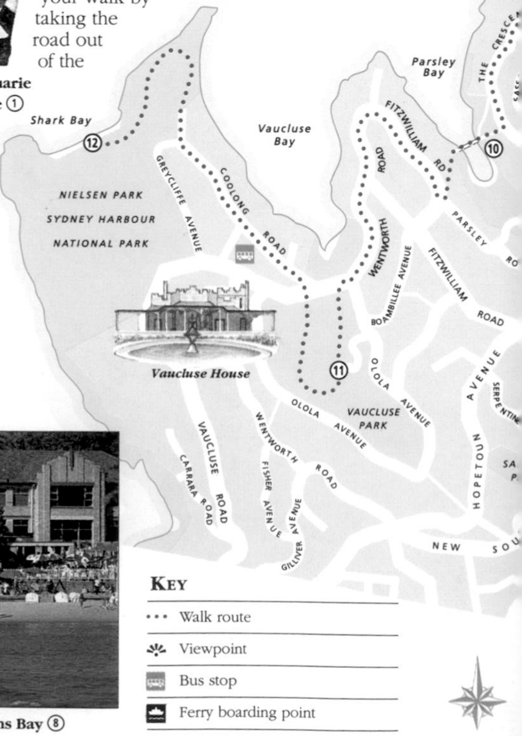

Camp Cove
Shark Bay
Parsley Bay
Vaucluse Bay
NIELSEN PARK
SYDNEY HARBOUR
NATIONAL PARK
GREYCLIFFE AVENUE
COOLONG ROAD
FITZWILLIAM RD
WENTWORTH ROAD
BOAMBILLEE AVENUE
PARSLEY
FITZWILLIAM ROAD
Vaucluse House
OLOLA AVENUE
VAUCLUSE PARK
VAUCLUSE ROAD
CARRARA ROAD
WENTWORTH ROAD
FISHER AVENUE
GILLIVER AVENUE
HOPETOUN AVENUE
NEW
KEY
Walk route
Viewpoint
Bus stop
Ferry boarding point

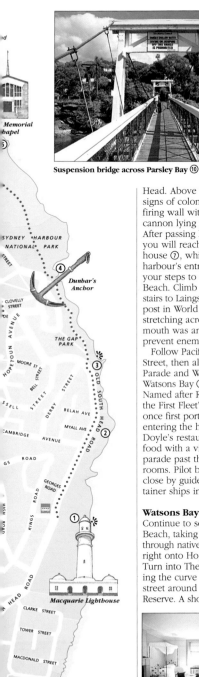

Suspension bridge across Parsley Bay ⑩

Head. Above the steps are signs of colonial defences: a firing wall with rifle slots; a cannon lying further along. After passing Lady Bay Beach, you will reach Hornby Lighthouse ⑦, which marks the harbour's entrance. Retrace your steps to Camp Cove Beach. Climb the western-end stairs to Laings Point, a defence post in World War II. A net stretching across the harbour mouth was anchored here to prevent enemy ships entering.

Follow Pacific Street to Cove Street, then along to Marine Parade and Wharf Beach in Watsons Bay ⑧ (see pp136–7). Named after Robert Watson of the First Fleet's *Sirius*, this was once first port of call for ships entering the harbour. Nearby, Doyle's restaurant offers seafood with a view. Follow the parade past the baths and tea rooms. Pilot boats ⑨ moored close by guide cruise and container ships into the harbour.

Watsons Bay to Vaucluse
Continue to secluded Gibsons Beach, taking the footpath left through native shrubbery, then right onto Hopetoun Avenue. Turn into The Crescent, tracing the curve of this exclusive street around to Parsley Bay Reserve. A short descent opens

onto a suspension bridge hung across the waters of tranquil Parsley Bay ⑩. Crossing the bridge, follow the pathway between two houses to arrive on Fitzwilliam Road. Continue right along Fitzwilliam Road, turning left into Wentworth Road to reach the extravagant Vaucluse House ⑪, surrounded by exotic gardens (see p136).

To finish your walk, make your way along Coolong Road to Nielsen Park (see p136) and Shark Bay ⑫. Protected from its namesake by a netted enclosure, the natural setting and safe waters of this beach make it a favourite for picnics.

Dramatic rock cleft known as Jacob's Ladder ③ near The Gap

TIPS FOR WALKERS

Starting point: Macquarie Lighthouse.
Length: 8 km (5 miles).
Getting there: Take Bus 324 from Circular Quay, or Bus 387 from Bondi Junction. Return by Bus 325 from Nielsen Park.
Stopping-off points: There are public toilets and showers at Camp Cove, Watsons Bay, Parsley Bay and Nielsen Park. Food and refreshments are available throughout the walk at Watsons Bay, Parsley Bay, Vaucluse and Nielsen Park. The tea rooms at Vaucluse House offer views of the gardens, and the café at Nielsen Park sells homemade fare in generous portions. The walk covers several harbour beaches where you can swim safely. In warm weather, bring a swimsuit, towel, hat and sunscreen, and allow time for swimming, sunbathing and picnicking.

Children's bedroom, one of the exhibits at Vaucluse House ⑪

BEYOND SYDNEY

Exploring Beyond Sydney

To the east, Sydney is bounded by the Pacific Ocean; to the west, by the Great Dividing Range. To the north and south, within easy distance of the city, are superb beaches and stretches of coastal scenery, while inland, you will encounter waterfalls, deep valleys and fascinating flora and wildlife. On the Hawkesbury River, to the north and west of the city, are settlements of historical as well as scenic interest while, further north, the Hunter River meanders through sloping vineyards. The excursions on pages 154–65 offer the visitor the chance to sample the rich variety of Sydney landscapes from the exhilarating to the tranquil.

Heritage Farm on the Hawkesbury River

Façade of Rothbury Estate in the Hunter Valley

SIGHTS AT A GLANCE

Blue Mountains ❹
Hawkesbury Tour ❷
Hunter Valley ❸
Pittwater and Ku-ring-gai Chase
  National Park ❶
Royal National Park ❻
Southern Highlands Tour ❺

GETTING AROUND

All the areas covered in these excursions can be easily reached by road from Sydney. Freeways and motorways take travellers part of the way to the Southern Highlands, Blue Mountains and Hunter Valley, while the other areas are accessible on sealed, well-signposted major roads. A number of tour operators offer guided one-day, or longer, tours to the Blue Mountains, Hunter Valley, Southern Highlands and South Coast, and parts of the Hawkesbury region. CityRail has regular train services to the Blue Mountains, Royal National Park and to parts of the area covered by the Southern Highlands Tour. Ferries offer access to some parts of the Hawkesbury River.

0 kilometres   50

0 miles   25

Grand old house in Kiama, near the Southern Highlands

Mudgee

Cap ... Ri

D... River

Orange,
Dubbo

BATHURST

Fish River

32

LITHGOW

90

BLUE
MOUNTAINS

KANANGRA-B...
NATIONAL P.

Wollondilly River

MOSS V...

Canberra

Wingecarribee River

Shoalhaven River

MORT...
NATIONAL...

Be...

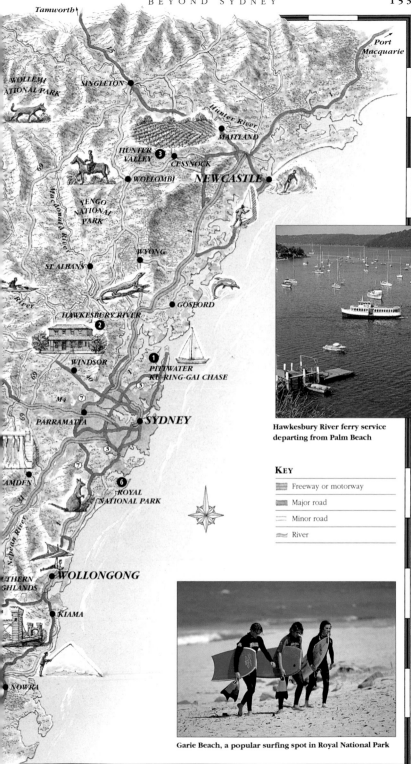

Tamworth

Port Macquarie

WOLLEMI NATIONAL PARK

SINGLETON

Hunter River

MAITLAND

HUNTER VALLEY ❸ CESSNOCK

WOLLOMBI

NEWCASTLE

YENGO NATIONAL PARK

WYONG

ST ALBANS

GOSFORD

HAWKESBURY RIVER ❷

WINDSOR

PITTWATER KU-RING-GAI CHASE ❶

M4

PARRAMATTA ● SYDNEY

CAMDEN

❻ ROYAL NATIONAL PARK

WOLLONGONG

KIAMA

SOUTHERN HIGHLANDS

NOWRA

Macdonald River

Nepean River

Hawkesbury River ferry service departing from Palm Beach

KEY

▬	Freeway or motorway
▬	Major road
▬	Minor road
▬	River

Garie Beach, a popular surfing spot in Royal National Park

Pittwater and Ku-ring-gai Chase ❶

Barrenjoey Lighthouse

PITTWATER AND THE ADJACENT Ku-ring-gai Chase National Park lie on Sydney's northernmost outskirts. They are bounded to the north by Broken Bay, at the mouth of the Hawkesbury River *(see pp156–7)*. Sparkling waterways and golden beaches are set against the unspoiled backdrop of the national park. Picnicking, bushwalking, surfing, boating, sailing and windsurfing are popular pastimes with visitors. The Hawkesbury River system curls around an ancient sandstone landscape rich in Aboriginal rock art, and flora and fauna.

Coal and Candle Creek
The pretty inlet is typical of eroded valleys formed during the last Ice Age. Water melted from the ice caps flooded the valleys to form the bays and creeks of Broken Bay.

Akuna Bay
The isolated marina, general store and café serve the Hawkesbury River boating fraternity.

Map labels: BRISBANE NATIONAL; Patonga; Hawkesbury; Juno Point; Gunyah Beach; Hungry Beach; River; Challenger Head; Refuge Bay; Cowan Creek; Cowan Point; KU-RING-GAI CHASE NATIONAL PARK; West Head Road; Coal and Candle Creek; Cottage Point; Smiths Creek; Akuna Bay; General San Martin Drive; McCarrs Creek Road; RYDE, CHATSWOOD

ABORIGINAL ART IN KU-RING-GAI CHASE

Ku-ring-gai Chase has literally hundreds of Aboriginal rock art sites, providing an insight into one of the world's oldest cultures. The most common are rock engravings, generally made in groups with as many as 100 individual figures. They include whales up to 8 m (26 ft) long, fish, sharks, wallabies, echidnas and Ancestral Spirits such as Daramulan, who created the land, its people and animals.

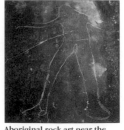

Aboriginal rock art near the Basin, Ku-ring-gai Chase

KEY

▬	Major road
═	Secondary road
═	Minor road
▢	National Park
- -	Ferry route
- -	Walk route
⚓	Boat hire
✍	Aboriginal rock art
☀	Viewpoint

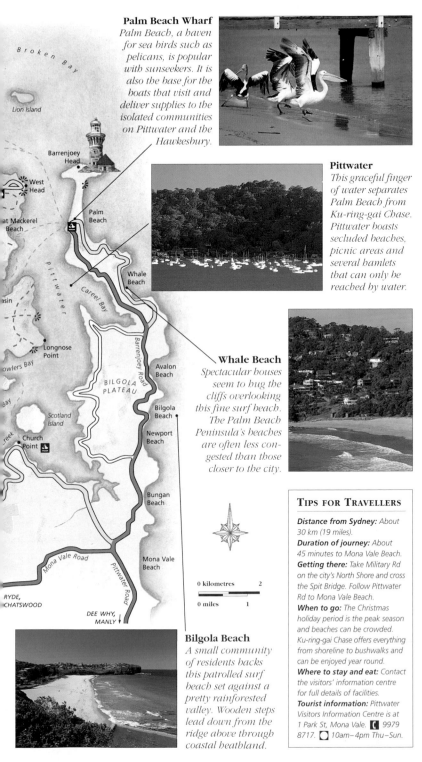

Palm Beach Wharf
Palm Beach, a haven for sea birds such as pelicans, is popular with sunseekers. It is also the base for the boats that visit and deliver supplies to the isolated communities on Pittwater and the Hawkesbury.

Pittwater
This graceful finger of water separates Palm Beach from Ku-ring-gai Chase. Pittwater boasts secluded beaches, picnic areas and several hamlets that can only be reached by water.

Whale Beach
Spectacular houses seem to hug the cliffs overlooking this fine surf beach. The Palm Beach Peninsula's beaches are often less congested than those closer to the city.

Bilgola Beach
A small community of residents backs this patrolled surf beach set against a pretty rainforested valley. Wooden steps lead down from the ridge above through coastal heathland.

0 kilometres 2

0 miles 1

TIPS FOR TRAVELLERS

Distance from Sydney: About 30 km (19 miles).
Duration of journey: About 45 minutes to Mona Vale Beach.
Getting there: Take Military Rd on the city's North Shore and cross the Spit Bridge. Follow Pittwater Rd to Mona Vale Beach.
When to go: The Christmas holiday period is the peak season and beaches can be crowded. Ku-ring-gai Chase offers everything from shoreline to bushwalks and can be enjoyed year round.
Where to stay and eat: Contact the visitors' information centre for full details of facilities.
Tourist information: Pittwater Visitors Information Centre is at 1 Park St, Mona Vale. 9979 8717. 10am–4pm Thu–Sun.

Hawkesbury Tour ❷

AUSTRALIA'S LONGEST eastward-flowing river, the Hawkesbury–Nepean, forms Sydney's northern and western boundaries. It was at first thought to be two separate rivers until further exploration revealed that they were in fact one. The section known as the Hawkesbury runs from the Colo River Valley to Broken Bay in the north *(see pp154–5)*.

Settled in 1794, by 1799 the Hawkesbury Valley's small farms produced three-quarters of the colony's grain. Its riverscape is little changed since then and much of the area remains a quiet backwater. It is an area rich in relics of the early colonial period, including towns and villages established during the Macquarie era of 1810–19 *(see p22)*. It is also a place of great scenic grandeur, with magnificent vistas of one of Australia's most beautiful rivers.

Tizzana Winery ⑤
A touch of Tuscany on the banks of the Hawkesbury, this sandstone winery was built in 1887 by Dr Thomas Fiaschi. It is open to visitors on Saturdays and public holidays.

Ebenezer Uniting Church ④
Built in 1809, the church and its 1817 schoolhouse have been superbly restored. The tree under which services were first held still stands.

Portland Reach ⑥
On the river, pleasure craft have replaced the grain barges of the past, but the area's farming community survives.

Colo River Drive ③
This pretty route travels along the Putty Road to Colo, then follows the river to Lower Portland.

Hawkesbury Heritage Farm ②
This collection of original pioneer buildings re-creates an early colonial village. At the centre is Rose Cottage (1811), built of iron-bark slabs with she-oak shingle roofing.

Sackville Ferry ⑦
It only takes a few minutes to cross the river by cable ferry.

Windsor ①
Built in 1815, the Macquarie Arms Hotel is just one of Windsor's fine early colonial buildings. Many others, including several by architect Francis Greenway *(see p114)*, remain from the town laid out in 1810.

Settlers Arms Inn ⑩
Once an overnight stop for stage coaches to the Hunter Valley *(see pp158–9)*, this atmospheric 1836 hotel is in the largely unchanged village of St Albans.

Webbs Creek Ferry ⑨
Opened in 1908, this cable ferry gives access to the western bank of the Hawkesbury for the drive beside the Macdonald River.

Old General Cemetery ⑪
A stark reminder of the hardships and tragedies of early settlement, this is the resting place of six First Fleeters *(see p20)*.

Portland Ferry ⑧
If taking the Colo River Drive, cross the river here by ferry for the River Road to Wisemans Ferry.

GOSFORD

Old Great North Road ⑫
The convict-built road with its massive buttresses was completed in 1828. Part of it still remains.

■ *Maroota*

● *Cornelia*

HORNSBY

Wisemans Ferry ⑬
This small village on a bend in the Hawkesbury River is where ex-convict Solomon Wiseman started his ferry service, Australia's oldest, in 1827.

TIPS FOR DRIVERS

Distance from Sydney: *55 km (35 miles) to Windsor.*
Duration of tour: *About 3½ hours, excluding stops.*
Getting there and back: *Follow M4 to James Ruse Drive (53) just before Parramatta, then Windsor Rd (40). To return from Wisemans Ferry, take the Old Northern Rd (36) to Middle Dural, then Galston Rd to Hornsby. From here, follow Pacific Hwy south.*
When to go: *Peak season is from December to February. The river, national parks and small towns can be enjoyed year round.*
Where to stay and eat: *Cafés, restaurants and accommodation can be found at Windsor and Wisemans Ferry. The Settlers Arms Inn at St Albans has a few rooms, and a bar and restaurant.*
Tourist information: *There is a visitors' centre at Hawkesbury Museum, Thompson Square, Windsor.* 📞 *4577 2310.*

KEY

▬▬▬	Tour route
▬ ▬ ▬	Scenic route
░░░	Other road
⛴	Cable ferry
🛈	Tourist information
☀	Viewpoint

0 kilometres   5

0 miles   3

Hunter Valley ❸

Cheese made by local producer

Some of the earliest vineyards to be planted in Australia were on the fertile flats of the Hunter River in the 1830s, when a thriving industry in fortified wine grew up in the area. Since the 1970s, one of the country's premium table wine districts has evolved *(see pp182–3)*. With more than 50 wineries and 30 restaurants, the Hunter Valley is a popular weekend trip for Sydney-siders. Hot air ballooning, golf courses, horse riding and cycling supplement vineyard visits. Most large wineries open daily for sales and tastings. Smaller establishments open at weekends or by appointment.

Lindemans
In 1842, Dr Henry John Lindeman resigned his naval commission to establish a vineyard in the Hunter. His company has been a major producer in the Australian wine industry ever since.

Golden Grape Estate
A popular coach stop, the winery has a vine gallery showing grape varieties found around the world. There is also a museum which features early wine-making equipment.

Map labels: SINGLETON, UPPER HUNTER · Sweetwater Creek · Old North Road · TERRACE RANGE · Hermitage Road · Rothbury Creek · Hunter Estate · Marsh Estate · Deaseys Road · ROSEMOUNT ESTATE, UPPER HUNTER · Mary Annes Creek · Broke Road · Tyrrell's Wines · Brokenwood · Tamb... · Pokolbin · Tu... · Debeyers · P... · Oakey · McWilliam's · Marro... · BROKEN BACK RANGE · Petersons

---

Personalities of the Hunter Valley

The wine industry seems to attract or create characters that are larger than life. Among the current generation of living legends is Len Evans, writer, wine judge, *bon vivant* and founder of the ambitious Rothbury Estate and Evans Family Wines. His contemporaries include Max Lake, a Sydney surgeon who started Lake's Folly as a weekend winery, and Murray Tyrrell, patriarch of a wine-making family that produced its first Hunter vintage in 1864 and proudly retains its independence.

Len Evans checking grape vines

Wyndham Estate

Established in the 1830s, this pioneering vineyard on the Wyndham family's property has a Georgian sandstone homestead that has been restored to its original condition.

Rothbury Estate

The grand inspiration of Len Evans, this winery is dedicated to wine excellence and education. Dinners and concerts held in the winery's cask hall are popular events.

Lake's Folly

Australian growers stopped planting Cabernet Sauvignon vines in the 19th century. But in the 1960s, Max Lake reintroduced the variety and his success has been repeated across Australia.

Convent at Pepper Tree

A restored 1909 convent is now an elegantly appointed guesthouse, with the Pepper Tree vineyard and winery and Robert's Restaurant only a short walk away.

Map labels:
BRANXTON, WYNDHAM ESTATE
Black Creek
Branxton Road
Rothbury
Palmers Lane
Calais Estates
Creek
GRETA
O'Connors Road
Oakey Creek
Allandale Road
Mount View Road
KURRI KURRI
CESSNOCK
SYDNEY
Bellbird Creek
Wollombi Road
WOLLOMBI, SYDNEY

KEY

═══ Main road

═══ Unsealed road

🏯 Winery

ℹ Tourist information

☼ Viewpoint

0 kilometres 2
0 miles 1

TIPS FOR TRAVELLERS

Distance from Sydney: *130 km (81 miles).*
Duration of journey: *About 2 hours from the centre of Sydney.*
Getting there and back: *Take the Sydney–Newcastle freeway north of Sydney and follow the signs to Cessnock. An alternative route is through the picturesque Wollombi Valley. Allow about 3 hours as this is a scenic route with some unsealed surfaces.*
When to go: *Year round. Vintage is Jan–Mar.*
Where to stay and eat: *There is a wide variety of motels, guesthouses, self-catering cottages and cabins, cafés and restaurants.*
Tourist information: *Visitor Information Centre, Turner Park, Aberdare Rd, Cessnock.*
📞 *4990 4477.*
Further afield: *The Upper Hunter vineyards are about 40 minutes by car northwest of Pokolbin.*

Blue Mountains ❹

For a quarter of a century after European settlement, the Blue Mountains prevented the colony's westward expansion. In 1813, an expedition led by the explorers Gregory Blaxland, William Lawson and William Charles Wentworth found a way across. The magnificent scenery, characterized by rugged cliffs and rock formations, ravines and waterfalls, is best appreciated on the bushwalks that wind along cliff tops and through valleys. The restaurants, cafés and antique shops will tempt the less energetic. The mountains are named for the perennial blue haze, caused by light striking eucalyptus oil particles in the air.

Zig Zag Railway
A steam train travels through cuttings and tunnels, and over three impressive viaducts built from 1866–9.

Grose Valley from Govetts Leap
Considered by many to be the most imposing view in the Blue Mountains, a great panorama with a series of ridges stretches into the far distance.

The Grose River flows between the two roads crossing the mountains.

ZIG ZAG RAILWAY

Victoria Falls

Mount York

JENOLAN CAVES

Three Sisters
This giant rock formation near Echo Point takes its name from an Aboriginal legend. The tale tells of three sisters turned to stone by their witch-doctor father to keep them safe from an evil bunyip or monster.

Jenolan Caves

About 55 km (34 miles) south-west of Mount Victoria is a magical series of spectacular underground limestone caves with icy blue rivers and fleecy limestone formations. They are surrounded by an extensive wildlife reserve. People have been making the trek here since the caves were discovered in 1838, staying originally in the Grand Arch cave and later in the Edwardian splendour of Jenolan Caves House, which still operates today.

The vividly coloured Pool of Cerberus at Jenolan Caves

Key

——	Major road
	Other road
•••	Suggested walk
🚶	Starting points for other walks
⛺	Campsite
🍽	Picnic area
ℹ	Tourist information
🔆	Viewpoint

Mount Wilson
A picturesque village with cultivated gardens and exotic trees, it has been called a "little corner of the northern hemisphere". Some gardens are open to the public in spring and autumn.

The Cathedral of Ferns is a remnant of the temperate rainforest that once covered this area.

Mount Tomah Botanic Gardens
This superbly landscaped garden, specializing in cool-climate plants, has sweeping views over the Grose Valley.

RICHMOND

Mount Banks

Yester Grange
The beautifully restored Victorian country house at Wentworth Falls has tea rooms and a restaurant, as well as a collection of antiques and crafts.

Kings Tableland

Jamison Valley

Leura village is classified by the National Trust. Nearby are Leura Cascades, floodlit at night and one of the prettiest sights in the mountains.

Wentworth Falls
An impressive double waterfall is the starting point for the National Pass track, a challenging four-hour return walk to the next valley.

0 kilometres   5

0 miles   3

TIPS FOR TRAVELLERS

Distance from Sydney: *About 105 km (65 miles).*
Duration of journey: *About 90 minutes to Wentworth Falls.*
Getting there and back: *Follow Metroad route 4 and the Great Western Highway to Wentworth Falls. Return by Bells Line of Road to Windsor. State Rail has regular services to the area. An Explorer Bus runs from Katoomba railway station at 9:30am on weekends and public holidays.*
When to go: *Year round. Always be prepared for the cold, especially when hiking, as the weather can change rapidly in all seasons.*
Where to stay and eat: *Contact the visitor information centre.*
Tourist information: *Blue Mountains Visitors' Information Centre, Echo Point, Katoomba.*
[1300 653 408.

Southern Highlands Tour [5]

Common wombat

THIS EASILY ACCESSIBLE area to the south of Sydney is often said to be more typical of Great Britain, particularly Scotland, than Australia. It is actually a delightful combination of both: Australian high country and coastal hinterland with many European qualities. It is a land of abrupt hills and valleys, waterfalls and fast-running streams; of quaint villages, cosy restaurants and cafés, antique shops and elegant places to stay. The tour takes in spectacular Seven Mile Beach and the pretty town of Berry before heading to Kangaroo Valley, sleepy Bundanoon and the antique shops of Berrima and Bowral. An exhilarating adjunct to the tour is nearby Minnamurra Falls with its boardwalk through rainforest.

Bowral ⑧
This highlands town holds a famous spring tulip festival every year and is home to cricket's Bradman Museum.

Berrima ⑦
By-passed by the railway in the 19th century, the only Georgian village in the highlands remains one of the most picturesque.

WOMBEYAN CAVES
31
Moss Vale
48
Sutton Forest
79
31
GOULBURN
Bundanoon Creek
Kangaroo
Tallowa Dam
MORTON NATIONAL PARK
Shoal

Bundanoon ⑥
Romantic guesthouses and a glow worm cave make this town a popular weekend destination.

Fitzroy Falls ⑤
Part of Morton National Park, the falls plunge 80 m (262 ft) into the subtropical rainforest below. The falls lookout has access for the disabled and walking trails with stunning views.

0 kilometres 10

0 miles 5

KEY

- Tour route
- Scenic route (alternative)
- Other roads
- Tourist information
- Viewpoint

Kangaroo Valley ④
Hampden Bridge, a castellated suspension bridge, crosses the Kangaroo River at this small village. The river is an idyllic place for canoeing.

BERRIMA GAOL

Completed in 1839 by convict labour, this Georgian sandstone jail is featured in Rolf Boldrewood's classic 1888 bushranging novel, *Robbery Under Arms*. The fictitious character Captain Starlight, who escapes from Berrima, describes it as "the largest, most severe, the most dreaded of all prisons in New South Wales".

Kiama ①
The historic town began life in the 1820s as a port for shipping cedar. Its blowhole can spurt water as high as 60 m (200 ft).

Seven Mile Beach ②
Part of a national park and best seen from Gerroa's Black Head, the beach is flanked by dunes and hardy coastal vegetation, including forest and swamp. It is a great fishing, swimming and picnicking spot.

TIPS FOR DRIVERS

Distance from Sydney: 120 km (75 miles).
Duration of tour: About 3½ hours, excluding stops.
Getting there and back: Take Metroad route 1, then follow the F3 freeway and Princes Hwy (1) to Kiama. Return via the F5 freeway (31) from Mittagong, then Metroad route 5 into the city.
When to go: Year round. The beaches are best in summer, the gardens in spring and autumn. Traditional Christmas fare is on offer at local restaurants and hotels during "Christmas in July".
Where to stay and eat: Eating places, hotels and guesthouses are found all over the South Coast and Southern Highlands.
Tourist information: Kiama Visitors Centre, Blowhole Point, Kiama. [] 4232 3322. Southern Highlands Visitors Information Centre, 62–70 Hume Hwy, Mittagong. [] 4871 2888.

Berry ③
This town, surrounded by lush dairy country, is well known for its main street lined with shady trees, antique and craft shops, tea rooms and historic buildings. The Berry Museum, built in 1886, is in a former bank.

Royal National Park ❻

DESIGNATED AS A NATIONAL PARK in 1879,
the "Royal" is the second oldest in the
world after Yellowstone in the United
States. It covers 15,014 ha (37,100 acres)
of landscape typical of the Sydney Basin
sandstone. To the east, waves from the Pacific
Ocean have undercut the sandstone and
produced majestic coastal cliffs broken occasionally by
small creeks and some spectacular beaches. Streams
flowing north and east have incised deep river valleys.
Heath vegetation on the plateaux merges with woodlands
on the upper slopes. The park is ideal for bushwalking,
picnicking, camping, swimming and birdwatching.

Waratah

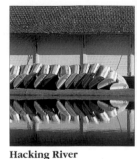

Hacking River
*Boating, fishing and canoe-
ing are common water sports.*

Audley
*A popular picnic area
since the Edwardian
era, its pavilion
was built in 1901.
The visitors'
centre is housed
in a 1920s
dance hall.*

Heathcote

Lady Carrington Drive
*Named after a governor's wife and now
closed to vehicles, the road is crossed by 15
creeks and is delightful to walk or cycle.
It also leads to the track to Palona Cave.*

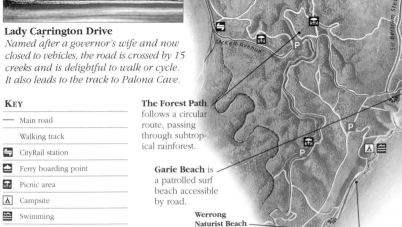

KEY

—	Main road
	Walking track
🚉	CityRail station
⛴	Ferry boarding point
🏞	Picnic area
△	Campsite
🏊	Swimming
P	Parking
🔭	Viewpoint

The Forest Path
follows a circular
route, passing
through subtrop-
ical rainforest.

Garie Beach is
a patrolled surf
beach accessible
by road.

**Werrong
Naturist Beach**

0 kilometres   4

0 miles   2

**Figure Eight
Pool**

Bundeena

Enclosed by national park on three sides, the small settlement at the mouth of the Hacking River may be reached by ferry from Cronulla or by road through the national park.

Jibbon Head

Aboriginal rock carvings such as this Jibbon Beach kangaroo may be up to 5,000 years old.

Deer Pool

One of many fresh-water pools in the park, this sheltered spot is on the track from Bundeena Drive to Marley and Little Marley.

Wattamolla Lagoon

This pretty picnic spot has a lagoon with a waterfall at its edge and a protected ocean beach.

Curracurrang

This rock formation is about halfway along the two-day Coast Walk. Sea eagles and terns nest in caves at the base of this rocky cove which also has a secluded swimming hole and waterfall.

TIPS FOR TRAVELLERS

Distance from Sydney: 34 km (21 miles).

Duration of journey: About 1 hour from the centre of Sydney.

Getting there: Follow Metroad route 1 south to Sutherland, then follow the signs to Heathcote and Wollongong. The turn-off to Farnell Avenue and the park entrance is shortly after Sutherland and well signposted.

When to go: Year round, but conditions for walking in summer can be hot so allow for this. If bushwalking, carry fresh water at all times and check on the fire danger at the Visitors' Centre before setting off.

Where to stay and eat: There are kiosks at Audley, Garie Beach and Wattamolla, but it is best to bring your own food. Camping information can be obtained at the Visitors' Centre.

Tourist information: Royal National Park Visitors' Centre, Farnell Ave, Audley.
📞 9542 0648.

TRAVELLERS' NEEDS

WHERE TO STAY

ITH AUSTRALIA's recent emergence as a major tourist destination, the urgent need for more high-quality and good-value accommodation became apparent. Previously, most Sydney hotels and guesthouses had been regarded as expensive and of varying standard. There has since been an enormous improvement in both quality and value, and there are excellent choices ranging from five-star luxury to the homeliness of a small, unpretentious hotel. In addition to hotels, Sydney has self-catering

Observatory Hotel doorman (p174)

apartments, homestay accommodation and budget and backpacker hostels for travellers on a budget. Information on these alternatives is given below. From a survey of various types of accommodation in different areas and price brackets, we have selected those offering good value for money. The chart *Choosing a Hotel* on pages 172–3 will help you to find at a glance the best to suit your needs. When you have selected the most likely hotels, you will find a more detailed description of each one by turning to pages 174–7.

A view of the rooftop pool at the Sydney Hilton Hotel *(see p175)*

WHERE TO LOOK

MOST OF the expensive hotels are in or near the city centre, but it is possible to find accommodation within most price ranges throughout Sydney. The city centre has the advantage of having many of the larger theatres, galleries and shops at hand, as well as easy transport access to more distant sights and attractions.

Cheaper accommodation can be found in the vibrant Kings Cross district. Choices here range from backpacker hostels to the small "boutique" hotels where the emphasis is on quality and personal service.

In The Rocks area, with its beautifully restored colonial buildings, you can choose from bed and breakfast in a traditional Sydney pub or the opulence of a five-star luxury hotel with good views of the Sydney Opera House.

The hotels around Darling Harbour and Chinatown offer good value for shoppers and are also within easy reach of

the city centre. Paddington has smaller hotels and self-catering apartments, while to the east are the up-market hotels of Double Bay. On the other side of Sydney Harbour Bridge, the leafy North Shore provides a more relaxed look at Sydney, and you can travel to and from the city centre by ferry.

The popular beachside suburbs of Bondi and Manly are a little way out of the centre of Sydney, but some visitors may like the opportunity to be close to superb beaches and yet still be reasonably near to the city.

You should also remember that in Australia a hotel can be a pub or a place to drink *(see pp196–7)*. Pubs do not always provide accommodation.

HOW TO BOOK

IT IS ADVISABLE to book well in advance, especially for the Christmas school holidays in December and January, the Gay and Lesbian Mardi Gras

Festival in February and Mardi Gras Parade in early March, the Easter holidays and July and September school holidays.

Bookings can be made by letter, phone, fax or through your local international travel agent. A credit card number or bank cheque in Australian dollars is usually required to secure your booking. Check cancellation requirements in case you have to change your plans, and reconfirm before you arrive in Sydney.

The **NSW Travel Centre** provides a booking service and also has a useful booklet on Sydney hotels, while the **NRMA** (National Roads and Motorists' Association) will arrange accommodation for members of motoring organizations, such as the British AA and RAC. The **Countrylink** agencies at the larger railway stations offer a comprehensive service and AFTA travel agencies, situated throughout the city, will book most hotels.

The indoor pool at the Observatory Hotel in The Rocks *(see p174)*

The curvilinear shape of the Hotel Nikko in Darling Harbour (see p176)

Some travel agencies specialize in specific areas. Tourist information centres can also offer valuable advice about where to stay in Sydney.

DISCOUNT RATES

WITH FEWER visitors staying in Sydney from April to October (except during the school holiday periods), some of the more expensive hotels may be willing to negotiate a better rate. This is particularly so if they think you will look elsewhere for accommodation. It is always worth asking for the corporate rate at which hotels give discounts for group or company bookings. Most hotels give these without question.

Stained glass at Simpsons hotel (see p176)

At the weekend there are fewer business clients around and so this is the time when prices are frequently cheaper in the top hotels. Money can also be saved by booking for a week at a time. Asking for a room without a harbour or ocean view is another good way of reducing the costs.

The NSW Travel Centre and the **Travellers Information Service** in the city can often arrange up to 50 per cent off regular hotel accommodation rates (this does not normally apply to budget hotels) to those who book in person on the day a room is required.

HIDDEN EXTRAS

BREAKFAST is usually charged on top of the room rate in the more expensive hotels. It is best to avoid consuming any of the contents of the mini-bar until you have checked the price. Alcohol is usually much more expensive here than in bottle shops. Also, be wary of the telephone charges. There will almost certainly be a considerable mark-up on any calls you make from your room. In general, tipping is not widespread, but it is expected in the more expensive hotels. You should make a note of the check-out time when you arrive, or negotiate a late check-out, as a surcharge may be incurred if you stay late.

SPECIAL OFFERS

HOTELS OFTEN cooperate with airlines, rail services, bus companies, theatres and entertainment promoters to provide package deals that include discounted accommodation. Booking agencies will have brochures with details of these seasonal offers, or ask the hotel for information on any special deals.

"Special occasion" packages (such as for anniversaries or honeymoons) are available at the top end of the market.

DISABLED TRAVELLERS

THE INFORMATION regarding wheelchair access that is given on pages 174–7 relies very much on each hotel's own assessment of its facilities.

ACROD NSW supplies a handbook for people who have mobility problems and **Barrier Free Travel** has a *Guide to Sydney for Travellers with Disabilities*. The **Centre for Leisure and Tourism Studies** also has information on accessible accommodation for those with disabilities.

TRAVELLING WITH CHILDREN

IT IS WORTH inquiring about special rates and facilities or deals that allow children to stay in their parents' room for no extra cost. Refer to *Choosing a Hotel* on pages 172–3 for hotels that cater for children.

SELF-CATERING FLATS

ACCOMMODATION including full kitchen and laundry facilities offers the traveller greater independence. It is also good value as the living space is larger than standard hotel rooms and the prices are competitive. The choice ranges from one- to three-bedroom luxury apartments in the inner city to basic flats at the beach. In *Choosing a Hotel* on pages 172–3, all the "apartment" hotels listed offer self-catering facilities.

Woolloomooloo Waters serviced apartments (see p176)

A luxurious room at the Regents Court hotel in Potts Point *(see p176)*

PRIVATE HOMES

EUROPEAN-STYLE bed-and-breakfast accommodation in a private home can be an ideal way to experience a city. It is fast becoming a popular alternative to more impersonal hotel rooms for many people who choose to visit Sydney.

People from all walks of life offer rooms in a wide variety of house styles and locations. Agencies such as **Bed and Breakfast Sydneyside** and the **Homestay Network** make every effort to match the host and guest if possible, so ring to discuss any preferences before making a reservation.

BUDGET ACCOMMODATION

AS A FAVOURED destination for many young travellers, Sydney has a large number of hostels that cater specifically for their needs. Despite fierce competition, standards vary widely. At their best, hostels offer excellent value.

While it is necessary to book in advance at some hostels, others do not take bookings and beds are on a first come, first served basis. Apartments,

Striking sculpture in the lobby of L'otel, Darlinghurst ***(see p176)***

rooms and dormitories are all available, but dormitories are often mixed sex; check before arriving. The backpacker scene changes quickly, so ask other travellers for the latest developments. Potts Point and Glebe have the largest concentration of cheap accommodation.

Halls of Residence

STUDENT ROOMS, with shared bathroom facilities, are available at the University of Sydney over the summer break from December to February. The university is conveniently close to the city and to public transport, and the moderate price includes breakfast.

Gay and Lesbian Accommodation

LESBIAN AND GAY visitors are welcome in all of Sydney's hotels. In fact, quite a number of them cater primarily, if not exclusively, for same-sex couples. Many of the small hotels in the inner city areas of Darlinghurst, Paddington, Newtown and Surry Hills are geared specifically towards gay and lesbian visitors, although most of them also welcome heterosexual guests.

The **AGLTA** (Australian Gay and Lesbian Travel Association) produces an accommodation guide which is available at no cost. There is a small charge for postage and handling if you are inquiring from overseas.

Travel agencies such as **Destination Downunder** and **Breakout Tours** specialize in holidays and accommodation for gay and lesbian travellers.

Camping

ALTHOUGH NOT AN option in the city itself, camping is available in several national parks close to Sydney. This can be a cheap and idyllic way of enjoying the natural beauty and wildlife of the bushland.

The **Royal National Park** *(see pp164–5)* has a campsite with facilities at Bonnie Vale. Advance booking is required all year round. Free bush or "walk-in" camping is allowed in several other places, but first ring the park to obtain the necessary camping permit.

At The Basin in **Ku-ring-gai Chase National Park** *(see pp154–5)*, bookings should be made and all fees paid before your stay or on arrival. There are toilets, cold showers, barbecue facilities and a phone.

There are basic campsites near Glenbrook, Woodford, Blackheath and Wentworth Falls in the **Blue Mountains National Park** *(see pp160–61)*. You will need to book if you want to camp at the Euroka Clearing near Glenbrook, but this is not necessary for the other sites. Bush camping is also permitted in the park, but there are some restrictions. Contact the national park for more details before you visit.

Manly Pacific Parkroyal ***(see p177)*****, overlooking Manly's ocean beach**

Using the Listings

Hotels are listed on pages 174–5. Each hotel is listed according to area and price category. The symbols summarize the facilities available at each of them.

🛁 all/number of rooms with bath and/or shower

[1] single-rate rooms available

👪 rooms for more than two people available

🧒 children welcome (eg babysitting service, cots etc)

[TV] television in all rooms

❄ air conditioning in all rooms

🏞 rooms with good views

🏊 hotel swimming pool or beach

♿ wheelchair access

⇅ lift

[P] hotel parking available

🌳 garden or grounds

🍴 restaurant

💳 credit and charge cards accepted:

AE American Express
DC Diners Club
MC MasterCard/Access
V Visa
JCB Japanese Credit Bureau

Price categories for a double room (not per person), including continental breakfast and service:

$ under $120
$$ $120–$200
$$$ $200–$280
$$$$ $280–$380
$$$$$ over $380

Choosing a Hotel

THE HOTELS AND SELF-CATERING APARTMENTS on the following pages have all been chosen and inspected specifically for this guide. This chart shows the selected hotels at a glance, and lists some of the factors that will help you to make an informed choice. A detailed description of each hotel appears on pages 174–7. They are listed by area of the city and all entries appear alphabetically within their price categories.

		Number of Rooms	Apartment Hotels	Children's Facilities	Business Facilities	Recommended Restaurant	Close to Shops and Restaurants	Quiet Location	24-hour Room Service
THE ROCKS AND CIRCULAR QUAY (see p174)									
Lord Nelson Brewery Hotel	$$	10		●		●	●	●	
Russell	$$	29		●		●	●		
Old Sydney Parkroyal	$$$	174		●	●	●	●		●
Stafford	$$$	61	●	●	●		●	●	
ANA Hotel Sydney	$$$$	570		●	●	●	●	●	●
Regent Sydney	$$$$	594		●	●	●	●		●
Renaissance Sydney	$$$$	579		●	●	●	●		●
Observatory	$$$$$	100		●	●	●	●	●	●
Park Hyatt Sydney	$$$$$	158		●	●	●	●		●
CITY CENTRE (see pp174–5)									
All Seasons Premier Menzies	$$	446		●	●		●		●
Castlereagh Inn	$$	83		●		●	●		
Savoy Serviced Apartments	$$	78	●	●			●		
Hyde Park Plaza	$$$	181	●	●			●		
Sydney Marriott	$$$	241		●	●	●	●		●
Wentworth	$$$	431		●	●	●	●		●
York Apartment Hotel	$$$	133	●	●	●	●	●		
Sheraton on the Park	$$$$	557		●	●	●	●		●
Sydney Hilton	$$$$	585		●	●	●	●		●
DARLING HARBOUR (see pp175–6)									
Aaron's	$	94		●			●		
Citistay Westend	$	90					●		
Carlton Crest	$$	251		●	●		●	●	
Country Comfort Sydney Central	$$	114		●	●		●		
Novotel Sydney on Darling Harbour	$$$	527		●	●		●		●
Parkroyal at Darling Harbour	$$$	354		●	●	●	●		●
Waldorf Apartment Hotel	$$$	61	●	●			●		
Hotel Nikko Darling Harbour	$$$$	645		●	●	●	●		●
BOTANIC GARDENS AND THE DOMAIN (see p176)									
Hotel Inter.Continental Sydney	$$$$	498		●	●	●	●		●
Ritz Carlton Sydney	$$$$	105		●	●	●	●		●
KINGS CROSS AND DARLINGHURST (see p176)									
Dorchester Inn	$	15	●	●			●		
L'otel	$	16			●	●	●		
Madison's Central City	$	39		●			●	●	
Crescent on Bayswater	$$	68	●	●	●		●		
Regents Court	$$	28	●	●			●	●	
Sebel of Sydney	$$	165		●	●	●	●		●
Simpsons of Potts Point	$$	14		●			●	●	
Woolloomooloo Waters	$$	69	●	●		●		●	

Price categories for a double room (not per person), including continental breakfast and service:
[$] under $120
[$][$] $120–$200
[$][$][$] $200–$280
[$][$][$][$] $280–$380
[$][$][$][$][$] Over $380

Family Rooms
Rooms equipped to cater for two adults and two children.

Children's Facilities
Child cots, a babysitting service, children's menu, high chairs in the breakfast room or restaurant.

Business Facilities
Conference rooms, desks, fax and computer service for guests.

Close to Shops and Restaurants
Within a 5-minute walk of a good centre for shops and restaurants.

Quiet Location
Quiet residential neighbourhood or quiet street in a busy area.

		Number of Rooms	Apartment Hotels	Children's Facilities	Business Facilities	Recommended Restaurant	Close to Shops and Restaurants	Quiet Location	24-hour Room Service
Paddington *(see p176–7)*									
Grand National	[$]	20				■	●	■	
Sullivans	[$]	64		■			●		
Hughenden	[$][$]	35		■			●	■	
Further Afield *(see p177)*									
Harbourside Apartments	[$][$]	82	●	■	●			■	
Mecure Hotel Lawson	[$][$]	96		■	●		●	■	●
McLaren	[$][$]	28		■	●		●	■	
Periwinkle Manly Cove	[$][$]	18		■			●	■	
Ravesi's on Bondi Beach	[$][$]	16		■	●	■	●		
Savoy Double Bay	[$][$]	39		■			●		
Sir Stamford Double Bay	[$][$]	72		■	●	■	●		
Manly Pacific Parkroyal	[$][$][$]	170		■	●	■	●	■	●
Medina Executive Apartments	[$][$][$][$]	48	●	■			●	■	
Ritz Carlton Double Bay	[$][$][$][$]	140		■	●	■	●	■	

THE ROCKS AND CIRCULAR QUAY

Lord Nelson Brewery Hotel

19 Kent St, The Rocks NSW 2000.
Map 1 A2. **(** 9251 4044.
FAX 9251 1532. **Rooms:** 10. 🏢 🏃
TV 🍴 🗪 AE, DC, MC, V. $$$$$

For 150 years, bar-room banter has resounded off the thick sandstone slab walls of this celebrated pub which is famous for its home brews. On the top floor, stone walls and rustic furnishings are a feature of the cosy bedrooms and there are shared bathrooms and a breakfast kitchenette for guests. This is a great place to meet the locals.

Russell

143a George St, The Rocks NSW 2000.
Map 1 B2. **(** 9241 3543. FAX 9252 1652. **Rooms:** 29. 🏢 18. 1 🏢 🏃
🔘 🍴 🗪 AE, DC, MC, V, JCB. $$$$$

The interior of this late 19th-century building is appealingly decorated, with chintzy materials, pretty wallpaper, country-style antiques and fresh flowers in abundance. A welcoming and intimate hotel, it has a rooftop garden which is the perfect spot for a quiet drink after a hectic day in the city.

Old Sydney Parkroyal

55 George St, The Rocks NSW 2000.
Map 1 B2. **(** 9252 0524. FAX 9251 2093. **Rooms:** 174. 🏢 🏢 🏃 TV
🍴 🗪 🗪 🔘 🗪 P 🍴 🗪 AE, DC, MC, V, JCB. $$$$$

The hotel is big enough to offer all the facilities found in a grand establishment, but small enough to offer personal attention. The decor is a little dated, but this may not be a consideration given the great location within the historic Rocks area and the proximity to Circular Quay and the Opera House.

Stafford

75 Harrington St, The Rocks NSW 2000. **Map** 1 B2. **(** 9251 6711.
FAX 9251 3458. **Rooms:** 61. 🏢 🏢
🏃 TV 🍴 🗪 🗪 🔘 P
🗪 AE, DC, MC, V, JCB. $$$$$

In this unusual apartment complex, guests are housed in either the central purpose-built property or in seven charmingly restored 1870 terrace houses nearby. All of the apartments have well-equipped kitchens but, if you prefer, room service breakfast can be arranged. There are a heated spa, swimming pool, sauna and gym for guests.

ANA Hotel Sydney

176 Cumberland St, The Rocks NSW 2000. **Map** 1 A3. **(** 9250 6000.
FAX 9250 6250. **Rooms:** 570. 🏢 🏢
🏃 TV 🍴 🗪 🔘 🗪 P 🍴
🗪 AE, DC, MC, V, JCB. $$$$$

Clever use of marble, glass, modern art and lush greenery gives this plush hotel a light and airy atmosphere. Service is exemplary and the spacious guest rooms and suites all have harbour views. Guests on the Executive Floor enjoy additional perks, but anyone can sip cocktails high up in the Horizon Bar where the glittering lights of the harbour at night are a magical backdrop.

Regent Sydney

199 George St, Sydney NSW 2000.
Map 1 B3. **(** 9238 0000.
FAX 9251 2851. **Rooms:** 594. 🏢 1
🏢 🏃 TV 🍴 🗪 🗪 🔘 🗪 P 🍴
🗪 AE, DC, MC, V, JCB. $$$$$

The imposing modern grandeur of the vast lobby is reflected in the elegant guest rooms. The superb location offers wonderful views of the harbour and city, while the state-of-the-art equipment in the Health Club gives you the chance to work up an appetite, which can easily be sated at one of the three first-class restaurants.

Renaissance Sydney

30 Pitt St, Sydney NSW 2000.
Map 1 B3. **(** 9372 2233.
FAX 9251 1122. **Rooms:** 579. 🏢 🏢
🏃 TV 🍴 🗪 🗪 🔘 🗪 P 🍴
🗪 AE, DC, MC, V, JCB. $$$$$

The three-tiered lobby, with an elaborate Italian mosaic centrepiece and sweeping staircase, sets a scene of some magnificence, but the hotel is surprisingly unstuffy. The rooms are large and offer all the features expected of a five-star hotel. The Renaissance Club, for those staying on the top four floors of the hotel, has a private lounge where breakfast, afternoon tea and cocktails are on the house.

Observatory

89–113 Kent St, Millers Point NSW 2000. **Map** 1 A2. **(** 9256 2222.
FAX 9256 2233. **Rooms:** 100. 🏃
TV 🍴 🗪 🗪 🔘 🗪 P 🍴
🗪 AE, DC, MC, V, JCB. $$$$$

Although relatively new, this smart boutique hotel blends successfully with the surrounding 19th-century buildings. It has been lavishly but tastefully furnished with original antiques, fine tapestries and paintings. All the guest rooms have luxurious marble bathrooms. The indoor pool has special lighting in the ceiling which makes it sparkle like a starry night sky.

Park Hyatt Sydney

7 Hickson Rd, The Rocks NSW 2000.
Map 1 B1. **(** 9241 1234. FAX 9256 1555. **Rooms:** 158. 🏢 🏢 🏃 TV
🍴 🗪 🗪 🔘 🗪 AE, DC, MC, V, JCB. $$$$$

This deluxe hotel, which hugs the harbour foreshore and is almost in the shadow of the Harbour Bridge, appears to be carved in sandstone. It is quiet, opulent and splendidly furnished in richly coloured fabrics and works of art. The guest rooms have every luxury, including a 24-hour butler service. The picture windows of the Art Deco lobby and the excellent restaurant are classy settings for watching the bustle of activity at Circular Quay.

CITY CENTRE

All Seasons Premier Menzies

14 Carrington St, Sydney NSW 2000.
Map 1 A4. **(** 9299 1000.
FAX 9290 3819. **Rooms:** 446. 🏢
🏢 🏃 TV 🍴 🗪 🗪 🔘 P 🍴
🗪 AE, DC, MC, V. $$$$$

For decades, the "Menzies" has been proud of its traditional, elegant atmosphere and the recent renovations retain the ambience of a gentlemen's club, with sumptuous green leather sofas on rich carpets over dark granite floors. Sports enthusiasts will revel in the Sporters Bar and Bistro where 15 monitors continuously show sporting events.

Castlereagh Inn

169–171 Castlereagh St, Sydney NSW 2000. **Map** 1 B5. **(** 9264 2281.
FAX 9283 2496. **Rooms:** 83. 🏢 1
🏢 🏃 TV 🍴 🍴 🗪 AE, DC, MC, V. $$$$$

The grand dining room is a special feature of this old-fashioned hotel. Crystal chandeliers illuminate crisp, white linen and furnishings reminiscent of a past era. Morning paper and continental breakfast are included in the affordable price.

Savoy Serviced Apartments

37–43 King St, Sydney NSW 2000. **Map** 1 A5. **(** 9267 9211. FAX 9262 2023.
Rooms: 78. 🏢 🏢 🏃 TV 🍴 🗪
🔘 P 🗪 AE, DC, MC, V, JCB. $$$$$

These one-bedroom apartments can accommodate up to four adults as the sofa converts to a double bed. Rooms are decorated in either frilly country-cottage style or a more modern design. The Savoy Deli is handy for stocking the fully equipped kitchens.

Hyde Park Plaza

38 College St, Sydney NSW 2010.
Map 4 F3. **[** 9331 6933.
FAX 9331 6022. **Rooms:** 181. 🛏 🎌
🏋 TV 🗄 🖼 🛉 P 🍴
🖨 AE, DC, MC, V, JCB. $$$

The hotel has a great location opposite the southern end of Hyde Park. The foyer is rather unprepossessing and dated, but the wide variety of self-contained suites, from studios to three-bedroom "flexi-suites", are roomy, comfortably furnished and fitted with every convenience.

Sydney Marriott

36 College St, Sydney NSW 2000.
Map 4 F3. **[** 9361 8400.
FAX 9361 8599. **Rooms:** 241. 🛏
🎌 🏋 TV 🗄 🖼 🛉 🛉 P 🍴
🖨 AE, DC, MC, V, JCB. $$$

This elegant hotel, overlooking Hyde Park, suits the business traveller very well, with its conference rooms, business centre and an executive lounge. The tastefully decorated rooms are fully appointed and even include microwave ovens. Some suites have hot plates, spa baths and fax lines.

Wentworth

61 Phillip St, Sydney NSW 2000.
Map 1 B4. **[** 9230 0700.
FAX 9227 9133. **Rooms:** 431. 🛏
🎌 🏋 TV 🗄 🖼 🛉 🛉 P 🍴
🖨 AE, DC, MC, V, JCB. $$$

Since 1966, this has been one of Sydney's most distinguished hotels. Now elegantly refurbished to expected international standards, the rooms have excellent facilities and all include a valet service. There are four non-smoking floors.

York Apartment Hotel

5 York St, Sydney NSW 2000.
Map 1 A3. **[** 9210 5000. FAX 9290 1487. **Rooms:** 133. 🛏 1 🎌 🏋 TV
🗄 🖼 🛉 🛉 limited. 🛉 P 🛉 🍴
🖨 AE, DC, MC, V, JCB. $$$

There is an understated elegance throughout this well-located hotel. All of its apartments, from studio to penthouse, are individually designed, beautifully furnished and have generous balconies, modern kitchens and large bathrooms.

Sheraton on the Park

161 Elizabeth St, Sydney NSW 2000.
Map 1 B5. **[** 9286 6000. FAX 9286 6686. **Rooms:** 557. 🛏 🎌 🏋 TV
🗄 🖼 🛉 P 🍴 🍴 🖨 AE, DC, MC, V, JCB. $$$$

Another relative newcomer in the city, there has been no expense spared on the interior design and

furnishings of this hotel. Centrally placed, it is convenient for both business and shopping, with the major department stores a short walk away. The peaceful oasis of Hyde Park is just across the road.

Sydney Hilton

259 Pitt St, Sydney NSW 2000.
Map 1 B5. **[** 9266 0610.
FAX 9265 6065. **Rooms:** 585. 🛏 🎌
🏋 TV 🗄 🖼 🛉 🛉 P 🍴
🖨 AE, DC, MC, V, JCB. $$$$

This *grande dame* of the central city's five-star hotels has the usual Hilton high standard of service and facilities, particularly for business people. There is a wide range of cuisine at the four hotel restaurants and a good choice of bars – do not miss the ornately decorated and historic Marble Bar *(see p82)*. Check out the small art gallery, which sometimes has special exhibitions.

DARLING HARBOUR

Aaron's

37 Ultimo Rd, Haymarket NSW 2000.
Map 4 D4. **[** 9281 5555. FAX 9281 2666. **Rooms:** 94. 🛏 🎌 🏋 TV 🛉
🛉 P 🍴 🖨 AE, DC, MC, V. $

This hotel offers apartments, rooms with en suite bathrooms and budget rooms with shared facilities. The decor is predominantly mushroom pink, with rather bland, although serviceable, furnishings, but you can overlook that for the price and the central location. An airport bus will call at the hotel on request.

Citistay Westend

412 Pitt St, Sydney NSW 2000. **Map** 4 E4. **[** 9211 4822. FAX 9281 9570.
Rooms: 90. 🛏 TV 🗄 🛉 🍴 breakfast only. 🖨 AE, DC, MC, V, JCB. $

Within walking distance of Central Railway Station, this older style hotel offers great value. Almost outside the door is Chinatown, while the city centre is just up the road. All rooms have a refrigerator and tea- and coffee-making facilities.

Carlton Crest

169–179 Thomas St, Haymarket NSW 2000. **Map** 4 D5. **[** 9281 6888.
FAX 9281 6688. **Rooms:** 251. 🛏 🎌
🏋 TV 🗄 🖼 🛉 🛉 P 🍴
🖨 AE, DC, MC, V, JCB. $$

The entrance, reception area and stairways are all part of the original 1902 Infants' Hospital building, now incorporated into an imposing façade for this modern hotel. All rooms and suites are extraordinarily large with excellent services for guests – including a rooftop pool, barbecue area and putting green.

Country Comfort Sydney Central

Cnr George & Quay Sts, Sydney NSW 2000. **Map** 4 D5. **[** 9212 2544.
FAX 9281 3794. **Rooms:** 114. 🎌
🏋 TV 🗄 🖼 🛉 🛉 P 🍴
🖨 AE, DC, MC, V, JCB. $$

Situated opposite Central Railway Station, the hotel is popular with visitors from country towns. The rooms, varying in style from standard to luxury spa suites, have been refurbished recently. Helpful staff maintain the Country Comfort reputation for friendly service.

Novotel Sydney on Darling Harbour

100 Murray St, Pyrmont NSW 2009.
Map 3 C2. **[** 9934 0000.
FAX 9934 0099. **Rooms:** 527. 🛏 🎌
🏋 TV 🗄 🖼 🛉 🛉 P 🍴
🖨 AE, DC, MC, V, JCB. $$$

This modern superstructure towers above Darling Harbour. With the monorail station virtually on the doorstep, the city centre is just a few minutes away. The rooms are good four-star quality and have views across the city, while pool, tennis court, sauna and gym are all on hand for energetic guests.

Parkroyal at Darling Harbour

150 Day St, Darling Harbour NSW 2000. **Map** 4 D3. **[** 9261 4444.
FAX 9261 8766. **Rooms:** 354. 🛏
🎌 🏋 TV 🗄 🖼 🛉 🛉 P 🍴
🖨 AE, DC, MC, V, JCB. $$$

A funnel-like atrium rises skyward through the centre of the lobby, and swirls of vivid colour through the murky greens almost create the sensation of swimming under water. The stylish guest rooms look out over the city skyline and Darling Harbour which, with its myriad lights reflecting on the water at night, seems almost to glitter.

Waldorf Apartment Hotel

57 Liverpool St, Sydney NSW 2000.
Map 4 E3. **[** 9261 5355.
FAX 9261 3753. **Rooms:** 61. 🛏
🎌 🏋 TV 🗄 🖼 🛉 🛉 P
🖨 AE, DC, MC, V, JCB. $$$

Everything is included in these spacious one- and two-bedroom apartments, from hair dryers and clock radio alarms to in-house movies and a rooftop pool. With a choice of over 50 restaurants in the area, the well-equipped kitchen may not be used much during a short stay. The balcony overlooking the city is a nice spot to relax with a drink after a day's sightseeing.

For key to symbols *see p171*

Hotel Nikko Darling Harbour

161 Sussex St, Sydney NSW 2000.
Map 4 D2. 🄲 *9299 1231.*
📠 *9299 3340.* ***Rooms:*** *645.* 🛏 🏋
🏋 📺 🍽 🌐 🅿 🛗 ⎕
⏚ *AE, DC, MC, V, JCB.* $$$$

Sleek modern design marries well
with several restored 19th-century
maritime buildings. A classic old
pub, the Dundee Arms, is now the
hotel's bar. All rooms are beautifully
appointed, some with views over
Darling Harbour. The top four executive floors offer the privacy and
services of a hotel within a hotel.

BOTANIC GARDENS AND THE DOMAIN

Hotel Inter.Continental Sydney

117 Macquarie St, Sydney NSW 2000.
Map 1 C3. 🄲 *9230 0200.* 📠 *9240
1240.* ***Rooms:*** *498.* 🏋 🏋 📺
🍽 🌐 🛗 🅿 🛗 ⏚ *AE,
DC, MC, V, JCB.* $$$$

The ingenious design of this hotel
blends colonial heritage with contemporary architecture. Part of the
old 1851 Treasury Building now
forms the foyer and lower storeys.
The dramatic lobby is constructed
beneath impressive vaulted sandstone arches reaching three storeys
above the marble floor. Here, small
music ensembles frequently perform
while guests sip tea or cocktails.

Ritz Carlton Sydney

93 Macquarie St, Sydney NSW 2000.
Map 1 C3. 🄲 *9252 4600.*
📠 *9252 4286.* ***Rooms:*** *105.* 🛏
🏋 🏋 📺 🍽 🌐 🛗 🅿 🛗
⏚ *AE, DC, MC, V, JCB.* $$$$

There is a refined but relaxed air
in this intimate hotel. Features
include open fireplaces, oriental
carpets, marble floors and 18th- and
19th-century antiques. Enjoy cocktails in the old-world atmosphere
in The Bar. The rooftop pool and
deck have wonderful views.

KINGS CROSS AND DARLINGHURST

Dorchester Inn

38 Macleay St, Potts Point NSW 2011.
Map 2 E5. 🄲 *9358 2400.*
📠 *9357 7579.* ***Rooms:*** *15.* 🛏 1️⃣
🏋 🏋 📺 🅿 🚻 🛗 ⏚ *AE, DC,
MC, V, JCB.* $

Hidden away in the quiet, leafy
part of Kings Cross is this charming
1886 hotel. Recently refurbished,

the colonial atmosphere has been
retained; the roomy, self-contained
serviced apartments are absolutely
up-to-date, but have kept those
elegant high ceilings and quaint
Victorian decorative features that
have such historic appeal.

L'otel

114 Darlinghurst Rd, Darlinghurst NSW
2010. **Map** 5 B1. 🄲 *9360 6868.*
📠 *9331 4536.* ***Rooms:*** *16.* 🛏 🏋
📺 🅿 🛗 ⏚ *AE, DC, MC, V.* $

Situated in the heart of Sydney's
café culture, this European-style
small hotel has individually styled
suites, either with French provincial decor or a more modern 1950s
Retro feel. The hallways provide a
fascinating art gallery, displaying
canvasses by young local artists.
Room service is available from the
bar and restaurant downstairs.

Madison's Central City

6–8 Ward Ave, Elizabeth Bay NSW
2011. **Map** 5 C1. 🄲 *9357 1155.*
📠 *9357 1193.* ***Rooms:*** *39.* 🛏 🏋
📺 🍽 🌐 🅿 ⏚ *AE, DC, MC, V.* $

A tropical garden courtyard separates two modern blocks of small
rooms and suites. Nothing fancy
here, but the rooms are clean with
standard fittings, modern furniture
and small bathrooms. It is also close
to all the action of Kings Cross.

Crescent on Bayswater

33 Bayswater Rd, Potts Point NSW
2011. **Map** 5 C1. 🄲 *9357 7266.*
📠 *9357 7418.* ***Rooms:*** *68.* 🛏 🏋
🏋 📺 🍽 🌐 🌐 🅿 🛗 ⏚ *AE, DC,
MC, V, JCB.* $$

The wrought-iron balconies of this
modern hotel have been designed
to blend harmoniously with the
graceful Victorian terraces nearby.
The French château-like staircase
sweeping up to the excellent restau-
rant from street level is much more
interesting than the basic lobby.
The guest rooms are self-contained
with kitchenettes and balconies.

Regents Court

18 Springfield Ave, Potts Point NSW
2011. **Map** 2 E5. 🄲 *9358 1533.*
📠 *9358 1833.* ***Rooms:*** *28.* 🛏 🏋
🏋 📺 🍽 🌐 🅿 🍴 ⏚ *AE, DC,
MC, V, JCB.* $$

An innovative design team has created one of Sydney's more stylish
and individual small hotels. The
serviced apartments have masses of
room and are equipped with high-
quality kitchen appliances – even
a Parmesan cheese grater. The collection of 20th-century designer
furniture used throughout belongs
to the owners, who make every
effort to ensure friendly service.

Sebel of Sydney

23 Elizabeth Bay Rd, Elizabeth Bay
NSW 2011. **Map** 2 F5. 🄲 *9358 3244.*
📠 *9357 1926.* ***Rooms:*** *165.* 🛏
🏋 🏋 📺 🍽 🌐 🅿 🛗
⏚ *AE, DC, MC, V, JCB.* $$

This sophisticated hotel has been
a favourite for years and has
always attracted visiting rock and
film celebrities, probably because
of the discreet and club-like atmo-
sphere. All the guest rooms have
excellent facilities – some even
have their own balconies and
dressing rooms. The suites have
mini-kitchens, sitting rooms and
spas. The rooftop pool is set in a
Mediterranean-style garden.

Simpsons of Potts Point

8 Challis Ave, Potts Point NSW 2011.
Map 2 E4. 🄲 *9356 2199.* 📠 *9356
4476.* ***Rooms:*** *14.* 🛏 1️⃣ 🏋 🏋 📺
🍽 🅿 ⏚ *AE, DC, MC, V, JCB.* $$

Built in 1892 as a family residence,
this historical hotel has been
exquisitely and expertly restored,
retaining the atmosphere of past
times with spacious and elegantly
designed rooms, grand hallways
and splendid stained-glass windows.
The hotel itself provides the same
impressive attention to detail, offering every comfort to guests.

Woolloomooloo Waters

88 Dowling St, Woolloomooloo NSW
2011. **Map** 2 E5. 🄲 *9358 3100.*
📠 *9356 4839.* ***Rooms:*** *69.* 🛏 🏋
🏋 📺 🍽 🌐 🅿 🛗
⏚ *AE, DC, MC, V, JCB.* $$

Clever reconstruction of a huge
warehouse in former docklands has
created a well-designed modern
hotel in a slightly offbeat area. The
large studios and apartments, com-
fortably and tastefully furnished in
grey and peach tones, have full
kitchen and laundry facilities. The
somewhat claustrophobic effect of
the indoor pool has been mini-
mized by an imaginative design.

PADDINGTON

Grand National

161 Underwood St, Paddington,
2021. **Map** 6 D4. 🄲 *9363 3096.*
📠 *9363 3542.* ***Rooms:*** *20.* 1️⃣ 🌐
🛗 ⏚ *AE, DC, MC, V.* $

Once just another of the back-street
Paddington pubs, this 100-year-old
building has been done up with
the help of an architect with a flair
for theatre design. The stylish
dining room and cocktail bar are

popular with the trend-setting locals. The accommodation is great value for those who do not mind packing their dressing gown for trips to the shared bathrooms.

Sullivans

21 Oxford St, Paddington NSW 2021. **Map** 5 B3. █ 9361 0211. FAX 9360 3735. **Rooms:** 64. 🛏 🏋 TV 🗐 ⚌ 🔽 P 🅾 🌊 AE, DC, MC, V. ⓢ

An uninspiring exterior belies the attractive minimalist interior of this family-owned small hotel. The rooms are not large, but are comfortable with good facilities. The central courtyard in terracotta tones has an inviting pool. Bicycles are available for guests to ride.

Hughenden

14 Queen St, Woollahra NSW 2025. **Map** 6 E4. █ 9363 4863. FAX 9362 0398. **Rooms:** 35. 🛏 🎫 🏋 TV P 🅗 🌊 AE, DC, MC, V. ⓢⓢ

After a chequered history, from being a family home in 1876, to a girls' school in later years and a boarding house for artistic types after World War II, this rambling old building is now restored to its original grandeur with beautifully carved staircases and marble fireplaces. The rooms are all quite comfortably furnished and the hotel has a very good restaurant.

FURTHER AFIELD

Harbourside Apartments

2a Henry Lawson Ave, McMahons Point NSW 2060. █ 9963 4300. FAX 9922 7998. **Rooms:** 82. 🛏 🎫 🔽 TV 🗐 🔽 P 🅾 🅗 🄯 AE, DC, MC, V. ⓢⓢ

Most of the executive- and family-serviced apartments in this 16-storey building close to the waterfront have what are probably some of the best views in Sydney. While the two-bedroom apartments are huge, the studios are a bit pokey, but all the apartments are comfortably furnished and have good kitchen facilities. The pool has a wonderful position right by the harbour's edge.

Mecure Hotel Lawson

383–389 Bulwara Rd, Ultimo NSW 2007. **Map** 3 C4. █ 9211 1499. FAX 9281 3764. **Rooms:** 96. 🛏 🎫 🏋 TV 🗐 🔽 P 🄯 AE, DC, MC, V, JCB. ⓢⓢ

This is a modern hotel but the use of stained wood throughout the rooms is reminiscent of an old country pub. The place is friendly

and relaxed and the rooms good value. The prints and memorabilia of 19th-century poet and short story writer, Henry Lawson, give a real Australian flavour.

McLaren

25 McLaren St, North Sydney NSW 2060. █ 9954 4622. FAX 9922 1868. **Rooms:** 28. 🛏 🎫 🏋 TV 🗐 🔽 P 🅾 🄯 AE, DC, MC, V. ⓢⓢ

The original stately mansion, now protected by National Trust listing, blends pleasingly with a new wing connected by the Atrium Garden. Here, cane furniture, hanging ferns and a glass ceiling evoke a seaside resort setting. All the facilities of a large hotel (including room service) are offered, with the friendly approach of a more intimate hotel.

Periwinkle Manly Cove

18-19 East Esplanade, Manly NSW 2095. █ 9977 4668. FAX 9977 6308. **Rooms:** 18. 🛏 11. 🗓 🎫 TV 🔽 P 🅾 🄯 MC, V. ⓢⓢ

Stylish rooms with high ceilings, wrought-iron verandas, and a leafy courtyard are features of this very pretty family-run guesthouse. The rooms all have ceiling fans and cane furniture, but bathrooms are shared. There are private outdoor areas where guests can enjoy the tranquillity of Manly Cove.

Ravesi's on Bondi Beach

Cnr Campbell Parade & Hall St, Bondi Beach NSW 2026. █ 9365 4422. FAX 9365 1481. **Rooms:** 16. 🛏 🎫 🏋 TV 🗐 🔽 limited. 🔽 11 🄯 AE, DC, MC, V. ⓢⓢ

Smart, laid-back and trendy, this busy small hotel epitomizes the relaxed style of beach life at Bondi. The rooms are furnished in cane and wood, and some of the suites have private balconies overlooking the surf of Bondi Beach. The hotel's restaurant is regarded as one of the best in the area *(see p189)*, but you will need to book ahead as it is always very popular with the local residents.

Savoy Double Bay

41–45 Knox St, Double Bay NSW 2028. █ 9326 1411. FAX 9327 8464. **Rooms:** 39. 🛏 🎫 🏋 TV 🗐 P 🄯 AE, DC, MC, V. ⓢⓢ

The rooms may be small and rather blandly furnished, but this small hotel, set among the outdoor cafés, exclusive shops and chic restaurants of up-market Double Bay, offers excellent value. Room rates include a continental breakfast, complimentary newspapers and coffee, all available to guests in the atrium.

Sir Stamford Double Bay

22 Knox St, Double Bay NSW 2028. █ 9363 0100. FAX 9327 3110. **Rooms:** 72. 🛏 🏋 TV 🗐 ⚌ 🔽 P 11 🄯 AE, DC, MC, V, JCB. ⓢⓢ

The lobby is sumptuously furnished and decorated in midnight blue and gold. The use of deep, rich colours continues in the bold design of the guest rooms, featuring exquisite furnishings, billowing silk curtains and canopied beds, or else New York loft-style rooms complete with mezzanine bedrooms. The elegant Romanesque-style pool is open to guests 24 hours a day.

Manly Pacific Parkroyal

55 North Steyne, Manly NSW 2095. █ 9977 7666. FAX 9977 7822. **Rooms:** 170. 🛏 🎫 🏋 TV 🗐 ⚌ 🔽 P 11 🄯 AE, DC, MC, V, JCB. ⓢⓢⓢ

Situated as it is right on Manly's ocean beach, the hotel has unbeatable views of sand and surf. All the rooms are light and spacious, with balconies and every modern convenience. There are bars, restaurants, a nightclub and a rooftop pool, and plenty of local pubs and cafés just a short stroll away.

Medina Executive Apartments

400 Glenmore Rd, Paddington NSW 2113. **Map** 6 D2. █ 9361 9000. FAX 9332 3484. **Rooms:** 48. 🛏 🎫 🏋 TV 🗐 P 🅾 🄯 AE, DC, MC, V. ⓢⓢⓢ

Set in landscaped gardens in a peaceful residential area, these huge two- and three-bedroom modern apartments offer all the conveniences of home, combined with hotel-style services. It is only a short walk to the supermarket to stock the refrigerator and buses directly to the beach or to the city are close by on New South Head Road.

Ritz Carlton Double Bay

33 Cross St, Double Bay NSW 2028. █ 9362 4455. FAX 9362 4744. **Rooms:** 140. 🛏 🎫 🏋 TV 🗐 ⚌ 🔽 P 🅾 11 🄯 AE, DC, MC, V, JCB. ⓢⓢⓢⓢ

This hotel reeks of sophistication, from the first-floor lounge and reception area to the classically decorated rooms and suites. The central courtyard is in the style of a Mediterranean villa garden, while the rooftop heated pool has fabulous views of Sydney Harbour.

For key to symbols *see p291*

RESTAURANTS, CAFÉS AND PUBS

S YDNEYSIDERS are justifiably proud of their dining scene. Australia's largest city has been populated by successive waves of migrants, all of whom have added something of their home countries to the communal table. These influences have spilled over into contemporary cuisine, which is often called "modern Australian". This term covers just about any ethnic style the chef may fancy, loosely based on French cuisine. The result is that, in terms of ethnic diversity, Sydney is able

Fresh seafood, Chinese style

to offer many dining options. For a summary of key features and prices of restaurants included in this guide, turn to *Choosing a Restaurant* on pages 186–7. There is a more detailed description of each restaurant in the listings on pages 188–93. Casual eating places, where you can often enjoy food that is as good as at a restaurant but cheaper, are featured on pages 194–7; here you will also find mention of pubs that have recommended bistros and dining areas.

WHERE TO EAT

C IRCULAR QUAY, The Rocks, Darlinghurst, Potts Point and Paddington are the areas where you will find the widest choice of places to eat. Just outside the city centre, and not covered in depth in these listings, are the inner-city "eat streets" of Glebe Point Road, Glebe *(see p131)*, and King Street, Newtown.

On the lower North Shore is Military Road, which extends from Neutral Bay to Mosman. It would be difficult to walk along any of these streets and not find a café or restaurant to suit your taste and budget.

All of the major hotels have at least one restaurant and a few of these, such as Kable's in the Regent Sydney *(see p174)*, serve some of the finest food that Sydney has to offer. Signature restaurants that are recommended in the grander

hotels include Raphael at the Sydney Renaissance, Unkai, a splendid Japanese dining room in the ANA Hotel and the very Venetian Galileo in the Observatory Hotel *(see pp174–7)*. They aim at the well-heeled diner on an expense account, but nonetheless offer a high standard of dining for people who want the best and are prepared to pay for it.

HOW MUCH TO PAY

C OMPARED WITH other major world capitals, dining out in Sydney is relatively inexpensive. The cost of a three-course meal in an average restaurant is probably 25 per cent lower than its equivalent in, say, New York or London. The cost is further reduced if you choose a BYO restaurant where you can avoid paying the marked-up price of restaurant wine by taking your own alcohol.

Understated chic at Darley Street Thai, Kings Cross *(see p191)*

OPENING TIMES

M OST RESTAURANTS serve lunch from noon to 3pm and dinner from 6pm to about 11pm, though last orders are often at 10:30pm. Cheap and cheerful ethnic kitchens may close earlier, around 9:30pm, but this largely depends on demand. Many restaurants close on some, if not all, public holidays *(see p51)*. This is particularly true of Christmas Day, Boxing Day and Good Friday.

RESERVATIONS

B OOKING IS recommended in most places – earlier in the day is usually adequate. If you want to be sure of a table for Friday or Saturday in a spot that is currently fashionable, however, you may need to make a reservation at least a week in advance. The more casual brasseries and bistros

The popular Fez Café in Victoria Street, Darlinghurst *(see p193)*

are the exceptions. Many are open all through the day and, as they aren't the sort of place where people linger over their meal, they do not take bookings. You may have to wait a few minutes for a table if you arrive at a busy time.

LICENSING LAWS

SYDNEY RESTAURANTS must be licensed to sell food, but when a place is described as licensed, this usually refers to its licence to sell alcohol. BYO (bring your own) restaurants are not licensed to sell liquor and you will need to buy it beforehand if you want to drink alcohol with your meal. A small amount will probably be charged for "corkage".

BYO restaurants not only reduce the cost of dining out, but also allow wine buffs to choose exactly the wines they wish to drink with their meal. At up-market establishments such as Claude's *(see p193)*, it is a good idea to inquire about the day's menu, so you can choose your wine accordingly.

Relaxing in a café at the top end of Oxford Street, Paddington

DRESS CODES

DRESS STANDARDS in Sydney restaurants are really quite relaxed, even in the more up-market establishments. Most restaurants will draw the line, however, at patrons in beachwear and flip flops.

Neat and tidy is the general rule. Smart casual dress is the safest option when considering

Surf watching from the balcony at Ravesi's on Bondi Beach *(see p190)*

what to wear. Jackets and ties are a rare sight unless the wearer has come straight from the office or is conducting a business meeting over a meal.

TAX AND TIPPING

AS IN THE REST of Australia, there are no government taxes or service charges added to bills in Sydney. While tipping is not compulsory, 10 to 15 per cent of the total bill is customary as a reward for good service. You can leave a cash tip on the table after you have paid or simply add it to the total if paying your bill by charge or credit card.

EATING WITH CHILDREN

MOST RESTAURANTS accept children who can sit still throughout a meal, although you may feel more comfortable in either Chinese restaurants or the cheap pasta eateries in East Sydney, where children are always welcome.

Hamburger chains such as McDonald's and Hungry Jacks have branches throughout the city. For families wanting to dine rather than snack, chains such as Pizza Hut and the Black Stump steakhouses offer special menus for children as well as alcohol for the adults.

The Hard Rock Café *(see p194)* in Darlinghurst has enough of a buzz to drown out any noise young children may make and the menu and upbeat atmosphere are popular with older kids. Perhaps the best spots to dine out with

children are those where they can play safely outside after they have eaten. The Bathers Pavilion *(see p188)* is right on Balmoral Beach *(see pp54–5)*, a sheltered harbour beach which has a netted swimming pool, while Centennial Park Café *(see p194)* is within supervisory range of grassy lawns and a children's playground.

USING THE LISTINGS

Key to symbols in the listings on pp188–93.

🍽 fixed-price menu
🍷 bring your own bottle
👶 children's portions
V vegetarian dishes available
♿ wheelchair access
▤ air conditioning
▦ tables outside
▨ tables with good views
🚭 non-smoking section
🍷 good wine list
★ highly recommended
💳 credit cards accepted:
AE American Express
DC Diners Club
MC MasterCard/Access
V Visa
JCB Japanese Credit Bureau

Price categories for a three-course evening meal for one person including cover charge and service (but not wine):
$ under $25
$$ $25–35
$$$ $35–50
$$$$ $50–70
$$$$$ Over $70

What to Eat in Sydney

Meat pie with tomato sauce

SYDNEYSIDERS take for granted the quality and variety of produce on offer. The pie with sauce has been pushed aside as restaurateurs seek out regional specialities. From New South Wales, you may sample Sydney rock oysters, honey from Mudgee, mushrooms from Orange, lamb from Illabo and the Southern Highlands' gourmet potatoes. From other states, try the olive oil of South Australia, salmon farmed in Tasmania, soft fruit and dairy produce from Victoria, reef fish and exotic fruit from Queensland and Western Australian farmhouse cheeses.

Eucalypt Honey
Imported bees seem to love the eucalypts. Leatherwood, light in colour, has the strongest flavour.

Potato Wedges
Coated with a spicy seasoning then fried in a two-step process, these chunky variations on the humble chip are usually served with sour cream and chilli sauce.

Yum Cha
Literally "drinking tea", this Chinese feast includes dim sum, or steamed dumplings stuffed with meat, fish or vegetables.

Focaccia
This Italian-inspired sandwich has gourmet antipasto, salad and meat slices between toasted slabs of crusty flat bread.

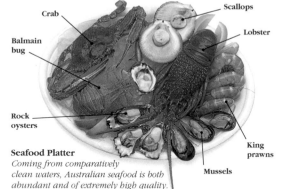

Crab

Scallops

Balmain bug

Lobster

Rock oysters

King prawns

Mussels

Lebanese Mezes
Expect an array of appetizers including pulse and vegetable dips, marinated and grilled vegetables and filled pastries.

Seafood Platter
Coming from comparatively clean waters, Australian seafood is both abundant and of extremely high quality.

Mixed Leaf Salad
Garden-fresh salad features on most menus. It is served here with feta cheese and grilled vegetables.

Char-grilled Kangaroo Fillet
A relatively recent addition to butchers' shelves, low-fat kangaroo fillet is usually served rare.

Thai Green Curry
Chicken is the favourite variety, but a tasty vegetarian version is also commonly served.

Kebabs

Chicken wings

Baby octopus

Seared Beef Fillet
Australian beef, here wrapped in paperbark, is usually served with the season's vegetables.

Barbecue
Char-grilled meat, poultry and fresh seafood such as baby octopus are served by themselves or in combination, usually accompanied by bread and green salad.

Freshwater Crayfish
Also known as "yabbies", this main dish is usually served simply on a bed of greens with a dipping sauce such as aïoli.

Blue-eyed Cod
Although known as cod, it is in fact trevalla, a deep sea fish of meaty texture and mild flavour. It is often served in thick steaks.

Lamb Loin Fillet
Thick slices of tender seared lamb served on a salad of rocket and fresh snow peas are ideal Sydney summer eating.

Baked Ricotta Cake
Indigenous Australian ingredients such as rosella buds may appear in contemporary desserts.

Pavlova
This meringue dessert is topped with fresh cream and summer fruit such as passionfruit.

Mixed Berry Ice Cream
Homemade ice creams, such as raspberry or honey, are often served with seasonal fruit.

shed rind
Salut   Jindi Brie   Heidi Gruyère

Mature sheep's cheese   Passionfruit   Mango   Macadamia nuts

Meredith Roquefort

Fresh goat's cheese   Tamarillo

Mature Cheddar   Lychee

Washed rind soft cheese

Rockmelon

Cheese Platter
Fresh and mature cheeses, usually accompanied by biscuits and dried fruit such as muscatels or figs, are the perfect way to finish a meal.

Fresh Fruit
Delicious tropical and exotic fruits are readily available year round.

What to Drink in Sydney

Semillon Chardonnay

THE DEFINITION OF a seven-course Australian meal, the old joke runs, is a meat pie and a six-pack (of beer, that is). It is true that Australians do love their beer, with a wide range of local products from which to choose. They can also select from some of the most acclaimed and best value wines in the world, produced by both local small businesses and corporate wineries. Imported wines, beers and spirits are also readily available.

SPARKLING WINE

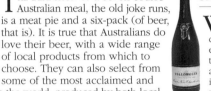

Pinot Noir Chardonnay

WITH PINOT NOIR and Chardonnay – the two classic Champagne varieties – responding well to the injection of expertise and capital from France in the 1980s, the sparkling wine shelves are stacked with premium products at affordable prices.

MAJOR WINE REGIONS

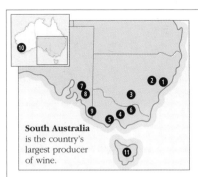

1. Hunter Valley
2. Mudgee
3. Riverina
4. Yarra Valley
5. Geelong
6. Northeastern Victoria
7. Clare Valley
8. Barossa Valley and Adelaide Hills
9. Coonawarra and Padthaway
10. Margaret River
11. Tasmania

South Australia is the country's largest producer of wine.

Grange Hermitage

WHITE WINE

Rhine Riesling   **Botrytis Semillon**

WHEN AUSTRALIANS first adopted table wines in the 1960s and 1970s, their preference was for a Moselle-type wine or Riesling and Gewürztraminer. Later, they embraced drier varieties such as Semillon, Chardonnay and Sauvignon Blanc, and showed a passion for wood-matured wines. Today, they can also choose from lesser known grapes such as Marsanne and *muscat à petits grains*. One of the most prized whites is Rosemount Estate's Roxburgh Chardonnay but, unfortunately, much of it is exported. In 1982, the De Bortolis made their first Botrytis Semillon, which started the dessert wine revolution. It remains the leader in this field.

Grape picking by hand in the Hunter Valley, north of Sydney

The Chardonnay grape lends its buttery, honeyed, rich notes to many of Australia's premium still and sparkling wines. It is regarded as the leading white wine grape worldwide.

GRAPE TYPE	BEST REGIONS	BEST PRODUCERS
Chardonnay	Barossa Valley	Penfolds, Saltram
	Hunter Valley	Petersons, Rosemount Estate, Scarborough, Tyrrell's
	Yarra Valley	Coldstream Hills, St Huberts
Riesling (Rhine Riesling)	Barossa Valley	Leo Buring, Orlando
	Clare Valley	Jud's Hill, Petaluma, Pikes
Semillon	Hunter Valley	Brokenwood, McWilliam's, Rothbury Estate
	Margaret River	Evans & Tate, Moss Wood
Semillon Chardonnay	Hunter Valley	Rosemount Estate
Semillon (dessert)	Riverina	De Bortoli
Muscat/Tokay	Northeastern Victoria	Baileys, Campbells, Chambers, Morris

Vast vineyards of Leeuwin Estate, Margaret River

RED WINE

AUSTRALIA'S BENCHMARK RED is Grange Hermitage, an invention of the late Max Schubert, in the 1950s. He preferred wines that required at least a decade's cellaring. In contrast, Wolf Blass, an architect of the current style, champions the "drink-now" approach with quickly maturing wines. Both men have created blends of varieties from different districts, with oak barrels an integral part of the process. Lighter reds, which may be served slightly chilled, have recently been introduced.

Shiraz   Pinot Noir

GRAPE TYPE	BEST REGIONS	BEST PRODUCERS
Cabernet Sauvignon	Barossa Valley	Henschke, Penfolds, Wolf Blass
	Coonawarra	Bowen Estate, Lindemans, Rouge Homme, Wynns
	Margaret River	Leeuwin Estate, Vasse Felix
Shiraz (Hermitage)	Barossa Valley	Henschke, Penfolds, Wolf Blass
	Hunter Valley	Brokenwood, Lindemans
	Margaret River	Cape Mentelle
Pinot Noir	Geelong	Bannockburn, Scotchman's Hill
	Hunter Valley	Calais, Rothbury Estate
	Yarra Valley	Coldstream Hills, Diamond Valley
Cabernet Shiraz	Barossa Valley	Penfolds, Wolf Blass
	Coonawarra	Leconfield, Lindemans, Mildara
	Margaret River	Cape Mentelle

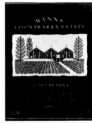
Cabernet Sauvignon from the Coonawarra district is one example of this increasingly popular quality red grape.

BEER

MOST AUSTRALIAN BEER is vat fermented, or lager, and consumed chilled. Full-strength beer has an alcohol content of around 4.8 per cent, mid-strength beers have around 3.5 per cent while "light" beers have less than 3 per cent. Traditionally heat sterilized, cold filtration is now popular. Aficionados of real ale should seek out one of the city's pub breweries. Beer is ordered by glass size and brand. A schooner is a 426 ml (15 fl oz) glass, while a middy is 284 ml (10 fl oz).

Tooheys   Cascade
Red Bitter   Premium Lager

Middy   Schooner

FRUIT JUICES

WITH THE FABULOUS fresh fruit at their disposal year round, cafés concoct an astonishing array of fruit-based non-alcoholic drinks. They include frappés of fruit pulp and juice blended with crushed ice; smoothies of fruit blended with milk or yoghurt; and pure juices, extracted from everything from carrots to watermelons.

Pear and   Banana   Strawberry
kiwi frappé   smoothie   juice

COFFEE

SYDNEY'S PASSION for coffee means that short black, macchiato, caffe latte, cappuccino and flat white (with milk) are now available at every neighbourhood café.

Flat white coffee   Caffe latte

OTHER DRINKS

TAP WATER in Sydney is fresh and clean, but local and imported bottled water is fashionable. The cola generation has graduated to alcoholic soft drinks and soda drinks. One brand, Two Dogs alcoholic lemonade, was born when a glut of lemons flooded the fruit market.

Alcoholic soda

Sydney's Best: Restaurants, Cafés and Pubs

SYDNEY IS THRICE BLESSED when it comes to eating houses. Not only are their quantity and quality staggering, but they are also remarkably good value when compared with other world centres. Even at the grandest establishment it is possible to enjoy a single course and a glass of wine for under $25. Within the areas covered by this guide, there is something for every taste, pocket and occasion. Full restaurant listings are on pages 188–93, while the more casual eating places are covered on pages 194–7.

Bennelong Restaurant
This is a grand dining experience with dramatic harbour views from the Opera House. (See p189.)

Rockpool
Asian flavours and splendid seafood are featured on the much-praised menu. (See p190.)

THE ROCKS AND
CIRCULAR QUAY

Customs House Bar
The crowds at this tiny business district haunt spill outside and under the trees. (See p196.)

BOTA
GAR
AND
DOM

CITY CENTRE

DARLING
HARBOUR

Il Edna's Table
Contemporary Australian dishes with "bush tucker" ingredients are the speciality here. (See p188.)

Silver Spring
Diners hail passing trolleys laden with dim sum *in the lunchtime ritual known as* yum cha *(to take tea) at this bustling Chinatown restaurant.* (See p191.)

Botanic Gardens Restaurant
Wisteria frames the view of the duck pond and gardens from the deck of this restaurant, which serves Mediterranean food. (See p188.)

Darley Street Thai
Considered the best Thai restaurant in Sydney, its chef was trained in Thailand and is renowned for his depth of knowledge of this complex cuisine. (See p191.)

Bayswater Brasserie
This brasserie is especially noted for its Sunday brunch. Some of the patrons have dined here daily since its 1982 opening. (See p189.)

Bar Coluzzi
Captains of industry, media types and anybody who is serious about coffee gravitate to this tiny café. (See p194.)

KINGS CROSS
AND
DARLINGHURST

PADDINGTON

Claude's
An elegant dining option for people who appreciate fine French-influenced fare, it has service to match. (See p193.)

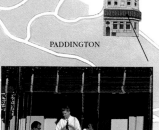

Royal Hotel
This busy pub bistro has veranda seating for watching the street life below. (See p196.)

0 metres	500
0 yards	500

Choosing a Restaurant

THE RESTAURANTS IN THIS GUIDE have been chosen for their good value or exceptional food. This chart, arranged by area and price category, highlights some of the factors which may influence your choice. Full restaurant reviews, arranged according to cuisine, are on pages 188–93. Information on cafés and pubs is given on pages 194–7.

	PAGE NUMBER	FIXED-PRICE MENU	GOOD VIEWS	TABLES OUTSIDE	VEGETARIAN SPECIALITIES	SEAFOOD SPECIALITIES	BYO	CHILDREN'S FACILITIES	LATE OPENING
THE ROCKS AND CIRCULAR QUAY									
Rock Fish Café (Seafood) $$	190				■	●		●	■
Zia Pina (Italian) $$	192								■
Sailor's Thai (Asian) $$$	191			●		●			
The Wharf Restaurant (Bistros and Brasseries) $$$	189		■	●	■	●		●	
Merrony's (Contemporary) ★ $$$$	188		■		■	●			
Bel Mondo (Italian) $$$$$	193		■	●	■				
Bennelong Restaurant (Contemporary) ★ $$$$$	189		■		■				
Rockpool (Seafood) ★ $$$$$	190					●			
CITY CENTRE									
Casa Asturiana (Mediterranean) $$	193				■	●			
Grand Taverna (Mediterranean) $$	193			●		●			
Hingara (Chinese) $$	191				■	●	■		
Edna's Table (Contemporary) ★ $$$	188			●	■	●		●	
Banc (Contemporary) ★ $$$$	188					●			
Criterion Brasserie (Middle Eastern) $$$$	193			●		●			■
Restaurant Suntory (Asian) $$$$	192	●			■	●			
Beppi's (Italian) $$$$$	192				■				■
Forty One (Contemporary) ★ $$$$$	189	●	■		■			●	
DARLING HARBOUR									
Kampung (Asian) $	191	●			■	●			
Regal (Chinese) $	190	●			■	●		●	■
Golden Century (Chinese) ★ $$	190				■	●			■
Golden Harbour (Chinese) $$	190	●			■	●			■
Malaya (Asian) $$	191	●			■	●			
Marigold (Chinese) $$	191				■	●			■
Silver Spring (Chinese) ★ $$	191				■	●			■
Jordons Seafood Restaurant (Seafood) $$$	190		■	●		●		●	■
Wokpool Darling Harbour (Asian) ★ $$$	191			●		●			
Kamogawa (Asian) $$$	192					●			
BOTANIC GARDENS AND THE DOMAIN									
Botanic Gardens Restaurant (Contemporary) ★ $$$	188		■	●	■			●	
KINGS CROSS AND DARLINGHURST									
No Names (Italian) $	192				■		■		
Fez Café (Middle Eastern) $$	193			●	■				
Fishface (Seafood) $$	190			●	■	●	■		
Oh! Calcutta! (Asian) $$	191				■		■		■
Yutaka One (Japanese) $$	191				■	●	■		
The Edge (Bistros and Brasseries) $$$	189			●	■	●		●	

Price categories for a three-course evening meal for one person including cover charge and service (but not wine):
$ under $25
$$ $25–$35
$$$ $35–$50
$$$$ $50–$70
$$$$$ Over $70

★ Means highly recommended.

FIXED-PRICE MENU
A menu of two to three courses for a set price which includes coffee but excludes wine and other drinks.

BYO
Bring your own alcohol. A small charge is often made for corkage.

LATE OPENING
Orders will still be accepted at or after 11pm.

	Price	Page Number	Fixed-Price Menu	Good Views	Tables Outside	Vegetarian Specialities	Seafood Specialities	BYO	Children's Facilities	Late Opening
Baywater Brasserie (Bistros and Brasseries) ★	$$$	189			●	●			●	●
Eleni's (Mediterranean)	$$$	193				●	●	●		●
Lime & Lemongrass (Asian)	$$$	191	●		●	●				●
Macleay Street Bistro (Bistros and Brasseries)	$$$	189			●	●		●		
Darley Street Thai (Asian) ★	$$$$	191	●			●	●			
Mezzaluna (Italian) ★	$$$$	193		●	●	●	●			
Paramount (Contemporary) ★	$$$$	188				●				
Cicada (Contemporary)	$$$$$	188			●	●				
PADDINGTON										
Lucio's (Italian)	$$$	192					●			
Bistro Moncur (French)	$$$$	193			●	●	●		●	
Claude's (French) ★	$$$$$	193	●						●	●
FURTHER AFIELD										
Frattini (Italian)	$$	192				●	●	●		
Gastronomia Chianti (Italian)	$$	192				●				
Mohr Fish (Seafood)	$$	190					●	●	●	
Sports Bard (Bistros and Brasseries)	$$	189		●		●			●	●
Veg-Italia (Italian)	$$	192				●		●		
Armstrong's Manly (Bistros and Brasseries)	$$$	189		●	●	●	●		●	
Barnaby's Riverside (Contemporary)	$$$	188	●	●	●	●	●			●
Gotham Bar & Brasserie (Bistros and Brasseries)	$$$	189		●		●	●			
Bathers Pavilion (Contemporary) ★	$$$$	188		●		●	●		●	●
Courtney's Brasserie (Bistros and Brasseries)	$$$$	189			●	●	●		●	
Darling Mills (Contemporary)	$$$$	188			●	●	●	●		●
The Pier (Seafood) ★	$$$$	190		●			●			
Ravesi's on Bondi Beach (Bistros and Brasseries)	$$$$	190		●	●	●	●			
Le Kiosk (Contemporary)	$$$$$	188		●	●	●	●		●	

CONTEMPORARY

In the 1980s, Sydney chefs started to embrace the multiculturalism of contemporary Australian society. Culinary influences from the many migrant countries were at last infiltrating the kitchens. At the same time, a movement began towards a lighter, fresher approach to both cooking and presentation. Now imaginative chefs, using superb ingredients, successfully produce delicious and unusual flavours while a few of the bolder ones experiment with formerly obscure native Australian or "bush tucker" foods.

Barnaby's Riverside

66 Phillip St, Parramatta.
[9633 3777. **]** noon–midnight Mon–Fri, 6pm–midnight Sat, noon–5pm Sun. ⬛🍴 ⬛ V ⬛ ⬛
⬛ ⬛ 🍷 AE, DC, MC, V. $$$

This colonial cottage overlooking the Parramatta River is a great setting for sampling a menu that combines Asian, Mediterranean and North African influences. Try the kangaroo fillet with plum sauce, *sashimi* of Atlantic salmon or baby squid with preserved lemon on couscous. Regular patrons always save room for the buffalo chips, whose only relationship to the animal is their chunky size.

Edna's Table

204 Clarence St. **Map** 1 B4. **[** 9267 3933. **]** noon–3pm Mon–Fri, 6–10pm Tue–Sat. V ⬛ ⬛ ⬛ 🍷 ★ 🍷 AE, DC, MC, V. $$$

Restaurant manager Jennice Kersh and her chef brother, Raymond, are ever-so-gently converting even the most conservative palates to the tastes of the outback with the menu they offer in this stylish space right in the heart of the city. Aboriginal art on the walls sets the scene for dishes such as ocean trout wrapped in ky choy and paperbark, and served with bush tomato *aïoli*. Aboriginal dancers and musicians perform here occasionally.

Bathers Pavilion

4 The Esplanade, Balmoral. **[** 9968 1133. **]** noon–3pm Mon–Fri, 9am–3pm Sat & Sun, 6:30pm–midnight daily. ⬛🍴 ⬛ V ⬛ ⬛ 🍷 ★ ⬛
AE, DC, MC, V, JCB. $$$$

The setting of this old Spanish-Mission-style beach pavilion in parkland at Balmoral Beach *(see pp54–5)* is quite magical, with its views across Middle and North Harbours to the open sea. The furniture may look a little faded, but the food is always fresh and inventively prepared in a variety

of ethnic styles. In the more casual and laid-back Refreshment Room, you can order wine by the glass, cakes, coffee and herbal teas.

Botanic Gardens Restaurant

Royal Botanic Gardens, Mrs Macquaries Rd. **Map** 2 D4. **[** 9241 2419.
] noon–2:30pm daily. ⬛ V ⬛
⬛ ⬛ ★ 🍷 AE, DC, MC, V.
$$$$

The wisteria-covered balcony looks out over the lovely Royal Botanic Gardens *(see pp104–5)* in this lunchtime venue, where the food has a Mediterranean accent. The combination of fine location and fine food is not lost on the business people from nearby Macquarie Street. If you plan to stop by when visiting the gardens, be sure to book ahead to ensure a table.

Darling Mills

134 Glebe Point Rd, Glebe. **Map** 3 A4.
[9660 5666. **]** noon–3pm Wed–Fri, 6–11pm Mon–Sat, 6–10pm Sun. ⬛ Sun–Thu. V ⬛ ⬛ ⬛ 🍷 🍷
🍷 AE, DC, MC, V. $$$$

This spacious sandstone building, completed in 1857 by Colonial Architect Edmund Blacket, was restored in the 1970s as a restaurant. A rooftop greenhouse means that the kitchen can harvest the freshest possible produce. Naturally the house salad should not be missed, but salmon, smoked on the premises, is another speciality.

Merrony's

2 Albert St, Circular Quay.
Map 1 C3. **[** 9247 9323. **]** noon–2:30pm Mon–Fri, 5:45–11pm Mon–Sat. V ⬛ ⬛ ⬛ 🍷 🍷 ★
🍷 AE, DC, MC, V. $$$$

Chef Paul Merrony worked his way through the Michelin stars of France and England before bringing his classical French training home. At this restaurant, which overlooks Circular Quay and the passing trains, the menu changes with the marketplace and has a strongly French influence.
Duck *confit* with sorrel and fried parsley, grilled sirloin with great chips, and prawn or seafood bisque are near constants, all served with a very impressive range of Australian wines. A good place for a delicious supper after the opera.

Paramount

73 Macleay St, Potts Point. **Map** 2 E5.
[9358 1652. **]** 6:30–11pm daily.
V ⬛ ⬛ 🍷 ★ 🍷 AE, DC, MC, V.
$$$$

The interior of this restaurant has been described as the sensuous

equivalent of sitting in a mother-of-pearl shell. Certainly, the moulded fibreglass interior, glass bar and white lighting create an impressive backdrop for the complex flavours of the refined fare the chef Chris Manfield dishes up. The menu changes monthly, as does the wine list, but regulars find it hard to pass up the fabulous moulded ice desserts made from fruits in season. In fact, Paramount is accustomed to welcoming guests just for their delicious desserts.

Bennelong Restaurant

Sydney Opera House, Bennelong Point. **Map** 1 C2. **[** 9250 7578.
] 5:30–11pm Mon–Sat. V
⬛ on request. ⬛ ⬛ ⬛ 🍷 ★
🍷 AE, DC, MC, V, JCB.
$$$$

Located in one of the shells of the Sydney Opera House *(see pp74–7)*, this restaurant has arguably the best location in Sydney, with its views across Circular Quay and the harbour. Dining here is almost as much of a drama as the daily performances at the nearby theatres. The serious dining area is at the lower end of the space with a mezzanine crustacea and oyster bar separating it from another bar on the top level. The main dining area has a brasserie-style menu ranging from seafood to more traditional roasts. On weekends, brunch is served for those seeking serious sustainance, with oysters, baked eggs, omelettes and waffles.

Banc

53 Martin Place. **Map** 1 B4. **[** 9233 5300. **]** noon–2:30pm Mon–Fri, 6–10:30pm Mon–Sat. ⬛ 🍷 🍷 ★
🍷 AE, DC, MC, V. $$$$$

Situated on the ground floor of a former bank, this restaurant retains many of the building's original Art Deco features and atmosphere – marble pillars, soaring ceilings and floor-to-ceiling windows. The fine food and remarkably unstuffy but excellent service match the luxurious surroundings without being intimidating. The unashamedly French-influenced menu is full of flavour and only the finest fresh produce is used. Truffles, duck confit, game and seafood all feature. Although lunch here may well seem the preserve of the business-suited diner, there is a sound reason the city's executives are drawn to Banc – the food.

Cicada

29 Challis Ave, Potts Point. **Map** 2 E4.
[9358 1255. **]** noon–2:30pm Wed–Fri, 6:30–10pm Mon–Sat.
V ⬛ ⬛ ⬛ 🍷 AE, DC, MC, V.
$$$$$

Robust Mediterranean and Middle Eastern flavours are given a subtle interpretation in this very popular restaurant, with its vine-covered terrace for outdoor eating. The menu changes seasonally, but the *escalivada* (aubergine) terrine with *tapenade* and black olive bread is a perennial favourite. There is an excellent wine list.

Forty One

Level 41, Chifley Tower, Chifley Square. **Map** 1 B4. (9221 2500. (noon–2pm Sun–Fri, 6:30–10:30pm Mon–Sat. ¶Ø V & ▤ ▨ ⚡ ★ ⚡ AE, DC, MC, V. $$$$$$

With impressive vistas of the city and Sydney Harbour, the view from this elegant establishment invites superlatives. So does the menu, which is French-based with occasional Asian influences. The crown roast of hare is a great treat when available and even the restaurant's most soigné clientele cannot resist the "variations on a theme", a chance to sample each of about five delectable desserts.

Le Kiosk

1 Marine Parade, Shelly Beach, Manly. (9977 4122. (noon–2:30pm Mon–Fri, noon–3pm Sat, noon–3:30pm Sun, 6:30–9pm Mon–Thu, 6:30–9:30pm Fri, 6:30–10pm Sat, 7–9pm Sun. V & ▤ ▨ ⚡ ¶ ⚡ AE, DC, MC, V. $$$$$

It would be hard to find a more pleasant way to punctuate a day at beachside Manly *(see p133)* than by strolling along the waterfront walkway to lunch in this charming sandstone cottage with outdoor tables set in a subtropical garden. Try the excellent seafood platter for two and a crisp white wine from the all-Australian list. Sunday breakfast is the full English extravaganza, buffet-style, starting with a glass of chilled sparkling wine.

BISTROS AND BRASSERIES

Sydney's dining-out pattern has changed in recent years, and there is now a demand for restaurants where people can drop in for just one dish – and perhaps a glass of house wine. Often styled along the lines of a French bistro or brasserie, these places are generally open throughout the day and evening. Diners can expect good food which has been imaginatively prepared, moderate prices and a bright and casual atmosphere. The Kings Cross and Darlinghurst areas in particular have a large concentration.

Armstrong's Manly

Manly Wharf, Manly. (9976 3835. (noon–9:30pm Sun–Thu, noon–10pm Fri & Sat. ¶ V & ▤ ▨ ⚡ AE, DC, MC, V, JCB. $$$

The harbour views from the Manly ferry wharf, a relaxed atmosphere and the best of produce with an emphasis on superb seafood make this a quintessential Sydney dining experience. You may order a full three-course meal with wine – the fish and chips here are second to none – a substantial snack, such as the mountainous Armstrong's Burger, or just coffee and a slice of cake. All will be excellent.

The Edge

60 Riley St, Darlinghurst. **Map** 5 A1. (9360 1372. (noon–11pm daily. ¶ V ▤ ▨ ⚡ ⚡ AE, DC, MC, V. $$$

The setting, with its wooden floors and marble bars, may seem austere, but 1930s French posters, friendly service and the almost clubby relationship between the staff and regulars lighten the atmosphere. With extensive vegetarian options, this is a place meat eaters can bring vegetarian friends. The pizzas from the wood-fired ovens are delicious and have imaginative toppings.

Gotham Bar & Brasserie

135 Rowntree St, Balmain. (9555 8008. (noon–3pm daily, 6–10pm Sun–Thu, 6–11pm Fri & Sat. ¶ V & limited. ▤ ▨ ⚡ ⚡ AE, MC, V. $$$

Friendly service from staff who know their food and wine is the hallmark of this former pub, built in 1863, and restored to its original condition. The atmosphere in the main dining room is buzzy, but there are three quieter rooms available with views towards the Harbour Bridge. The menu encompasses Mediterranean, Asian and Creole with a classical French finish. On weekends, people willingly queue for the brunch.

Macleay Street Bistro

73a Macleay St, Potts Point. **Map** 2 E5. (9358 4891. (noon–3pm Fri–Sun, 6–11pm daily. ¶ V ▤ ⚡ AE, DC, MC, V. $$$

The French-style menu sits quite comfortably with the former bohemian tradition of Kings Cross. Those who are particular about their steak tartare and brandade of salt cod all swear by the versions served here. Frequently nominated as Sydney's best BYO, this place is busy so make sure you get there early on Fridays and at weekends as they do not take bookings.

Sports Bard

32 Campbell Parade, Bondi Beach. (9130 4582. (5pm–midnight Mon–Fri, 10am–midnight Sat. ¶ V ▤ ▨ ⚡ ⚡ AE, MC, V. $$$

Somehow this upbeat spot on the southern end of Sydney's most famous beach *(see p137)* manages to hold as much appeal for families as it does for trendy young couples. Perhaps it is the house special risottos, or the decadent desserts, or the breakfast of poached egg, smoked salmon and spinach on a potato pancake. Maybe it is the pool room out the back. Whatever the attraction, lots of people want to share it, so be prepared to wait for a table at the weekend.

The Wharf Restaurant

Pier 4, Hickson Rd, Millers Point. **Map** 1 A1. (9250 1761. (noon–3pm Mon–Sat, 6–10:30pm Mon–Sat. V & phone beforehand. ▤ ▨ ⚡ AE, DC, MC, V. $$$

The perfect venue for a meal either before or after a performance, this restaurant, on the wharf that's home to the Sydney Theatre Company *(see p69)*, is worth a visit in its own right. It has dress-circle views of the harbour and the Sydney Harbour Bridge – try an outdoor table – and good simple fare, such as pasta, risotto and seafood. There is also 'fast' food for theatre-goers.

Bayswater Brasserie

32 Bayswater Rd, Potts Point. **Map** 5 B1. (9357 2749. (noon–midnight Mon–Sat. V ▤ ▨ ⚡ ★ ⚡ AE, DC, MC, V, JCB. $$$$

The Thai chicken curry has been everyone's favourite since 1982, but the chef also recommends the river rock oysters or Pacific oysters from Tasmania's clear waters, the succulent Illabo lamb from the west of New South Wales, and the South Australian squid with black ink pasta. The bread, pastries and ice cream, all made on the premises, are superb, and Sunday brunch has become an institution.

Courtney's Brasserie

2 Horwood Pl, Parramatta. (9635 3288. (noon–10:30pm Mon–Fri, 6–10:30pm Sat. ¶ V ▤ ▨ ⚡ ⚡ AE, DC, MC, V. $$$

This convict-brick building first opened its doors in 1830 as a soldiers' mess. Located in the business centre of Sydney's west, this spot tends to have a loyal clientele. It is well worth a visit during or after a busy day touring Parramatta's many historic buildings *(see p138–9)*.

For key to symbols *see p291*

Ravesi's on Bondi Beach

Cnr Campbell Parade & Hall St, Bondi Beach. **☎** 9365 4422. **◯** 7:30am–10pm Mon–Fri, 7:30am–10:30pm Sat & Sun. **V ⅋ ⯐ ▩ ⮹ 𝄐** AE, DC, MC, V. **$$$$**

Sit on the balcony to catch the sea breeze, and uninterrupted views of the surf and beach. The house special, fish and chips with *aïoli*, the tuna with avocado, corn and Spanish onion salsa, and the mango brûlée are delicious. Breakfast is a speciality; snacks served all day.

SEAFOOD

Sydney is blessed when it comes to seafood – not only with abundance, but also with quality and freshness *(see p202)*. Most restaurants have daily seafood specials and a handful have exclusively seafood menus. The traditional purveyors of fish and chips in the city are the Doyle family – their Watsons Bay beachfront establishment is almost an institution *(see p136)*. They also have branches at Circular Quay and the Sydney Fish Market *(see p131)*.

Fishface

132 Darlinghurst Rd, Darlinghurst. **Map** 5 B1. **☎** 9332 4803. **◯** noon–3pm Sun, 6–11pm Mon–Sat, 6–10pm Sun. **⯐ V ▤ ⮹** AE, DC, MC, V. **$$**

The menu changes daily in this tiny café, where patrons sit on bar stools at high tables to eat some of the best-value seafood on offer. Seafood risotto is always popular as, of course, is the fish of the day. You cannot make a reservation, but staff will collect diners from the bar of the nearby hotel when a table becomes available.

Mohr Fish

202 Devonshire St, Surry Hills. **☎** 9318 1326. **◯** 10am–10pm daily. **⯐ ⑩ ⯐ $$**

Regulars happily repair to the bar of the pub across the road to wait for one of the four tables at this superior seafood café which also does a roaring takeaway trade. Fish of the day in beer batter and bouillabaisse are firm favourites.

Rock Fish Café

14 Loftus St. **Map** 1 B3. **☎** 9252 3114. **◯** noon–3pm Mon–Fri, 6pm–late Mon–Fri. **V ⅋ ⮹ 𝄐** AE, DC, MC, V. **$$**

The city's Gallipoli Club for war veterans may seem an unlikely location for this bustling seafood bistro, but the suits from the city know good value and brisk service when they find it and always keep the place packed at lunchtime. The blackboard menu changes often, but green chilli curry and Parmesan-crumbed sardines are frequently chalked up because of demand.

Jordons Seafood Restaurant

Harbourside Festival Marketplace, Darling Harbour. **Map** 3 C2. **☎** 9281 3711. **◯** noon–3pm Mon–Fri, 6–10pm Sun–Fri, noon–11pm Sat. **⯐ ⅋ ⯐ ▩ 𝄐** AE, DC, MC, V, JCB. **$$$**

"Seafood as fresh as this morning" the menu proclaims at this venue overlooking Darling Harbour *(see pp90–101)*. Sushi, *sashimi* and char-grilled baby octopus sit alongside deep-fried snapper and salmon. The indecisive can opt for the deluxe platter for two, a hot and cold selection of the market's best.

The Pier

594 New South Head Rd, Rose Bay. **☎** 9327 6561. **◯** noon–3pm daily, 6–10pm Mon–Sat, 6–9pm Sun. **▤ ⯐ ★ 𝄐** AE, DC, MC, V. **$$$$**

An elegant harbourside restaurant where the menu, with its Asian and Mediterranean influences, is almost as impressive as the stunning water views. Simplicity is the keynote – from classic fish and chips to a whole John Dory baked with ginger, chilli and green onions. Dine here on a sunny day and you will gain an inkling of why some fervently patriotic T-shirts proclaim Sydney the "best address on earth".

Rockpool

107 George St, The Rocks. **Map** 1 B3. **☎** 9252 1888. **◯** noon–2:30pm Mon–Fri, 6–11pm Mon–Sat. **▤ ⯐ ⯐ ★ 𝄐** AE, DC, MC, V. **$$$$$**

The modish lounge bar at the front of the restaurant sets the scene for seriously good food with a particular emphasis on Asian-influenced seafood. Although the menu is changed seasonally, herb- and spice-encrusted tuna steaks and John Dory in Indian pastry with cardamom sauce are regulars. It is said Sydney's first taste of sticky date tart took place here and many will claim it is still the best.

CHINESE

Sydney's Chinatown spreads from Darling Harbour to Central Railway Station, but Chinese restaurants can be found throughout the city and suburbs. Today, hot and spicy food from the western province of Sichuan, delicate Shanghai-style dishes and Peking-style food are all available, but Cantonese cuisine remains the dominant tradition. *Yum cha (dim sum)*, the brunch-type dumplings and snacks enjoyed with tea, is among the most reasonably priced dining in town.

Golden Century

393–399 Sussex St. **Map** 4 E4. **☎** 9212 3901. **◯** noon–4am daily. **V ▤ ⯐ ★ 𝄐** AE, DC, MC, V, JCB. **$$**

Eight tanks brimming with live scallops, pippies, prawns, lobster, abalone, King Island crab, parrot fish, coral trout, perch and barramundi tell the story of this excellent Cantonese restaurant. Customers usually select their dinner from the tank then discuss with the waiter how it should be prepared. Shift workers, hotel staff, taxi drivers, night owls and jet-lagged overseas visitors also appreciate the Golden Century because it is one of the few spots in the city where they can be sure of a fine meal at 3am.

Regal

347 Sussex St. **Map** 4 E3. **☎** 9261 8988. **◯** 10am–3pm daily, 5:30pm–midnight daily. **⑩ ⯐ V ⅋ ▤ ⯐ 𝄐** AE, DC, MC, V, JCB. **$**

The glittering chandeliers, private rooms downstairs, people queueing for tables and waiters dashing everywhere with *dim sum*-laden trolleys serve to make this venue reminiscent of the *yum cha* palaces of Hong Kong. The pace is somewhat gentler at dinner. Cantonese seafood is the star and King Island crab is available for those who fancy a real indulgence. Best ordered by groups of six or eight people, these massive crustaceans – they start at about 5 kg (11 lb) – are served in several appetizing guises.

Golden Harbour

31–33 Dixon St. **Map** 4 D3. **☎** 9212 5987. **◯** 10am–4pm Mon–Fri, 9am–4pm Sat & Sun, 5:30–11pm Sun–Thu, 5:30pm–1am Fri & Sat. **V ▤ ⯐ 𝄐** AE, DC, MC, V, JCB. **$$**

On Sundays, the queues for *yum cha* wind out into Dixon Street. Regulars say it is worth the wait for the splendid dumplings filled with snowpea leaves or garlic chives, "silky noodles" (pan-fried rice noodles) or pippies in black bean sauce. In the evenings, the Cantonese menu emphasizes seafood fresh from the tanks with specials such ast king prawns steamed whole with garlic, squid in spicy salt and curried mud crab.

Hingara

82 Dixon Street. **Map** 4 D3. ☎ *9212 2169.* 🕐 *9:30am–3pm, 5–9:30pm Sun–Thu, 10am–3pm, 5–10:30pm Fri & Sat.* 🍾 [V] 💳 *AE, MC, V.* $$

The décor is rather old-fashioned and casual in this Chinatown restaurant, but this only reflects the unpretentious and simple nature of the menu. Expect authentic, consistently tasty Chinese cuisine here, with seafood a particular speciality. Start with the crispy spring rolls and then try the fried fish with corn sauce. Bring your own wine with you, but expect to pay a small corkage charge.

Marigold

299–305 Sussex St. **Map** 4 D3. ☎ *9264 6744.* 🕐 *10am–3pm daily, 5:30–11:30pm daily.* [V] ▤ 💳 *AE, DC, MC, V, JCB.* $$

This restaurant is the original of a triumvirate that includes the Marigold Citymark and the Regal. It was something of an innovator on the Chinatown landscape when it was opened in the early 1980s, with its daily *yum cha* and seafood taken live from the tanks. Although it is now more of a fixture, there is still an inclination to set the pace and try out new ingredients, such as crocodile meat (served either with chilli or on a sizzling plate with satay sauce).

Silver Spring

1st Floor, Sydney Central, Cnr Hay & Pitt Sts. **Map** 4 E4. ☎ *9211 2232.* 🕐 *10am–3pm Mon–Fri, 9am–3pm Sat & Sun, 5–11pm daily.* [V] ♿ ▤ 🚭 ★ 💳 *AE, DC, MC, V, JCB.* $$

Waiters communicate by walkie-talkies when they are busy turning over the tables to new diners at this multi-roomed upstairs restaurant. On an average Saturday or Sunday morning, *yum cha* will be served to 1,500 people. The scene is more sedate at night, with Cantonese specialities such as barbecued suckling pig, and shark's fin soup.

OTHER ASIAN

The growing number of Korean, Thai, Japanese, Indonesian, Indian, Vietnamese and Malaysian restaurants reflects the successive waves of migration into Australia. The restaurants here are all highly recommended, but you will also find authentic fare in most of the many population centres, such as Thai and Vietnamese in Marrickville and Cabramatta *(see pp40–43)*, Malay and Indonesian in Randwick and Korean in Campsie.

Kampung

Royal Garden International Hotel, 431–439 Pitt St. **Map** 4 E4. ☎ *9281 6999.* 🕐 *noon–2:30pm daily, 6–10pm daily.* 🍴 [V] ♿ ▤ 🚭 💳 *AE, DC, MC, V, JCB.* $

This second-floor hotel restaurant in the heart of Chinatown serves predominantly Malaysian cuisine. There are *halal* and vegetarian dishes, along with the popular house special of chilli crab, beef *rendang, nasi lemak, nasi goreng* and *laksa.* A special menu for children is also available.

Malaya

761 George St. **Map** 4 E5. ☎ *9211 0946.* 🕐 *noon–3pm Mon–Fri, 5:30–10pm Mon–Sat.* 🍴 [V] ♿ ▤ 🚭 💳 *AE, DC, MC, V.* $$

Located a short distance from three major media offices and close to Central Railway Station, this bustling two-level restaurant has, for more than 30 years, served as an alternative staff canteen for Sydney's journalists. The menu includes Indonesian, Malaysian, Sichuan, Singaporean and *halal* dishes, along with the ever-popular *laksas, sambals* and *rendang.*

Oh! Calcutta!

251 Victoria St, Darlinghurst. **Map** 5 B2. ☎ *9360 3650.* 🕐 *noon–4pm Fri, 6–midnight daily.* 🍾 [V] ▤ 🚭 💳 *AE, MC, V.* $$

There are no Indian clichés in this modern, sparsely decorated restaurant with its bentwood chairs, stainless steel fittings, white linen and stylish sandstone sculptures. The menu here is similarly non-conformist and changes constantly. It spans the entire subcontinent from Pakistan and Afghanistan to Sri Lanka and India. Afghani *mantu* or steamed dumplings filled with ground lamb and celery are a very popular dish, while Goan mussels with chilli and coriander are also recommended if available.

Yutaka One

200 Crown St, Darlinghurst. **Map** 5 A1. ☎ *9361 3818.* 🕐 *noon–2pm Mon–Fri, 6–10:30pm Mon–Sat, 6–10pm Sun.* 🍾 [V] ▤ 💳 *AE, MC, V.* $$

Do not be fooled by the modest entrance, vinyl chairs and plastic tablecloths, the food served here is freshly prepared and tasty. Yutaka One and its sister establishment just along the road are popular with the city's Japanese residents, as well as with Japanese travellers looking for a less expensive meal. All the standards from miso soup to sushi are on the menu, and the service is brisk and friendly.

Wockpool Darling Harbour

Panasonic Imax Theatre, Southern Promenade, Darling Harbour. **Map** 4 D3. ☎ *9368 2911.* 🕐 *noon–3pm daily, 6–10pm Sun–Thu, 6–11pm Fri & Sat.* [V] ♿ ☀ 🍸 🚭 ★ 💳 *AE, DC, MC, V.* $$$

Superb seafood, Malaysian *laksas,* Vietnamese *phos* and other noodle dishes are on the menu at nigth for Imax theatre-goers at the laid-back little brother of the Rockpool restaurant *(see p190).* Here, chef Neil Perry offers the rustic dishes he cannot serve at the other more sophisticated venue.

Lime & Lemongrass

42 Kellett St, Potts Point. **Map** 5 B1. ☎ *9358 5577.* 🕐 *6:30–11pm Mon–Thu & Sun, 6:30–11:30pm Fri & Sat.* 🍴 [V] ▤ 🍸 💳 *AE, DC, MC, V.* $$$

Sunthree Pancharoen has been a leader of Sydney's Thai revolution since the early 1980s. She now spreads the word from this smart terrace house with balcony and courtyard seating in the heart of the Kings Cross district. Sunthree's menu is drawn from all over Thailand. Special dishes are the tapioca balls with peanuts and vegetable pickles and freshly steamed spring rolls, packed with cucumber, sprouts, eggs and Chinese sausage, served with tamarind sauce.

Sailor's Thai

106 George St, The Rocks. **Map** 1 B2. ☎ *9251 2466.* 🕐 *noon–2pm Mon–Fri, 6–10pm Mon–Sat.* **Noodle Bar** 🕐 *noon–8pm daily.* 🍸 🚭 💳 *AE, DC, MC, V.* $$$

This restaurant located in the Sailors' Home in the heart of The Rocks has a canteen noodle bar with one long communal dining table upstairs where your neighbour may be an actress or a judge. An offshoot of the renowned Darley Street Thai, it serves great Thai food at less expensive prices. The chef learnt his trade from a Bangkok matriarch and the food he offers here, at prices more suited to a budget, is Thai cuisine of a standard that would certainly be a cut above most.

Darley Street Thai

30 Bayswater Rd, Potts Point. **Map** 5 B1. ☎ *9358 6530.* 🕐 *6:30–10:30pm Mon–Thu, 6:30–11pm Fri & Sat, 6:30–10pm Sun.* 🍴 [V] ♿ *limited.* 🚭 ★ 💳 *AE, DC, MC, V.* $$$$

Even when the names are familiar, the dishes are head and shoulders above their peers at this respected establishment. The chef David Thompson is well known for the research he has done into the Thai table using centuries-old cookbooks. His dishes are much more complicated than those normally served at Thai restaurants. The chef also pays scant regard to the cost of the labour involved. The coconut cream, for example, takes three days to prepare. The water is first smoked using a jasmine candle, then infused with flowers before being combined with fresh coconut flesh. The cost of such indulgence may make this restaurant more expensive than the average Thai eatery, but the resulting excellence is definitely worth every cent.

Kamogawa

1st Floor, 177 Sussex St. **Map** 1 A5.
(9299 5533. **)** 6–10:30pm
daily. 🍴 🗐 *AE, DC, MC, V, JCB.*
$$$$$

Stately *kaiseki* menus, in which the presentation is almost as important as the food, range from seven to 12 courses in this elegant establishment. Ten private *tatami* rooms, where you sit on the floor, cater for groups of two to 20. With a large Japanese clientele, lobster and *awabi* (abalone) *sashimi* are popular choices from the main dining room's extensive à la carte menu.

Restaurant Suntory

529 Kent St. **Map** 4 E3. **(** 9267 2900.
) noon–2pm Mon–Fri, 6:30–10pm
Mon–Sat, 6–9pm Sun. 🍴🐟🖥🗐
🗐 *AE, DC, MC, V, JCB.* $$$$

Here, the outlook onto a tranquil Japanese garden provides a welcome break from the bustle out on the city streets. The restaurant has a *teppanyaki* (barbecue at table) room, an à la carte section and four *tatami* rooms for groups of four to 16. *Shabu shabu* and *suki-yaki* are firm favourites, along with the hot rock barbecue which features beef specially selected from a Victorian producer.

ITALIAN

Italians were prominent among postwar migrants to Australia and one of their legacies has been the large number of Italian eateries to be found all over Sydney. They range from the cheap and cheerful spaghetti houses of Darlinghurst to the home-style pizza, pasta and veal-based menus found in the restaurants of the inner western suburb of Leichhardt, Sydney's Little Italy. A growing number of city-smart dining rooms also present the refined fare and suave service of Italy's northern regions.

No Names

1st Floor, 81 Stanley St, Darlinghurst.
Map 5 A1. **(** 9360 4711.
) noon–2:30pm daily, 6–10pm
daily. 🍴 🗙 🖥 $

Despite there being no sign, you will have little trouble finding this spaghetti canteen. Just look for the queue on the stairs waiting for some of the best-value food in town. A few grills and *gelati* have been added to the basic spaghetti *bolognese* or *napoletana* choice, but little else has altered – the bread and cordial are still free. Be prepared to share a table if you are in a hurry.

Frattini

122 Marion St, Leichhardt.
(9569 2997. **)** noon–3pm
Mon–Fri & Sun, 6–10pm Mon–Sat,
6–9:30pm Sun. 🍴🐟🗙🖥🖥
🗐 *AE, DC, MC, V.* $$

One of the outstanding restaurants in Sydney's Little Italy, this trattoria's approach could not be further removed from many of its neighbours, who still seem to be caught in a spag-bol-and-garlic-bread time warp. The salmon *carpaccio* is always popular, as are *neonata* (fritters of New Zealand whitebait) and asparagus with Parmesan. Try to leave room for mascarpone-filled crêpes with liqueur-poached strawberries. There never seems to be a quiet day here, so be sure to book well in advance.

Gastronomia Chianti

444 Elizabeth St, Surry Hills. **Map** 4 E5.
(9319 4748. **)** 10:30am–4pm
Mon–Fri, 6–10:30pm Fri. 🖥 🖥
🗐 *AE, DC, MC, V.* $$

Doreen Orsatti has been a part of the Surry Hills *(see p130)* scene since she and her late husband, Francesco, opened Chianti in 1955. In the early 1990s, she remodelled her place as a delicatessen, café and restaurant. Patrons range from local workers stocking up on their salami or *antipasti*, footsore bargain shoppers grabbing a filled *focaccia* and coffee while touring the area's factory outlets to people simply in search of three imaginative courses. The mushroom risotto is a menu constant, and there will always be chunky Italian sausages, grilled liver, fish and pasta specials.

Veg-Italia

353-355 Crown St, Surry Hills. **Map** 5
A3. **(** 9360 5349. **)** noon–11pm
daily. 🗙 🖥 🗐 *AE, DC, MC, V.* $$

The contemporary décor of this restaurant, with its tiled floor, black metal chairs and large windows, attracts an avant-garde crowd of locals, and makes it a fun and

trendy place to eat. Specialities include gnocchi sautéed in garlic, with mushrooms and tomatoes and *tortelloti* – cheese ravioli with pinenuts, capsicum and chiles.

Zia Pina

93 George St, The Rocks. **Map** 1 B3.
(9247 2255. **)** noon–3pm daily,
5–9pm Sun & Mon, 5–10:30pm
Tue–Thu, 5–11:30pm Fri & Sat. 🗐
AE, DC, MC, V. $$

This tiny Italian restaurant is always busy, and has become one of the most popular places to eat in the area. The wooden floor and red and white checked tablecloths give it a traditional, rustic feel. The menu is, as you would expect, predominately pizza and pasta. The pizzas come in two sizes, the large being very large, and have a wide variety of toppings from which to choose. The pasta dishes include ravioli and canneloni accompanied by one of six different sauces. Expect simple but tasty food.

Lucio's

47 Windsor St, Paddington. **Map** 6 D3.
(9380 5996. **)** 12:30–3pm Mon–
Sat, 6:30–11pm Mon–Sat. 🖥
🍴 🗐 *AE, DC, MC, V.* $$$

Phone a day ahead and order *pesce al sale* (fish baked in a rock salt mould) at this institution famed for the consistency of its up-market northern Italian menu. It is also known for the professionalism of its waiting staff, who are accustomed to dealing with the barons of industry. There are always several varieties of ravioli available and the grilled Tasmanian salmon is another constant. Regulars say you should not pass up the *gamberi e fagioli* (prawns, cannellini beans and caviar with olive oil).

Mezzaluna

123 Victoria St, Potts Point. **Map** 2 E5.
(9357 1988. **)** noon–3pm Tue–
Fri & Sun, 6–11pm Tue–Sat, 6–10pm
Sun. 🖥 🖥 🍳 🍴 ★ 🗐 *AE,
DC, MC, V, JCB.* $$$$

The chance to dine here should not be missed: the finest of northern Italian cuisine, excellent wines and wonderful views of the city skyline from the covered terrace. This is the perfect place to eat on a balmy summer's evening or sunny winter's day. Norma and Marc Polese (wife and son of the owner of Beppi's) are in charge in these modernized twin terrace houses, producing the almost faultless cuisine for which Sydney is becoming known.

Bel Mondo

Level 3, Argyle Department Store.
12–24 Argyle St, The Rocks. **Map** 1 B2.

C *9241 3700.* ○ *noon–2:30pm Mon–Fri, noon–midnight Sun, 6:30–10:30pm Mon–Thu, 6:30–11pm Fri & Sat.* **V** 目 目 ﹏ ﹏ 🅿 ★ 🅲 *AE, DC, MC, V.* ⑤⑤⑤⑤⑤

Chef Stefano Manfredi has deemed his establishment a "true Italian/Australian restaurant". It serves northern Italian cuisine prepared using quality local produce. The menu, combined with the views across Circular Quay to the Opera House, provides one of the best dining experiences in the city. Wines by the glass and *antipasti* are served all day at the Anti bar, while the more formal dining area opens for lunch and dinner.

Beppi's

Cnr Stanley & Young Sts, Darlinghurst. **Map** 4 F3. **C** *9360 4558.* ○ *noon–3:30pm Mon–Fri, 6pm–late Mon–Sat.* **V** 🅑 目 目 🅿 *AE, DC, MC, V, JCB.* ⑤⑤⑤⑤⑤

In 1956, when Beppi Polese took over a humble Yugoslav café, he gradually set about introducing the Italian dishes that would transform it into a Sydney landmark. In those days, Beppi would get up to catch the low tide and harvest mussels from the pylons of the then wooden Spit Bridge. Today, mussels are readily available at the markets, but Beppi is still known as a man who will go to the most extraordinary lengths to give his diners the best. His cellar is quite exemplary and the outstanding wine list is supplemented by a selected vintage wine list which offers Australian reds dating back to 1952. A visit to this temple of gastronomy is a real treat for anyone who is serious about good food, wine and service.

FRENCH

These days, Sydney's dining public is notoriously fickle, embracing Vietnamese noodle dishes one day and Moroccan *tagines* the next. Yet the French tradition just seems to go on forever, and even the most ardent supporters of the best contemporary Australian cooking probably have a firm grounding in classical French cuisine. Francophiles are lucky, though, as the city has a number of purists who use wonderful fresh produce to provide excellent French fare.

Bistro Moncur

Woollahra Hotel, 116 Queen St, Woollahra. **Map** 6 E4. **C** *9363 2782.* ○ *noon–3pm Tue–Sun, 6–10:30pm Tue–Sat, 6–9pm Sun.* 🅧 **V** 目 ﹏ 🅲 *AE, DC, MC, V.* ⑤⑤⑤⑤

Damien Pignolet uses the term *habitué* (regular) to describe the clientele he aims to attract to his bistro. One wall is covered by an amusing Michael Fitzjames mural of people who like to lunch. However, the absence of "attitude" and, more importantly, food that you would consider yourself lucky to find in a classic Parisian bistro have helped Pignolet achieve his goal. Officially, you cannot book to enjoy the *tripes Lyonnaise*, classic Provençal fish soup and *entrecôte café de Paris*, but if you phone ahead a table will usually be held for 30 minutes.

Claude's

10 Oxford St, Woollahra. **Map** 6 D4. **C** *9331 2325.* ○ *7:30–9:30p,m Tue–Sat.* 🍴🅑 🅧 目 ﹏ ★ 🅲 *AE, MC, V.* ⑤⑤⑤⑤⑤

Discretion and fine service are the bywords in this dining room, which has gained its renown from the skills of the chef Tim Pak Poy. The wine you bring will be treated with the same degree of reverence accorded the preparation of the superlative dishes and you may possibly feel you have accidentally joined a very special gathering of a very serious epicurean society.

MEDITERRANEAN AND MIDDLE EASTERN

The bold flavours and relaxed style of the Mediterranean fit well with Sydney's climate, waterfront and outdoor lifestyle. The readily available prime-quality seafood also lends itself easily to Greek and Spanish cuisine. For decades, the city's Little Lebanon has been at the western end of Cleveland Street in Surry Hills *(see p130)*, where diners were introduced to the delights of the *meze* platter of appetizers, grilled meats and sausages or meatballs for main courses, and pastry desserts rich in honey and nuts.

Casa Asturiana

77 Liverpool St. **Map** 4 E3. **C** *9264 1010.* ○ *noon–3pm Tue–Fri & Sun, 5:30–10:45pm daily.* **V** 🅑 *limited.* 目 🅲 *AE, DC, MC, V.* ⑤⑤

With more than 20 choices, *tapas*, or tasting portions, are the main attraction in this two-storey former warehouse which has a traditional Castilian ground floor and a modernist space with marble bar above. It is family run, and the recipes are reworkings of well-known northern favourites such as *paella*, squid cooked in its own ink and stuffed sardine fillets. There are *sangría*, Asturian cider and Tio Pepe to wash it all down and *casadiellas* or little walnut pastries to go with stiff black coffee and "cognac".

Fez Café

247 Victoria St, Darlinghurst. **Map** 5 B1. **C** *9360 9581.* ○ *7am–10:30pm Mon–Fri, 8am–10:30pm Sat & Sun.* 🅧 **V** ﹏ ﹏ ⑤⑤

On weekends, patrons line up to sip thick coffee on the cushioned window seats and to breakfast on couscous, compote of spiced dried fruit with nuts, and yoghurt. The menu spans the crescent from Turkey to Morocco, beginning with a *meze* platter of dips and pickled vegetables with Turkish bread and travels through to Moroccan *tagines* and duck in pomegranate sauce.

Grand Taverna

Sir John Young Hotel, 557 George St. **Map** 4 E3. **C** *9267 3608.* ○ *noon–3pm Mon–Sat, 5:30–10pm Mon–Wed, 5:30–11pm Thu–Sat.* 🅑 目 ﹏ 🅲 *AE, DC, MC, V.* ⑤⑤

You can sit at the bar or at a table inside or outside in this popular pub bistro with all the traditional Spanish dishes. Prawns come in garlic or tomato-based sauces; octopus, fish and *chorizo* sausage come from the barbecue and dishes for two include mixed seafood Sevillana (tomato and garlic sauce) and *paella*. A jug of *sangría* from the bar will complete your meal, for which you pay beforehand.

Eleni's

185a Bourke St, Darlinghurst. **Map** 5 A1. **C** *9331 5306.* ○ *noon–2:30pm Mon–Fri, 6:30pm–late Mon–Sat.* 🅧 **V** 🅑 ﹏ 🅲 *AE, DC, MC, V.* ⑤⑤⑤

A setting as bold as an Aegean sunset, matched by an enticing Greek menu, has earned the restaurant a chorus of fans. The owner/chef comes from central Greece, where food is kept simple to emphasize pure flavours. You can sample translations to contemporary cuisine with offerings such as pies filled with rabbit and black olives, or *moussaka* of aubergine, scallops and *taramasalata*.

Criterion Brasserie

Lobby Level, MLC Centre, Martin Place. **Map** 1 B4. **C** *9233 1234.* ○ *noon–9:30pm Mon–Fri, 5:30pm–late Sat.* **V** 🅑 目 ﹏ ﹏ 🅲 *AE, DC, MC, V.* ⑤⑤⑤⑤

This restaurant manages a rare combination of slick city good looks with Mediterranean-influenced cuisine and old-fashioned Lebanese family service. The house special *meze* platter, with yoghurt balls, marinated vegetables and pastries, will appeal to vegetarians. There are tables on the outdoor terrace or overlooking the MLC steps.

Light Meals and Snacks

SYDNEY'S CASUAL EATING SCENE is extremely competitive and wherever you choose to take a break you will probably enjoy good-value food that approaches the high standards set by more formal establishments. The eateries listed here all have a staunch local following and are particularly recommended for those hungry travellers whose time and budget are limited.

CAFÉS

FOOD COLUMNISTS frequently note the mercurial nature of Sydney's dining scene, by chronicling the multitude of establishments that open and close each year. With cafés, this situation is magnified and, as a result of this competition, the standards are quite high.

Most places serve breakfast in either the eggs-and-bacon or croissant-and-pastry guises, and then move into the day with a menu offering burgers, cheese melts, *focaccia* and salads, pasta and risotto. The night owls can enjoy cakes and desserts, and choose from espresso coffee, *caffe latte* and *cappuccino*, or from a range of teas, juices, milk shakes, fruit *frappés* and smoothies.

COFFEE AND TEA

DARLINGHURST is the caffeine kingdom of Sydney and **Bar Coluzzi**, with its boxing pictures on the walls, is its capital. Media heavies, lawyers and taxi drivers throng here both for the company and the coffee. Across the road at the **Tropicana Coffee Lounge**, the clientele is more likely to be involved in the theatre or the film industry. At **Café Hernandez**, aficionados flock in for a Spanish short black and supplies of coffee beans.

Enjoy tea and scones at the **Gumnut Café**, housed in an old, crooked cottage. Sit by the fire if it's cold, or in the pretty courtyard in the summer. **Gina's Café**, in the city centre, is for those who know their coffee, and so too is the popular Paradiso family of cafés, which includes the **Obelisk Café** in Macquarie Place, **Paradiso** in the MLC Centre and the **Paradiso Lunch Bar** in Darling Park, close to Chinatown.

There has been a **Roma Caffè Ristorante** near Central Railway Station since the early 1970s and, while the address may have changed, the winning formula of good Italian coffee, pasta, pastries and great gelato has not.

SNACKS AND LIGHT MEALS

SHOULD YOU want to start the day in a sun-drenched spot, **Bill's** is a favourite place. You can breakfast on ricotta hot cakes with honeycomb butter or lunch on a delicious steak sandwich. There is a similar mood at **La Passion du Fruit** in Surry Hills, which has a big following for its fruit *frappés*, fresh salads and the hot olive bread pockets filled with any selection from the *antipasto* table. Just a few blocks away, on Crown Street, **Prasit Thai** offers imaginative and aromatic Thai fare from a tiny shopfront that is easy to miss.

Set amid the bustle of Circular Quay, the trattoria-style **Rossini Restaurant** serves reasonably priced Italian standards such as crancini, scallopine and pasta. The service is brisk and cheery, and the venue is popular with city workers and visitors alike.

Shoppers in Paddington usually fit in a lunch at one of the cafés – but on Saturdays there may be queues as this is when the Paddington Bazaar is held *(see p126)*. The **Hot Gossip Deli** has a handy delicatessen adjacent, where you can buy healthy fare to take away. **Sloane Rangers** is a real home away from home, with lots to keep vegetarians happy and a small courtyard at the back. For a quick snack before seeing a movie at the Academy Twin, try the nearby **Flicks Café**. In Darlinghurst,

you will find **Betty's Soup Kitchen** which serves a wide range of soups and delicious desserts. Nearby **Dov** is a mixture of Mediterranean Jewish and Middle European cuisine.

At **Una's Coffee Lounge**, the regular clientele are often joined by homesick Germans longing for *schnitzel*, soup and *spaëtzle* (noodles). The **Hard Rock Café** remains true to its international formula, but weekend queues suggest that the demand for burgers and T shirts has not lessened. **Le Petit Crème** is an oasis of *brioche* and *croque madame* (toasted cheese sandwich with chicken).

In Potts Point, vegetarian food and changing art on the walls are the order of the day at **Roy's Famous**.

GALLERIES AND GARDENS

THESE DAYS, most of the city's galleries, museums and larger parks have good cafés or restaurants – the following are a cut above the average.

Most of the clientele at the **Centennial Park Café** are there to take in the passing parade of joggers, horse riders and cyclists as they tuck into pasta, risotto, salad or a roasted tuna steak with African spices. Wine is available by the bottle or the glass. At the **Concourse Restaurant** in the forecourt of the Opera House, stylish Mediterranean fare is on the menu. Directly across Circular Quay, the **MCA Fish Café** is run by the same team as at the up-market Rockpool restaurant *(see p190)*. The menu here is also strongly Mediterranean.

The food is often influenced by visiting exhibitions at the **Art Gallery Restaurant** and this café is worth a visit even if you do not have time to see the collections. The **Hyde Park Barracks Café** has seating in the courtyard of these convict-built Georgian barracks and dishes such as potted goat's milk cheese with slow-roasted garlic on toast and delicious open sandwiches to stir up the appetite. You can enjoy sandwiches, soups and cream teas in the palm-studded surrounds of **Vaucluse House Tea Rooms**, in the garden of the former home of statesman and explorer, WC Wentworth.

TAKEAWAY FOOD

THE FILLED baguettes practically march out the door of the city's **Deli on Market**. There is also good coffee and a selection of their own cakes, chutneys, cheeses and vinaigrettes to take away. For a far more down-to-earth dining experience, you can drop in to **Harry's Café de Wheels** in Woolloomooloo, to sample an Aussie meat pie and sauce

from the stand-up bar at this caravan diner. This Sydney institution has been satisfying the late-night food cravings of both locals and visitors for decades, and is particularly popular with the sailors from the adjacent naval dockyard. An entirely different sort of treat can be found at the **Maya Indian Sweets Centre** in Surry Hills, where a particularly luscious array of desserts and cakes is available – there are a few tables for tea if you are desperate to eat.

At the opposite end of the spectrum are the food courts in the basements or ground floors of major city buildings.

These serve the city's office workers at lunchtime with a grand assortment of foods to take away or eat at tables nearby. Australia Square, the MLC Centre, Chifley Tower, the Mid City Centre and the American Express Tower all have food courts with shops offering everything from Asian noodles and Mexican nachos to pizza and sushi.

Most of Sydney's markets *(see p203)* have food stalls where a large mixed plate of Indian, Mexican or Asian food will cost only a few dollars. Paddington Bazaar has good, cheap vegetarian food in the hall at the back of the market.

DIRECTORY

THE ROCKS AND CIRCULAR QUAY

Obelisk Café
7 Macquarie Place.
Map 1 B3. ☎ 9241 2141.

Concourse Restaurant
Sydney Opera House.
Map 1 C2. ☎ 9250 7300.

Gumnut Café
28 Harrington St,
Map 1 B3.
☎ 9247 9591.

MCA Fish Café
Museum of Contemporary Art, Circular Quay West.
Map 1 B2. ☎ 9241 4253.

Rossini Restaurant
Wharf 5, Circular Quay.
Map 1 B3. ☎ 9247 8026.

CITY CENTRE

Paradiso
MLC Centre, Martin Place.
Map 1 B4. ☎ 9221 0527.

Deli on Market
30–32 Market St.
Map 4 E2. ☎ 9262 6906.

Gina's Café
106 Bathurst St. **Map** 4 E3.
☎ 9267 2480.

DARLING HARBOUR

Paradiso Lunch Bar
Darling Park,
201 Sussex St. **Map** 4 D2.
☎ 9283 1906.

Roma Caffè Ristorante
Sydney Central, 181 Hay St Haymarket. **Map** 4 E4.
☎ 9211 3909.

BOTANIC GARDENS AND THE DOMAIN

Art Gallery Restaurant
Art Gallery Rd, The Domain.
Map 2 D4. ☎ 9225 1819.

Hyde Park Barracks Café
Queens Square,
Macquarie St. **Map** 1 C5.
☎ 9223 1155.

KINGS CROSS AND DARLINGHURST

Bar Coluzzi
322 Victoria St,
Darlinghurst. **Map** 5 B1.
☎ 9380 5420.

Betty's Soup Kitchen
269 Crown St,
Darlinghurst. **Map** 5 A2.
☎ 9360 9698.

Bill's
433 Liverpool St,
Darlinghurst. **Map** 5 B2.
☎ 9360 9631.

Café Hernandez
60 Kings Cross Rd,
Potts Point. **Map** 5 C1.
☎ 9331 2343.

Dov
Cnr Burton & Forbes St,
Darlinghurst. **Map** 5 A2.
☎ 9360 9594.

Hard Rock Café
121–129 Crown St,
Darlinghurst. **Map** 5 A1.
☎ 9331 1116.

Harry's Café de Wheels
Cowper Wharf Rd,
Woolloomooloo.
Map 2 E5. ☎ 9357 3074.

Le Petit Crème
118 Darlinghurst Rd,
Darlinghurst. **Map** 5 B1.
☎ 9361 4738.

Roy's Famous
176 Victoria St, Potts Point.
Map 5 B1.☎ 9357 3579.

Tropicana Coffee Lounge
227b Victoria St,
Darlinghurst. **Map** 5 B1.
☎ 9360 9809.

Una's Coffee Lounge
340 Victoria St,
Darlinghurst. **Map** 5 B1.
☎ 9360 6885.

PADDINGTON

Centennial Park Café
Cnr Grand & Parkes Drives,
Centennial Park.
Map 6 E5. ☎ 9380 6922.

Flicks Café
3 Oxford St, Paddington.
Map 5 B3. ☎ 9331 7412.

Hot Gossip Deli
436 Oxford St, Paddington.
Map 6 D4. ☎ 9380 5305.

Sloane Rangers
312 Oxford St, Paddington.
Map 5 C3. ☎ 9331 6717.

FURTHER AFIELD

La Passion du Fruit
633 Bourke St, Surry Hills.
Map 5 B3. ☎ 9690 1894.

Maya Indian Sweets Centre
470 Cleveland St, Surry Hills.
Map 5 A5. ☎ 9699 8663.

Prasit Thai
415 Crown St, Surry Hills.
Map 5 A3. ☎ 9319 0748.

Vaucluse House Tea Rooms
Vaucluse House,
Wentworth Rd, Vaucluse.
☎ 9388 8188.

Sydney Pubs and Bars

CONFUSINGLY for the overseas visitor, Australian pubs and bars are more commonly known as hotels. This is because licensing laws originally required any place serving alcohol to provide accommodation, too. In the cities, at least, hotels have changed radically and what were once the domains of beer-swilling males have now evolved into far more civilized spots.

Pub menus have also undergone a metamorphosis. In place of the former meat pie and sauce, most pubs now offer hearty snacks, such as *nachos*, *focaccia*, pasta, grills and salads, at remarkably low prices. All pubs serve basic mixed spirit-based drinks and often wine by the glass, but cocktails tend to be the preserve of the more up-market venues. Pubs are also often good venues for entertainment ranging from rock to jazz *(see pp214–15)*.

RULES AND CONVENTIONS

IN THEORY, pubs are open from 10am to 10pm every day. This often extends to midnight closing on Fridays and Saturdays, and even to 3am when live entertainment is provided. Some pubs, in areas where there are large numbers of shift workers, will open at 6am and are known as "early openers". Others, particularly in tourist haunts, have a 24-hour licence. You must be at least 18 years of age (and able to provide the proof) to buy or consume any alcohol. However, children under 18 may accompany adults into beer gardens and into hotel restaurants. Dress requirements are purely at the discretion of the publican and the management always has the right to refuse service.

One aspect of traditional pub culture is the custom of "shouting", or buying drinks for your companions. It can be very expensive to become involved in buying "rounds" – when someone buys you a drink, it is considered bad form if you do not return the favour. If you are on a budget and do not want to offend, simply explain that you are only staying for one drink or make some other excuse.

Apart from being very good places to soak up some local atmosphere, pubs are also ideal spots for watching any televised major international or local sporting matches in the company of like-minded people. Many hotels broadcast matches on a big screen and locals gather to watch.

Pubs are also excellent spots for live entertainment – many Australian rock music names first performed in hotels. The daily newspapers are a good source of information on dates, times and venues *(see p221)*.

JOIN THE LOCALS

PUBS PROVIDE the chance to observe Sydney at play. At Circular Quay, the **Customs House Bar** has been serving drinks since 1826. On Friday nights, up to 2,000 people spill out into Macquarie Place to talk shop and gossip under the trees. **Miro Tapas Bar** is an equally trendy destination, with floor-to-ceiling murals and Spanish-style snacks to go with the *sangria* and melon and peach "shooters". The **Dendy Bar & Bistro** is in the Dendy cinema complex *(see p210)*; here office workers mix with film-goers and coffee is served alongside cocktails.

Cowboy boots and country music set the scene at the **Arizona Bar & Restaurant**, where American beers and margaritas wash down New Mexican spiced ribs and grills. Situated close to the State Theatre *(see p82)*, it is a very popular haunt of film-festival patrons. A little further afield in Surry Hills, the **Elephant's Foot Hotel** boasts everything from cocktails and coffee to cake and pasta, plus a pool table. There are also pool tables at the busy **Palace Hotel**

in Darlinghurst, which has a popular restaurant, and the **Green Park Hotel**, which does not offer any bar food apart from potato crisps.

There are plenty of "locals" in Paddington, most of which serve above-average bar food to their discerning clientele. The **London Tavern** opened in 1876 and claims to be the suburb's oldest pub. The sign outside welcomes all except for dogs, giraffes, elephants and children under 18 for drinks. Five Ways *(see p126)* is dominated by the **Royal Hotel**, an 1880s three-storey corner establishment, where cocktails are served in the upstairs Elephant Bar and the restaurant below extends out onto an iron-lace encrusted veranda. Both the bistro at the **Paddington Inn** and the dining room of the **Bellevue Hotel** offer good contemporary Mediterranean-style fare.

Just about any Sydneysider who has partied through the night has ended up at the **Bourbon & Beefsteak** in the wee hours. This bar undergoes an amazing transformation around dawn. The cigarette smoke clears to reveal a full breakfast room extravaganza, with the signed portraits of famous patrons on the walls, masses of fresh flowers and starched white napery.

UP-MARKET BARS

IF YOU ARE looking for a more elegant atmosphere, head for **Horizon's Bar** at the top of the ANA Hotel *(see p174)*. You can admire views extending from Botany Bay to Manly while you sip a Toblerone (liquid chocolate with a kick). Or drop into **The Cortile** in the glamorous lobby of the Hotel Inter-Continental and sip a cocktail in the comfort of the cane armchairs. There is imported Champagne by the glass at **Wine Banc**, as well as cocktails, an excellent selection of wines and fine food in the stylish bar in the city's central business district.

The **Regent Club Bar** in the Regent Sydney *(see p174)* is another hotel lounge which is ideal either for pre- or post-theatre drinks and nibbles. The stylish **L'otel** *(see p176)* has a cocktail bar, where the staff especially recommend the margaritas, and quite a decent restaurant. Try the delicious crispy squid with chilli salt.

HISTORIC PUBS

A WALK ALONG George Street will reveal some of The Rocks' old pubs, but two of the more significant ones are a few streets back. The **Hero of Waterloo**, built in 1843, has a maze of stone cellars underneath which testify to its nefarious past *(see p69)*. The **Lord Nelson Brewery Hotel** was first licensed in 1841 and is now a "pub brewery" with a range of ales brewed on the premises. It also has Nelson's Bistro and, upstairs, six guest rooms *(see p174)*.

The **Sydney Cove Oyster Bar**, on the eastern side of Circular Quay, operates from a remodelled tram terminus. Its outdoor tables are certainly a treat in fine weather, as is the range of Australian wines and beers. The latter includes Coopers and Redback wheat beer. Enjoy a glass with the small but satisfying seafood menu which offers oysters prepared in five ways (there is steak for die-hard meat eaters).

At the **Marble Bar** *(see p82)*, the sumptuous decoration on its walls is Italian Renaissance in style with hunting scenes, exotic flora and fruit complementing the cocktail list.

ENTERTAINMENT

A S A VENUE for both new and established comics, stage comedies and other comic gatherings, Glebe's **Comedy Hotel** stands alone. There is a bistro in the evenings, but the food may be overshadowed by the stimulating company.

Also in Glebe is the **Nag's Head**, where soloists and duettists perform everything from Neil Diamond to Pearl Jam, Wednesday to Sunday nights. The pub bistro serves a variety of grills and salads.

In Surry Hills, there are live bands every Saturday night at the **Hopetoun Hotel** and there is a DJ playing old funk, jazz and blues on Friday and Sunday evenings. The bar menu has *focaccia*, pies and pasta. In Rozelle, there is folk and blues on weekends and a bistro serving pasta and grills at the **Rose, Shamrock and Thistle**. The **Orient Hotel** in the heart of The Rocks is very popular with both locals and tourists. On New Year's Eve, it practically bursts at the seams. There are cover bands daily and jazz on weekends, plus a restaurant and a cook-your-own barbecue which has an accompanying pianist.

DIRECTORY			
THE ROCKS AND CIRCULAR QUAY	**Sydney Cove Oyster Bar** 1 Circular Quay East. **Map** 1 C2. 9247 2937.	**KINGS CROSS AND DARLINGHURST**	**Royal Hotel** 237 Glenmore Rd, Paddington. **Map** 5 C3. 9331 2604.
Customs House Bar Sydney Renaissance Hotel, Macquarie Place. **Map** 1 B3. 9259 7000.	**CITY CENTRE** **Arizona Bar & Restaurant** 247 Pitt St. **Map** 1 B5. 9261 1077.	**Bourbon & Beefsteak Bar** 24 Darlinghurst Rd, Potts Point **Map** 5 B1. 9358 1144.	**FURTHER AFIELD** **Elephant's Foot Hotel** 505 Crown St, Surry Hills. 9319 6802.
Hero of Waterloo 81 Lower Fort St, Millers Point. **Map** 1 A2. 9252 4553.	**Dendy Bar & Bistro** 19 Martin Place. **Map** 1 B4. 9221 1243.	**Green Park Hotel** 360 Victoria St, Darlinghurst. **Map** 5 B2. 9380 5311.	**Comedy Hotel** 115 Wigram Rd, Glebe. 9552 1791.
Horizon's Bar Level 36, ANA Hotel, 176 Cumberland St, The Rocks. **Map** 1 A3. 9250 6000.	**Marble Bar** Sydney Hilton Hotel, 259 Pitt St. **Map** 1 B5. 9266 0610.	**L'otel** 114 Darlinghurst Rd, Darlinghurst. **Map** 5 B1. 9360 6868.	**Hopetoun Hotel** 416 Bourke St, Surry Hills. **Map** 5 A3. 9361 5257.
Lord Nelson Brewery Hotel 19 Kent St, Millers Point. **Map** 1 A2. 9251 4044.	**Miro Tapas Bar** 76 Liverpool St. **Map** 4 E3. 9267 3126. **Wine Banc** 53 Martin Place. **Map** 1 B4. 9233 5399.	**PADDINGTON** **Bellevue Hotel** 159 Hargrave St, Paddington. **Map** 6 E3. 9363 2293.	**Nag's Head Hotel** 162 St Johns Rd, Glebe. **Map** 3 A5. 9660 1591.
Orient Hotel 89 Argyle St, The Rocks. **Map** 1 B2. 9251 1255.	**BOTANIC GARDENS AND THE DOMAIN**	**London Tavern** 85 Underwood St, Paddington. **Map** 6 D3. 9331 3200.	**Palace Hotel** 122 Flinders St, Darlinghurst. **Map** 5 A3. 9361 5170.
Regent Club Bar Regent Sydney, 199 George St. **Map** 1 B3. 9238 0000.	**The Cortile** Hotel Inter.Continental, 117 Macquarie St. **Map** 1 C3. 9230 0200.	**Paddington Inn** 338 Oxford St, Paddington. **Map** 6 D4. 9380 5277.	**Rose, Shamrock & Thistle** 193 Evans St, Rozelle. 9810 2244.

SHOPS AND MARKETS

Souvenir
boomerangs

FOR MOST TRAVELLERS, shopping can be as much of a voyage of discovery as sightseeing. The variety of shops in Sydney is wide and the quality of merchandise is usually good. The city has many elegant arcades and shopping galleries, with plenty of nooks and crannies to explore. The range of goods on offer is vast – most international labels are imported and local talent in many fields, notably jewellery, fashion and indigenous arts and crafts, is promoted. Nor does the most interesting shopping stop at the city centre; there are several "satellite" alternatives. The best shopping areas are highlighted on pages 200–201.

A typical junk-shop-cum-café in Balmain *(see p131)*

SHOPPING HOURS

MOST SHOPS ARE open from 9am to 5:30pm during the week, and from 9am to 4pm on Saturdays. On Thursdays, many shops stay open until 9pm. Some are open late every evening and most of these also open on Sundays.

HOW TO PAY

MAJOR CREDIT cards are accepted at many shops, but there may be a minimum purchase requirement. You will need identification, such as a valid passport or driver's licence, when using traveller's cheques. Shops will generally exchange goods or refund your money if you are not satisfied, provided you have some proof of purchase. This does not usually apply to items bought on sale. Australia has no goods or service tax – the price you see is what you pay.

SALES

MANY SHOPS conduct sales all year round. The big department stores of **David Jones** and **Grace Bros** have two clearance sales a year. The post-Christmas sales start on 26 December and last into January. Keen bargain-hunters queue from dawn for substantial savings. The other major sale time is during July, after the end of the financial year.

TAX-FREE SALES

DUTY-FREE SHOPS are found in the centre of the city as well as at Kingsford Smith Airport. Some shops also have branches in the larger suburbs. Overseas visitors can save around 30 per cent on goods such as perfume, jewellery, cameras and alcohol at shops that offer duty-free shopping. You must show your passport and onward ticket when the goods are collected.

Most duty-free merchandise must be kept in its sealed bag until you leave. Cameras and video cameras are exceptions. Some duty-free shops in the city will deliver your goods to the airport where you can pick them up on your departure.

Chifley Tower, with the Chifley Plaza shopping arcade at its base

ARCADES AND MALLS

ARCADES AND shopping malls in Sydney range from the ornately Victorian to modern marble and glass. The **Queen Victoria Building** *(see p82)* is Sydney's most palatial shopping space. Four levels contain more than 200 shops. The top level, Victoria Walk, is devoted to merchandise such as silver, antiques, designer knitwear and high-quality souvenirs.

The elegant **Strand Arcade** *(see p84)* was originally built in 1892. Jewellery, lingerie, high fashion, fine antiques and gourmet coffee shops and tea rooms are its stock in trade.

Pitt Street Mall is home to several other shopping centres. **Skygarden** is the place for

Interior design shop on William Street in Paddington *(see p124)*

homeware, classy fashion from Australian and international designers, and art galleries of distinction. A spacious food gallery offers everything from antipasto to Thai takeaway. The bustling **Mid City Centre** is home to the huge HMV music store and shops selling clothes, accessories and gifts. **Centrepoint** has more than 140 speciality shops that stock everything from avant-garde jewellery to leather goods.

Nearby in Pitt Street, the marble and glass of **Piccadilly** houses flashy boutiques, good shoe shops (including Bruno Magli and Raymond Castles), quality jewellers and cafés.

Both the **MLC Centre** and the nearby **Chifley Plaza** cater to the prestige shopper. Gucci, Cartier, Tiffany & Co, MaxMara, Kenzo and Moschino are just some of the shops found here.

The **Harbourside Shopping Centre** has dozens of shops, plus several waterfront restaurants. The atmosphere is festive and the merchandise includes fine arts, jewellery, duty-free shopping, beachwear and Australiana.

BEST OF THE DEPARTMENT STORES

THE SPRING and Mother's Day floral displays in the **David Jones** Elizabeth Street store are legendary, as is the luxurious perfumery and cosmetics hall on the ground

Greengrocer's display of fresh fruit and vegetables

Gowings menswear store logo

floor. The building has seven floors of quality merchandise, including women's clothing, lingerie, baby goods, toys and stationery. The Market Street store nearby specializes in menswear, kitchenware, furniture, china, crystal and silver. The food hall on the lower ground floor is famous for its range of gourmet food and fine wines.

Grace Bros is a good pit stop for the visitor in need of cosmetics, hats, sunscreen or casual clothing, while the **Argyle Department Store** in The Rocks *(see p68)* is chock full of fashion boutiques.

Gowings, which has operated continuously since 1868, is a Sydney institution. This unpretentious family-owned and family-run menswear store also sells such things as sunglasses, watches, Swiss army knives, fishing gear, miners' lamps and genuine Australiana such as kangaroo leather wallets and plaited leather belts.

SHOPPING FURTHER AFIELD

GOOD SHOPPING is also found outside central Sydney. Other areas well worth visiting include Double Bay, with its sophisticated, village-style shopping, to the east, and the Left Bank-style student haunts of Newtown to the south and Glebe to the west. Bargains can be found at the clothing and homeware factory outlets at Surry Hills and Redfern to the south of the city (east of Redfern railway station).

Part of the spring floral display, David Jones department store

Sydney's Best: Shopping Streets and Markets

SYDNEY'S BEST SHOPPING AREAS range from galleries, arcades and department stores selling expensive gifts and jewellery *(see pp198–9)*, to boutiques of extroverted or elegant cutting-edge fashion and its accessories. The range of styles is impressive – both international couture brands and acclaimed local designer labels *(pp204–5)*. The city's hip fringe areas are alive with street fashion and its accoutrements.

Colourful markets are a delight for collectors and bargain-hunters alike *(p203)*, while those who seek out the quirky and one-off items are well catered for, as are those looking to take home quality craft and indigenous art as mementos of their visit. Specialist browsers will find a tempting selection of book and music shops *(pp206–7)* from which to choose.

The Rocks Market
At weekends, the stalls offer affordable arts and crafts and jewellery. (See p203.)

THE RO
AND CIR
QUA

Darling Harbour
Quality Australiana, surf and beach wear, souvenir ideas, children's clothes, colourful knits and art and craft shops abound.

Queen Victoria Building
This elegant shopping gallery offers four floors of designer wear, gifts, and speciality stores amid cafés.

DARLING
HARBOUR

Sydney Fish Market
You can buy fresh seafood daily in the colourful fishmongers' halls or order from the cafés which spill out on to the sunny terrace alongside the marina. (See p202.)

Chinatown
This is the place to fin discounts on watches gold jewellery opals and eve fabrics. There are also Chine butchers' shop herbalists and supermarkets

| 0 metres | 500 |
| 0 yards | 500 |

City Centre
Dazzling shopping arcades and smart malls are dotted throughout the city centre, notably Pitt Street Mall, Strand and Piccadilly Arcades, and Centrepoint.

Castlereagh Street
The city's designer row is home to Chanel, Moschino, Gucci and Hermés. The most exclusive names cluster near the King Street intersection.

BOTANIC GARDENS AND THE DOMAIN

Darlinghurst and Surry Hills
These suburbs are the youth culture barometer: young designers, leather à la mode, gay fashion, hot music and gifts for those who love quirky collectables.

KINGS CROSS AND DARLINGHURST

PADDINGTON

Paddington and Woollahra
Up-market clothing, shoes, homeware and jewellery are on show. Bookshops, cafés and galleries add to the allure. Queen Street, Woollahra, is the antique shop strip.

Paddington Bazaar
Considered by many to be Sydney's best market and a showcase for the up-and-coming fashions, it is held every Saturday. (See p203.)

Sydney Fish Market

EACH YEAR, 16 million kilograms (35 million pounds) of fresh fish and other seafood are sold at the Fish Market's Dutch Clock auction. In this system, prices start high, and gradually descend on a computerized "clock", until a buyer puts in a bid. At this

Balmain bug

point, no other bids are accepted, and the deal is made. This unusually quiet auction starts at 5:30am every Monday to Friday, and runs for two to three hours until all the seafood is sold. Members of the public can follow the auction proceedings from a viewing area.

The waterfront cafés offering fine seafood at reasonable prices make dining here a rare treat.

Blue swimmer crabs have a mild flavour and are found all around the Australian coastline.

About 30 wholesalers, many of them family concerns, buy bulk quantities of the day's catch; some also have retail outlets at the market itself.

Local fishermen arrive at the market between 4pm the previous day and 8am on the day of the auction. About 80 per cent of the catch is from the far coasts of New South Wales.

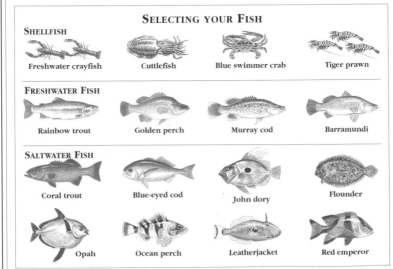

SELECTING YOUR FISH

SHELLFISH

Freshwater crayfish	Cuttlefish	Blue swimmer crab	Tiger prawn

FRESHWATER FISH

Rainbow trout	Golden perch	Murray cod	Barramundi

SALTWATER FISH

Coral trout	Blue-eyed cod	John dory	Flounder
Opah	Ocean perch	Leatherjacket	Red emperor

Markets

SCOURING MARKETS FOR THE CHEAP, the cheerful and the chic has become a popular weekend pastime in Sydney. Weekly or monthly markets that suit both the bargain-hunter and the serious shopper have sprung up all over Sydney's suburbs. Caps, souvenir T-shirts, bargain leather jackets, high-class art – there is bound to be something to suit every taste. Just as popular are the Sydney Fish Market and the produce markets, which have turned shopping for staples into a big day out.

Balmain Market

Cnr Darling St and Curtis Rd, Balmain. 442, 434. 7:30am–4pm Sat.

Held in the grounds of the Balmain Congregational Church, in the shade of a fig tree said to be more than 150 years old, this compact, high-calibre market attracts both locals and tourists. Fees from stallholders contribute to the ongoing restoration of the church which was built in 1853. As well as children's wear, second-hand books, contemporary and antique jewellery, arty mirrors, recycled stationery, stained-glass mobiles and Chinese healing balls, there's a food hall where you can find fresh and aromatic Japanese, Thai, Indian and specialist vegetarian dishes in the making.

Bondi Beach Market

Bondi Beach Public School, Campbell Parade, North Bondi. 380, 382, 389. 9am–5pm Sun in summer (4pm in winter).

Arrive early (some of the stalls are all set up by 9am) for the best second-hand clothing buys; funky 1970s gear is particularly popular. The best bargain clothes are near the back of the market. Expect to see the odd pop star and stars of Australian television soap operas among the browsers. The market is also noted for its cactus plants, glassware and tourist art – scenes of Bondi Beach are a speciality.

Glebe Market

Glebe Public School, Glebe Point Road, Glebe. **Map** 3 B5. 431, 433. 10am–4pm Sat.

A treasure-trove for the junk shop enthusiast and canny scavenger, this market is bright, changeable and popular with the inner-city grunge set. Best buys are bric-a-brac (get there early for bargain porcelain and, if you're lucky, the odd undervalued lithograph) and crafts made from recycled wood, metal and glass. Eccentricities include patchwork velvet jesters' caps, suitcases full of amber and turquoise beads, and handpainted light bulbs. Second-hand clothes are a good buy here, as are leather wallets, silver rings and pendants, amulets and plaited friendship bands, books, CDs and records.

Paddington Bazaar

(See p126.)

Like Paddington itself, this market reflects the latest trends and fashions in the contents of its stalls. From nouveau to novelties, there is always something tempting here, and it is unlikely you will come away empty-handed. You can preview clothes and fashion trends before they hit the shops. Silver jewellery is abundant, so prices are very competitive; there are also smart children's clothes, leather goods, unusual buckles, belts, stationery, candles, handcrafts and oddities such as babies' baseball caps and rubbery novelty masks.

Paddy's Market

(See p99.)

In the 19th century, Paddy's in the Haymarket was the city's fringe market and also the location of fairgrounds and circuses. Today it has between 500 and 800 stalls under one roof. Early birds will get the best flowers, fruit, vegetables and seafood. There are also good buys in caneware, luggage, leather goods, tools, homeware, ornaments, gifts, souvenirs and toys . . . not to mention pet rabbits, puppies, kittens and cockatoos.

The Rocks Market

George St, The Rocks. **Map** 1 B2. 431, 432, 433, 434. 10am–5pm Sat & Sun.

At weekends, rain or shine, a sail-like canopy is erected at the top end of George Street, transforming the area into an atmospheric marketplace. Get there early to beat the afternoon crowds. The market was established with Sydneysiders in mind, but it has now become just as popular with visitors. There are about 140 stalls, whose wares are unique rather than inexpensive. Quality is a priority here. Look out for wind chimes, pewter picture frames, pub poster prins, stained-glass homeware, lace, oils, leather goods, wooden toys, gold-plated bush leaves, and jewellery made from wood, shell, silver or crystal. There are also new paperbacks for sale at half price. You can watch a sculptor making art out of stone, immortalize your visit with a calico "Sydney" bag or have your portrait sketched in charcoal.

Sydney Fish Market

(See p131.)

Sydney is famous for its fresh seafood and the Sydney Fish Market is the ideal place to buy it. You can choose from over 100 species, both live and prepared, in the fishmongers' halls. The displays of seafood are arresting, with coral reds, marble pinks, blacks, greys and iridescent yellows to take your mind off the sloshy floors and the smell of the sea. The market also has sushi bars; fish cafés (where you can sit inside or outside on the waterfront); a bakery; a fine foods delicatessen (their chutneys and olives are delicious); a poultry and game specialist; a shop selling fine wines to complement the gourmet meal you are planning; and a fresh fruit and vegetable shop. The Sydney Seafood School operates above the market, offering lessons in preparing and serving seafood.

The Tarpeian Market

Western Boardwalk, Sydney Opera House. **Map** 1 C2. 438. 9am–6pm Sun & public hols.

Sir Joseph Banks named what is now the southern rock face and walkway of the Opera House after the Tarpeian Rock in Rome, hence this market's unusual name. Under calico market umbrellas, you will find arts and crafts in a spectacular setting. Some call this a distillation of the best, and certainly you won't find T-shirts and cheap souvenirs, but rather goods that have been either hand-made or hand-finished. It is an eclectic mix: from English porcelain thimbles to welded art (such as miniature motorcycles), ornate wooden smoking pipes, framed prints of Sydney, jewellery, groovy hats and healing crystals. If you are lucky, you can catch performance artists – who are often happy to pose for pictures. The morning may be a more pleasant time to go in summer, but you will miss the afternoon entertainment.

Clothes and Accessories

SMART CASUAL IS A TERM often heard in Sydney, applied to both dress and occasion. Particularly in summer, the style is visibly relaxed with warm weather encouraging dressing down rather than dressing up. Shops do not neglect the formal dresser, however, and stylish Australian labels vie with the international designer names on offer.

WOMEN'S CLOTHES

SMART DAYWEAR and casual clothes in classic, if a little unadventurous, styles are the province of **Country Road**, which has shops throughout Sydney. **Carla Zampatti** is an Australian designer whose speciality is elegant day and evening wear. **David Jones** stocks innovative Australian names such as Robert Burton, Leonie Levy and Jodie Boffa, while international labels such as Sonia Rykiel, Donna Karan and Missoni are to be found on the exclusive seventh floor. **Grace Bros** carries impressive Australian designers such as Jane Lamerton, Covers, Anthea Crawford and Trent Nathan.

Emporio Armani can also be found in Sydney, with its trademark quality fabric, cut and design excellence. The **Sportsgirl** stores are great for bright accessories and up-to-the-minute fashions. **Collette Dinnigan** uses Italian and French lace, silk and tulle to make exquisite lingerie that includes teddies, bustiers and decadent pyjamas.

MEN'S CLOTHES

THE EXCELLENT menswear department in **David Jones** stocks everything from casual to formal dress. **Polo Ralph Lauren** has shoes, sweaters, jackets, shirts and accessories for the designer-orientated. **Stewart's Gentlemen's Outfitters** also stocks up-market men's labels, including Bally, Zegna and Gant. **Marcs** has locally-made clothing (for both men and women), and top imports such as Yohji Yamamato and Issey Miyake.

For men who do not enjoy fussy shopping, **Gowing Bros** is the answer. This department store stocks absolutely everything imaginable from socks, shirts and detachable collars

to made-to-measure suits, pyjamas, hats and even regulation whites for lawn bowling – all at very competitive prices.

AVANT-GARDE AND STREET FASHION

PADDINGTON, Darlinghurst, Surry Hills and King Street in Newtown are the places to find some of Sydney's best street fashion. **Bracewell** and **Leona Edmiston** design for women and men. Their clothes are in demand by rock stars, models and everyone in between. **Lisa Ho** and **Black Vanity** also cater for the style-conscious woman.

Skin Deep has retro gear for men – Hollywood-style shirts, suits from the 1940s and 1950s, old silk ties and great tie pins. Watch the markets, Glebe and Paddington in particular *(see p203)*, for the up-and-coming designers. **Aussie Boys**, popular with the gay crowd, stocks

cheeky casual clothes for men and women, as well as trendy gym gear and the latest party wear. **Dangerfield** is another shop filled with funky fashion.

ESSENTIALLY AUSTRALIAN

AUSTRALIAN "outback fashion", from elastic-sided riding boots and Akubra hats to the stylish Driza-bone oilskin coats, are found at **R. M. Williams**. Beach and surf wear labels to look for are Hot Tuna, 100% Mambo, Rip Curl, Speedo and Brian Rochford. Shops carrying these brands include **Hot Tuna**, **Surf Dive 'n Ski** and major department stores. The **Mambo Friendship Store** carries Mambo label surf and street wear and accessories. **General Pants Co.** is another retail outlet for Mambo.

KNITWEAR

CHUNKY HANDKNITS adorned with Australian motifs are sold at **Dorian Scott**, alongside children's wear, hats and an eclectic range of casual wear. You will also find the rainbow-coloured Coogi knits here. The **Great Australian Jumper Company** has classic knitwear

SIZE CHART

Women's clothes							
Australian	6	8	10	12	14	16	18	20
American	4	6	8	10	12	14	16	18
British	6	8	10	12	14	16	18	20
Continental	38	40	42	44	46	48	50	52
Women's shoes							
Australian	6–6½	7	7½–8	8½	9–9½	10	10½–11	
American	5	6	7	8	9	10	11	
British	3	4	5	6	7	8	9	
Continental	36	37	38	39	40	41	42	
Men's suits							
Australian	44	46	48	50	52	54	56	58
American	34	36	38	40	42	44	46	48
British	34	36	38	40	42	44	46	48
Continental	44	46	48	50	52	54	56	58
Men's shirts							
Australian	36	38	39	41	42	43	44	45
American	14	15	15½	16	16½	17	17½	18
British	14	15	15½	16	16½	17	17½	18
Continental	36	38	39	41	42	43	44	45
Men's shoes							
Australian	7	7½	8	8½	9	10	11	12
American	7	7½	8	8½	9½	10½	11	11½
British	6	7	7½	8	9	10	11	12
Continental	39	40	41	42	43	44	45	46

designed by Adele Weiss and made from Australian wool. **Vivian Chan Shaw** specializes in feathery evening knits made from superfine wool.

SHOES

THE SHOE FETISHIST is very well served in Sydney, with shops like **Edward Meller**, **Evelyn Miles** and **Raymond Castles** appealing to all tastes. **Bally** and **Bruno Magli** have top-notch styles at matching prices. **Grace Bros** and **David Jones** carry the smart designs of Elle Effe, as well as a good range of men's shoes. **Josephs Shoe Store** stocks top-quality shoes for men, including Bally.

HATS

SYDNEY'S MARKETS (see p203) have hats galore, ranging from raffia to plush velvet. **Helen Kaminski** sells her original designs in the historic Argyle Centre (see p68). The **Strand Hatters** stocks a wide range of styles for men and women, from typical bush hats to wide-brimmed straw creations. **Rochelle** also sells casual and formal hats.

Vic Cooper Hats is where fashion magazines go for hats for their photo shoots. Helen Kaminski's distinctive raffia and felt hats are sold at David Jones and Dorian Scott.

DIRECTORY

WOMEN'S CLOTHES

Carla Zampatti
143 Elizabeth St. **Map** 1 B5.
(9264 3257.

Collette Dinnigan
39 William St, Paddington.
Map 6 D3. **(** 9360 6691.

Country Road
142 Pitt St. **Map** 1 B5.
(9394 1818.
One of several branches.

David Jones
See p199.

Emporio Armani
4 Martin Place. **Map** 1 B4.
(9231 3655.

Grace Bros
See p199.

Sportsgirl
Skygarden. **Map** 1 B5.
(9223 8255.
One of several branches.

MEN'S CLOTHES

David Jones
See p199.

Gowing Bros
See p199.

Stewart's Gentlemen's Outfitters
Sheraton Wentworth Hotel, Phillip Street.
Map 1 B4. **(** 9221 2203.

Marcs
Mid City Centre.
Map 1 B5.
(9221 4583.
One of several branches.

Polo Ralph Lauren
Queen Victoria Building.
Map 1 B5.
(9267 1630.

AVANT-GARDE AND STREET FASHION

Aussie Boys
102 Oxford St,
Darlinghurst. **Map** 5 A2.
(9360 7011.

Black Vanity
400 Oxford St,
Paddington. **Map** 6 D4.
(9360 5130.
One of three branches.

Bracewell
264 Oxford St,
Paddington. **Map** 5 C3.
(9360 6192.
One of two branches.
Menswear
274 Oxford St,
Paddington. **Map** 5 C3.
(9331 5844.

Dangerfield
330 Crown St, Surry Hills.
Map 5 A2.
(9380 6924.

Lisa Ho
2a–6a Queen St,
Woollahra. **Map** 6 E4.
(9360 2345.

Leona Edmiston Man
Strand Arcade. **Map** 1 B5.
(9221 5616.

Leona Edmiston Woman
Strand Arcade. **Map** 1 B5.
(9232 7606.

Skin Deep
141 Elizabeth St.
Map 1 B5. **(** 9264 1239.

ESSENTIALLY AUSTRALIAN

General Pants Co.
391 George St. **Map** 1 B5.
(9299 3565.
One of several branches.

Hot Tuna
180 Oxford St,
Paddington. **Map** 5 C3.
(9361 5049.

Mambo Friendship Store
17 Oxford St,
Paddington. **Map** 5 B3.
(9331 8034.

R. M. Williams
389 George St. **Map** 1 B5.
(9262 2228.
One of three branches.

Surf Dive 'n Ski
462 George St. **Map** 1 B5.
(9267 3408.
One of several branches.

KNITWEAR

Dorian Scott
105 George St, The Rocks.
Map 1 B2.
(9221 8145.

Great Australian Jumper Company
Chifley Plaza. **Map** 1 B4.
(9231 3511.
One of three branches.

Vivian Chan Shaw
Queen Victoria Building.
Map 1 B5. **(** 9264 3019.

SHOES

Bally
Queen Victoria Building.
Map 1 B5.
(9267 3887.

Bruno Magli
Piccadilly. **Map** 1 B5.
(9267 4712.

David Jones
See p199.

Edward Meller
St James Centre.
Map 1 B5. **(** 9232 1807.
One of three branches.

Evelyn Miles
MLC Centre. **Map** 1 B4.
(9233 1569.

Grace Bros
See p199.

Josephs Shoe Store
Strand Arcade. **Map** 1 B5.
(9233 1879.

Raymond Castles
Centrepoint. **Map** 1 B5.
(9232 2147.
One of three branches.

HATS

David Jones
See p199.

Dorian Scott
See Knitwear.

Rochelle by John Court
Queen Victoria Building.
Map 1 B5.
(9283 4070.

Strand Hatters
Strand Arcade. **Map** 1 B5.
(9231 6884.

Vic Cooper Hats
Royal Arcade, 255 Pitt St.
Map 1 B5. **(** 9267 3713.

Helen Kaminski
Argyle Department Store,
12–24 Argyle St, The
Rocks. **Map** 1 B2.
(9251 9850.

Specialist Shops and Souvenirs

Sydney offers an extensive range of gift and souvenir ideas, from unset opals and jewellery to Aboriginal art and hand-crafted souvenirs. Museum shops, such as at the Museum of Sydney *(see p85)* and the Art Gallery of NSW *(see pp108–11)*, often have specially commissioned items that make great presents or reminders of your visit.

One-Offs

Specialist shops abound in Sydney – some practical, some eccentric, others simply indulgent. **Ausfurs** sells everything from luxurious sheepskin coats and jackets to pure wool handknits and mohair rugs.

Red Earth sells reasonably priced natural oils, vegetable soaps, skincare products and cosmetics.

Wheels & Doll Baby is a rock'n'roll heaven – loads of leather, belts, shoes and rocker accessories. For hip watches with a high-tech look and unusual telephones, explore **Hello Darling**. **The Watch Gallery** stocks more traditional watches. Designer sunglasses such as Armani and Jean Paul Gaultier can be found at **The Looking Glass**.

Australiana

Australiana has become more than just a souvenir genre; it is now an art form in itself. **Australian Craftworks** sells souvenirs that double as desirable art, including woodwork, pottery and leather goods.

Done Art and Design has distinctive prints by Ken and Judy Done on a wide range of clothes, swimwear and accessories, while at **Weiss Art** you will find tasteful, mainly black and white, minimalist designs on clothes, umbrellas, baseball caps and cups. **Makers Mark** is a showcase for exquisite work by artisans in wood, glass and silver. The Queen Victoria Building's Victoria Walk *(see p82)* is dominated by shops selling Australiana: souvenirs, silver, antiques, art and crafts.

The **Australian Museum** *(see pp88–9)* has a small shop on the ground floor. It sells slightly unusual gift items such as native flower presses, bark paintings and Australian animal puppets, puzzles and games.

Books

The larger chains such as **Dymocks** and **Angus & Robertson's Bookworld** have a good range of guide books and maps on Sydney.

For more eclectic browsing, **Abbey's Bookshop**, **Ariel** (open until midnight), **New Edition Bookshop** and **Gleebooks**. **The Bookshop** specializes in gay and lesbian fiction and non-fiction. The **State Library of NSW** *(see p112)* bookshop has a good choice of Australian books, particularly on history.

Music

Several specialist music shops of international repute can be found in Sydney. **Red Eye Records** is for the streetwise, with its collectables, rarities, alternative music and concert tickets. At **Timewarp Records** the vinyl comeback is heralded. Classic jukebox-style vinyl 45s are a speciality here, as are reissues on CD from the 1950s, 1960s and 1970s. **Central Station Records and Tapes** has mainstream grooves, plus rap, hip hop and cutting edge dance music. **Birdland** stocks blues, jazz, soul and avant-garde, while **Anthem Records** is the home of funk, soul and R&B. **Folkways** specializes in world music, **Waterfront** independent rock and grunge and **Utopia Records** heavy metal. **Michael's Music Room** sells classical music only.

Aboriginal Art

Traditional paintings, fabric, jewellery, boomerangs, carvings and cards can be bought at the **Aboriginal and Tribal Art Centre**. At **New Guinea Primitive Arts** you will find a range of tribal artifacts from Aboriginal Australia, Papua New Guinea and Oceania.

The **Coo-ee Aboriginal Art Gallery** boasts a large selection of limited edition prints, hand-printed fabrics, books and Aboriginal music. The long-established **Hogarth Galleries Aboriginal Art Centre** has a fine reputation and usually holds work by Papunya Tula and Balgo artists and respected painters such as Clifford Possum Tjapaltjarri *(see p111)*. Works by urban indigenous artists can be found at the **Boomalli Artists' Cooperative**.

Opals

Sydney offers a variety of opals in myriad settings. Both **Flame Opals** and **Opal Fields** sell opals from all the major Australian opal fields. At **The Rocks Opal Mine** you can board a mine shaft elevator for some simulated opal mining – and buy gems into the bargain. **Giulian's** has unset opals, including blacks from Lightning Ridge, whites from Coober Pedy and boulder opals from Quilpie. The **Gemstone Boutique** sells an extensive range of opals, and also stocks coral, pearls, jade and gold nugget jewellery.

Jewellery

Long-established Sydney jewellers with 24-carat reputations include **Fairfax & Roberts**, **Hardy Brothers** and **Percy Marks**. World-class pearls are found in the waters off the northwestern coast of Australia. Rare and beautiful examples can be found at **Paspaley Pearls**.

Victoria Spring Designs evokes costume jewellery's glory days, with filigree and glass beading worked into its sumptuous pendants, rings, earrings and Gothic crosses. **Dinosaur Designs** made its name with colourful, chunky resin jewellery, while at **Love & Hatred**, jewelled wrist cuffs, rings and crosses recall lush medieval treasures.

Glitz Bijouterie has lots of affordable hip silver and glitzy gold necklaces in up-to-the minute styles.

DIRECTORY

ONE-OFFS

Ausfurs
Queen Victoria Building.
Map 1 B5.
9264 6072.

Hello Darling
Queen Victoria Building.
Map 1 B5.
9264 8303.

The Looking Glass
Queen Victoria Building.
Map 1 B5.
9261 4997.

Red Earth
Queen Victoria Building.
Map 1 B5.
9264 4019.
One of several branches.

The Watch Gallery
142 King St.
Map 1 B5.
9221 2288.

Wheels & Doll Baby
259 Crown St,
Darlinghurst.
Map 5 A2.
9361 3286.

AUSTRALIANA

Australian Craftworks
127 George St, The Rocks.
Map 1 B2.
9247 7156.
One of two branches.

Australian Museum
6 College St.
Map 4 F3.
9320 6150.
One of two branches.

Done Art and Design
123 George St, The Rocks.
Map 1 B2.
9251 6099.
One of several branches.

Makers Mark
Chifley Plaza. **Map** 1 B4.
9231 6800.

Weiss Art
85 George St, The Rocks.
Map 1 B2.
9241 3819.

Also: Harbourside
Shopping Centre, Darling
Harbour. **Map** 3 C2.
9281 4614.

BOOKS

Abbey's Bookshop
131 York St. **Map** 1 A5.
9264 3111.

Angus & Robertson Bookworld
Imperial Arcade
168 Pitt St. **Map** 1 B5.
9235 1188.
One of many branches.

Ariel
42 Oxford St, Paddington.
Map 5 B3.
9332 4581.

The Bookshop
207 Oxford St,
Darlinghurst. **Map** 5 A2.
9331 4140.

Dymocks
424–428 George St.
Map 1 B5.
9235 0155.
One of many branches.

Gleebooks
49 Glebe Point Rd, Glebe.
Map 3 B5.
9660 2333.

New Edition Bookshop
328a Oxford St,
Paddington. **Map** 6 D4.
9360 6913.

State Library of NSW
Macquarie St. **Map** 1 C4.
9273 1414.

MUSIC

Anthem Records
9 Albion Place. **Map** 4 E3.
9267 7931.

Birdland
3 Barrack St. **Map** 1 A4.
9299 8527.

Central Station Records and Tapes
46 Oxford St,
Darlinghurst. **Map** 4 F4.
9361 5222.

Folkways
282 Oxford St,
Paddington. **Map** 5 C3.
9361 3980.

Michael's Music Room
19 Town Hall Arcade.
Map 4 E3.
9267 1351.

Red Eye Records
Tank Stream Arcade,
Cnr King and Pitt Sts.
Map 1 B4.
9233 8177.

Timewarp Records
289 Clarence St.
Map 1 A5. 9283 1555.

Utopia Records
636 George St. **Map** 1 A4.
9283 2423.

Waterfront Records
89 York St. **Map** 1 A5.
9262 4120.

ABORIGINAL ART

Aboriginal and Tribal Art Centre
117 George St, The Rocks.
Map 1 B2. 9241 5998.
One of several branches.

Boomalli Artists' Cooperative
27 Abercrombie St,
Chippendale. **Map** 3 C5.
9698 2047.

Coo-ee Aboriginal Art Gallery
98 Oxford St, Paddington.
Map 5 B3. 9332 1544.

Hogarth Galleries Aboriginal Art Centre
7 Walker Lane, off Brown
St, Paddington. **Map** 5 C3.
9360 6839.
One of two branches.

New Guinea Primitive Arts
8th Flr, Dymocks Building,
428 George St. **Map** 1 B5.
9232 4737.
One of two branches.

OPALS

Flame Opals
119 George Street,
The Rocks. **Map** 1 B2.
9247 3446.

Gemstone Boutique
388 George St.
Map 1 B5.
9223 2140.

Giulian's
2 Bridge St. **Map** 1 B3.
9247 5119.

Opal Fields
155 George St, The Rocks.
Map 1 B2.
9247 6800.
One of two branches.

Rocks Opal Mine
Clocktower Square,
35 Harrington St,
The Rocks. **Map** 1 B2.
9247 4974.

JEWELLERY

Dinosaur Designs
Strand Arcade.
Map 1 B5.
9223 2953.
One of several branches.

Fairfax & Roberts
44 Martin Place.
Map 1 B4.
9232 8511.
One of two branches.

Glitz Bijouterie
Imperial Arcade.
Map 1 B5.
9231 1383.

Hardy Brothers
77 Castlereagh St.
Map 1 B5.
9232 2422.
One of two branches.

Love & Hatred
Strand Arcade.
Map 1 B5.
9233 3441.

Paspaley Pearls
142 King St. **Map** 1 A4.
9232 7633.

Percy Marks
60–70 Elizabeth St.
Map 1 B4.
9233 1355.

Victoria Spring Designs
33 William St, Paddington.
Map 6 D3.
9331 7862.

ENTERTAINMENT IN SYDNEY

SYDNEY HAS THE STANDARD of entertainment and nightlife you would expect from a cosmopolitan city. Everything from opera and ballet at Sydney Opera House to Shakespeare by the sea at the Balmoral Beach amphitheatre is on offer. Venues such as the Capitol, Her Majesty's Theatre and the Theatre Royal play host to the latest musicals, while Sydney's many smaller theatres are home to interesting fringe theatre,

A Wharf Theatre production poster

modern dance and rock and pop concerts. Pub rock thrives in the inner city and beyond; and there are many nightspots for jazz, dance and alternative music. Movie buffs are well catered for with film festivals, art-house films and foreign titles, as well as the latest Hollywood blockbusters. One of the features of harbourside living is the free outdoor entertainment so, for children, a Sydney visit can be especially memorable.

Signs outside the Dendy repertory cinema in Martin Place (see p210)

INFORMATION

FOR DETAILS OF events in the city, you should check the daily newspapers first. They carry cinema, and often arts and theatre, advertisements daily. The most comprehensive listings appear in the *Sydney Morning Herald*'s "Metro" guide every Friday. The *Daily Telegraph* has a gig guide on Thursdays, with opportunities to win free tickets to special events. The *Australian*'s main arts pages appear on Fridays and all the papers review new films in weekend editions.

The **NSW Travel Centre**'s tourist information kiosks and most of the major hotels have invaluable free guides such as *What's on in Sydney*, which is published quarterly, and the weekly *Where Magazine*.

Music fans are well served by the free weekly guides *On the Street*, *Drum Media* and *3D World*, with youth culture information, interviews and tour guides. They are found at video and music shops, pubs and clubs. *3D World* has the best dance club information.

Many venues have leaflets about forthcoming attractions, while the major centres have information telephone lines.

BUYING TICKETS

SOME OF THE popular operas, shows, plays and ballets in Sydney are sold out months in advance. While it is better to book ahead, many theatres do set aside tickets to be sold at the door on the night.

You can buy tickets from the box office or by telephone. Some orchestral performances do not admit children under seven, so check with the box office before buying. If you make a phone booking using a credit card, the tickets can be mailed to you. Alternatively, tickets can be collected from the box office half an hour before the show. The major agencies will take overseas bookings.

If you are desperate to see a sold-out rock concert, there may be touts selling tickets

A busker at Circular Quay

outside, but often at hugely inflated prices. If all else fails, hotel concierges have a reputation for being able to secure hard-to-get tickets.

BOOKING AGENCIES

SYDNEY HAS two main ticket agencies: **Ticketek** and **Firstcall**. Between them, they represent all the major entertainment and sporting events.

Ticketek has more than 50 outlets throughout the state, open from 9am to 5pm weekdays, and Saturdays from noon to 4pm. Bookings by phone can be made from 8:30am–9pm, Monday to Saturday, and 10am–7pm Sundays. Overseas bookings can be faxed to Ticketek.

The main Firstcall office is open Monday to Friday, from 9am–6pm. Other offices are open 10am–9pm and can be

The annual Gay and Lesbian Mardi Gras Festival's Dog Show (see p49)

found at all the Greater Union cinemas, the State Theatre, Theatre Royal, Capitol Theatre and Footbridge Theatre *(see pp210–11)*. Firstcall has a 24-hour telephone service.

Agencies accept traveller's cheques, bank cheques, cash, Visa, MasterCard (Access) and American Express. However, some agencies do not accept Diners Club. A booking fee applies, with a postage and handling charge also added if tickets are mailed out. There are generally no refunds (unless a show is cancelled) or exchanges available.

If one agency has sold out its allocation for a show, it is worth checking to see if the

Halftix booth selling cut-price tickets in Martin Place

DISCOUNT TICKETS

WHEN A SHOW isn't sold out, **Halftix** offers half-price tickets (plus a small booking fee) for the theatre, concerts, opera and ballet from noon on the day of the performance only (except for matinees and Sunday performances, tickets to which can be bought the day before). Bus tour, theatre restaurant, harbour cruise, art gallery and film tickets are also available at half price. Payment is by cash or credit card, and there is no limit on the number of tickets you can buy.

You can ring Halftix from 11am for recorded information on which shows are offering discounts. Be there early to beat the queues during the Sydney Festival *(see p49)*. Halftix is also a Ticketek agency for regular advance sales.

Tuesday is budget-price day at most cinemas. Some independent cinemas have special prices throughout the week. The **Sydney Symphony Orchestra** *(see p212)* offers a special Student Rush price to full-time students when tickets

The Spanish firedancers Els Comediants at the Sydney Festival *(p49)*

are available. These can only be bought on the day of the performance, from the box office at the relevant venue. A student card must be shown.

CHOOSING SEATS

IF BOOKING IN person at either the venue or the agency, you will be able to look at a seating plan. Be aware that in the State Theatre's stalls, row A is the back row. In Sydney, there is not as much difference in price between stalls and dress circle as in other cities.

If booking by phone with Ticketek, you will only be able to get a rough idea of where your seats are. The computer will select the "best" tickets.

DISABLED VISITORS

MANY OLDER venues were not designed with the disabled visitor in mind, but this has been redressed in most newer buildings. It is best to phone the box office beforehand to request special seating

The highly respected Australian Chamber Orchestra *(see p212)*

and other requirements. Ask about the best street entrance. The Sydney Town Hall has wheelchair access at its Druitt Street entrance. The **Sydney Opera House** has disabled parking, wheelchair access and a loop system in the Concert Hall for the hearing impaired. A brochure, *Services for the Disabled*, is also available.

Theatre and Film

Sydney's theatrical venues are notable for both their atmosphere and their quality. There is a stimulating mix of productions, from musicals, classic plays and Shakespeare-by-the-sea (and in the park) to contemporary, fringe and experimental theatre. Comedy is also finding a strong niche as a mainstream performance art. Prominent playwrights include David Williamson, Steve J Spears, Stephen Sewell and Louis Nowra.

Australian film-making has earned an international reputation in recent years and there is a rich variety of both local and international films to see, plus annual film festivals showcasing the best local and overseas offerings.

THEATRE

THE LARGER, mainstream musicals, such as those of Andrew Lloyd Webber, are staged at the **Theatre Royal**, the opulent **State Theatre** (see p82), **Her Majesty's** and the **Capitol Theatre** (p99). The **Star City** casino has a showroom and a lyric theatre for musical productions and stage shows.

The smaller venues offer a range of interesting plays and performances. These include the **Seymour Theatre Centre**, which has three theatres; the **Belvoir Street Theatre**, which has two; the **Ensemble**, a theatre-in-the-round by the water; **NIDA Theatre** and the **Footbridge Theatre**. The **Stables Theatre** specializes in works by new Australian playwrights.

The well-respected **Sydney Theatre Company** (STC) is the city's premier theatre company. Most STC productions are at **The Wharf** at Walsh Bay or in the Drama Theatre of the **Sydney Opera House**. The **Bell Shakespeare Company** gives the Bard an innovative slant without tampering with the original text. Its productions are ideal for young or wary theatregoers. While venues vary, there are two Sydney seasons – one in the autumn and one at the beginning of summer.

Street performance and open-air theatre are popular during the summer months when life in Sydney, in general, moves outdoors. Especially popular is the **Shakespeare by the Sea** production, which is performed at Balmoral Beach (see p55). Visitors can purchase tickets through Ticketek (see p209).

For the more adventurous theatre-goer, **Sydney Fringe Festival** offers a celebration of original Australian theatre, film, dance, music and visual arts. Contrary to its "fringe" tag, the festival is accessible in its approach to performances and all works staged are usually of a high standard. It is held over the second half of January at the Bondi Pavilion (see p144) and satellite venues, among them Bondi Beach.

CHILDREN'S THEATRE

SYDNEY THRIVES on spectacles that delight children. You will often find jugglers, mime artists and buskers at Circular Quay. Free entertainment of this sort can also be found in Darling Harbour's Tumbalong Park on most days. Nearby, Harbourside Festival Marketplace often has street theatre and magic shows.

In the suburb of Killara, the **Marian Street Children's Theatre** puts on the occasional theatrical production. If you are lucky, you may be able to see the athletic **Flying Fruit Fly Circus**. This troupe, aged from eight to eighteen, excels in aerial gymnastics and performs in Sydney every year.

FILM

THE CITY'S MAIN commercial cinema strip is in George Street, just one block south of Town Hall. **Hoyts**, **Village** and **Greater Union** show all the latest blockbusters. Similar multi-screen complexes can be found in many suburbs. **The Pitt Centre** can be relied upon for its interesting mainstream and art-house selection.

Film buffs and cinephiles have plenty to choose from at the Paddington end of Oxford Street (the **Academy Twin** and the **Verona**, and the **Chauvel** in Paddington Town Hall).

The **Dendy** cinemas show the latest art-house films – the Martin Place Dendy has a bar and bistro, plus a shop filled with movie memorabilia: soundtracks, videos, books, posters and magazines. The **Walker Cinema** is another popular repertory venue.

Most cinemas offer half-price tickets on Tuesdays, although competition has seen budget prices extend to other days of the week.

The **Imax Theatre** in Darling Harbour has a giant, 8-storey screen and shows 2D and 3D films made specifically for the large screen.

The **Movie Room** shows art-house films and mainstream blockbusters. This cinema is situated above a restaurant, food from which is included in the cost of admission. At the **Australia Cinema**, the latest Chinese movies, with English subtitles, are shown regularly.

Night owls will find late screenings of films at the major cinema complexes and some of the independent cinemas.

FILM FESTIVALS

ONE OF THE BEST events in Sydney's calendar is the **Sydney Film Festival** (see p51). The main venue is the State Theatre, with satellite

---

FILM CENSORSHIP RATINGS

G For general exhibition
PG Parental guidance recommended for those under 15 years
M 15+ Recommended for mature audiences aged 15 and over
MA 15+ Restricted to people 15 years and over
R 18+ Restricted to adults 18 years and over

screenings at other venues. Dozens of new features, shorts and documentaries from all over the globe are presented, and there are often tribute sessions and retrospectives.

Held under the stars at the Bondi Pavilion Amphitheatre at Bondi Beach, **Flickerfest International Short Film Festival** is run over ten days in January. The Short Poppies Festival is staged in tandem with Flickerfest and is a feast of student films and videos.

Sydney's Festival of Jewish Cinema, held at the **Academy Twin** in Paddington, begins in mid-November and lasts for ten days. Highly acclaimed international films with a Jewish theme are screened.

The Gay and Lesbian Film Festival runs over two weeks, starting mid-February. Films are shown at various inner-city venues, as part of the **Gay and Lesbian Mardi Gras** *(p49)*.

COMEDY

SYDNEY'S MOST established comedy venue, the **Comedy Store**, is only minutes by train from Central Railway Station. There are stand-up comics, sketches or revues every night except Monday. Thursday is the night new comedians try out their stand-up skills.

Monday night is Comics in the Park at the **Comedy Hotel**, when new and established comics have a chance at the microphone. Other comedy shows are held throughout the week. Monday is also the night for laughs at the Fringe Bar in the **Unicorn Hotel**. On Tuesdays, comedians perform at the **Hopetoun Hotel**, while Thursday night is stand-up comedy night at the **Bat and Ball Hotel**.

DIRECTORY

THEATRE

Bell Shakespeare Company
📞 9241 2722.

Belvoir Street Theatre
25 Belvoir St, Surry Hills.
📞 9699 3444.

Capitol Theatre
13 Campbell St,
Haymarket. **Map** 4 E4.
📞 9320 5000.

Ensemble Theatre
78 McDougall St, Kirribilli.
📞 9929 0644.

Footbridge Theatre
University of Sydney,
Parramatta Rd, Glebe.
Map 3 A5.
📞 9692 9955.

Her Majesty's Theatre
107 Quay St (near Railway Square), Haymarket.
Map 4 D5.
📞 9212 3411.

NIDA Theatre
215 Anzac Parade,
Kensington.
📞 9697 7613.

Seymour Theatre Centre
Cnr Cleveland St & City
Rd, Chippendale.
📞 9364 9400.

Shakespeare by the Sea
📞 9557 3065.

Stables Theatre
10 Nimrod St, Kings
Cross. **Map** 5 B1.
📞 9361 3817.

Star City
80 Pyrmont St,
Pyrmont. **Map** 3 B1.
📞 9777 9000.
Lyric Theatre
Box office 📞 9657 8000.

State Theatre
49 Market St. **Map** 1 B5.
📞 9373 6655.

Sydney Fringe Festival
📞 9365 0112.

Sydney Opera House
Bennelong Point.
Map 1 C2. 📞 9250 7111.

Theatre Royal
MLC Centre, King St.
Map 1 B5. 📞 9320 9191.

The Wharf
Pier 4, Hickson Rd,
Millers Point. **Map** 1 A1.
📞 9250 1777.

CHILDREN'S THEATRE

Flying Fruit Fly Circus
📞 6021 7044.

Marian Street Children's Theatre
2 Marian Street, Killara.
📞 9498 3166.

FILM

Academy Twin
3a Oxford St, Paddington.
Map 5 B3. 📞 9361 4453.

Australia Cinema
59 Goulburn St.
Map 4 E4. 📞 9281 2883.

Chauvel Twin Cinemas
249 Oxford St, Paddington.
Map 5 C3. 📞 9361 5398.

Dendy Cinema
Martin Place
MLC Centre, 19 Martin
Place. **Map** 1 B4.
📞 9233 8558.
George Street
624 George St. **Map** 4 E3.
📞 9264 1577.
Newtown
354 King St, Newtown.
📞 9519 5081.

Greater Union
525 George St. **Map** 4 E3.
📞 9267 8666.

Hoyts Centre
505 George St. **Map** 4 E3.
📞 9273 7431.

Imax Theatre
Southern Promenade,
Darling Harbour. **Map** 4 D3.
📞 9281 3300.

Movie Room
112 Darlinghurst Rd,
Darlinghurst.
📞 9360 7853.

Verona Cinema
17 Oxford St, Paddington.
Map 5 B3.
📞 9360 6099.

Village
545 George St.
Map 4 E3.
📞 9264 6701.

Walker Cinema
121 Walker St,
North Sydney.
📞 9959 4222.

FILM FESTIVALS

Flickerfest
📞 9211 7133.

Gay and Lesbian Mardi Gras
📞 9557 4332.

Sydney Film Festival
📞 9660 3844.

COMEDY

Bat and Ball Hotel
495 Cleveland St,
Redfern. **Map** 5 A5.
📞 9699 3782.

Comedy Hotel
115 Wigram Rd, Glebe.
📞 9552 1791.

Comedy Store
450 Parramatta Rd,
Petersham. 📞 9692 0564.

Hopetoun Hotel
416 Bourke St,
Surry Hills. **Map** 5 A3.
📞 9361 5257.

Unicorn Hotel
106 Oxford St,
Paddington. **Map** 5 B3.
📞 9360 3554.

Opera, Classical Music and Dance

MUSIC BUFFS CANNOT POSSIBLY visit Sydney without seeing an opera or hearing the city's premier orchestra perform in the Sydney Opera House. And that is just the start. Since the 1970s, music played in Sydney has considerably broadened its base, opening the door to all manner of influences from Asia, Europe and the Pacific, not to mention local compositions. For the visitor, there is a wealth of orchestral, choral, chamber and contemporary music from which to choose.

OPERA

AUSTRALIA has produced a number of world-class opera singers, including Joan Sutherland, and eminent conductors such as Sir Charles Mackerras, Simone Young and Stuart Challender. The first recorded performance of an opera in Sydney was in 1834. For the next 120 years, most opera seen by Sydneysiders was imported from overseas.

In 1956, the Australian Opera (AO) was formed and it presented four Mozart operas in its first year. But it was the opening of the **Sydney Opera House** (see pp74–7) in 1973 that heralded a new interest in opera. The AO's summer season is held from early January to early March; the winter season from June to the end of October. Performances are held in the Opera Theatre of the Sydney Opera House. Crowd pleasers over the years have included *Turandot* and *La Bohème*. Every year at the hugely popular Opera in the Park (see p49), members of the Australian Opera perform excerpts from classical operas.

ORCHESTRAL MUSIC

SYDNEY'S main provider of orchestral music and recitals is the **Sydney Symphony Orchestra** (SSO). Numerous concerts are given each year, mostly in the Sydney Opera House Concert Hall or the **Sydney Town Hall** (see p87).

This season is complemented by the Meet the Music series – twilight concerts aimed at adventurous younger classical fans. These feature a new Australian work introduced by the composer, a masterpiece and a concerto. There's a Tea and Symphony series mid-year, held on Friday mornings at the Sydney Opera House. For one week in November, the Babies' Proms are held in the **Eugene Goossens Hall** for children under five years of age.

The **Conservatorium of Music** (see p106), with its picturesque location in the Royal Botanic Gardens and castle-like architecture, provides an atmospheric concert setting. There are inexpensive concert evenings throughout the year at which you can listen to the Conservatorium's symphony,

wind or chamber orchestras, or jazz big bands. The **Sydney Youth Orchestra** was formed in 1973 and is highly praised for its talent, enthusiasm and impressive young soloists. It performs each year at Carols in The Domain (see p49), and once every couple of months at the Sydney Opera House or Sydney Town Hall.

CONTEMPORARY MUSIC

THE VERY FIRST concert held by **Musica Viva** was in December 1945, at the New South Wales Conservatorium of Music. What began with just a string chamber ensemble today promotes concerts of all kinds. Chamber music was Musica Viva's first love, but it now presents string quartets, jazz, piano groups, percussionists, soloists and international avant-garde artists as well. Concerts are held at the Sydney Opera House, the **Seymour Theatre Centre** and, on rare occasions, Sydney Town Hall.

Synergy is one of Sydney's best contemporary music groups and one of Australia's foremost percussion quartets. The group commissions works from all over the world and gives its own concert series at Eugene Goossens Hall every year. Synergy also collaborates with dance and theatre groups.

CHAMBER MUSIC

UNDER DIRECTOR Richard Tognetti, the **Australian Chamber Orchestra** has considerably raised the profile of large chamber orchestras. This internationally acclaimed orchestra is noted for its creativity and interesting choice of venues, including museums, churches and even wineries. Its main concerts are held at the Sydney Opera House, with dates throughout the year. There is also a smaller concert series at the Sydney Town Hall, plus a Church Series, which is held over the Easter period.

The **Australia Ensemble** is the resident chamber music group at the University of New South Wales. It performs six times a year at the **Sir John**

FREE CONCERTS

Lunchtime concerts are very much part of Sydney life. There are free performances every weekday in the Martin Place amphitheatre (see p84). Solo graduate students and small ensembles from the Conservatorium of Music give a free recital in Martin Place every Wednesday. The half-hour organ recital in St Andrew's Cathedral (see p87), at 1:15pm on Thursdays, is a long-standing tradition. You will find buskers, jazz bands, string ensembles, guitarists or dancers most weekends and right through school holiday periods at Circular Quay, The Rocks and Darling Harbour. If the weather is fine, the Sydney Opera House provides free entertainment from noon on Sundays and public holidays on the Forecourt or Northern Boardwalk. During the Sydney Festival (see p49), there are free concerts aplenty, the most popular being Opera in the Park, Symphony under the Stars and the Australia Day Concert, all held in The Domain.

Clancy Auditorium and also appears for Musica Viva. Many choral groups and ensembles, such as the **Macquarie Trio** of violin, piano and cello, like to book **St James' Church** because of its atmosphere and acoustics (which, it must be said, are kinder than the seats). The trio also performs at the **Macquarie Theatre**.

CHORAL MUSIC

COMPRISING THE 200-strong Sydney Philharmonia Symphonic Choir and the 40-member Sydney Philharmonia Motet Choir, the **Sydney Philharmonia Choirs** are the city's finest. They perform at the Sydney Opera House every two months or so and, in December, are the focal point of the Sydney Symphony *Messiah* concerts and Carols in The Domain *(see p49)*.

The **Australian Youth Choir** is booked for many private functions, but if lucky, you may catch one of their two major annual performances at the Sydney Town Hall in June and December. One of the city's most impressive vocal

groups is the **Café at the Gate of Salvation**, described as "a feral Aussie blend of *a cappella* gospel". Check the weekly listings *(see p208)* for performance dates.

DANCE

THERE IS AN eclectic variety of dance on offer in Sydney. The Australian Ballet has two seven-week Sydney seasons at the Sydney Opera House: one in March/April, the other in November/December. The company's repertoire spans traditional through to modern, although it is perhaps most noted for classical ballets such as *Swan Lake* and *Giselle*.

Sydney Dance Company is the city's leading modern dance group, often combining its vigorous productions with innovative musical scores. It has performed in Italy, New York, London and China. Productions are mostly staged at the Sydney Opera House, but are, on occasion, held at their studio at **The Wharf**.

The **Performance Space** is very popular for experimental dance and movement theatre.

Artists with backgrounds in everything from dance, mime and circus work to Butoh and performance art are likely to appear here. It is also where the challenging modernist troupe, **Dance Exchange**, performs its work each year.

Bangarra Dance Theatre uses traditional Aboriginal and Torres Strait Islander dance and music as its inspiration, infused with contemporary elements. The troupe makes international, outback and interstate tours, but is based in Sydney. The **Aboriginal Islander Dance Theatre** is also contemporary with a traditional flavour. Its Sydney performances are usually at the Seymour Theatre Centre.

The smaller experimental companies rely on year-to-year funding or community-based work. These include Kinetic Energy Theatre Co., which has the **Edge Theatre** as its head-quarters, the collaborative **One Extra Company**, and **Darc Swan**. **ACE**, established by *Strictly Ballroom* star Paul Mercurio, draws on a range of movement from contemporary ballet to street dance.

DIRECTORY

ORCHESTRAS AND CHOIRS

Australian Chamber Orchestra
[9357 4111.

Australia Ensemble
[9385 4872.

Australian Youth Choir
[9808 5561.

Café at the Gate of Salvation
[9144 5501.

Macquarie Trio
[9850 9447.

Musica Viva
[9698 1711.

Sydney Philharmonia Choirs
[9251 2024.

Sydney Symphony Orchestra
[9334 4644.

Sydney Youth Orchestra
[9281 1666.

DANCE COMPANIES

Aboriginal Islander Dance Theatre
[9252 0199.

ACE
[9314 3133.

Bangarra Dance Theatre
[9251 5333.

Dance Exchange
[9357 3576.

Darc Swan
[9818 3039.

One Extra Company
[9364 9468.

Sydney Dance Company
[9221 4811.

CONCERT AND DANCE VENUES

Conservatorium of Music
Macquarie St. **Map** 1 C3.
[9351 1222.

Edge Theatre
642 King St, Newtown South. [9516 1954.

Eugene Goossens Hall
Australian Broadcasting Commission, 700 Harris St, Ultimo. **Map** 4 D5.
[9333 1500.

Macquarie Theatre
Macquarie University, Cnr Epping and Balaclava Rds, North Ryde.
[9850 7586.

Performance Space
199 Cleveland St, Redfern.
[9319 5091.

St James' Church
173 King St. **Map** 1 B5.
[9232 3022.

Seymour Theatre Centre
See p211.

Sir John Clancy Auditorium
University of NSW, Anzac Pde, Kensington.
[9385 3471.

Sydney Opera House
See p211.

Sydney Town Hall
Cnr George and Druitt Sts. **Map** 4 E2.
[9265 9189.

The Wharf
See p211.

Music Venues and Nightclubs

SYDNEY DRAWS the biggest names in contemporary music all year round. Venues range from the cavernous Sydney Entertainment Centre to small and noisy back rooms in pubs. Most of the venues cater for a variety of music tastes – rock one night, jazz, blues or folk the next. The many weekly gig guides *(see p208)* will tell you what to see and when to see it.

GETTING IN

FOR THE MAJOR shows and outdoor concerts you can buy tickets through booking agencies such as Ticketek and Firstcall *(see p208)*. There can be a large price variation, depending on the act. You may pay from $10 to $35 for something at the Metro, but nearly $100 for the best seats at a Rolling Stones concert.

With smaller venues, you pay at the door on the night. The price often depends on the band's popularity and the takings are usually the band's total earnings for the night.

Dance clubs often have a cover charge, but some venues will admit you free before a certain time in the evening.

ROCK MUSIC

THE ROCK WORLD'S biggest names usually perform at the **Sydney Entertainment Centre**. Alternative venues which are frequently used are sports grounds such as the **Eastern Creek Raceway**, **Sydney Football Stadium** and **Sydney Cricket Ground**.

There are also more intimate locations for esteemed local and international rock acts. Many are old theatres, including the **State Theatre**, the **Enmore Theatre** and the musically adventurous **Metro**, opposite the city's cinema strip.

The Australia Day Concert *(see p49)*, a free evening event which takes place on 26 January, brings the best of Australia's rock acts together at **The Domain** *(see p107)*.

Pub rock is a constantly changing scene in Sydney. Weekly listings, appearing in papers such as the *Sydney Morning Herald*, have the latest news on when and where to see bands *(p208)*. Hotel venues such as the

Sandringham Hotel, **Annandale Hotel**, **Bridge Hotel**, **Hopetoun Hotel** and Selina's at **Coogee Bay Hotel** draw big crowds to their everchanging rota of bands and performers.

You can drop into **Round Midnight** most nights for a dose of funk, soul or blues.

JAZZ

FOR CONSISTENTLY excellent contemporary jazz **The Basement** is almost an institution among Sydney jazz fans. This popular venue has both local and international artists, and the music played here includes blues and, at times, even respectable pop.

Soup Plus is another option for those wanting to hear excellent music and good inexpensive food is also served. Alternatives are the **Harbourside Brasserie** and the **Orient Hotel** on weekends. A jazz cruise, the **Rocks Rhythmboat**, leaves Pier 1 at noon every Sunday.

BLUES

THE BEST SPOTS to hear blues in Sydney are the **Bridge Hotel**, the **Rose, Shamrock & Thistle** (commonly referred to as the "Three Weeds"), the **Cat & Fiddle**, **The Basement** and the Harbourside Brasserie. The **Rose of Australia** has a a big blues jam on the last Sunday of every month.

NIGHTCLUBS

DANCE CLUBS may come and go in Sydney as they do in every city, but there are still several constants on the scene. Nightspots playing a broad range of dance, soul, funk, disco and rock include the **Cauldron**, Juliana's in the **Sydney Hilton**, **Riva Night**

Club and **Kinselas**. Clubs into dance music, house and hip hop include the **Bentley Bar**, **Mister Goodbar**, **Soho Lounge Bar** and **Q**. Hard-core dance music starts on Saturday night at **Blackmarket** and continues all day Sunday with the Dayclub. Thursday night is the renowned Hellfire Club for the S&M crowd. **DCM** has a large dance floor and good music. **Axis** plays black beats, soul funk and all the latest grooves, while **Power Cuts** is the venue for reggae.

GAY AND LESBIAN VENUES

SUNDAY NIGHT is the big night out for many of Sydney's inner-city gay community, although there is plenty of action all through the week. Popular hotspots include the **Beresford**, **Beauchamp**, **Flinders** and **Oxford** hotels, and the **Midnight Shift**. The Phoenix Bar at the **Exchange** draws big crowds on Thursday and Sunday nights. The **Albury Hotel** has entertainment all week, including drag shows.

For cocktails to kick off a night out, there's the Lizard Lounge at the **Exchange**, a favourite spot with lesbians, and the Oxford Cocktail Bar at the **Oxford Hotel**. One of the best lesbian nights out is On the Other Side upstairs at **Kinselas** on Sundays.

In Newtown, the **Imperial** and the **Newtown** hotels are popular gay and lesbian venues. The Imperial Hotel was featured in the movie *Priscilla, Queen of the Desert.*

CABARET

THERE'S ENTERTAINMENT most nights at the **Harbourside Brasserie**, ranging from dinner shows to jazz, rock and late-night dance bands. The **Tilbury Hotel** – a cosy and atmospheric cabaret venue – also has dinner shows most nights of the week. At the Sydney Hilton, international acts of Al Jarreau and Pointer Sisters calibre are booked for its dinner and supper shows.

DIRECTORY

ROCK MUSIC

Annandale Hotel
17 Parramatta Rd,
Annandale.
9550 1078.

Bridge Hotel
135 Victoria Rd,
Rozelle.
9810 1260.

Coogee Bay Hotel
Cnr Coogee Bay Rd and
Arden St, Coogee.
9665 0000.

The Domain
Art Gallery Road.
Map 1 C5.

**Eastern Creek
Raceway**
Horsley Rd, Eastern Creek.
9672 1000.

Enmore Theatre
130 Enmore Rd,
Newtown.
9550 3666.

Hopetoun Hotel
416 Bourke St,
Surry Hills.
9361 5257.

Metro
624 George St.
Map 4 E3.
9264 2666.

Round Midnight
2 Roslyn St,
Potts Point. **Map** 5 C1.
9356 4045.

**Sandringham
Hotel**
387 King St,
Newtown.
9557 1254.

State Theatre
49 Market St. **Map** 1 B5.
9373 6655.

**Sydney Cricket
Ground**
Driver Ave,
Moore Park. **Map** 5 C5.
9360 6601.

**Sydney
Entertainment
Centre**
Harbour St, Haymarket.
Map 4 D4.
9320 4200.
1900 957 333.

**Sydney Football
Stadium**
Moore Park Rd and Driver
Ave, Moore Park.
9360 6601.

JAZZ

The Basement
29 Reiby Place.
Map 1 B3.
9251 2797.

**Harbourside
Brasserie**
Pier 1, Hickson Rd,
Millers Point.
Map 1 B1.
9252 3000.

Orient Hotel
89 George St, The Rocks.
Map 1 B2.
9251 1255.

Rocks Rhythmboat
Departs Pier 1, Hickson Rd,
Millers Point.
Map 1 B1.
9247 2979.

Soup Plus
383 George St.
Map 1 B5.
9299 7728.

BLUES

The Basement
See Jazz.

Bridge Hotel
See Rock
Music.

Cat & Fiddle Hotel
456 Darling St, Balmain.
9810 7931.

**Harbourside
Brasserie**
See Jazz.

Rose of Australia
1 Swanson St, Erskineville.
9565 1441.

**Rose, Shamrock &
Thistle Hotel**
193 Evans St, Rozelle.
9810 2244.

NIGHTCLUBS

Axis
195 Oxford St, Bondi
Junction. 9386 1006.

Bentley Bar
320 Crown St, Surry Hills.
Map 5 A2.
9331 1186.

Blackmarket
111 Regent St,
Chippendale.
9698 8863.

Cauldron
207 Darlinghurst Rd,
Darlinghurst. **Map** 5 B1.
9331 1523.

DCM
33 Oxford St,
Darlinghurst. **Map** 4 F4.
9267 7380.

Kinselas
383 Bourke St,
Darlinghurst. **Map** 5 A2.
9331 3299.

Mister Goodbar
11a Oxford St, Paddington.
Map 5 B3.
9360 6759.

Power Cuts
150 Elizabeth St.
Map 4 F4.
9264 5380.

Q
Level 2, 44 Oxford St,
Darlinghurst. **Map** 4 F4.
9360 1375.

Riva Night Club
Sheraton on the Park,
130 Castlereagh St.
Map 1 B5.
9286 6666.

Soho Lounge Bar
171 Victoria St, Potts
Point.
9358 4221.

Sydney Hilton
259 Pitt St. **Map** 1 B5.
9266 2000.

GAY AND LESBIAN
VENUES

Albury Hotel
2–8 Oxford St,
Paddington. **Map** 5 B3.
9361 6555.

Beauchamp Hotel
267 Oxford St,
Darlinghurst. **Map** 5 A2.
9331 2575.

Beresford Hotel
354 Bourke St,
Darlinghurst. **Map** 5 A3.
9331 1045.

Exchange Hotel
34 Oxford St,
Darlinghurst. **Map** 4 F4.
9331 1936.

Flinders Hotel
63 Flinders St,
Darlinghurst. **Map** 5 A3.
9360 4929.

Imperial Hotel
35 Erskineville Rd,
Erskineville.
9519 9899.

Kinselas
See Nightclubs.

Midnight Shift
85 Oxford St, Darlinghurst.
Map 5 A2.
9360 4319.

Newtown Hotel
174 King St, Newtown.
9557 1329.

Oxford Hotel
134 Oxford St, Darlinghurst.
Map 5 A2.
9331 3467.

CABARET

**Harbourside
Brasserie**
See Jazz.

Sydney Hilton
See Nightclubs.

Tilbury Hotel
22 Forbes St,
Woolloomooloo.
Map 2 D5. 9368 1955.

SURVIVAL
GUIDE

PRACTICAL INFORMATION

Lifesavers at Coogee Surf Carnival

ALTHOUGH SYDNEY has only fairly recently become a major destination for international tourists, facilities are now well established and most services are of a very high standard. Hotels in the city are generally expensive, but clean, comfortable cheaper accommodation is available *(see pp168–77)*. There are cafés and restaurants in all price brackets that offer a wide range of international cuisines *(see pp178–97)*. Public transport is reliable and inexpensive, especially if you take advantage of the numerous composite travelcards that offer combined bus, ferry and train travel *(see p230)*. Bureaux de change and cash dispensers are conveniently located throughout the city and major credit cards are accepted by most hotels, restaurants and shops. Visitors will find Sydney a safe, clean and welcoming city. They should encounter few practical problems as long as they follow a few common-sense guidelines about personal security *(see pp222–3)*.

Visitor information kiosk inside Central Railway Station

TOURIST INFORMATION

SYDNEY'S PRINCIPAL tourist information and booking centre for accommodation, tours and travel is the state-run **NSW Information Line**. Information booths can also be found at Sydney's major attractions and beaches, and at several central Sydney locations. As well as providing information and advice, these booths have maps, brochures and entertainment listings *(see p208)* available for free.

For visitors arriving by air, there is another branch of the NSW Information Line at Sydney Airport, open from 5am to midnight, or while flights are operating.

If you would like to find out about Sydney and the rest of Australia before you travel, the **Australian Tourist Commission** can provide useful information and brochures.

MUSEUMS AND GALLERIES

MOST OF SYDNEY'S major museums and galleries are close to the city centre and readily accessible by public transport *(see pp230–35)*.

Although opening hours and admission charges vary, the majority of museums and galleries are open 10am–5pm daily (smaller galleries are usually closed on Mondays). Admission is quite often free or else only a moderate fee is charged. There are concessions available for senior citizens, students and children.

Museums and galleries are often at their busiest on weekends, particularly when special exhibitions are being staged.

Art Gallery of New South Wales

SMOKING

SMOKING is strictly forbidden in shops and department stores and many workplaces; on public transport and outside the designated smoking areas in restaurants, theatres and entertainment venues. It is best to ask about smoking policies when making reservations in hotels and restaurants.

AUSTRALIAN TOURIST COMMISSION OFFICES

UK
Gemini House, 10–18 Putney Hill Rd, London SW15 6AA.
📞 0181 780 2229.
FAX 0181 780 1496.

USA and Canada
2049 Century Park East, Suite 1920, Los Angeles, CA 90067.
📞 1310 229 4870.
FAX 1310 552 1215.

TOURIST INFORMATION

NSW Information Line
City Centre
📞 132077.
Kingsford Smith Airport
International Arrivals Hall.
📞 9667 9431.

Sydney Visitor Centre
106 George St, The Rocks.
Map 1 B2. 📞 9255 1788.
⭕ Feb–Nov: 9am–5pm daily; Dec–Jan: 9am–6pm daily.

Darling Harbour Visitors Centre
Palm Grove Carousel, Darling Harbour. **Map** 3 D3.
📞 9286 0111.
⭕ 10am–6pm daily.

Central Railway Station
Sydney Terminal. **Map** 4 E5.
⭕ 6am–10pm daily.

Casual dress at a beachside café

ETIQUETTE AND TIPPING

WHILE SYDNEY customs are generally casual, there are a few rules to follow. Eating and drinking is frowned at on public transport, and also when travelling in taxis.

Dress code is generally smart casual, but is more relaxed in summer – although people do like to go all out for formal occasions. Topless bathing is accepted on most beaches, but not at public swimming pools.

People do not depend on tips for their livelihood so this is generally optional. However, it is the custom to leave a little extra for good service in cafés and restaurants (see p179), to tip hotel porters (see p169) and to leave any small change for bartenders and taxi drivers.

GUIDED TOURS AND EXCURSIONS

TOURS AND EXCURSIONS offer the visitor many different ways of exploring the city and its surroundings – from bus tours of the city's night spots, jaunts on the back of a Harley Davidson, guided nature walks, harbour cruises and river runs, to aerial adventures by hot-air balloon, seaplane or helicopter.

As well as being an easy way to take in the sights, a guided tour can help you to get a feel for your new surroundings.

Perhaps the most economical and flexible introductions to Sydney's attractions are the unregimented tours provided by the State Transit Explorer Buses (see p231). The **State Transit Tourist Ferries** also run special sightseeing routes. In addition, commuter ferries (see pp234–5) provide a less costly alternative to all-out commercial harbour cruises.

Top-sail schooner *Solway Lass*

STUDENT TRAVELLERS

STUDENT TRAVELLERS carrying the International Student Identity card are eligible for discounts in museums, theatres and cinemas, as well as a 40 per cent reduction on internal air fares and 15 per cent off interstate coach travel.

Overseas visitors who are full-time students in Australia can purchase an International Student Identity card (with a guidebook included) for $10 from Sydney branches of the **Student Travel Association**.

DIRECTORY

COACH AND MOTORCYCLE TOURS

Australian Pacific Tours
102 George St. **Map** 1 B4.
(9252 2988.

Eastcoast Motorcycle Tours
(9247 5151.

HARBOUR AND RIVER CRUISES

Captain Cook Cruises
Wharf 6, Circular Quay.
Map 1 B3. (9206 1111.

Matilda Cruises (Solway Lass)
Pier 26, Darling Harbour.
Map 4 D2. (9264 7377.

State Transit Tourist Ferries
Wharves 4 and 5, Circular Quay.
Map 1 B3. (131500.

The Bounty
29 George Street, The Rocks.
Map 1 B2. (9247 1789.

WALKING TOURS

Maureen Fry Sydney Guided Tours
15 Arcadia Rd, Glebe.
(9660 7157.

The Rocks Walking Tours
106 George St, The Rocks.
Map 1 B2. (9247 6678.

AIR TOURS

Cloud Nine Balloon Flights
(9686 7777.

Sydney Harbour Seaplanes
(9388 1978.

Sydney Helicopter Service
(9637 4455.

STUDENT INFORMATION

Student Travel Association
(9212 1255.

Seaplane moored at Rose Bay, available for scenic flight charter

DISABLED TRAVELLERS

SYDNEY HAS RECENTLY made much-needed advances in catering for the disabled. State Transit is phasing in specially designed buses with doors at pavement level and ramps that allow people in wheelchairs to use the bus service. There is also priority seating for those with a disability and bus hand-rails and steps are marked with bright yellow paint to assist visually impaired passengers.

The Circular Quay railway station is completely accessible to wheelchair users. Several other stations have wide entrance gates and most have ramps installed. The Public Transport Infoline *(see p230)* can give details on disabled access at each station.

Museums, newer hotels and some major sights cater to the less mobile, including those in wheelchairs, as well as people with other disabilities. You are strongly advised to phone all sights in advance to check on facilities, allowing the most effective forward planning.

For detailed information on accessible services and venues, ACROD's *Accessing Sydney (see p170)* is available from all major bookshops. A map and directory for people who have limited mobility can be obtained from the **Sydney City Council One-Stop Shop**.

Sydney City Council One-Stop Shop
Town Hall House, Sydney Square, George St. **Map** 4 E3. **[C]** *9265 9333.*

SYDNEY TIME

Sydney is in the Australian Eastern Standard Time zone (AEST). Daylight saving in New South Wales starts on the last Sunday in October and finishes on the last Sunday in March. The Northern Territory, Queensland and Western Australia do not observe daylight saving, so check time differences when you are there.

Australian Time Zones

City and Country	Hours + or – AEST
Adelaide (Australia)	–½
Brisbane (Australia)	same
Canberra (Australia)	same
Darwin (Australia)	–½
Hobart (Australia)	same
Melbourne (Australia)	same
Perth (Australia)	–2
London (UK)	–9
Los Angeles (USA)	–17
Singapore	–2
Toronto (Canada)	–14

IMMIGRATION AND CUSTOMS

ALL VISITORS TO Australia, with the exception of New Zealand passport holders, are required to hold a valid pass-port and visa, as well as an onward ticket and proof that they have sufficient funds for the duration of their visit.

The customs allowance per person over 18 years of age entering Australia is gifts up to value of A$400, 1.125 litres (about 2 pints) of alcohol and a carton of 250 cigarettes.

Quarantine regulations in Australia are very strict because of the debilitating effect that introduced pests and diseases would have, not only on the agricultural industry, but also on the country's unique flora and fauna. The importation of

Overseas cruise ship in port at Circular Quay passenger terminal

fresh or packaged food, fruit, vegetables, seeds, live plants and plant products is prohibit-ed. It is also illegal to bring in any items or products made from endangered species.

On all international flights to Sydney, the aircraft cabin is sprayed with insecticide just before landing. The customs declaration forms issued on the plane must be filled out and given to customs officers as you enter the country. The penalties for importing illegal drugs of any sort are severe.

DEPARTURE TAX

AS IN MANY other countries, Australia has a departure tax. All passengers aged 12 or over are required to fill out a form and pay a A$27 departure tax when leaving the country. This tax is usually included in the cost of your airline ticket.

If you have not already paid departure tax, airport check-in staff will refer you to a post office *(see p227)*. Departure tax can be paid for in advance at most Australia Post offices.

Entrance gates with wheelchair access at Circular Quay railway station

MEDIA

SYDNEY'S CHIEF daily morning newspaper is the *Sydney Morning Herald*. It includes a comprehensive listing of local entertainment on Fridays and Saturdays. The other Sydney daily is the *Daily Telegraph*.

The *Australian* is a daily national paper with the most comprehensive coverage of overseas news, and the weekly *Bulletin* is Australia's leading international news magazine. Foreign newspapers and magazines are widely available for sale at many newsstands.

Sydney is well served with AM and FM radio stations. The state-run ABC (Australian Broadcasting Corporation) stations cater for various tastes, from rock to classical, as well as providing current affairs and magazine-style programmes. The commercial stations offer popular music, news and talk-back shows. There are also radio stations with programmes in community languages.

Sydney has two state-run television stations, the ABC's Channel 2 and the multicultural Special Broadcasting Service (SBS). Channels 7, 9 and 10 are commercially operated and offer the usual soap operas, news, sport and gameshows.

A selection of daily newspapers

PUBLIC TOILETS

FREE PUBLIC TOILETS are to be found in Sydney's public places, galleries and museums, department stores and all bus and railway stations. They are generally well serviced and clean. Baby changing facilities

Drinking fountain in the city

are also quite common, particularly in department stores and major museums and galleries.

Clean drinking fountains can be found throughout the city. Spring, or distilled, water is also often freely available from dispensers in waiting areas of chemist shops, travel agents and offices.

Standard Australian three-pin plug

ELECTRICAL APPLIANCES

AUSTRALIA'S ELECTRICAL current is 240–250 volts AC. Electrical plugs can have either two or three pins. Most good hotels will provide 110-volt shaver sockets and hair dryers, but a flat, two- or three-pin adaptor will be necessary for other appliances. These can be bought from electrical stores.

CONVERSION TABLE

Imperial to Metric
1 inch = 2.54 centimetres
1 foot = 30 centimetres
1 mile = 1.6 kilometres
1 ounce = 28 grams
1 pound = 454 grams
1 pint = 0.6 litres
1 gallon = 4.6 litres

Metric to Imperial
1 centimetre = 0.4 inches
1 metre = 3 feet, 3 inches
1 kilometre = 0.6 miles
1 gram = 0.04 ounces
1 kilogram = 2.2 pounds
1 litre = 1.8 pints

DIRECTORY

EMBASSIES AND CONSULATES

Canada
Level 5, 111 Harrington St.
Map 1 B3. [9364 3000.

New Zealand
Level 14, Goldfields House,
1 Alfred St. **Map** 1 B3.
[9247 1344.

Republic of Ireland
20 Arkana St, Yarralumla
ACT 2600. [6273 3022.

United Kingdom
Level 16, The Gateway,
1 Macquarie Place. **Map** 1 B3.
[9247 7521.

USA
MLC Centre, 19–29 Martin Place.
Map 1 B4. [9373 9200.

RELIGIOUS SERVICES

Anglican
St Andrew's Cathedral,
Sydney Square, George St.
Map 4 E3. [9265 1661.

Baptist
Central Baptist Church,
619 George St. **Map** 4 E4.
[9211 1833.

Catholic
St Mary's Cathedral, Cathedral St.
Map 1 C5. [9220 0400.

Interdenominational
Wayside Chapel of the Cross,
29 Hughes St, Potts Point.
Map 2 E5. [9358 6577.

Islamic
Surry Hills Mosque,
175 Commonwealth St,
Surry Hills. **Map** 4 F4.
[9281 0440.

Jewish Orthodox
The Great Synagogue,
187 Elizabeth St. **Map** 1 B5.
[9267 2477.

Presbyterian
Scots Church, 44 Margaret St.
Map 1 A4. [9299 1804.

Uniting
St Stephen's Church,
197 Macquarie St. **Map** 1 C4.
[9221 1688.

Personal Security and Health

STREET CRIME IN SYDNEY IS LESS prevalent than in many other large cities, but it does exist. You can minimize your risk of becoming a victim of crime by exercising reasonable caution. Members of Sydney's police patrol the city's streets and public transport system in pairs. Mobile police stations, set up at crowded tourist areas and at public events, have proved particularly successful and are popular with the public. Further afield, the surf beaches and natural bushland can present a few dangers of their own, and the following information offers some practical advice for coping with environmental hazards.

Police vehicle

Fire engine

Intensive care ambulance

LOOKING AFTER YOUR PROPERTY

LEAVE VALUABLES and important documents in your hotel safe, and don't carry large sums of cash with you. Traveller's cheques are generally regarded as the safest way to carry large sums of money. It is also worth photocopying vital douments in case of loss or theft.

Be on guard against purse snatchers and pickpockets in places where big crowds gather. Prime areas for petty theft are popular tourist areas, beaches, markets, sporting venues and on public transport.

Never carry your wallet in an outside pocket where it is an easy target for a thief and wear shoulder bags and cameras with the strap across your body and the bag or camera in front with the

Ambulance paramedic

clasp fastened. If you have a car, always try to park in well-lit, reasonably busy streets. Remember to lock the vehicle securely. It is also important not to leave any valuables or property visible inside the car that might attract a thief.

PERSONAL SAFETY

SYDNEY HAS NO definite off-limit areas during the day, but it is probably wise to avoid the more unsavoury side streets and lanes of areas such as Kings Cross. If you take reasonable care, you can go into most areas at night, although visitors are advised to stay clear of deserted, poorly lit streets and toilets in parks.

When travelling by train at night, stay close to security points on platforms and use those parts of the train in the

marked "Nightsafe" area of the platform. Although more expensive, taxis are probably the safest, most efficient means of travel at night, especially for shorter journeys.

MEDICAL TREATMENT AND INSURANCE

SYDNEY HAS excellent medical services, with highly trained doctors and modern hospitals. However, overseas visitors are not covered by Australia's "Medicare" government health scheme, and medical, dental and ambulance costs are quite expensive. Before leaving your own country, be sure to purchase adequate insurance for any medical, hospital or dental costs you may incur during your stay. Under a reciprocal arrangement, British passport holders are entitled to free basic emergency medical and hospital treatment.

If you are in need of urgent medical attention, dial 000 for an ambulance or go to the emergency department of the nearest main public hospital. For less urgent treatment, look under "Medical Centres" in the Yellow Pages of the Sydney telephone directory.

The **Traveller's Clinic** offers medical treatment for travel-related illnesses as well as a vaccination service. For non-urgent dental treatment, look under "Dentists" in the Yellow Pages of the telephone directory. The **Emergency Dental Service** has an after-hours phone line for urgent cases.

Policewoman

Policeman

Fire officer

PHARMACIES

PHARMACIES ARE generally known as "chemist shops" in Sydney and are liberally scattered throughout the city and suburbs. They sell a wide range of unrestricted drugs and other medical supplies over the counter. Pharmacists can be a source of advice on simple ailments such as colds and stomach upsets. You can ring **After-Hours Pharmacy** information if you need to find one that is open outside normal business hours.

Doctor's prescriptions from your own country cannot be filled by an Australian pharmacist unless they are first endorsed by a medical practitioner practising locally.

Chemist shop in The Rocks

ENVIRONMENTAL HAZARDS

TAKE CARE WHEN going out in the sun – the ultraviolet rays are very intense, even on cloudy days. You should wear SPF 15+ sun block at all times and re-apply it regularly.

A hat and sunglasses are also recommended, as is staying out of the sun between 10am and 2pm (11am and 3pm during daylight saving). When swimming at an ocean beach, always check that there are lifesavers on patrol and swim within the "flagged" areas.

In their red and yellow caps, surf lifesavers keep an eye out for changing surf conditions, people in difficulty and surfers coming too close to areas set aside for swimmers only (see p54). If signs on the beach indicate that the surf is dangerous, do not go in under any circumstances. Popular beaches have loudspeakers to warn people of hazards that may suddenly arise. If you plan to bushwalk, do not hike alone.

Lifesaving flag Always tell someone where you are going and when you will be back. It is wise to take a map and a basic first-aid kit, as well as food and fresh water, and warm, waterproof clothing.

When walking through the bush, be aware that you are passing through the habitat of native animals, including some poisonous snakes and spiders. It is very unlikely that you will encounter any, but you should wear substantial footwear, keep a close eye on where you step and check around logs and rocks before sitting on them.

Snake bite victims should be kept calm and, most important, remain still while emergency medical help is sought. Try to identify the snake by size and colour so that the correct anti-venom can be administered.

The funnel-web (see p89) and the redback spider are both poisonous species found in the Sydney region. Anyone bitten by either of these should seek urgent medical attention.

Surf lifesaving sign indicating a dangerous undertow or "rip"

Banking and Local Currency

SYDNEY IS AUSTRALIA'S financial capital. In the central business district are the imposing headquarters of several of the country's leading banks, as well as the Australian head offices of major foreign banks. Visitors will find local, state and national bank branches dotted at convenient intervals throughout the city and suburbs.

There is no limit to the amount of personal funds that visitors can bring into Australia. Most currencies can be exchanged on arrival at the airport (beyond immigration and customs). Although banks generally offer the best exchange rates, money can also be changed at bureaux de change, larger department stores and major hotels.

High street bank logos

BANKING

BANK TRADING hours are generally from 9:30am to 4pm Monday to Thursday, and 9:30am to 5pm on Fridays. Some are also open to mid-day on Saturdays. Major city banks open 8:30am to 5pm on weekdays.

A valid passport or another form of photographic ID is usually needed if you are cashing traveller's cheques. The current exchange rates, which can vary considerably from day to day, are displayed in the windows or foyers of many banks.

Automatic cash dispenser

AUTOMATIC CASH DISPENSERS

AUTOMATIC CASH dispensers can be found in most bank lobbies or on an external wall near the bank's entrance. Ask your own bank which Sydney banks and cash dispensers will accept your card and what the transaction charges will be.

Australian currency (in $20 and $50 denominations) can be withdrawn from your bank or credit account. Most cash dispensers will accept various Australian bank cards, Visa and MasterCard (Access), as well as certain others. They are not only convenient, but may also provide a better exchange rate than cash transactions.

CREDIT CARDS

ALL WELL-KNOWN international credit cards are widely accepted in Australia. Major credit cards such as American Express, MasterCard (Access), Visa and Diners Club can be used to book and pay for hotel rooms, airline tickets, car hire, tours and concert and theatre tickets. Credit cards are accepted in most restaurants and shops, where the logos of all recognized cards are usually shown on doors and counter tops. You can also use credit cards in automatic cash dispensers at most banks to withdraw cash.

Credit cards are a convenient way to make phone bookings and avoid the need to carry large sums of cash. They can be especially useful in emergencies or if you need to fly home at short notice.

CASHING TRAVELLER'S CHEQUES

AUSTRALIAN DOLLAR traveller's cheques issued by major names like Thomas Cook and American Express are usually accepted (with a passport) in larger shops in Sydney. You may have problems, however, in smaller outlets. Foreign currency cheques can be cashed at banks, bureaux de change and established hotels.

Banks are generally the best places to go as their fees are lower. Westpac Bank will cash traveller's cheques in Australian dollars without charge. Other banks have varying transaction charges, so shop around.

BUREAUX DE CHANGE

SYDNEY HAS MANY bureaux de change in the popular shopping districts. Most are open Monday to Saturday from 9am to 5:30pm. Some branches also operate on Sunday.

While their extended hours can make bureaux de change a convenient alternative to a bank, their commissions and fees are generally higher than those charged by major banks.

DIRECTORY

FOREIGN CURRENCY EXCHANGE

American Express
92 Pitt St.
Map 1 B4.
[9236 9261.
One of several branches.

Thomas Cook
175 Pitt St.
Map 1 B4.
[9231 2877.
One of several branches.

AFTER-HOURS BUREAUX DE CHANGE

Thomas Cook
Shop 64, Queen Victoria Building,
455 George St.
Map 1 B5.
[9264 1133.
⏲ *9am–6pm Mon–Wed, Fri &*
Sat, 9am–9pm Thu,
11am–5pm Sun.

Travelex
37–49 Pitt St. **Map** 1 B3.
[9241 5722.
⏲ *8am–7pm daily.*

Interforex
Wharf 6, Circular Quay. **Map** 1 B2.
[9247 2082. ⏲ *8am–10pm*
daily. ⬤ *25 Dec.*

LOCAL CURRENCY

THE AUSTRALIAN currency is the Australian dollar ($ or A$), which breaks down into 100 cents (c). The decimal currency system now in place has been in operation since 1966.

Single cents may still be used for some prices, but as the Australian 1c and 2c coins are no longer being circulated, the total amount to be paid will be rounded up or down to the nearest five cent amount.

It can be difficult to get $50 and $100 notes changed, so avoid using them in smaller shops and cafés and, more particularly, when paying for taxi fares. If you do not have change, it is always wise to tell the taxi driver before you start your journey to avoid any misunderstandings. Otherwise, when you arrive at your destination, you may have to find change at the nearest shop or automatic cash dispenser.

To improve security, as well as increase their circulation life, all Australian bank notes have now been plasticized.

Bank Notes

Australian bank notes are produced in denominations of $5, $10, $20, $50 and $100. There are two types of bank note in circulation: the older paper notes, which are still legal tender, and plasticized notes in similar colours.

$100 note

$50 note

$20 note

$10 note

$5 note

5 cents (5c)

10 cents (10c)

20 cents (20c)

50 cents (50c)

1 dollar ($1)

2 dollars ($2)

Coins

Coins currently in use are 5c, 10c, 20c, 50c, $1 and $2 (shown here at actual sizes). There are several 50c coins in circulation; all are the same shape, but have different commemorative images on the face. The 10c and 20c coins are useful for local telephone calls (see p226).

Using Sydney's Telephones

SYDNEY'S PUBLIC PAYPHONES are generally maintained in good working order. Their prevalence on streets throughout the city and suburbs – as well as in hotels, cafés, shops and public buildings – means that users seldom have to queue to make calls. To save money, avoid making calls from hotel rooms. Hotels set their own rates and a call from your room will invariably cost more than one made from a payphone in the hotel lobby.

Using a mobile phone at Bondi

Telstra Corporation logo

PUBLIC TELEPHONES

MOST PAYPHONES accept both coins and phonecards, although some operate solely on phonecards and major credit cards.

Phonecards can be bought from selected newsagents and news kiosks, as well as from the many other outlets displaying the blue and orange Telstra sign.

Although slightly varied in shape and colour, all public telephones have a hand receiver and 12-button key pad, as well as clear instructions (in English only) and a list of useful phone numbers. The **Telstra Phone Centre** has ten payphones and is open 24 hours a day.

Telstra payphones

PAYPHONE CHARGES

LOCAL CALLS (those with the 02 area code) are untimed and cost 40 cents. Charges for long-distance calls can be obtained at no cost by calling 012 (for within Australia) and 0102 (for international). Phonecard and credit card phones debit 40-cent units in the same way as other telephones; however, all credit card calls have a $1.20 minimum fee, making them uneconomical for local calls. Long-distance calls are less expensive if you dial without the help of an operator. Most international calls can be dialled direct and there is little need for operator assistance unless you wish to make a reverse-charge call. Savings can be made on both national and international calls by phoning during off-peak periods. In general, peak and discount calling times fall into three ascending price brackets: economy, 6pm Sat–8am Mon, or 10pm–8am daily; night rate, 6pm–10pm Mon–Fri; day rate, 8am–6pm Mon–Sat. Special rates and times may apply to calls to certain countries.

MOBILE PHONES

MOBILE TELEPHONES are used extensively in Australia. They are available for short-term rental from the NSW Travel Centre's branch at the international airport *(see p218)*. Rates are approximately $23 per day or $125 per week.

Other rental companies are listed in the Yellow Pages of the telephone directory under "Mobile Telephones". Ask your service provider about whether your own digital mobile phone will work in Australia.

FAX SERVICES

MOST SYDNEY POST offices offer a fax service. There are also many copy shops that will send or receive faxes on your behalf. Look under the heading "Facsimile &/or Telex Communication Services" in the Yellow Pages phone directory for an agency near you.

Post offices charge per-page fees to send a fax to another fax machine within Australia. The cost per page is reduced after the first page. A fax can be sent to a postal address for the same charge, in which case the fax is sent to the local post office and delivered with the mail, usually the following day. A same-day fax to a postal

USING A COIN/PHONECARD OPERATED PHONE

1 Lift the receiver and wait for the dialling tone.

2 Insert the coins required or insert a Telstra phonecard in the direction of the arrows shown on the card.

3 Dial the number and wait to be connected.

4 The display shows you how much value is left on your phonecard or coins. When your coins or phonecard run out you will hear a warning beep. To continue, insert more coins if using coins. If using a phonecard, remove the old card and insert a new one.

5 Replace the receiver at the end of the call and withdraw your card or collect any unused coins. Payphones do not give change.

6 When you finish your call, the phonecard is returned to you with a hole punched in it showing the approximate remaining value.

Phonecards
Telstra phonecards are available in $2, $5, $10, $20 and $50 denominations.

address must be dispatched by 1pm, and there is a delivery fee. Delivery within 2 hours is available for a higher charge.

Overseas faxes can also be faxed to another fax machine or sent to a postal address. The cost is on a per-page rate, as with faxes to local numbers.

USEFUL INFORMATION

Telstra Phone Centre
100 King St. **Map** 1 B5.

Time
C 1194.

REACHING THE RIGHT NUMBER

• To ring Sydney from the UK, dial 0061 2, then the local number.
• To ring Sydney from the USA and Canada, dial 011 61 2, then the local number.
• For long-distance direct-dial calls outside your local area code, but within Australia (STD calls), dial the appropriate area code, then the number.
• For international direct-dial calls (IDD calls): dial **0011**, followed by the country code (USA and Canada: 1; UK: 44; New Zealand: 64), then the city or area code (omit initial 0) and then the local number.
• International directory enquiries: dial **1225**.
• Local directory enquiries: dial **1223**.
• STD directory enquiries: dial **1223**.
• International operator assistance: dial **1234**.
• Local operator assistance: dial **1234**.
• Reverse charge calls within Australia: dial **12550**.
• International reverse charge calls: dial **12550** or **1800 801 800** to access operator in home country.
• Numbers beginning with **1800** are toll-free numbers.
• Numbers with the prefix **014, 015, 018, 019** or **041** are mobile or car phones.
• *See also* Emergency Numbers, *p223*.

Postal Services

Australia Post logo

POST OFFICES ARE open 9am–5pm week days. Almost all post offices offer a wide range of services, including poste restante, fax, money orders, electronic post, express delivery, parcel post and telegrams, as well as stamps, envelopes, packaging, stationery and post-cards. Stamps can also be bought from hotels and shops where postcards are sold, and from some newsagents.

Australia Post postman

POSTAL SERVICES

ALL DOMESTIC MAIL is first class and usually arrives within one to five days, depending on distance. Be sure to include postcodes on mailing addresses to avoid delays in delivery.

Express Post, for which you need to buy one of the special yellow and white envelopes sold in post offices, guarantees next-day delivery in designated areas of Australia. International air mail takes from five to ten days to reach most countries.

Labels used for overseas mail

Typical stamps used for local mail

Stamp from a scenic series issue

There are two types of inter-national express mail. EMS International Courier is the fastest service and will reach nearly all overseas destinations within two to three days. Alternatively, Express Post International will reach most destinations throughout the world in four to five days.

Standard and express postboxes

POSTBOXES

SYDNEY HAS BOTH red and yellow postboxes. The red boxes are for normal postal service; yellow boxes are used exclusively for Express Post within Australia. Both types of postbox can be found on most busy street corners as well as outside post offices.

POSTE RESTANTE

POSTE RESTANTE letters can be sent to the General Post Office. Address mail to Poste Restante, GPO Sydney, NSW 2000. You will need to show your passport or other proof of identity before collecting mail sent to you poste restante.

USEFUL INFORMATION

General Post Office (GPO)
159 Pitt St (near Martin Place).
Map 1 B4. **C** 131317.
◐ 8:30am–5:30pm Mon–Fri,
8:30am–noon Sat.
Poste restante C 9244 3732.

TRAVEL INFORMATION

RAVELLING TO SYDNEY can involve a long and tiring flight. Visitors from Europe can take advantage of stopovers in Asia; those from the United States could break their journey in Hawaii or one of the other Pacific Islands. A break can mean the difference between arriving in Sydney jet-lagged or stepping off the plane refreshed and ready to take in the sights. Sydney is linked to Australia's other state capitals

Countrylink and Indian Pacific train logos

by efficient air, rail and coach connections. Long-distance coach travel is comfortable and relatively inexpensive; interstate trains are more expensive, but they are generally a great deal faster. People travelling by coach should consider taking one of the scenic routes with stopovers offered by some coach companies. Car travellers can also plan their journey to Sydney to pass through scenic areas.

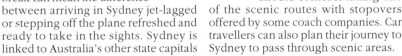

ARRIVING BY AIR

INTERNATIONAL FLIGHTS to Sydney can be expensive. They are also often heavily booked, especially between the months of December and February. December is peak season, and therefore the most expensive time to fly. Shoulder season, from 1 January to 12 April, is slightly less costly.

APEX fares are often the cheapest. Some stipulate set arrival and departure dates, or carry penalties if you cancel your flight. Round-the-world fares can be good value and are increasingly popular. **Qantas Airways** and **Ansett Australia**, Australia's international and major domestic carriers, link Sydney with other state capitals and major tourist destinations. Other domestic airlines service shorter routes. Flights within Australia are not cheap, but you can save by booking in

Airport Express bus into the city centre

advance (although restrictions apply). Overseas visitors with international tickets are eligible for discounts on internal flights.

ARRIVING AT SYDNEY AIRPORT

THE MAIN GATEWAY to Australia is Sydney (Kingsford Smith) Airport. As a result of this, congestion, especially at peak periods, can sometimes cause irritating delays. There is a duty-free shop for arriving passengers on the incoming side of the baggage collection and customs area. Just beyond this is the NSW Travel Centre's information desk *(see p218)*, as well as gift shops, a bureau de change and car hire desks.

Flight arrivals and departures are displayed on TV monitors and the whereabouts of toilets and other airport facilities are indicated using internationally recognized symbols.

Queueing for taxis at the Sydney Airport domestic terminal

GETTING INTO THE CITY

SYDNEY AIRPORT is about 9 km (5½ miles) from the centre of the city, about a 30-minute express bus journey. Bus and taxi ranks are located directly outside the international and domestic terminals.

State Transit has four airport buses: Airport Express 300 to Circular Quay, Airport Express 350 to Kings Cross, Metro route 400 from Burwood to Bondi Junction via the airport and Metro route 100 to Dee Why.

Kingsford Smith Bus Service leaves for various city hotels every 30 minutes 6am–5pm, then as required until 12:40am. The Airporter Clipper goes to all city and Kings Cross hotels and hostels 4:30am–11pm.

Taxis are usually plentiful, but queues may form at peak times. The fare to the centre of Sydney is around $20.

ARRIVING BY SEA

THE MOST delightful way to arrive in Sydney is by ship. Passenger ships berth at the overseas passenger terminals at Circular Quay and Darling

International flight arriving at Sydney Airport

The *QEII* passenger ship berthed at Circular Quay

Harbour. At either terminal, you will find the city on the doorstep. Information booths, tour booking centres, buses, trains, ferries, taxis and water taxis are all close at hand.

ARRIVING BY COACH

M OST LONG-DISTANCE bus or coach services arrive at the **Sydney Coach Terminal** at Central Railway Station. The terminal has left-luggage lockers, while shower facilities and food outlets are found in the station above.

Competition between the coach companies is fierce, so it is worth shopping around to get the best price.

ARRIVING BY CAR

T HE FOUR MAJOR routes into Sydney are the Pacific Highway from the north; the Great Western Highway from the west; the Princes Highway, which follows the coast from Melbourne; and the Hume Highway, which runs inland from Melbourne.

As they approach Sydney, these routes feed into freeways or motorways, which in turn lead to priority routes known as "Metroads" (marked by blue and white hexagonal badges). When you reach the city outskirts, look for the Metroad signs and stay in the lanes as marked for the city centre.

ARRIVING BY TRAIN

A LL INTERSTATE and regional trains arrive at Central Railway Station. Australia's nationwide rail network is known by a different name in each state, but it still operates cohesively. The **Countrylink** reservations line will answer queries and take bookings (6:30am–10pm daily) for train services throughout Australia.

CityRail also has slower, but cheaper, services from nearby centres on which seats cannot be booked. The Bus, Train & Ferry Infoline *(see p230)* has information about CityRail's country services.

Country service passenger train waiting at Central Railway Station

---

DIRECTORY

SYDNEY AIRPORT

Airport Information
📞 9667 9111.

AIRLINE INFORMATION

Air New Zealand
Reservations 📞 132476.
Arrivals and departures
📞 9937 5299.

Ansett Australia
Domestic reservations
📞 131300.
International reservations
📞 131414.
Domestic arrivals and departures 📞 131515.
International arrivals and departures 📞 9352 7878.

British Airways
Reservations
📞 8904 8800.
Arrivals 📞 131223.
Departures 📞 8904 8838.

Canadian Airlines
Reservations
📞 1300 655 767.
Arrivals and departures
📞 131 223.

Japan Airlines
Reservations and flight information
📞 9272 1111.

Qantas Airways
Domestic reservations
📞 131313.
International reservations
📞 131211.
Domestic arrivals and departures 📞 131223.
International arrivals and departures 📞 131223.

Singapore Airlines
Reservations 📞 131011.
Arrivals 📞 131223.

United Airlines
Reservations 📞 131777.
Arrivals and departures
📞 131177.

AIRPORT HOTELS

Sydney Airport Hilton
📞 9518 2000.

Sheraton Sydney Airport
📞 9317 2200.

LONG-DISTANCE COACH SERVICES

Sydney Coach Terminal
Eddy Ave. **Map** 4 E5.
📞 9281 9366.

Greyhound Pioneer Australia
📞 132030.

Pioneer Motor Service
📞 1300 368 100.

McCafferty's Express Coaches
📞 131499.

TRAIN INFORMATION

Central Railway Station
General inquiries
📞 131 500.
Lost property
📞 9379 4757.

Countrylink
Reservations 📞 132232.
Arrivals 📞 132232.

Getting Around Sydney

SydneyPass ticket

IN GENERAL, THE BEST WAY to see Sydney's many sights and attractions is on foot, coupled with use of the public transport system. Buses, trains and the new light railway will take visitors to within easy walking distance of anywhere in the inner city. They also serve the suburbs and outlying areas. Passenger ferries provide a fast and scenic means of travel between the city and harbourside suburbs. The best selection of maps, plus fascinating aerial and satellite views and historical maps, can be found at the excellent **Sydney Map Shop**.

People crossing at pedestrian lights in the centre of the city

WALKING

TAKE CARE when walking around the city. Vehicles are driven on the left and often move quickly. It is wise to use pedestrian crossings. There are two types. Push-button crossings are found at traffic lights. Wait for the green man signal and do not cross at lights if the red warning sign is on or flashing. Zebra crossings are marked by yellow and black signs. Make sure vehicles are stopping before you cross.

COMPOSITE TICKETS

TRAVELLING ON Sydney's trains buses and harbour ferries is not expensive, especially if you use of one of the composite tickets or TravelPasses that are readily available.

These can be bought from **State Transit Information and Ticket Kiosks**, railway stations, newsagents and news-stands where the yellow and

black "bus tickets sold here" sign is on display. For some visitors, TravelTen or FerryTen (see p234) tickets, which can be used on buses and ferries respectively, may prove useful.

TRAVELTEN TICKETS

TRAVELTEN TICKETS entitle you to make ten bus journeys by public transport. Bus routes are divided into parts, or "sections". Tickets are colour-coded according to the number of sections for which they can be used on each journey.

These tickets are useful if you need to travel the same route a number of times. Most visitors will require either a Blue TravelTen, valid for 1–2 sections, or a Red TravelTen, valid for 3–9 sections.

TravelTen tickets can be transferred from one user to another and can be shared by more than one passenger on the same journey.

A Blue Weekly TravelPass, Red TravelTen and Blue TravelTen

TRAVELPASSES

THE MOST ECONOMICAL of the composite tickets are the TravelPasses. These allow you unlimited seven-day travel on Sydney's public buses, trains and ferries as long as you travel within stipulated zones.

They are sold in "bus only" or "bus–ferry" or "bus–ferry–train" combinations. The Red TravelPass, a combined bus–ferry–train ticket, covers all zones included in the usual tourist jaunts. The slightly more expensive Green TravelPass allows for bus, train and ferry travel over a wider area.

SydneyPass

The SydneyPass allows either three or five days' use in any seven-day period, or seven consecutive days of unlimited bus and ferry travel, including trips on the Manly Jetcat, three Sydney Harbour cruises (see p234), the Sydney Explorer and the Bondi & Bay Explorer buses and the Airport Express services (see p228).

You can buy a SydneyPass direct from the driver on any Airport Express or Explorer bus, travel agents where you see the SydneyPass sign on display, Circular Quay ferry wharf and State Transit Information and Ticket Kiosks.

All-Day Tickets

If you only have one day for sightseeing, a BusTripper or DayPass ticket may be useful. These allow unlimited travel for one day on as many regular services as you like. BusTripper tickets can only be used on buses, while DayPasses can be used on buses and ferries.

USEFUL INFORMATION

Sydney Map Shop
Land Information Centre, 23 Bridge St. **Map** 1 B3. (*9228 6315.*

State Transit Information and Ticket Kiosks
Sydney Airport
Outside arrivals halls at international, Ansett domestic and Qantas domestic terminals.
Circular Quay
Cnr Loftus and Alfred Sts.
Map 1 B3.
Queen Victoria Building
York St. **Map** 1 A5.
Wynyard Park
Carrington St. **Map** 1 A4.

Bus, Train & Ferry Infoline
(*131 500.*

Sydney Ferries Information Office
Opposite Wharf No. 4, Circular Quay.
Map 1 B3. (*9207 3166.*

Travelling by Bus

S TATE TRANSIT'S SYDNEY BUSES provides a punctual service that links up conveniently with the city's rail and ferry systems. As well as covering city and suburban areas, there are two Airport Express services *(see p228)* and two excellent sightseeing buses – the Sydney Explorer and the Bondi & Bay Explorer. The **Public Transport Infoline** can advise you on routes, fares and journey times for all Sydney Buses. Armed with the map on the inside back cover of this book and a composite ticket, you can avoid the difficulties and expense of city parking.

Automatic stamping machine for validating composite bus tickets

USING SYDNEY BUSES

R OUTE NUMBERS and journey destinations are displayed on the front, back and left side of all State Transit buses. An "X" in front of the number means that it is an express bus. Only single-journey tickets can be purchased on board regular buses. Single fares are bought from the driver. Try to have coins at hand as drivers are not always able to change large notes. You will be given a ticket valid for that journey only – if you change buses you will have to pay again.

If using a TravelTen ticket or TravelPass, you must insert it in the automatic stamping machine as you board. Ensure the arrow is facing you and pointing downwards. If sharing a TravelTen, insert it into the machine once for each person.

Front seats must be given up to elderly or disabled people. Eating, drinking, smoking or playing music is prohibited on buses. To signal that you wish to alight, press one of the red buttons – they are mounted on the vertical handrails on each seat – well before the bus reaches your stop. The doors are operated by the drivers.

BUS STOPS

B US STOPS are indicated by yellow and black signs displaying a profile of a bus and a boarding passenger. Below this symbol, the numbers of all buses travelling along the route are clearly listed.

Timetables are usually found on the bus stop sign or nearby shelter. The Sunday timetable also applies to public holidays, except when they fall on a Saturday. In this case, Saturday timetables apply after 6pm. While bus stop timetables are usually kept as up-to-date as possible, it is best to carry a current bus timetable with you. They are available from State Transit Authority Information and Ticket Kiosks in the city, as well as at Bondi Junction and the Manly ferry wharf.

Express bus

SIGHTSEEING BY BUS

T WO SYDNEY BUS services, the distinctive red Sydney Explorer and the blue Bondi & Bay Explorer, offer flexible sightseeing with informative commentaries. The Sydney Explorer bus covers a 26-km (16-mile) circuit and stops at 22 of the city's most popular sights and attractions. The Bondi & Bay Explorer travels through a number of Sydney's eastern suburbs, taking in much of the area's coastal and bayside scenery along the way.

These buses operate daily at intervals of 15–25 minutes. The great advantage of these services is that passengers can explore at will, getting on and off the buses as often as they wish in the course of a day. The best way to make the most of your journey is to choose the sights you most want to see and plan a basic itinerary. Make sure you take account of the opening times of museums, art galleries and shops; the bus drivers can advise you about these. Explorer bus stops are clearly marked by the colours of the bus (red or blue).

Tickets can be bought on board the buses or from State Transit Authority Information and Ticket Kiosks.

A typical Sydney Bus used for standard services

The Bondi & Bay Explorer bus

The Sydney Explorer bus

Travelling by Train and Monorail

CityRail logo

A S WELL AS PROVIDING the key transport link between the city and suburbs, Sydney's railway network also serves a large part of the central business district. The City Circle loop is the main line running through the city centre stopping at Central, Town Hall, Wynyard, Circular Quay, St James and Museum. All suburban lines connect with the City Circle at Central and Town Hall stations. An easy way of exploring the museums and shops of Darling Harbour is to use the Light Rail.

FINDING YOUR WAY AROUND BY RAIL

O PERATING IN the Darling Harbour Area, the new Sydney Light Rail (SLR) links Central Station with Wentworth Park in Wattle Street, Pyrmont. These environmentally friendly trains offer a quicker and quieter way of visiting many places of interest including Chinatown, Paddy's Market, the Convention and Exhibition Centre, Harbourside Shopping Centre, the National Maritime Museum, Star City, John Street Square and the Fish Market.

User-friendly ticket machines are located at every stop. The service runs seven days a week, with trains every five-and-a-half minutes during peak periods and every 11 minutes off-peak.

The most efficient way of travelling to and from outlying suburbs such as Parramatta, Cronulla and Cabramatta is to make use of the CityRail system. Trains run from 4:30am to around midnight. Take care when travelling at night: stand in the "Nightsafe" areas, which are marked clearly on platforms, and only use carriages near the train guard, signalled by a blue light.

SIGHTSEEING BY MONORAIL

M ORE NOVEL THAN practical, the Monorail runs along a scenic loop through central Sydney, Chinatown and Darling Harbour. Covering a short distance between the city centre and Darling Harbour, it can be a convenient way to travel if you do not feel like walking.

There are seven stops on the Monorail route: City Centre, Darling Park, Harbourside, Convention, Haymarket, World Square and Park Plaza. It runs from 7am–10pm, Mondays to Wednesdays, 7am–midnight Thursday to Saturdays and 8am–10pm on Sundays. Trains run every five minutes and the circuit takes about 12 minutes.

Pedestrian concourse outside Central Railway Station

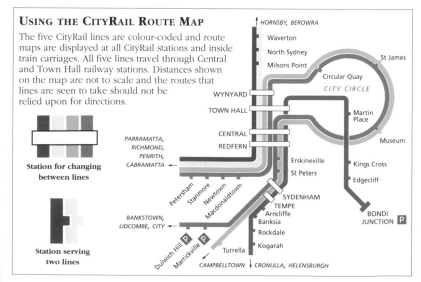

USING THE CITYRAIL ROUTE MAP

The five CityRail lines are colour-coded and route maps are displayed at all CityRail stations and inside train carriages. All five lines travel through Central and Town Hall railway stations. Distances shown on the map are not to scale and the routes that lines are seen to take should not be relied upon for directions.

Station for changing between lines

Station serving two lines

HORNSBY, BEROWRA

Waverton

North Sydney

Milsons Point

St James

Circular Quay

CITY CIRCLE

WYNYARD

Martin Place

TOWN HALL

CENTRAL

Museum

REDFERN

PARRAMATTA, RICHMOND, PENRITH, CABRAMATTA

Erskineville

Kings Cross

St Peters

Edgecliff

Petersham

Stanmore

Newtown

Macdonaldtown

SYDENHAM

TEMPE

Arncliffe

BANKSTOWN, LIDCOMBE, CITY

Banksia

BONDI JUNCTION P

Rockdale

Dulwich Hill P

Marrickville P

Kogarah

Turrella

CAMPBELLTOWN

CRONULLA, HELENSBURGH

Token vending machines are found at each station. These accept most notes and coins and give change. Tokens are then used to pass through the turnstiles. A Monorail Day Pass allows unlimited rides all day. It can be bought at any of the monorail information booths.

Monorail leaving the city centre, with Sydney Tower in background

COUNTRY AND INTERURBAN TRAINS

STATE RAIL has **Countrylink Travel Centres** throughout the city and suburbs, which provide information about its country rail and coach services and also take bookings. The NSW Discovery Pass, valid for one month, allows unlimited economy travel by rail and coach in New South Wales.

Interurban trains run to the Blue Mountains to Sydney's west, Wollongong in the south and Gosford and Newcastle to the north *(see p229)*.

USEFUL INFORMATION

CityRail Information
Central Railway Station
Map 4 E5. 9379 4054.
Circular Quay Railway Station
Map 1 B3. 9224 3553.

Countrylink Travel Centres
Central Railway Station
Sydney Terminal.
Map 4 E5. 9379 4976.
Circular Quay Railway Station
Map 1 B3. 9224 3400.
Town Hall Railway Station
Map 4 E3. 9379 3600.

Sydney Light Rail
9660 5285.

MAKING A JOURNEY BY CITYRAIL

1 Study the CityRail route map. Route lines are distinguished by colour, so simply trace the line from where you are to your destination, noting where you need to change and make connections.

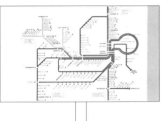

2 Tickets can be bought from newsagents, ticket dispensing machines or ticket booths at stations. To obtain your ticket from a dispensing machine, press the button to indicate destination, then the button that shows the ticket type required (single, return, adult, child etc). Insert money into the slot and then collect your ticket and any change.

3 To pass through the ticket barrier, insert your ticket (arrow side up) into the slot at the front of barrier machines (indicated by green arrows). Take your ticket as it comes out of the machine and the barrier gates or turnstile will open.

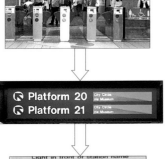

4 To find the right platform, follow the signs with the same colour code as the line you need and the name of the line's final station.

5 On the platform, display signs show all the stations the line travels through. Stations at which the next train will stop are lit up and are announced as the train arrives at the station.

Tickets
Keep your ticket – you will need it at the end of your journey and possibly to show a ticket inspector on the train. A TravelPass (left) and a single-fare ticket (right) are shown.

Travelling by Ferry and Water Taxi

FOR MORE THAN A CENTURY, harbour ferries have been a picturesque, as well as a practical, feature of the Sydney scene. Today, they are as popular as ever. Travelling by ferry is both a pleasure and an efficient way to travel between Sydney's harbour suburbs. Sight-seeing cruises are operated by various private companies as well as by State Transit *(see p219)*. Water taxis can be a convenient, but pricey, alternative to the ferry.

MUNICIPALITY OF LEICHHARDT
DARLING STREET · BALMAIN

Sign for Darling Street Wharf

Harbour ferries coming and going at Circular Quay Ferry Terminal

USING SYDNEY'S FERRIES

THERE IS a constant procession of State Transit Sydney Ferries traversing the harbour between 6am and 10pm daily. They service most of Sydney Harbour and several stops along the Parramatta River.

Frequent services run to and from Darling Harbour, Manly, Balmain, Parramatta, Hunters Hill, Taronga Zoo, Neutral Bay, Mosman and Rose Bay, with numerous stops en route. State Transit's Sydney Buses *(see p231)* provide convenient connections at most wharves.

Staff at the Sydney Ferries Information Office *(see p230)*, open 7am–7pm daily, will answer passenger queries and provide ferry timetables. You can also phone the Public Transport Infoline *(see p230)* for advice about connections, destinations and fares between 6am and 10pm daily.

MAKING A JOURNEY BY FERRY

ALL FERRY JOURNEYS start at the Circular Quay Ferry Terminal. Electronic destination boards at the entrance to each wharf indicate the wharf from which your ferry will leave, and also give departure times and all stops made en route.

Tickets and TravelPasses can be bought from the Sydney Ferries Information Office *(see p230)*. You can also buy your ticket from the machines on each wharf. Only at Manly and Circular Quay are tickets checked through a turnstile. When boarding a ferry at any other point, you are usually able to purchase a ticket from a ticket seller on board, or from the machines when you arrive at Circular Quay.

Manly's large ferry terminal is serviced both by ferries and speedy Jetcats. Tickets and information can be obtained from the ticket windows located in the centre of the

A State Transit harbour ferry

A State Transit JetCat ferry

HOW TO USE FERRY TICKET MACHINES

A coin-only ticket machine on each Circular Quay wharf sells the range of tickets from TravelTens and weekly TravelPasses *(p230)* to single-journey. Change machines dispense coins.

1 Press the button indicating the type of ticket you need – composite, single or return.

HOW TO BUY A TICKET

Press TICKET type.
FARE will be displayed.
Insert COINS
Collect TICKET & CHANGE

2 The fare will be displayed. Insert your coins in the slot found at the top of the ticket machine.

3 Your ticket and change will be dispensed. Use your ticket to go through any of the ticket barriers indicated with a green arrow.

SYDNEY FERRIES

Automatic Ticket Barriers
Insert the ticket in the barrier in the direction indicated by the arrows. Remove and pass through.

A State Transit RiverCat ferry

Electronic destination board for all ferries leaving Circular Quay

terminal. To pass through to the embarkation area you must feed your ticket into the turnstiles. No food or drink is permitted on JetCat ferries, but the larger and slower ferries have snack bars on board.

SIGHTSEEING BY FERRY

STATE TRANSIT has a variety of well-priced harbour cruises which take in the history and colourful sights of Sydney Harbour. They are a refreshingly cheap alternative to the commercial harbour cruises. There are morning, afternoon and evening tours, all with a commentary throughout. Food and drinks are available on board, but passengers can, if they wish, bring their own.

Morning River Cruise
This 2½-hour cruise travels close to Sydney Opera House and several islands before turning westward. It then goes

under the Harbour Bridge and along Parramatta River, passing picturesque bays and coves.
Departures Wharf 4, Circular Quay. 10am daily.

Afternoon Harbour Cruise
The cruise to Watsons Bay and Middle Harbour takes 2½ hours.
Departures Wharf 4, Circular Quay. 1pm Mon–Fri, 1:30pm Sat, Sun & pub hols.

Evening Harbour Lights
Spectacular night-time views of the city are features of this 1½-hour cruise.
Departures Wharf 5, Circular Quay. 8pm Mon–Sat.

Other Cruises
There is also an abundance of commercial sightseeing cruises. **Australian Travel Specialists** has information about all river and harbour cruises from Circular Quay and Darling Harbour. They do not charge a booking fee.

WATER TAXIS

SMALL, FAST TAXI boats carry passengers around the harbour. You can flag them down like normal cabs if you spot one cruising for a fare. Circular Quay near the Overseas Passenger Terminal is the place to look. You can also telephone for a water taxi. They will pick up and drop off at any navigable pier. Rates begin at around $35.00 for the first person and $5.00 for each additional passenger.

A water taxi on Sydney Harbour

USEFUL INFORMATION

Australian Travel Specialists
Wharves 2 & 6, Circular Quay.
Map 1 B3. ☎ 9247 5151.

Sydney Ferries Lost Property
Wharf 5, Circular Quay. **Map** 1 B3.
☎ 9207 3166.

Water Taxi Companies
Harbour Taxis ☎ 9555 1155.
Taxis Afloat ☎ 9955 3222.

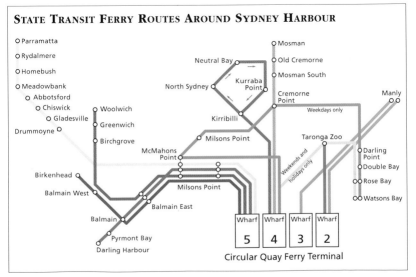

STATE TRANSIT FERRY ROUTES AROUND SYDNEY HARBOUR

Parramatta
Rydalmere
Homebush
Meadowbank
Abbotsford
Chiswick
Gladesville
Drummoyne
Woolwich
Greenwich
Birchgrove
McMahons Point
Birkenhead
Balmain West
Balmain
Balmain East
Pyrmont Bay
Darling Harbour

Mosman
Old Cremorne
Neutral Bay
Mosman South
Kurraba Point
North Sydney
Cremorne Point
Kirribilli
Milsons Point
Taronga Zoo
Darling Point
Double Bay
Rose Bay
Watsons Bay
Manly

Weekdays only
Weekends and holidays only

Wharf 5 Wharf 4 Wharf 3 Wharf 2

Circular Quay Ferry Terminal

Travelling by Car and Bicycle

D RIVING IS NOT THE IDEAL way to get around central
Sydney, although cars can be very convenient for
journeys into the suburbs and further afield. The city
road network is confusing, traffic is congested and
parking can be expensive. If arriving in Sydney by car,
make sure that your hotel provides parking. Cycling in
the city can also be difficult and dangerous for those
unfamiliar with Sydney's traffic and road conditions.

**Petrol station with full driveway
service in Balmain** *(see p131)*

DRIVING IN SYDNEY

I F YOU ARE planning to use a
car to drive around greater
Sydney, you will need a good
street directory. It is best to
avoid the peak-hour traffic
periods (about 7:30–9:30am
and 5–7:30pm). Regular traffic
update reports are broadcast
on many radio stations.

On a positive note, petrol is
relatively cheap, being a little
more expensive than in North
America, but about half the
price of petrol in Europe. Dispensed by the litre, it comes
in super, regular unleaded,
premium unleaded and diesel
grades. Most petrol stations
are self-service and many of
them accept major credit cards.

Kerbside Traffic Signs
*Always pay strict attention to
Sydney's parking and traffic
signs as fines for infringements
can be very expensive.*

DRIVING REGULATIONS

O VERSEAS VISITORS can use
their usual driving licences
to drive in New South Wales,
but must have proof that they
are simply visiting. You must
have your licence or an International Driver's Permit with
you whenever you are driving.

Australians drive on the left-
hand side of the road and
overtake on the right. Speed
limits and distances are given
in metric measurements. The
speed limit is 60 km/h (35
mph) in the city and
most suburbs, and
100–110 km/h
(60–65 mph) on
motorways, free-
ways and highways,
unless otherwise indi-
cated. The wearing
of seat belts is com-
pulsory for drivers
and passengers.

Drivers must give
way to all police
vehicles, fire engines
and ambulances. At
some intersections,
which are clearly signposted,
drivers are allowed to make a
left-hand turn at a red light
after stopping, but must give
way to pedestrians.

The 0.05 per cent maximum
blood alcohol level for drivers
is enforced by random breath
tests. Drivers who are found
to be over the legal limit will
incur heavy fines, suspension
or loss of licence, and even
prison sentences. Should you
be involved in an accident
while over the limit (whether
or not you are at fault), your
insurance may be invalidated.

The NRMA *(see p223)* has a
free 24-hour roadside service
for members. Non-members
are charged a service fee and
joining fee. Most car hire companies provide their own free
roadside emergency service.

**Beware of
kangaroos crossing**

Traffic on the Harbour Bridge

PARKING

P ARKING IN SYDNEY is strictly
regulated with fines for any
infringements. In certain areas,
particularly along clearways
(indicated by signposts),
vehicles are towed
away if parked ille-
gally. Contact the
**Sydney Traffic
Control Centre** to
find out where your
vehicle has been
impounded if this
happens. There are
car parks scattered
around the city area.
They vary widely,
both in how much
they charge and their
opening hours. Most
close after midnight,
but many close earlier – check
carefully before parking your
car for the evening.

Look out for the blue and
white "P" signs or seek out one
of the metered parking zones.
Almost all metered parking
zones are free after 6:30pm on
weekdays, on Saturday afternoon and all day on Sunday.

CAR HIRE

M ETROPOLITAN RATES offered
by the major agencies
(**Avis**, **Budget**, **Hertz** and
Thrifty) range from about $75
a day for a small car to $100 a
day for a large car. These rates
usually include comprehensive
insurance. However, many of
the other agencies listed in the
Yellow Pages telephone directory offer highly competitive

prices, and rentals can be obtained for as little as $35–$40 a day. Be sure to read the fine print on hire agreements as deals may not be as attractive as they first seem – and be aware of the costs you could incur in the event of an accident if you opt for less than full insurance cover.

Generally, rates are lower if you hire for more than three days, or if you take a limited, low-kilometre deal. Extra charges may apply if you drive over 100 km (60 miles) a day, travel over rough rural roads or return your vehicle late.

You must be at least 21 years old to hire a car. If you do not have a recognized credit card, you will need to leave a sizeable deposit. Hire company fuel refills are usually at prices comparable to petrol stations.

TAXIS

TAXIS ARE PLENTIFUL in Sydney and you should have little difficulty in flagging one down in the city and inner suburbs. There are taxi ranks at many city locations and taxis are often found outside the large city hotels. The four main taxi companies provide a reliable telephone service, but you should book your taxi at least 15 minutes before you need it.

Meters indicate the fare plus any extras, such as booking fees and waiting time. Fares, as well as extra charges, are regulated and are the same for any time of the day or night. Tips are not normally expected, but it is customary to round the fare up to the next dollar.

Sydney has a new fleet of taxis designed to accommodate disabled passengers, including

Cycling in Centennial Park

those in wheelchairs. These taxis can be booked through any of the major companies. Smoking in taxis is forbidden by law in New South Wales.

SYDNEY BY BICYCLE

WHILE CYCLING IS permitted on all city and suburban roads, visitors would be well advised to restrict their cycling to designated cycling tracks, or to areas where motor traffic is likely to be light. Helmets are compulsory by law.

Keen cyclists who wish to take advantage of Sydney's undulating terrain and pleasant weather can seek advice from **Bicycle New South Wales**. It published a handbook, *Cycling around Sydney*, which has a map of good cycling routes.

Centennial Park is one of the most popular spots; on weekends and every evening packs of riders can be seen cycling through the park. You can take your bicycle on CityRail trains (*see p232*), but you will have to pay an extra adult fare.

Cabcharge is for account customers only, but some taxis also accept American Express and Diners Club.

The orange light, when lit, shows the taxi is available.

Taxi licence number

The taxi company name and phone number are displayed on front driver and passenger doors.

The taxi driver's photo licence must be on clear display within the taxi.

DIRECTORY

CAR HIRE COMPANIES

Avis
📞 9353 9000.

Budget
📞 132727.

Hertz
📞 133039.

Thrifty
📞 1300 367 227.

TAXI COMPANIES

Legion Cabs
📞 9289 9000.

Premier Taxis
📞 9897 4000.

RSL Cabs
📞 9581 1111.

Taxis Combined
📞 9332 8888.

CYCLE HIRE AND INFORMATION

The Australian Cycle Company
28 Clovelly Rd, Randwick.
(Near Centennial Park.)
📞 9399 3475.

Bicycle New South Wales
Level 2, 209 Castlereagh St.
Map 4 E3. 📞 9283 5200.

Centennial Park Cycles
50 Clovelly Rd, Randwick.
(Near Centennial Park.)
📞 9398 5027.

Woolys Wheels
82 Oxford St, Paddington.
Map 5 B3. 📞 9331 2671.

USEFUL NUMBERS

Infringement Processing Bureau
130 George St, Parramatta.
📞 9841 8000.

Sydney Traffic Control Centre
📞 9211 3000. 24-hour service.

Taxi Complaints
Department of Transport,
418a Elizabeth St, Surry Hills.
Map 4 E3. 📞 9270 6122.

SYDNEY STREET FINDER

THE PAGE GRID superimposed on the *Area by Area* map below shows which parts of Sydney are covered in this *Street Finder*. Map references given for all sights, hotels, restaurants, shopping and entertainment venues described in this guide refer to the maps in this section. All the major sights are clearly marked so they are easy to locate. A complete index of the street names and places of interest follows on pages 246–9. The key, set out below, indicates the scale of the maps and shows what other features are marked on them, including railway stations, bus terminals, ferry boarding points, emergency services, post offices and tourist information centres.

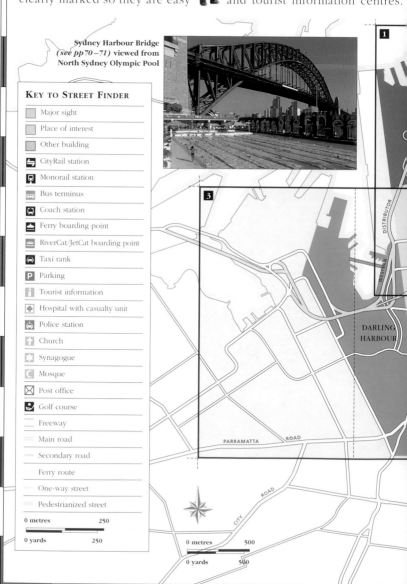

Sydney Harbour Bridge *(see pp70–71)* **viewed from North Sydney Olympic Pool**

KEY TO STREET FINDER

- Major sight
- Place of interest
- Other building
- CityRail station
- Monorail station
- Bus terminus
- Coach station
- Ferry boarding point
- RiverCat/JetCat boarding point
- Taxi rank
- P Parking
- Tourist information
- Hospital with casualty unit
- Police station
- Church
- Synagogue
- Mosque
- Post office
- Golf course
- Freeway
- Main road
- Secondary road
- Ferry route
- One-way street
- Pedestrianized street

| 0 metres | 250 |
| 0 yards | 250 |

| 0 metres | 500 |
| 0 yards | 500 |

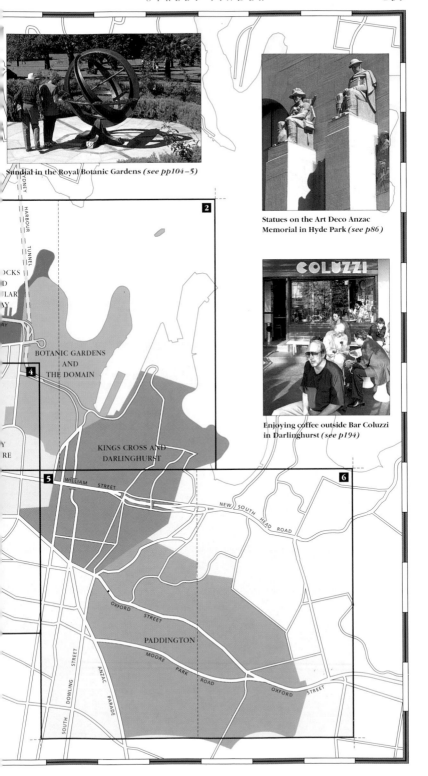

Sundial in the Royal Botanic Gardens *(see pp104–5)*

Statues on the Art Deco Anzac Memorial in Hyde Park *(see p86)*

Enjoying coffee outside Bar Coluzzi in Darlinghurst *(see p194)*

BOTANIC GARDENS AND THE DOMAIN

KINGS CROSS AND DARLINGHURST

WILLIAM STREET

NEW SOUTH HEAD ROAD

OXFORD STREET

PADDINGTON

MOORE PARK ROAD

OXFORD STREET

SOUTH DOWLING STREET

ANZAC PARADE

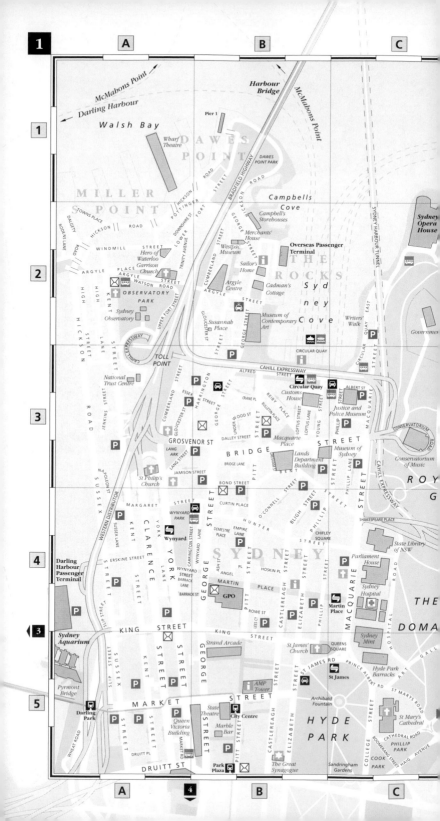

1

A   B   C

1

McMahons Point

Darling Harbour

Walsh Bay

Pier 1

Harbour Bridge

McMahons Point

Wharf Theatre

DAWES POINT

DAWES POINT PARK

BRADFIELD HIGHWAY

SYDNEY HARBOUR TUNNEL

Sydney Opera House

MILLER POINT

STOWNS PLACE

HICKSON   ROAD

WINDMILL   STREET

Hero of Waterloo

Garrison Church

Campbells Cove

Campbell's Storehouses

Merchants' House

Westpac Museum

Sailor's Home

Overseas Passenger Terminal

THE ROCKS

2

DALGETY ROAD

ROSA NG LANE

ARGYLE   STREET

HICKSON   ROAD

KENT   STREET

HIGH   STREET

HIGH   LANE

OBSERVATORY PARK

ARGYLE   PLACE

Sydney Observatory

WATSON   ROAD

UPPER FORT STREET

LOWER   FORT   STREET

TRINITY AVENUE

DOWNSHIRE ST

POTTINGER   ST

HICKSON   ST

GEORGE   STREET

CUMBERLAND   STREET

GLOUCESTER   ST

ARGYLE   STREET

Argyle Centre

Cadman's Cottage

Susannah Place

Museum of Contemporary Art

GEORGE   STREET

Syd ney Cove

Writers' Walk

Governmer

3

HICKSON   ROAD

SUSSEX   ROAD

CAHILL EXPRESSWAY

TOLL POINT

National Trust Centre

JENKINS STREET

CUMBERLAND   STREET

GLOUCESTER   STREET

ESSEX   STREET

HARRINGTON   STREET

GEORGE   STREET

CRANE PL

REIBY   PLACE

RUELINE PLACE

LOFTUS STREET

LOFTUS LANE

YOUNG   STREET

YOUNG   STREET

ALFRED   STREET

CAHILL   EXPRESSWAY

Circular Quay

Customs House

CIRCULAR QUAY

Justice and Police Museum

ALBERT ST

PHILLIP   STREET

MACQUARIE   STREET

CIRCULAR QUAY EAST

CONSERVATORIUM ROAD

CONSERVATORIUM of Music

ROY G

GROSVENOR ST

WOOD ST

DALLEY STREET

LANG PARK

LANG STREET

JAMISON STREET

BRIDGE   STREET

BRIDGE LANE

PITT   STREET

Macquarie Place

Lands Department Building

BENT

Museum of Sydney

PHILLIP LANE

St Philip's Church

NAPOLEON ST

WESTERN DISTRIBUTOR

BOND STREET

Lands Department Building

4

Darling Harbour Passenger Terminal

MARGARET   STREET

ERSKINE STREET

SUSSEX   LANE

KENT   STREET

CLARENCE   STREET

YORK   STREET

YORK   LANE

CARRINGTON STREET

WYNYARD   LANE

WYNYARD STREET

WYNYARD BARRACK LANE

BARRACK   ST

GEORGE   STREET

Wynyard Park

Wynyard

DEMESTRE PLACE

EMPIRE LANE

ANGEL PL

HUNTER   STREET

ASH ST

HOSKIN PL

CURTIN PLACE

O'CONNELL   STREET

BLIGH   STREET

CHIFLEY SQUARE

PHILLIP   STREET

SHAKESPEARE PLACE

State Library of NSW

Parliament House

CAHILL EXPRESSWAY

SYDNEY

MARTIN   PLACE

GPO

PITT   STREET

ROWE ST

CASTLEREAGH   STREET

ELIZABETH   STREET

Martin Place

MACQUARIE   STREET

Sydney Hospital

THE DOMA

3

Sydney Aquarium

SLIP   STREET

SUSSEX   STREET

KENT   STREET

CLARENCE   STREET

YORK   STREET

KING   STREET

KING   STREET

LEE ST

Strand Arcade

GEORGE   STREET

St James' Church

QUEENS SQUARE

Sydney Mint

HOSPITAL ROAD

Hyde Park Barracks

ST JAMES RD

St James

PRINCE ALBERT RD

5

Pyrmont Bridge

WHEAT ROAD

Darling Park

MARKET   STREET

Queen Victoria Building

State Theatre

DRUITT PL

MARKET   ST

Marble Bar

PITT   STREET

City Centre

AMP Tower

The Great Synagogue

HYDE PARK

Archibald Fountain

ST JAMES   STREET

CASTLEREAGH   STREET

ELIZABETH   STREET

COLLEGE   STREET

St Mary's Cathedral

PRINCE ALBERT RD

ST MARYS RD

CATHEDRAL ROAD

PHILLIP PARK

BOOMERANG STREET

HAIG   AVENUE

COOK PARK

Park Plaza

DRUITT ST

Sandringham Gardens

A   **4**   B   C

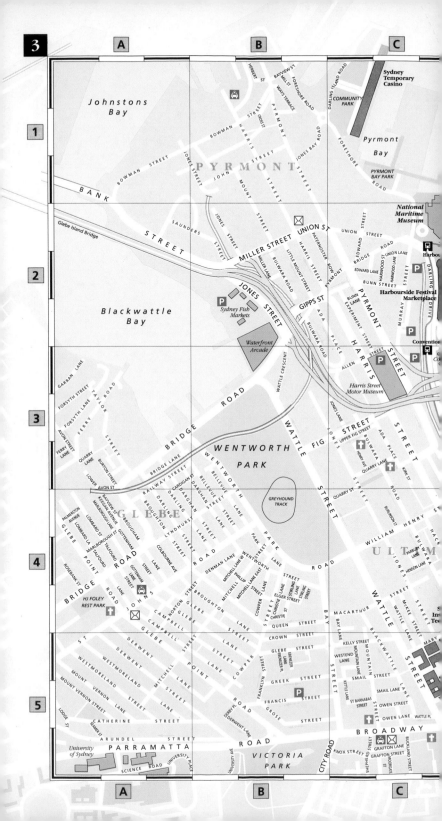

3

A **B** **C**

1

2

3

4

5

Johnstons Bay

BOWMAN STREET

BANK STREET

Glebe Island Bridge

SAUNDERS STREET

Blackwattle Bay

P
Sydney Fish Markets

Waterfront Arcade

BRIDGE ROAD

WENTWORTH PARK

GARRAN LANE

FORSYTH STREET
FORSYTH LANE

TAYLOR STREET

FERRY ROAD

AVON STREET
FERRY LANE

QUARRY LANE

BURTON STREET

LOWER AVON ST

RAILWAY STREET

BRIDGE LANE

CARDIGAN ST

DARLING STREET
DARGHAN LANE

BROGHTON STREET

LYNDHURST STREET

WENTWORTH STREET

BELLEVUE STREET

DARGHAN STREET

GLEBE

PALMERSTON AVENUE

BAYVIEW STREET

LOMBARD STREET

BEGGAN STREET
MARLBOROUGH LANE

GOTTENHAM

TALFORD STREET

MARLBOROUGH STREET

COLBOURNE AVE

LYNDHURST STREET

DARLING STREET

PARK LANE

MITCHELL LANE

DENMAN LANE

WENTWORTH STREET

ROEBANK ST

GLEBE POINT ROAD

LOMBARD ST
MALCOLM

GOTTENHAM STREET
LANE

JOHN STREET

HJ FOLEY REST PARK

CAMPBELL STREET

GLEBE STREET

NORTON STREET

BROUGHTON STREET

MITCHELL LANE WENTWORTH

MITCHELL LANE EAST

PHILLIP LANE

COWPER STREET

CHRISTIE ST

ELGER STREET

STIRLING LANE
STIRLING STREET

DERWENT STREET

WESTMORELAND STREET

MOUNT VERNON STREET

GLEBE POINT ROAD

CAMPBELL LANE

MITCHELL LANE

DERWENT LANE

WESTMORELAND LANE

MOUNT VERNON LANE

LODGE ST

SEAMER ST

CATHERINE STREET

ARUNDEL STREET

PARRAMATTA

University of Sydney

SCIENCE ROAD

UNIVERSITY PLACE

GLEBE STREET

CAMPBELL STREET

POINT ROAD

COWPER STREET

GLEBE STREET

CROWN STREET

GLEBE LANE
EBENEZER LANE
EBENEZER ST

FRANKLYN STREET

GREEK STREET

FRANCIS STREET

DERWENT LANE

GROSE STREET

DERBY PL

P

VICTORIA PARK

UNIVERSITY AVE

BROADWAY

CITY ROAD

HERBERT ST

BAYVIEW ST
MILL ST
FORESHORE ROAD
WAYS TERRACE

CROSS STREET

BOWMAN STREET

HARRIS STREET

JONES STREET

MOUNT STREET

PYRMONT STREET

JOHN STREET

PYRMONT

JONES BAY ROAD

JONES STREET

MILLER STREET

MILLER LANE

JONES STREET

JONES STREET

BULWARA ROAD

UNION ST

PATERNOSTER ROW

LITTLE MOUNT STREET

HARRIS STREET

BULWARA ROAD

GIPPS ST

ADA STREET

BULWARA ROAD

WATTLE CRESCENT

WATTLE STREET

FIG STREET

WATTLE STREET

PARK ROAD

PARK LANE

BAY STREET

MACARTHUR STREET

COWPER STREET

QUEEN STREET

BAY STREET

WESTEND LANE

MOUNTAIN LANE

KELLY STREET

SMAIL STREET

KETTLE LANE

SMAIL LANE

ST BARNABAS STREET

OWEN STREET

OWEN LANE

BROADWAY

KNOX STREET

SHEPHEARD RD LANE

GRAFTON STREET

GRAFTON STREET

BUCKLAND STREET

MORT ST

PARBURY LANE

DARLING ISLAND ROAD

COMMUNITY PARK

Sydney Temporary Casino

Pyrmont Bay

FORESHORE

PYRMONT BAY PARK

PYRMONT BAY ROAD

National Maritime Museum

UNION STREET

EDWARD ROAD

BRIDGE STREET
UNION LANE

HARWOOD ST
HARWOOD LANE

Harbou

P

EDWARD LANE

BUNN STREET

PYRMONT STREET

EXPERIMENT STREET

Harbourside Festival Marketplace

BUNN LANE

MURRAY STREET

DARLING DRIVE

P

Convention

P

HARRIS STREET

ALLEN STREET

P

Harris Street Motor Museum

JONES LANE

JONES STREET

UPPER FIG STREET

HENRY AVE

BULWARA

QUARRY LANE

ADA PLACE

ADA PLACE

KIRK ST

ROAD

QUARRY ST

STREET

BURLINGTON STREET

WILLIAM HENRY STREET

HACK

BULWARA STREET

ULTIMO

WATTLE STREET

HENSON LANE

JONES STREET

MCKEE STREET

WATTLE LANE

MARY

S In Te

WATTLE PL
WATTLE LANE

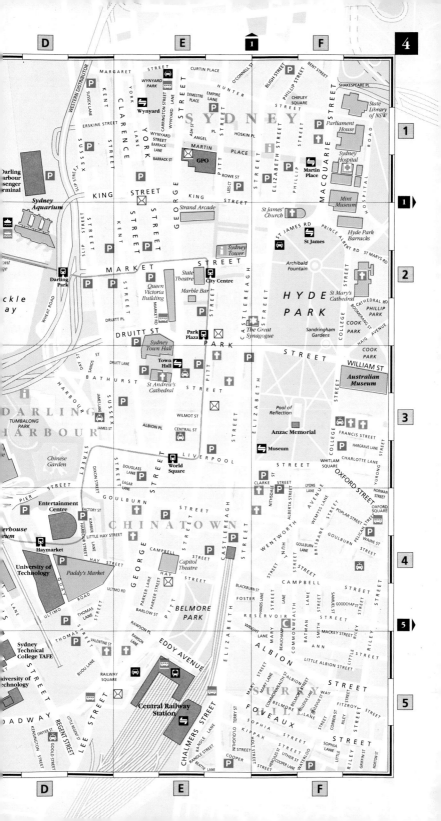

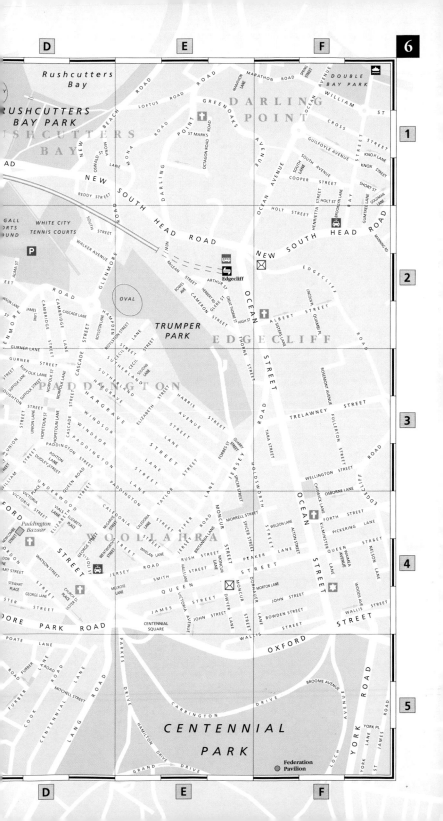

Street Finder Index

General Index

cknowledgments

ORLING KINDERSLEY would like to thank the
llowing people whose help and assistance
ontributed to the preparation of this book.

AIN CONTRIBUTORS

en Brass grew up on Sydney's Bondi Beach. He
egan his career in journalism with the *Sydney
orning Herald* and later worked as one of its
ondon correspondents before becoming a staff
riter on national daily newspapers in the United
ingdom. Returning home, he worked on the
ustralian Women's Weekly, Weekend Australian
ewspaper and *Australian Geographic* magazine.
is photographs appear regularly in a range of
ustralian magazines.

irsty McKenzie grew up on a sheep station in
utback Queensland. She entered journalism after
ompleting an arts degree. After making Sydney
er home in 1980, she worked on a number of
estyle and travel publications. Since becoming a
eelance writer in 1987, she has regularly contrib-
ed to food, interior design and travel magazines.

DDITIONAL TEXT AND RESEARCH

ith Hillard, Siobhán O'Connor.

DDITIONAL PHOTOGRAPHY

aire Edwards, Leanne Hogbin, Siobhán O'Connor.

DDITIONAL ILLUSTRATIONS

eslye Cole, Stephen Conlin, Jon Gittoes, Steve
raham, Ray Grinaway, Helen Halliday, David
rshner, Alex Lavroff, Iain McKellar, Chris Orr,
liver Rennert.

DDITIONAL CARTOGRAPHY

and Information Centre, Sydney.
orling Kindersley Cartography, Sydway.

DITORIAL AND DESIGN

EPUTY EDITORIAL DIRECTOR Douglas Amrine
EPUTY ART DIRECTORS Gillian Allan, Gaye Allen
AP CO-ORDINATORS Michael Ellis, David Pugh
RODUCTION David Proffit
CTURE RESEARCH Wendy Canning
TP DESIGNER Leanne Hogbin
APS Gary Bowes, Fiona Casey, Anna Nilsson,
hristine Purcell, Richard Toomey (Era-Maptec Ltd)
DITORIAL AND DESIGN ASSISTANCE Charis Atlas,
nny Cattell, Joy Fitzsimmons, Clare Forte, Emily
reen, Gail Jones, Lisa Kosky, Jim Marks,
ebecca Milner, Kylie Mulquin, Louise Parsons,
elen Partington, Clare Pierotti, Tracey Timpson.

NDEX

nny Cattell.

PECIAL ASSISTANCE

rt Gallery of New South Wales, in particular
herrie Joseph; Australian Museum, in particular
z Wilson; Ann-Marie Bulat; the staff of Elizabeth
ay House; Historic Houses Trust; Lara Hookham;
fo Direct, in particular Frank Tortora; Professor
ax Kelly; Lou MacDonald; Adam Moore; Museum
Sydney, in particular Michelle Andringa; National

Maritime Museum, in particular Jeffrey Mellefont
and Bill Richards; National Trust of Australia (NSW),
in particular Stewart Watters; Bridget O'Regan;
Royal Botanic Gardens, in particular Anna Hallett
and Ed Wilson; State Transit Authority; Sydney
Opera House, in particular David Brown and
Valerie Tring; Diane Wallis.

PHOTOGRAPHY PERMISSIONS

DORLING KINDERSLEY would like to thank all those
who gave permission to photograph at various
cathedrals, churches, museums, restaurants, hotels,
shops, galleries and other sights too numerous to
thank individually.

PICTURE CREDITS

t = top; tl = top left; tlc = top left centre; tc = top
centre; trc = top right centre; tr = top right;
cla = centre left above; ca = centre above; cra =
centre right above; cl = centre left; c = centre;
cr = centre right; clb = centre left below;
cb = centre below; crb = centre right below;
bl = bottom left; b = bottom; bc = bottom centre;
bcl = bottom centre left; br = bottom right;
brb = bottom right below; d = detail.

Every effort has been made to trace the copyright
holders. Dorling Kindersley apologizes for any
unintentional omissions and would be pleased, in
such cases, to add an acknowledgment in future
editions.

Works of art have been reproduced with the
permission of the following copyright holders:
© MUSEUM OF SYDNEY 1996: *Edge of the Trees*
Janet Laurence and Fiona Foley, on the site of
First Government House: 32tr, 85b; © LIN ONUS
1996 – Lin Onus (1948–) *Fruit Bats* 1991, 95
fibreglass polychrome fruit bats, Hills Hoist, polychrome wooden disks, Art Gallery of New South
Wales: 111cr.

The publisher would like to thank the following
individuals, companies and picture libraries for
their kind permission to reproduce their
photographs:

ACP: 27cb, 28bc; ANTHONY CRICKMAY: 76cla;
EMANUEL ANGELICAS: 42br; ART GALLERY OF NEW
SOUTH WALES: 25cb; © Sir William Dobell Art
Foundation 1996 *Dame Mary Gilmore* 1957
William Dobell (1899–1970), oil on hardboard
90.2 x 73.7 cm, gift of Dame Mary Gilmore 1960:
29ca; © Bundanon Trust 1996 *The Expulsion*
1947–48 Arthur Boyd (1920–), oil on hardboard
99.5 x 119.6 cm: 31c; © Ms Stephenson-Meere
1996 *Australian Beach Pattern* 1940 Charles
Meere (1890–1961) oil on canvas 91.5 x 122 cm:
33tl; 34b; © The Cazneaux family 1996 *Bridge
Pattern* Harold Cazneaux (1890–1961), gelatin
silver photograph 29.6 x 21.4 cm, gift of the
Cazneaux family 1975: 58bc(d); © Lady Drysdale
1996 *Sofala* 1947 Russell Drysdale (1912–81), oil
on canvas on hardboard 71.7 x 93.1 cm: 108tr;
108ca; 108clb; © Tiwi Design Executive 1996
Pukumani Grave Posts, Melville Island 1958

various artists, natural pigments on wood 165.1 x 29.2 cm, gift of Dr Stuart Scougall 1959: 109tc; © DACS 1996 *Nude in a Rocking Chair* 1956 Pablo Picasso (1881–1973), oil on canvas 195 x 130 cm: 109ca; 109crb; 109bc; © Estate of Francis Bacon *Study for Self Portrait* 1976 Francis Bacon (1901–92), oil and pastel on canvas 198 x 147.5 cm: 110tr; 110cla; © Wendy and Arkie Whiteley 1996 *The Balcony 2* 1975 Brett Whiteley (1939–92), oil on canvas 203.5 x 364.5 cm: 110bl; *Warlugulong* 1976 Clifford Possum Tjapaltjarri (1932–) and Tim Leura Tjapaltjarri (1939–84), synthetic polymer paint on canvas 168.5 x 170.5 cm: 111tr; AUSCAPE INTERNATIONAL: Kevin Deacon 96br; AUSTRALIAN INFORMATION SERVICE: 29tl(d); AUSTRALIAN MUSEUM: C. Bento 18tl, 18clb, 18cb, 19tl, 19c, 19crb; Carl Bento/Nature Focus 32cla; AUSTRALIAN PICTURE LIBRARY: John Carnemolla 28clb.

BANGARRA DANCE THEATRE: Greg Barrett 42cla; GREG BARRETT: 209bc; BARTEL PHOTO LIBRARY: 160bc; MERVYN G BISHOP: 20crb; BRUCE COLEMAN: John Cancalosi 45bc; Francisco Futil 44tr; BULA'BULA ARTS: Tony Dhanyula *Nyoka* (Mud Crabs), circa 1984, ochres and synthetic polymer on bark, J.W. Power Bequest, purchased 1984 by the Museum of Contemporary Art, Sydney: 32clb.

CENTREPOINT MANAGEMENT: 83br; CIRCUS SOLARUS: 48cr; COO-EE HISTORICAL PICTURE LIBRARY: 9ca, 61ca, 151ca, 167ca, 217ca; CORBIS: E. O. Hoppé 65cra.

DAVID JONES (AUSTRALIA) P/L: 23crb(d); DIXSON GALLERIES, STATE LIBRARY OF NEW SOUTH WALES: 8–9, 18tr, 20blb(d), 24cla, 70tr, 138br; MAX DUPAIN: 77br.

FAIRFAX PHOTO LIBRARY: 26bl; 52ca; 71bra; 114cl(d); 77tc; ASCUI 51br; Dallen 29cra; Gerrit Fokkema 28br; Ken James 209tr; McNeil 120bl; White 41bl.

GOVERNMENT PRINTING OFFICE COLLECTION, STATE LIBRARY OF NEW SOUTH WALES: 24clb, 26clb, 76blb.

HAPPY MEDIUM PHOTOS: 41tc; C MOORE HARDY: 208br; HOOD COLLECTION, STATE LIBRARY OF NEW SOUTH WALES: 71bl, 137br(d).

THE IRISH-AUSTRALIAN: 43cla.

LAKE'S FOLLY VINEYARDS: 159cr; LUNA PARK TRUST: 128

MAZZ IMAGES: 28–9; MITCHELL LIBRARY, STATE LIBRARY OF NEW SOUTH WALES: 19br, 19bcb, 20br(d), 20–21 21tl, 21ca(d), 21cb, 22clb(d), 22cb(d), 22bl, 23tl, 23ca(d), 23bl(d), 24cr, 24bc, 24br, 25tl, 25br, 27ca(d), 27blb, 29cb, 44tl, 71cra, 112tl; DAVID MOORE: 28cla.

NATIONAL GALLERY OF VICTORIA: © Ann M Mills 199 *The Bridge in Curve* Grace Cossington Smith 1930: 71tl; NATIONAL LIBRARY OF AUSTRALIA, CANBERRA: 22tl, 22cla, 23brb(d), 25bc; NATIONAL MARITIME MUSEUM: 20cl, 34tl, 42tl; NATURE FOCUS: Kevin Diletti 47br(d); John Fields 44bl; Pavel German 47tr.

OLYMPIC CO-ORDINATION AUTHORITY: 139t/b.

PARLIAMENT HOUSE: The Hon Max Willis, RFD, ED LLB, MLC, President, Legislative Council, Parliame of New South Wales. The Hon J Murray, MP, Speaker, Legislative Assembly, Parliament of New South Wales. Artist's original sketch of the historical painting in oils by Algernon Talmage, RA, *The Founding of Australia*. Kindly loaned to the Parliament of New South Wales by Mr Arthur Chard of Adelaide: 73bl; PARRAMATTA CITY COUNCI S. Thomas 40tr, 43tr; POWERHOUSE MUSEUM: 20tl, 21br, 22bcb, 24tl, 26tl, 26cla, 26cb, 26bc, 27crb, 27bc, 32t, 32br; Tyrrell Collection 106tc.

ROYAL BOTANIC GARDENS: Jaime Plaza 48bl.

STATE LIBRARY OF TASMANIA: 20clb; STOPMOTION: 160tr; SUZIE THOMAS PUBLISHING: Thomas O'Flynn 74bc, 76clb; SYDNEY FILM FESTIVAL: 51clb, SYDNEY FREELANCE: J Boland 49cl; SYDNEY JEWISH MUSEUM: 33br; SYDNEY OPERA HOUSE TRUST: 74tr, 74cla, 75t 75br, 75blb, 76br, 77cla, 77ca, 77cra, 77c; Willi Ulmer Collection 77bc.

VINTAGE ESTATES: 158bc.

WESTPAC BANKING CORPORATION: 68br.

Jacket: All special photography except WORLD PICTURES: front t; TELEGRAPH COLOUR LIBRARY: Colorific/Phillip Hayson front tl.

DORLING KINDERSLEY SPECIAL EDITIONS

DORLING KINDERSLEY books can be purchased in bulk quantities at discounted prices for use in promotions or as premiums. We are also able to offer special editions and personalized jackets, corporate imprints, and excerpts from all of our books, tailored specifically to meet your own needs.

To find out more, please contact: (in the United Kingdom) – SPECIAL SALES, DORLING KINDERSLEY LIMITED, 9 HENRIETTA STREET, COVENT GARDEN, LONDON WC2E 8PS; TEL. 020 7753 3572;

(in the United States) – SPECIAL MARKETS DEPARTMENT, DORLING KINDERSLEY, INC., 95 MADISON AVENUE, NEW YORK, NY 10016.

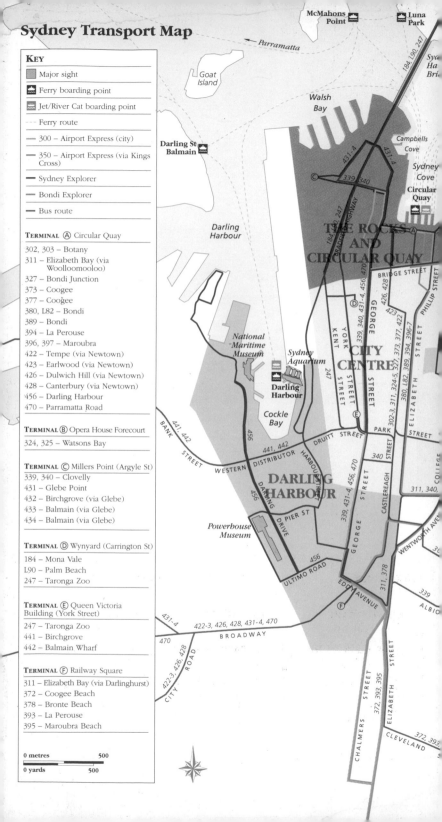